THE NEW
KIERKEGAARD

THE NEW KIERKEGAARD

EDITED BY
ELSEBET JEGSTRUP

INDIANA UNIVERSITY PRESS

BLOOMINGTON & INDIANAPOLIS

Publication of this book is made possible in part with the
assistance of a Challenge Grant from the National
Endowment for the Humanities, a federal agency that
supports research, education, and public programming in the
humanities.

This book is a publication of

Indiana University Press
601 North Morton Street
Bloomington, Indiana 47404-3797 USA

http://iupress.indiana.edu

Telephone orders	800-842-6796
Fax orders	812-855-7931
Orders by e-mail	iuporder@indiana.edu

© 2004 by Indiana University Press

The paper used in this publication meets the minimum
requirements of American National Standard for Information
Sciences—Permanence of Paper for Printed Library
Materials, ANSI Z39.48-1984.

Manufactured in the United States of America

Library of Congress Cataloging-in-Publication Data

The new Kierkegaard / edited by Elsebet Jegstrup.
   p.   cm.—(Studies in Continental thought)
Includes bibliographical references and index.
ISBN 0–253-34284–8 (alk. paper)—ISBN 0–253-21623–0
(pbk. : alk. paper)
1. Kierkegaard, Søren, 1813–1855. I. Jegstrup, Elsebet,
date II. Series.
B4377.N39 2004
198'.9—dc21
                                        2003012812

1 2 3 4 5 09 08 07 06 05 04

Til min Mor

CONTENTS

ACKNOWLEDGMENTS

The New Kierkegaard completes a long-held dream of mine to provide a collection of deconstructive readings of the Danish philosopher Søren Kierkegaard so that more young Continental philosophers might begin to read this extraordinary philosopher as a bona fide contributor to the philosophical tradition whose work falls within both modern and post/modern thinking. The dream became an idea that I first aired to John Sallis on a bus returning to Perugia from one of the many outings that make the yearly Collegium Phenomenologicum so charming, and where during two summers at these gatherings I learned to read Kierkegaard without ever reading his works. My first thanks will therefore go to Kierkegaard himself for the gifts of his unusual thinking and writing—may he still rest in peace with this publication. My sincere gratitude also goes to John Sallis, who guided me into this wonderful realm of Continental philosophy, listened with encouragement to my idea about assembling this amazing group of philosophers to concentrate for a few days, without interruption, on the thought of Kierkegaard, and finally accepted this publication into his series Studies in Continental Thought. Moreover, I am deeply thankful to Peter S. Knox IV of Augusta, whose generosity made the International Kierkegaard Forum possible, and to the Augusta State University Foundation, and especially to former vice president Bill Bompart, who readily made up the difference and wholeheartedly agreed to host the gathering at Augusta State University in March 2001—a gathering that precipitated this volume—and whose attentiveness at this gathering became a shining example for faculty and students alike. I am most grateful to Joseph Roberts and Ray Whiting for their generous advice on how to put all this together, and I want especially to thank Dee Mortensen, my sponsoring editor at Indiana University Press, for her kindness, her helpfulness, and her immense patience. I also want to thank the Menil Collection and the Artists Rights Society for securing the permission to reproduce Magritte's *The Listening Room* on the front cover. I am forever indebted to Margaret Kirby, whose philosophical passions are matched only by her generous nature, which made all this possible this quickly. Finally, I want to express my gratitude and joy to all the contributors to this volume for their intelligence, their love of Kierkegaard's thought, and their willingness to participate in this endeavor. Understanding Kierkegaard's thought is still a work in progress that awaits all Continental philosophy.

ABBREVIATIONS

Most references will be to *Kierkegaard's Writings* (Princeton University Press, 1978–2001). See the sigla below, which constitute the authoritative abbreviations for *International Kierkegaard Commentary,* edited by Robert Perkins and published by Mercer University Press, which has graciously given permission for their use here. Some contributors, however, have used other translations of Kierkegaard's writings, which are cited in endnotes following each essay. Some essays refer to the Danish edition of Kierkegaard's oeuvre: *Søren Kierkegaard Samlede Værker* (SV), 3d ed., 20 volumes, edited by A. B. Drachmann, J. L. Heiberg, and H. O. Lange (Copenhagen: Gyldendal, 1962–64), as well as *Søren Kierkegaards Papirer* (PAP), 2d ed., 16 volumes, including index, edited by P. A. Heiberg and V. Kuhr (Copenhagen: Gyldendal, 1909–70).

Sigla

BA *The Book on Adler.* Translated by Howard V. Hong and Edna H. Hong. Princeton, N.J.: Princeton University Press, 1995.

CA *The Concept of Anxiety.* Translated by Reidar Thomte, in collaboration with Albert B. Anderson. Princeton, N.J.: Princeton University Press, 1980.

CD *Christian Discourses; The Crisis and a Crisis in the Life of an Actress.* Translated by Howard V. Hong and Edna H. Hong. Princeton, N.J.: Princeton University Press, 1997.

CI *The Concept of Irony;* together with "Notes of Schelling's Berlin Lectures." Translated by Howard V. Hong and Edna H. Hong. Princeton, N.J.: Princeton University Press, 1989.

COR *The Corsair Affair.* Translated by Howard V. Hong and Edna H. Hong. Princeton, N.J.: Princeton University Press, 1982.

CUP *Concluding Unscientific Postscript to "Philosophical Fragments."* 2 vols. Translated by Howard V. Hong and Edna H. Hong. Princeton, N.J.: Princeton University Press, 1992.

EO,1 *Either/Or.* Vol. 1. Translated by Howard V. Hong and Edna H. Hong. Princeton, N.J.: Princeton University Press, 1987.

EO,2 *Either/Or.* Vol. 2. Translated by Howard V. Hong and Edna H. Hong. Princeton, N.J.: Princeton University Press, 1987.

EUD   *Eighteen Upbuilding Discourses.* Translated by Howard V. Hong and Edna H. Hong. Princeton, N.J.: Princeton University Press, 1990.

FSE   *For Self-Examination; Judge for Yourself!* Translated by Howard V. Hong and Edna H. Hong. Princeton, N.J.: Princeton University Press, 1990.

FT   *Fear and Trembling; Repetition.* Translated by Howard V. Hong and Edna H. Hong. Princeton, N.J.: Princeton University Press, 1983.

JC   *Johannes Climacus, or "De omnibus dubitandum est."* See *Philosophical Fragments.*

JFY   *Judge for Yourself!* See *For Self-Examination.*

JP   *Søren Kierkegaard's Journals and Papers.* 7 vols. Edited and translated by Howard V. Hong and Edna H. Hong, assisted by Gregor Malantschuk. Bloomington: Indiana University Press, 1967–78.

LD   *Letters and Documents.* Translated by Hendrik Rosenmeier. Princeton, N.J.: Princeton University Press, 1978.

P   *Prefaces; Writing Sampler.* Translated by Todd W. Nichol. Princeton, N.J.: Princeton University Press, 1998.

PC   *Practice in Christianity.* Translated by Howard V. Hong and Edna H. Hong. Princeton, N.J.: Princeton University Press, 1991.

PF   *Philosophical Fragments; Johannes Climacus.* Translated by Howard V. Hong and Edna H. Hong. Princeton, N.J.: Princeton University Press, 1985.

POV   *Point of View.* Translated by Howard V. Hong and Edna H. Hong. Princeton, N.J.: Princeton University Press, 1998.

R   *Repetition.* See *Fear and Trembling.*

SLW   *Stages on Life's Way.* Translated by Howard V. Hong and Edna H. Hong. Princeton, N.J.: Princeton University Press, 1988.

SUD   *The Sickness unto Death.* Translated by Howard V. Hong and Edna H. Hong. Princeton, N.J.: Princeton University Press, 1980.

TA   *Two Ages: The Age of Revolution and the Present Age: A Literary Review.* Translated by Howard V. Hong and Edna H. Hong. Princeton, N.J.: Princeton University Press, 1978.

TDIO   *Three Discourses on Imagined Occasions.* Translated by Howard V. Hong and Edna H. Hong. Princeton, N.J.: Princeton University Press, 1993.

TM   *The Moment and Late Writings.* Translated by Howard V. Hong and Edna H. Hong. Princeton, N.J.: Princeton University Press, 1998.

UDVS   *Upbuilding Discourses in Various Spirits.* Translated by Howard V. Hong and Edna H. Hong. Princeton, N.J.: Princeton University Press, 1993.

WA   *Without Authority.* Translated by Howard V. Hong and Edna H. Hong. Princeton, N.J.: Princeton University Press, 1997.

WL   *Works of Love.* Translated by Howard V. Hong and Edna H. Hong. Princeton, N.J.: Princeton University Press, 1995.

THE NEW
KIERKEGAARD

Introduction

WHY PRESENT A COLLECTION OF ESSAYS on the thought of Søren Kierkegaard (1813–55) exclusively in the deconstructive mode? Is this a beneficial way to present his authorship: does it reveal a different (better?) thinking, or does it produce a better interpretation of his texts than those heretofore presented in Kierkegaard scholarship? Or, might a deconstructive reading be a way to undermine, even de-struct, Kierkegaard's philosophy? The best answers to these questions are to be found in the following essays, which, as a whole, will demonstrate that perhaps the best way to approach his thinking is precisely to read his texts deconstructively, to focus on the textuality of the text and let the play of that textuality inform the reading. Why? Because Kierkegaard is himself, for all intents and purposes, a deconstructive philosopher. However, much depends on how the deconstructive approach is understood, what is meant by deconstruction, especially considering that this approach to reading texts has so often been *mis*understood, *mis*interpreted. Historically, but also presently, many Kierkegaard scholars have engaged in interpretations of Kierkegaard that are grounded in logocentrism. By virtue of this type of analysis, which mainly ignores how Kierkegaard understands existence, conclusions have been drawn from his texts about Kierkegaard himself, as well as about his thought, that seem to contradict his own intentionally deconstructive approach. In addition, such readings of Kierkegaard's authorship have often been driven by agendas in the same way that early Anglo/American translations of Kierkegaard's writings were driven by agendas, religious and otherwise. But Kierkegaard's philosophy, if it is anything, is a philosophy of existence, of *Existents,* Kierkegaard's technical term for being-in-the-world. It is a philosophy that through a complex non-methodical method involving various forms of communication devices, plenty of ironic discourse, and multiple pseudonyms—all characteristics of Kierkegaard's deconstructive approach—attempts to engender self-knowledge in the reader and, perhaps, in Kierkegaard himself. What we as readers get is a philosophy that addresses singularity, addresses a way *to be* that emphasizes the height of singularity but also the aporias of such height—Abraham in *Fear and Trembling* who stands above the community, above what is generally true, and thus renders singularity silent.

But what constitutes a deconstructive reading of texts? Is this Kierkegaard's way?

What is meant by logocentrism? The deconstructive and the logocentric modes of reading texts need to be addressed simultaneously, for only then can there be some clarification. Importantly, deconstruction is *not* one thing. It proposes no unitary meaning, but that does not mean that it commits the reader to the "recommendation of meaninglessness." It does not entail the "equivalence in value of all different readings (rather the singularity of each), and indeed demands the most rigorous textual evidence for readings proposed."[1] In other words, the deconstructive approach throws the issue of the authoritativeness of the interpretation back upon the integrity of singularity. Where the logocentric approach appeals to the rules of logic, to something outside singularity making poor interpretations a problem of mistake, the deconstructive approach challenges the very character of singularity. This would seem, once and for all, to render the frivolous charges of the relativity of deconstructive readings mute. Nevertheless, such readings can never insist on being the dominant readings, as they will never be able to claim to have exhausted the textual evidence. Rather, deconstruction distinguishes multiple perspectives from which no one meaning can be discerned, and yet deconstruction should not be understood to result in a kind of total relativism or nihilism. As Derrida clarifies, "deconstruction is or should be an affirmation linked to promises, to involvement, to responsibility."[2] Deconstruction is existential. It respects singularity, and, most profoundly, it recognizes otherness and the fact that we may not always be able to say what constitutes otherness. It realizes that although much experience can be shared, there will always be areas of experience, understood in physical as well as metaphysical terms, that cannot be shared. I will never know how an orange tastes to you. We may share that it is sour, has too many seeds, and is not as juicy as we would like. But how sour tastes to you, I will never know, just as I will never know your love nor you mine. Deconstruction celebrates singularity, celebrates the ambiguities of human experience in the world and thus discloses the tensions so characteristic of existence. In contrast, logocentrism rests on a systemic approach that promises to expose truth, promises to reveal reality, promises one unitary meaning that has its ground in a logical understanding of textual evidence. With logocentrism, so-called objectivity can be obtained, meaning we can share in the disclosed truths or realities this approach recognizes. Deconstruction, however, will question the possibility of such truths or realities. John Caputo insists that preceding such "truths" or "realities" there is "unreality and irreality [making] 'reality' possible, making possible and impossible what would dare to pass itself off as reality."[3]

While there are no rules per se in a deconstructive approach to reading texts, a logocentric approach must adhere to certain rules, rules that make it necessary to circumscribe what it cannot explain. For example, logocentrism cannot accept logical contradictions. However, as Heidegger clarifies in *An Introduction to Metaphysics,* the rules of logic can keep us from seeing the possibility of nonbeing and being at the same time: "[W]e find ourselves standing in the very middle of this contradiction ['the determinate and wholly indeterminate being']. And this 'stand' of ours is more real than just about anything else that we call real."[4] That is to say, the logocentric approach necessarily leaves out what its rules cannot comprehend. Descartes argued with a great deal of overbearance that if only we have the right method, we can know the truth.[5] But Kierkegaard is not fooled. "By disregarding *Existents* and what it means to exist, [abstract thinking] suspends [*hæve*][6] the difficulty and the contradiction. But the subjective thinker is an existing person, and yet he is a thinking person. He does not abstract from existence and from the contradiction, but he is in them, and yet he is supposed to think" (CUP, 1:351, trans. amended).

The notion of "method" could perhaps also be understood from the perspective of the proverbial scientific box within which 'normal science' is accomplished. The problem is, as Thomas Kuhn has suggested, 'normal science' constitutes "mopping-up operations," operations that force nature into a box that resists new sorts of phenomena,[7] allows experiment and hypotheses within a given realm, but anything outside that realm it considers forbidden territory until someone, accidentally, makes a repeatable discovery.[8] Agreement within the community will eventually enclose this discovery within the box, within the method, and thereby it becomes 'normal science.' This is how a logocentric approach to reading can be understood. Deconstruction, in contrast, reads whatever there is to read, does not limit itself to what external rules may dictate, and accepts whatever it finds. It accepts that there are some things that it is unable to explain or even describe, things that are unnameable: in the case of Kierkegaard, the divine, "the god," the wholly other, alterity, things that, nevertheless, have meaning. Logocentrism cannot do this, and perhaps more problematically, refuses to do it. In other words, what is *other* cannot be the territory of a logocentric reading of text. Logocentrism has to reduce what is other to the same in order to examine it using the rules of the box. Logocentrism is exclusive, while deconstruction is inclusive.

Kierkegaard's deconstructive approach more or less follows the above outline of deconstruction generally. It does not fixate on the ambitious attempts of pure reason; it does not recognize totalizing theory such as Hegel's dialectic, which claims to explain absolutely everything. For Kierkegaard (as for Kant) there is a dimension of human experience that remains hidden, inaccessible to logocentrism's need to explain. That is not to say logocentric approaches to reading texts are somehow illegitimate. Rational analysis is simply one among many ways of reading texts. However, the deconstructive approach to Kierkegaard's writings appears to reach deeper into the complexities of his texts, unfolds them, considers the intricacies of his thinking—pseudonyms, communication devices, ironies—examines the many meanings of them, a necessity especially with a Danish text. The Danish language is quite limited, with individual words having many significations, all of which Kierkegaard toys with and sometimes uses to excess. Kierkegaard's deconstructive approach cuts through these meanings, adopts a multiplicity of perspectives, illuminating and disclosing various interpretations of the human condition not in terms of things themselves, but as fraught with ambiguities, with arbitrariness, with accident and bad decisions. The thing itself always slips away, "always eludes the play of signifiers in virtue of which any such so called real thing is signified in the first place."[9] Or as Kierkegaard would have it with no small amount of irony:

> The systematic idea is subject-object, is the unity of thinking and being; existence, in contrast, is precisely the separation. . . . Objectively understood, thinking is pure thinking, which just as abstractly-objectively corresponds to its object, which in turn is therefore itself, and truth is the correspondence of thinking with itself. This objective thinking has no relation to the existing subjectivity, and while the difficult question always remains—namely, how the existing subject gains entrance into this objectivity in which subjectivity is pure abstract subjectivity . . . it is certain that the existing subjectivity evaporates more and more. And finally, if it is possible that a human being can become such a thing and that all this is not something of which he at best can become cognizant through imagination, this existing subjectivity becomes a pure abstract co-knowledge (*Medviden*) in and knowledge of this pure relation between thinking and being, this pure identity, indeed this tautology, because here being does not mean that the thinking person is, but basically only that he is a thinker. (CUP, 1:123–24)

Kierkegaard rejects the subject-object paradigm of logocentrism, insisting that singularity is located "smack in the middle" of existence, is, as Heidegger would say, always already within the world relating to it. It is this circumstance of human experience that Kierkegaard's deconstructive approach exposes. Deconstruction opens us to possibilities, and importantly, in the case of Kierkegaard, opens us to impossibilities such as the *im*possible confrontations between existential commitment to the unnameable and communal responsibility, neither of which reason alone can justify or make meaningful. As Derrida reiterates, "deconstruction is not an enclosure in nothingness, but an openness toward the other."[10] Objectifying the unnameable, says Kierkegaard, is to deprive it of its otherness, reducing what is other to the Same (CUP, 1:42–43, 577–78). Gasché argues that with the advent of logocentrism, thinking toward otherness, toward exteriority, has been repressed as the project of Western philosophy attempts to "domesticate Otherness,"[11] and thereby avoids the uncomfortable contradictions or (logical) impossibilities in which deconstruction delights. What we learn from Kierkegaard is that deconstruction penetrates the possibilities and impossibilities of existence. Thus deconstruction discloses human experience as subject to the aporias of existence, aporias that defy all explanation. A deconstructive reading of Kierkegaard's texts therefore emphasizes his indirect communication, for "[n]o one who can speak only directly will be able to understand this" (CUP, 1:83). Kierkegaard elsewhere refers to this as the "inwardness of self-activity" (CUP, 1:243). Because the scholars included in this collection of essays all demand deep penetration into any given text, this collection will present essays on Kierkegaard's writings exclusively in the deconstructive mode and at the same time demonstrate that deconstruction is *not* one thing.

Let us now look at how Kierkegaard uses the deconstructive approach. When Kierkegaard begins his publishing career with the two-volume *Either–Or* and on the title page asks, "Is reason alone baptized, are the passions pagan?" he signals his approach to the authorship to come, namely that he intends to call into question the status quo of philosophy. Kierkegaard's deconstruction is aimed directly at Hegel's dialectic and indirectly at all systemic ambitions attempting to explain existence abstractly.[12] In a footnote in *Concluding Unscientific Postscript,* his best deconstructive guise is revealed in all its sardonic splendor: "Hegel himself has staked his whole reputation on the point of the method. But a method possesses the peculiar quality that, viewed abstractly, it is nothing at all; it is a method precisely in the process of being carried out; in being carried out it is a method, and where it is not carried out, it is not *the* method [*Metoden*], and if there is no other method, then there is no method at all" (CUP, 1:109 n, emphasis added).

From Kierkegaard's perspective, an approach to philosophical inquiry grounded in logocentrism leaves out too much of what makes up human experience, such as the passions—love, faith, responsibility—and is therefore incapable of rendering human experience in the world meaningful. Insofar as Kierkegaard understands the human condition as existential decision, he believes what the original philosophical paradigm required: namely, that an inquiry into this condition would also have to include the multiple discursive vocabularies of music, narrative, poetry, art, and love as well as the moral, political, and religious concerns that together with the rational (logical) element impose on human existence. Deconstruction, I emphasize once again, is all-inclusive. That is to say, Kierkegaard's deconstructive approach questions the Enlightenment's belief in the *exclusive* power of reason (logic) to produce truth and meaning, questions the modern philosophical tradition, claiming that neither epistemological systems nor metaphysical theorems can provide an adequate philosophy of existence: "a logical system can be given; . . . but a system of existence cannot be given" (CUP, 1:109). Let us now look at some examples of Kierkegaard's deconstructive approach.

Either–Or is the title of Kierkegaard's first publication, but "either-or" is also a recurring theme in Kierkegaard's authorship, suggesting the human condition is understood as existential decision.[13] That is to say, Kierkegaard also understands this "either-or" deconstructively, and he demonstrates not only the agility of a deconstructive understanding but also its many possibilities through multiple pseudonymous perspectives—which is why we can never claim that his texts represent his own thinking. In a journal note he emphasizes that the title of *Either–Or* is not a title, it is an activity (PAP IV B 59). He understands that there is a tendency to read titles as just that, but his purpose is larger. The same is true of the cumbersome title of an early work, *Johannes Climacus, or De omnibus dubitandum est*. This too signifies an "either-or," signifies an activity, a decision, but this time he presents the choices: *either* existence *or* logocentrism. There is an awakening to the fact that the two cannot coexist inasmuch as singularity, existence, is the focus of Kierkegaard's philosophy. His penetration into the deeper meaning of existence, of the "either-or," discloses the space between determinacy and chaos, between totalizing absolutes and anarchic relativity, a space of the in-between (*inter-esse*), the space of existence (*Existents*). It is a space that holds apart and discloses difference, precisely what Hegelian dialectic reconciles. Kierkegaard's deconstructive "reading" of existence retracts from the ho-mogeneity of the dialectic and the calculable and instead pursues what is only "ostensibly a paradox . . . [that] opens the field of decision and decid-ability."[14] Deconstruction intends to disturb by disclosing the condition of undecidability, a condition that nevertheless requires decision. Singularity must always already decide—*that* is the ethic of deconstruction. Simon Critchley refers to such moments as "*ethical transcendence*,"[15] a dimension of deconstruction too often ignored by its critics. That is not to say that Kier-kegaard's deconstruction abandons all reason. However, it does abandon the circumscribed rationality of modern philosophy in favor of a larger embrace to which contemporary deconstruction also subscribes. "We must affirm this—that is, deconstruction must affirm and say 'Yes' to the unnameable," says Derrida, echoing Kierkegaard.[16] It is an ethical moment of affirmation that encourages deconstruction to address an alterity "that can neither be excluded from nor included within logocentric conceptuality."[17] Kierkegaard is not asking that singularity express freedom in terms of a choice between *either* reason *or* passion. He is saying that human experience is constituted by more than that which reason (logic) can make meaningful, by more than Hegelian abstractions; it also involves passions such as the human capacity toward love, toward responsibility, toward faith. Deconstruction is not fazed by what logocentric conceptuality considers "messy details" of human ex-perience that would be better ignored. Deconstruction delights in such messy details.

Another example of Kierkegaard's deconstructive approach is his under-standing of "idleness" in the essay with the funny title "Rotation of Crops" in *Either–Or*. While traditional (logocentric) interpretations of idleness tend to understand it as "the root of all evil," Kierkegaard thinks of idleness as time, idle time, spare time, time to be put to good use, not to boredom's obsessive activity, but to thinking in its most human sense. Thus from his deconstructive perspective, idleness constitutes a true good. "Idleness is not the evil; indeed, it may be said that everyone who lacks a sense for it thereby shows that he has not raised himself to the human level" (EO, 1:289). Idleness is the time for thinking, perhaps for creative thinking—a gesture of a deconstructive reading of human experience.

Importantly, then, the purpose of Kierkegaard's deconstructive project is not to do away with (destruct) the need for reason, for cognitive knowledge and objective truths. Rather, and in concert with contemporary philosophy, he argues that reason does have a place in human experience and in understanding this experience, but that "it provides only one, among many, ways of describing ourselves."[18] Kierkegaard's aim is to (re)construct, indeed increase the scope of, philosophical inquiry more in accordance with the original (Platonic/Socratic) purpose of the philosophical paradigm: that it constitute a symbolic signification of the meaningfulness of human experience in the world *and* a way of life. Unlike the Enlightenment tradition, Kierkegaard's non-methodical method has no overarching scheme. He rejects the objective method's requirement for results and instead emphasizes singularity's continuous striving. "Results are nothing but junk," inasmuch as what counts is the "self-activity of appropriation," something which cannot be directly communicated (CUP, 1:242).[19] The most prominent feature of Kierkegaard's deconstructive approach is precisely the indirect communication, for what he wants to communicate cannot be directly communicated. Kierkegaard's thinking deals with the impossible, deals with how to make sense of a dissonant actuality. Thus he assumes a total break with actuality and instead asks at the very beginning of his authorship: "What is a poet?" a question that for Kierkegaard has a typically cryptic, and yet existentially meaningful, answer: "An unhappy person who conceals anguish in his heart but whose lips are so formed that as sighs and cries pass over them they sound like beautiful music" (EO, 1:19). This is deconstruction's territory, a territory Kierkegaard's thinking constantly falls into, a territory that always already withdraws from our grasp yet shows itself without language as deconstruction circles it, approaches it from all angles without ever being able to say what it is—because it remains unnameable. What Kierkegaard wants to know, therefore, is the *how* of singularity's relation to the unnameable, not logocentrism's *what* of the unnameable itself (CUP, 1:202). "The process of becoming is the thinker's very existence" (CUP, 1:91); it "is the spacing that holds apart," emphasizes difference, while the systematic represents the "conclusiveness that gathers" (CUP, 1:118, trans. amended). John Caputo has passionately described this aim of deconstruction with both Kierkegaard and Derrida in mind:

> to keep the system open, to prevent the play of differences from regathering and reassembling in a systematic whole with infinite warrant, and to take its

stand with everyone and everything that is rejected and expelled by this carnivorous gathering.[20]

Thus Kierkegaard puts everything into question; *he* begins the deconstructive project, and he does so in order to show that grand theoretical constructs are just that and hence ripe for deconstruction. We are indebted to Jacques Derrida for having brought "renewed life and renewed language" to the deconstructive approach "in a time when the dogmatics of theory, the dogmatics of fundamentalism, just like in Kierkegaard's time, seem to breed everywhere."[21] We are grateful, because now the hermeneutic project of the Kierkegaardian texts is again relevant.

Although deconstruction can send us in the direction of the negative, it should not be "mistaken for a nihilism, nor for a metaphysics of absence, nor for a negative theology." Continuing his interpretation of Derrida's thinking, Rodolphe Gasché says that deconstruction does not constitute a "demolition and a dismantling to be opposed by a calling for rebuilding or a reconstruction."[22] Reading Kierkegaard carefully, not bluntly, discloses the importance of the negative's presence in existence, and because it is "present everywhere (because being there, existence [*Existents*], is continually in the process of becoming), the only deliverance from it is to become continually aware of it" (CUP, 1:81–82). What does it mean to be aware of the negative in existence? It means to be aware that there are some things we cannot know but which, nevertheless, present themselves to us—thus Kierkegaard's emphasis on indirect communication, a deconstructive move in and of itself. Importantly, then, for both Kierkegaard and Derrida, deconstruction is the vehicle that opens us to the possibility of something more and indeed to impossibility, what always already confronts singularity (CUP, 1:267), to something beyond itself, to something undeconstructible. Thinking's passion is to think what cannot be thought, says Kierkegaard in *Philosophical Fragments* (PF, 37), and thus he challenges the boundaries of reason that modern philosophy has imposed.

★   ★   ★

The present collection distinguishes itself sharply from the several other collections on Kierkegaard that have been published in the last few years, all of which are heavily influenced by the requirements of modern philosophy. This collection distinguishes itself inasmuch as it presents *new* deconstructive essays on Kierkegaard exclusively as discussed above. Only the collection *Kierkegaard: A Critical Reader,* edited by Jonathan Rée and Jane Chamberlain (1998), contains essays by a variety of interesting and in some cases deconstructive philosophers such as Paul Ricoeur, Emmanuel Levinas, George Steiner, Sylviane Agacinski, and Jacques Derrida, as well as a couple of authors also represented in the present volume. However, all but two of these essays were first published elsewhere. In contrast, *Kierkegaard and Post/Modernity,* edited by Martin Matustik and Merold Westphal (1995), presents only one or two deconstructive essays, those by Caputo and Schrag, while the rest of the essays are more or less typical traditional interpretations by mostly recognized Kierkegaard scholars. *The Cambridge Companion to Kierkegaard,* edited by Alastair Hannay and Gordon Marino (1998), contains only one, perhaps two, deconstructive essays, namely those of Roger Poole and Herman Deuser. The rest of the essays are by the same people, more or less, as in the former collection. Appearing most recently, *Kierkegaard after MacIntyre,* edited by John Davenport and Anthony Rudd (2001), presents exclusively analytical essays on Kierkegaard. What characterizes the latter three collections is their lack of imagination; but, I suppose, the same could be said of a collection with exclusively deconstructive essays. The difference is that the present collection presents a number of scholars who have not before published on Kierkegaard. However, being familiar with their work and seeing their appeals to Kierkegaard everywhere, often revealing new and intriguing insights into his thinking, I found their selection for this volume easy. Recognition of these insights is what precipitated the International Kierkegaard Forum held at Augusta State University in March 2001, and forms the foundation for the present collection; although, it should be said, the essays for that forum have been reworked to present themselves even better, and several others have been added. Importantly, they all engage in a deconstructive effort to seek more deeply into and thereby gather a better understanding of Kierkegaard's philosophy, which offers a thinking that, nevertheless, will always present a puzzle. What is of fundamental importance to us when reading Kierkegaard is, then, to accept that his words can never be said to represent his own thoughts, and the perspectives that he does present are never complete—thus the (intentional?) puzzle. These circumstances the present authors all accept, and, it seems, embrace, allowing for the play that often is the generosity of deconstructive philosophy.

★   ★   ★

At this point convention suggests that I describe and perhaps categorize and explain the positioning of the essays in this collection. To do so, however, would be untrue to Kierkegaard's thinking, untrue to the deconstructive approach. First, it would suggest that there is a "correct," singular interpretation of these essays, and at the same time suggest that these essays represent a "correct," singular reading of Kierkegaard's works as such. Second, it would suggest that these essays somehow connect, somehow form a relationship, that an overarching scheme somehow embraces them and gathers them together. And at the same time it would suggest that Kierkegaard's entire authorship embraces such an overarching scheme, that his individual texts, pseudonymous and not, somehow form a cohesive whole. But most of his writings, including some of the discourses such as *Works of Love,* and certainly the pseudonymous works, signify only independent perspectives that represent nothing more than perspectives as such, but perspectives that may, nevertheless, make a serious reader more aware of, more alert to, existence. To make more out of them than that would be to impose upon a most peculiar thinking, a thinking that, once again, addresses singularity, addresses the possibilities and impossibilities of human experience, and thereby attempts to satisfy the requirements of philosophy. As Kierkegaard concedes in *The Point of View for My Work as an Author,* "What I write here is for orientation and attestation—it is not a defense or an apologetics. . . . [T]he duplexity, the equivocalness, is deliberate, is something the author knows about more than anyone else, is the essential dialectical qualification of the whole authorship, and therefore has the deeper basis" (POV, 24, 29, trans. amended). Nevertheless, it is possible to give some guidance to the reading of these essays. Although the International Kierkegaard Forum that precipitated this volume focused on Kierkegaard's first publication, namely *Either–Or,* or tried to, presenters were not limited to this work. It is possible, then, to at least identify the Kierkegaard writings that particular essays address. To do more than that, such as an exegesis on the various essays, would be counterproductive to the understanding of Kierkegaard's writings a particular author is trying to get across. For example, his "categories" of indirect communication, pseudonymity, irony, and so on do not lend themselves to a synoptic elaboration inasmuch as this may all too easily lead to the reductive belief that these "categories" have just one meaning. In fact, Kierkegaard often assigns different meanings to these so-called categories in his various writings, a meaning that is often tied to the particular pseudonym (perspective) assigned to present the text. Different meanings of these "categories" are precisely the reason for his use of different pseudonyms. Were it otherwise, he would have used only one pseudonym, if any at all. Thus the intention is to forestall a reductive reading of the present essays on Kierkegaard. For these reasons, only practical concerns have guided the placing of the essays in this collection. Generally speaking, they have been located in a non-hierarchical sequence that presupposes no connections, no links, no relationships. They appear here only for the purpose of showing the breadth and depth of Kierkegaard's unusual and complex thinking.

The essays by Caputo, Poole, and Garff all deal essentially with *Either–Or* in its entirety, but as is often the case when one tries to understand Kierkegaard, his other works occasionally sneak in, and this is true in these essays as well. In addition, Caputo purposely draws Derrida into the discussion on undecidability, the very condition of *Either–Or,* in order to expose the irony of this very situation that confronts us. In so doing, the depth and the seriousness of the ironic, as Kierkegaard apparently perceived it, reveals itself, interrupting any comfort we may have had about this mood that seemingly pervades Kierkegaard's thinking. Poole questions whether we have been reading *Either–Or* correctly in view of the past fifteen years' onslaught of a "greater Alexandrianism" of interpretation and commentary, while Garff provides an engaging and clever exposé on the possible ménage à trois between A, B, and C (his synonym for Judge Wilhelm's unnamed wife). Jegstrup's essay, in contrast, is all over the place, so to speak, making use of many of Kierkegaard's works, especially his Journals, *Either–Or, Fear and Trembling,* the *Postscript,* and *Works of Love,* in an attempt to understand the *non*-methodical method that is Kierkegaard's alone—an insanity, methodologically speaking, that drives any serious reader to the very brink of another kind of insanity, the one that appears when one is rendered overwhelmed, exhausted, and utterly confounded and the (rational?) ego protests. Only accidentally, John Llewelyn's essay follows, taking its cue from *Philosophical Fragments* but also leaning heavily on Kierkegaard's Journal notes as well as on Kant and Hegel in order to expose another madness, or at least the borderline of this madness, namely that which, as he says, issues from Kierkegaard's seemingly contrary "warning against commonness . . . [which] would drive you mad," yet madness is a most common way of "distinguishing someone's uncommonness." Jacob Bøggild concentrates on a rhetorical reading of two of Kierkegaard's early upbuilding discourses, "The Lord gave and the Lord has taken away, Blessed be the name of the Lord" and "The Thorn in the Flesh," while David Wood plays with the aesthetics of the "Diary of the Seducer" in volume 1 of *Either–Or,* juxtaposing it to Judge Wilhelm and "the ethical transformation" in volume 2. Robert Gibbs brings us to the "other" end of Kierkegaard's authorship, discussing the problem of writing in a tight focus on certain texts in *Works of Love* and the ethical proposition "love of the other." Vanessa Rumble also concentrates on *Works of Love* and the "alterity and unattainability of such love," while John Vignaux Smyth introduces us, for the first time and long awaited, to a serious connection between Kierkegaard and Isak Dinesen in a reading of the latter's *Ehrengard* as a response to the "Diary of the Seducer." Finally, Mark Dooley tries to understand differences between Kierkegaard and Derrida by reading Levinas; Jason Wirth introduces us to a new reading (with Derrida) of *Fear and Trembling* focusing on the question of responsibility; and Richard Kearney, in a brilliant display of humor and seriousness, rounds up this collection with a discussion of the hermeneutical model that suggests that "if every text . . . involves someone talking about something to someone, then this one [the "appendix" to the fourth part of *Stages on Life's Way*] is, when closely decrypted, nothing more nor less than Kierkegaard talking about Kierkegaard to himself."

So I ask that you read these essays, dear reader, that together indeed represent a new Kierkegaard, and take joy in these deconstructive efforts, which bring us to a greater understanding of an extraordinary authorship and, perhaps, of ourselves.

Notes

1. Geoffrey Bennington, *Interrupting Derrida* (New York: Routledge, 2000), 11.

2. Jacques Derrida, "A Discussion of Architecture (with Christopher Norris)," *Aesthetics,* eds. David Goldblatt and Lee B. Brown (Upper Saddle River, N.J.: Prentice Hall, 1997), 184.

3. John D. Caputo, "For Love of the Things Themselves: Derrida's Hyper-Realism," *Social Semiotics* 11, no. 1 (2001). Quotation taken from Internet: http://www.jcrt.org/archives/01.3/caputo.shtml, 1 (Jan. 2002).

4. Martin Heidegger, *An Introduction to Metaphysics,* trans. Ralph Manheim (New Haven, Conn.: Yale University Press, 1959), 78.

5. René Descartes, "Discourse on Method," in *Philosophical Works of Descartes,* trans. Elizabeth S. Haldane and G.R.T. Ross (Cambridge: Cambridge University Press, 1968), 82.

6. Kierkegaard plays on the Danish language here. *Ophæve* and *hæve* can both be used to mean the same thing. He is teasing Hegel by not using the word that would properly correspond to the German *aufheben.* Both in German and in Danish these words are ambiguous; they mean both to raise and to cancel.

7. Thomas Kuhn, *The Structure of Scientific Revolutions,* 2d ed. (Chicago: University of Chicago Press, 1970), 24.

8. Martin Heidegger, *Being and Time,* trans. Joan Stambaugh (Albany: State University of New York Press, 1996), 8.

9. Caputo, "For Love of the Things Themselves," 1.

10. Richard Kearney, "Deconstruction and the Other," *Dialogues with Contemporary Continental Thinkers* (Manchester, England: Manchester University Press, 1984), 124.

11. Rodolphe Gasché, *The Tain of the Mirror* (Cambridge, Mass.: Harvard University Press, 1986), 101.

12. See, for example, his deconstruction of systemic philosophy in *Johannes Climacus, or De omnibus dubitandum est* (PF, 129–72).

13. It is most regrettable that the Hongs chose to impose a slash in the title of Kierkegaard's first publication. The original title, *Enten–Eller,* contains the all-important dash, which in the Danish is *tankestreg*—translation: "thought line." Nothing could be more important than the admonition *to think* when confronted by decision and, ultimately, by *undecidability.* All essays in this volume style the title as *Either–Or,* with the dash, except in note citations of English translations that use the slash.

14. Jacques Derrida, *Limited Inc.* (Evanston, Ill.: Northwestern University Press, 1988), 116.

15. Simon Critchley, *The Ethics of Deconstruction: Derrida and Levinas* (Oxford: Blackwell, 1992), 30.

16. Jacques Derrida, *Margins of Philosophy* (Chicago: University of Chicago Press, 1982), 27. See especially Kierkegaard's *Philosophical Fragments,* where he addresses what is absolutely other: "What, then, is the unknown? It is the frontier that is continually arrived at, and therefore when the category of motion is replaced by the category of rest it is the different in which there is no distinguishing mark. Defined as the absolutely different, it seems to be at the point of being disclosed, but not so, because the understanding cannot even think the absolutely different; it cannot absolutely negate itself but uses itself for that purpose and consequently thinks the difference in itself, which it thinks by itself. . . . If the unknown (the god) is not solely the frontier, then the one idea about the different is confused with the many ideas about the different" (PF, 44–45). Incidentally, this is where the difference between Kierkegaard and Levinas becomes clear inasmuch as Levinas makes no distinction between the Other of a higher order and your neighbor.

17. Critchley, *Ethics of Deconstruction,* 41.

18. Richard Rorty, *Philosophy and the Mirror of Nature* (Princeton, N.J.: Princeton University Press, 1979), 361.

19. For more on Kierkegaard's indirect communication, see Elsebet Jegstrup, "Text and the Performative Act: Kierkegaard's (Im/possible) Direct Communications," *Philosophy Today* 45, no. 2 (summer 2001): 121–31.

20. John D. Caputo, *The Prayers and Tears of Jacques Derrida* (Bloomington: Indiana University Press, 1997), 246.

21. Elsebet Jegstrup, "Kierkegaard and Deconstruction: Is Kierkegaard *inter alia* Anywhere in Jacques Derrida's *The Gift of Death?*" *Søren Kierkegaard Newsletter* 41 (February 2001): 19–23.

22. Rodolphe Gasché, *Inventions of Difference* (Cambridge, Mass.: Harvard University Press, 1994), 25.

1

Either–Or, Undecidability, and Two Concepts of Irony: Kierkegaard and Derrida

John D. Caputo

THE CRITICS OF DECONSTRUCTION often sound like Judge Wilhelm upbraiding the aesthete for his indecisiveness. Either–Or is the whole passion of my personality, the judge proclaims, the energy of my life, that has stood me in good stead at every turning point in my life. But as for you, Jacques the Seducer, apostle of undecidability, when you use the words "Either–Or" it is to mock them. You use them with a wink: do it or do not do it, and you will regret it either way. You do not treat these hallowed words as a true and incisive disjunctive; for you they are but a single word, a mishmash, an interjection that you hurl at all those poor fellows helplessly caught up in the rush of existence. But when you mock Either–Or, *Monsieur Indécidabilité,* when you say that all life is a masquerade, "inexhaustible material for amusement," you mock yourself. For do you not know "that there comes a midnight hour when everyone must unmask; do you believe one can sneak away just before midnight in order to avoid it?" Why do you fear becoming "completely transparent" to yourself? Are you not appalled at the abyss that yawns before you, the "disintegration"—shall we say the dissemination—"of your essence into a multiplicity," the breakup and loss of all that is "most inward and holy in a human being, the binding power of the personality?" (EO, 2:158–60).

Do you not realize that at any moment the veils of life may part and a voice will say to you, "This day your soul is required in eternity"? Deconstruction, for such critics, is the sickness unto death, the despair over oneself, the despair of infinitude that loses itself in an infinite play without being concretely anchored in the finite; or else it is despair over oneself in finitude that loses itself by losing the thought of true infinity. Do you not know, *Monsieur le Texte,* that when the hourglass of time runs out, when the noise of worldly life has subsided, when we will all stand in stillness before eternity, eternity will want to know not whether we have held an important post in life or invented another reading, but whether we have lived in faith or in despair (SUD, 27).

Hear, hear! Well said! Enough said for Mr. Both–And, for all deconstructionists everywhere, for all indecision and indecisiveness, for Godless relativism and faithless anti-realism![1] For deconstruction is the demonic despair of disintegration and down-building (which is betrayed by its very name!), passionlessness and disengagement from life, the bad infinity of melancholy. What would happen if our most promising young people, "with that lovable confidence that is the ornament of youth," were to go to deconstruction for advice? Would that not spell the end of the liberal arts, of scholarship, of religion, of science, of all objectivity, of the university, of the West?

The judge denounces the aesthete for trying to hover in a never-never land, shall we say a Derrida-da land, *prior* to the Either–Or, that is, to principle of contradiction. The judge, steady, decent man that he is, takes the bull by the horns and chooses one of the alternatives, the horn of the good no doubt, which reconciles the dilemma not by mediation but by excluding one of the alternatives (EO, 2:175). Of course, the ironic outcome, as we learn in the "Ultimatum," is that the judge, in an important way, makes the wrong choice by not choosing to be *in* the wrong, since before God one is essentially in the wrong. That is repentance, which also reconciles the dilemma not by mediation but by excluding the possibility that we are in the right, which means that we are in this sense infinitely responsible.

But the irony that drives the judges of deconstruction into a lather, that leaves them sputtering with frustration, is that Derrida's position is most closely approximated not by the aesthete, nor by the proud and self-approving Judge, but by the Jutland pastor. For like the good pastor, Derrida too holds that before the *tout autre* we are infinitely responsible, that good conscience is a ruse, that the good sense of a "finite responsibility"—that we do the best we can and take the rest of the day off—is the real masquerade. So, if we are looking for a suitable pseudonym for Derrida, we should forget about Jacques the Seducer and try "Reb Rida" (WD, 78)[2] or perhaps "Rabbi Augustinus Judaeus."[3]

Still we must proceed with caution here. We must not let our affection for the prayers and tears of Jacques Derrida blind us to the fact that the Either–Or of decision in the pseudonyms and in the signed works is not the same as the movement of deciding-in-the-midst-of-undecidability in Derrida. While it is true that we must look to the "religious" stage for a Kierkegaardian analogy to deconstruction, still Derrida's religion is a "religion without religion" (GD, 49), a religion marked by a *sans,* that is importantly different from the religion of the pseudonyms, which is a religion *with* religion, with the historically particular and determinate Christian religion. That is what I will try to sort out in what follows by way of two different figures of Socrates and Socratic irony, Kierkegaard's Christian Socratism and what I shall call Derrida's "khoral" Socratism.

De-construction as an Up-Building Discourse

To begin with, let us establish the decisiveness of decision in deconstruction and its up-building character. Like the pseudonymous authorship itself, deconstruction pursues a two-pronged strategy: it visits upon us the idea that before the *tout autre* we are always "responsible," always "in the wrong," even while clothing itself in the garments of irony and humor, that which are the incognitos of its religion without religion. One cannot be *finitely* unconditional, for that would be to give not unconditionally but only under certain conditions, to forgive not unconditionally but only up to a point; one would be committed to the Unconditioned, but only if certain conditions are met. When Rorty objected to all the "hype" about "infinity" in Levinas and Derrida, Derrida rightly responded:

> I believe that we cannot give up on the concept of infinite responsibility.
> . . . I would say, for Levinas and for myself, that if you give up the infinitude
> of responsibility, there is no responsibility. It is because we act and we live
> in infinitude that the responsibility with regard to the other (*autrui*) is irre-
> ducible. If responsibility were not infinite, if every time that I have to take
> an ethical or a political decision with regard to the other (*autrui*) this were
> not infinite, then I would not be able to engage myself in an infinite debt
> with regard to each singularity. I owe myself infinitely to each and every
> singularity. . . . There are only moral and political problems . . . from the mo-
> ment when responsibility is not limitable. (DP, 86)

One cannot be finitely responsible, Derrida says: if you take away the infinity, then you take away the responsibility; if the weight of responsibility is *finite* you can always dodge it, remove it, lift the weight. Without the infinity, one can always say that, all things considered, I really am not all that responsible. Indeed, while I may have my faults, I am on the whole a rel-atively steady and decent fellow, especially when compared to these other chaps, who really need to be told a thing or two.

Thus "deconstruction," *s'il y en a*, by the very definition provided by the "Ultimatum" that concludes *Either–Or*, and disregarding a too literal reading of its name, is the most "edifying"—the most constructive or up-building—thing of all, because the only thing that is genuinely edifying according to the unnamed parson is the thought that before the infinite one is always in the wrong. Love alone puts itself in the wrong for the love of the beloved. To wish to be in the right is to abolish the love and the edification, and to persist in adopting a finite and comparative point of view, on the perfectly sensible premise that God would not require the impossible of us (EO, 2: 345). So let us keep our heads, the finite understanding says, and stick to

what is possible. Let us do what we can do, and then get a good—a finite—
night's sleep and we will feel much better about things in the morning. From
the "Ultimatum" at the end of *Either–Or* to the "Unchangeableness of God,"
Kierkegaard located the essence of the edifying in the same thought: that
none is good but God, that every good and perfect gift is from God, that
before God we are in the wrong, that without God a man can do nothing.
The edifying is to stand before God, the Father of lights, in whom there is
no change or shadowy fluctuation. The edifying is to stand, *coram deo*, as
before an absolute white light in which we understand ourselves.[4]

That is why for Kierkegaard and Derrida (and also for Heidegger and
Levinas) there is nothing good about a good conscience. Very much like the
parson in the "Ultimatum," Derrida says that I can never say "I have taken
a decision," or "I have assumed my responsibilities." I can never have a good
conscience about having a good conscience, not if I am responsible, unconditionally responsible:

> And that is why undecidability is not a moment to be traversed and over-
> come. Conflicts of duty—and there is only duty in conflict—are intermi-
> nable and even when I take my decision and do something, undecidability
> is not at an end. I know that I have not done enough and it is in this way
> that morality continues, that history and politics continue. There is politi-
> cization and ethicization because undecidability is not simply a moment to
> be overcome by the occurrence of the decision. Undecidability continues to
> inhabit the decision and the latter does not close itself off from the former.
> . . . Even when I believe myself to have opted for a decision, I do not know
> if I have in fact taken a decision, but it is necessary that I refer myself to the
> possibility of the decision and think it, *s'il y en a.* (DP, 87)

Undecidability is first, last, and constant; it is the element of the decision,
like air is the element of the bird. Undecidability is the thing that gives the
decision its bite, which is why there would always be a notion of "repetition"
in deconstruction, a "yes, yes," for deciding-in-the-midst-of-undecidability
is constituted as a movement that must be continually repeated, again and
again; it is never over and done with. Undecidability is not indecision but
the ongoing condition of possibility of decision demanding the constant
renewal of decision. The opposite of undecidability for Derrida is not decisiveness but programmability, formal decidability. Then the decision can be
made in virtue of the axioms that govern the problem, or by means of an
algorithm, or more generally in virtue of formal rules that need merely be
applied to the case at hand, which does not require good judgment but good
software (FL, 24–26; OH, 41, 45–46). One need only run the program and
there is no need for decision or decisiveness at all, no need for judgment,
everything having been turned into what Climacus calls an "objective problem." When Derrida says that undecidability describes a situation that is not
"programmable," this corresponds to Johannes Climacus saying that an

"existential system" is not possible. The only thing that is programmable is a logical system; an existential system is formally undecidable; that is, it is not a system.

What Does the Fire Chief Say?

The question of decision in the Kierkegaardian authorship is not framed by the problem of programmability but by what Kierkegaard calls "ambiguity," thinking we know what we do not know, that we are precisely what we are not, a difficulty that calls for a thoroughly Socratic therapy, which means one that is both maieutic and ironic. The pseudonyms try to find a way to urge the single individual to embrace the Either–Or, to take up in earnest the task of becoming Christian, all the while maintaining a safe distance from the individual so as not to defraud God of the individual's God relationship. The authorial task is edifying, because it concerns the God-relationship, but it is also aesthetic, because it is executed without authority, with unbroken irony and constant laughter, which are meant to draw a circle of respect around the individual's personal responsibility. Thus the authorship is both aesthetic and edifying, "both–and," as Michael Strawser argues very nicely.[5]

The spiritual situation that calls for this Socratic solution is described in the hilarious fire scene. "It's the same at a fire," Kierkegaard quips. No sooner has the alarm sounded than a crowd gathers at a scene, this fellow with his pail, that one with his spray pump, and all of them blocking the path of the fire department. So what does the fire chief say? "Hey! Get the hell out of here with your pails and your spray pumps." Now, we must understand that the fire chief is otherwise a quiet and respectable gentleman, but at the fire he has a job to do. So when he sees this crowd of bumblers getting in the way of his firefighters he loses his decorum and shouts, "Where the hell are the police?" And when the police arrive, he says to them, "Get rid of these damned people with their pails and spray pumps," and if they won't go quietly, "then tan their hides" (TM, 217–20).

The fire chief is not to be blamed. On the contrary, he is taking command of the situation, which is just what is needed. For a fire is a serious thing, an earnest matter, and when it comes to earnest matters the rule is Either–Or. *Either* you are someone who can truly do something to help, *or* you are in the way, in which case the earnest thing to do is to get the hell out of the way. The worst thing to do is to stand around cluttering up the fire lane with your pail or spray pump and looking like you are an important part of the operation. "It is the same in the world of the spirit as at a fire": either you are in earnest or you are in the way. Either you heed the Christian requirement in all earnestness, with fear and trembling, or you stand around in a crowd blathering about it. That crowd of blatherers is, alas, what the blood of the martyrs has come down to. For the historical process of

Christianity is an inverted chemical process, a process not of purification, but of impurification, so that instead of gradually filtering out the impure components, we have ruined the idea, muddled it into gibberish and illusion (TM, 347), botched, babbled, and prattled the idea into the ground, so that nothing is left of it except a mockery. The idea was never purer than at the beginning, but by now, at the end of the history of Christian "perfectibility," after the 1,840—or rather the 2,000—years, all we have are fellows standing around with their Christian pails and ecclesiastical spray pumps doing nothing but getting in the way: "Wherever there is truly to be earnestness, the law is: Either–Or; either I am the one who is involved with this cause in earnest, is called to it and is unconditionally willing to venture decisively or, if this is not the case, then the earnestness is: have nothing at all to do with it . . . *Aut—aut: aut Caesar aut nihil*" (TM, 220). Either become a Christian, or get the hell out of the way. Nothing is worse than to try to split the difference with earnestness about the unconditional, which means to undermine the decisive with the indecisive, with a certain disastrous "to a certain degree." If one undertakes the task of becoming Christian to a certain degree, then all is lost. "I understand that," says Kierkegaard, I who am known to the children on the street as "Mr. Either–Or." Either–Or "gives admittance to the unconditional," as opposed to a "cowardly sagacity" that turns Christianity into blather (TM, 94).

The complicating factor is the ambiguity. The Christian Socratic author is not a missionary who has landed on a distant island where the natives have never heard of Christianity, where he can simply plant a cross in the sand and proclaim the gospel to them directly and unequivocally. The complication is that the crowd that is standing around already takes itself to be Christian, so that the more anyone would urge Christian life upon them the more furiously they would nod their heads in agreement. But the more heartily they agree, the less they hear of what is being urged. That is what he means by "ambiguity" (TA, 77–78): double-mindedness, *Zwei-deutigkeit*, in German, like those figures in Parmenides who wander about two-headed saying both "it is" and "it is not," where to say "it is" is quite precisely the very best way possible to say "it is not." It is the same with Christianity as with death. The best way to show that one is not in earnest is to make a showy claim of the fact that one is in earnest: all men are mortal, yes indeed, and we are all Christian, yes, indeed, and we take these matters very seriously, thank you very much.

That means that the Christian Socratic author cannot come forth straightforwardly proclaiming that he is a Christian and that others should do likewise; he must be more circumspect and ironic. The strategy called for here is ironically to turn the tables and assume the posture of one who is not a Christian addressing a thoroughly Christian people. That makes the idea of "being" Christian problematic and shifts the focus to "becoming" one. *Being* a Christian for Kierkegaard is like the coming of the Messiah in Derrida: it never actually happens, but the *becoming,* the repetition, the push forward, the call to come, *viens, oui, oui,* is what drives us, impels and moves us on. Being Christian is, it seems, impossible, *the* impossible, coming as it does at an absurdly, paradoxically, impossibly high price. So we need to ironically expose the ruse that Christianity is not available on the cheap and that "in a world where millions and millions call themselves Christians," the honest Socratic move is not to call oneself Christian (TM, 49). Kierkegaard's gift, if it is a gift, his task, if he has a task, is, having stated plainly that he is not a Christian, to make it manifest that the millions and millions are also not Christian (TM, 340). In this Socratic task Christendom is the sophistry, the blathering confusion, the double-mindedness of the millions standing around with their pails and their spray pumps. The only edge the religious author has is Socratic: knowing what the millions do not know, that they are not Christian, which makes their position even more desperate than his, for he at least knows what he is not while they are not what they think they are.

Christendom is deconstructible, but Christianity, *s'il y en a,* is not deconstructible. *S'il y en a:* if there is such a thing, if such a thing exists. "Christianity," according to Kierkegaard, "does not exist all." Indeed, he goes so far as to say that this is his "thesis," what he was sent into the world to say, having said which he can die in peace (TM, 521). There are indeed "churches, bells, organs, offering boxes, collection boxes, hymn boards, hearses, etc.," but far from constituting evidence of Christianity, this inventory is positively dangerous, for it only serves to contribute to the illusion that Christianity exists (TM, 35).

Christianity has something of the structure of the quasi-transcendental: the very conditions that make it possible—the earnestness, the honesty, the decisiveness, the Either–Or—also make it impossible, make it clear that such an earnest one is at best, on his very best day, still in a process of becoming, earnestly striving to become what today he still is not. Insofar as Christianity is, it is not, but is only an infinite task. Conversely, to the extent that Christianity lays claim to worldly presence, to be actually found among the world's existing structures, Christianity tends to annul itself and to take the form of Christendom. Indeed, as Kierkegaard noted, long before the story of the "Grand Inquisitor," if Jesus dared return to earth the Church would persecute him. Having a divine gadfly like Jesus around would not be good for the Church and so we would have to sacrifice him once again, albeit for the good of the Church (so perhaps he would understand that it was for a good cause). Nothing is as pure as the beginning, but as soon as it begins, it begins to unravel, to undergo the reverse chemical process, the *im*-purification process that accompanies existence.

So whatever the difference may be between Kierkegaard and Derrida, the difference is *not,* if this still needs to be said, that Kierkegaard is a Knight of Decision and Decisiveness while Derrida is Jacques the Seducer, whispering the subversive news that there is nothing outside the text into the ears of an innocent maid while her aunt is in the kitchen making tea. Kierkegaard and Derrida, the one no less than the other, are sublime pranksters in a deadly serious game; under the masks of irony and humor, they stake everything on the need to decide in the midst of undecidability, which is the very thing that raises the price of faith to infinity, which blocks the confusion that faith can be had at a bargain rate in a market town—or in *la haute culture* of Paris.

They differ, then, not as the decisive differs from the indecisive, but in terms of two differing conceptions of decision. Their conceptions of decision differ, in my view, in two ways: (1) the decisiveness of a "decision" in the pseudonyms has the structure of an "Either–Or" that is governed by a *binary logic* that is precisely denied by the *logic of undecidability* in deconstruction; (2) the decisiveness of a decision for Derrida has an *indeterminateness* that is foreign to the commitment of the pseudonyms to the *historical determinacy* of Christianity, with the result that Derrida has a more pervasive, invasive notion of irony than is deployed in the authorship. Let us examine these two points in turn, for they are not unconnected.

Binary Logic and the Logic of Undecidability

For Kierkegaard and the pseudonyms, "every cause that is not served as an Either/Or (but as a both/and) is *eo ipso* not God's cause" (TM, 425). The badge of "Either–Or" can be worn as a symbol of a man laboring in the service of God's cause, whereas the badge of "both–and" is the badge of mediocrity (TM, 24). Derrida, on the other hand, thinks that the "both–and" invades the *situation of the choice* and blurs the lines of demarcation between the terms of the choice. So Derrida thinks that it is *never a matter of Either–Or, never a matter of choosing between* X and Y—between the pure gift and economy, between the two sorts of interpretation, between justice and the law, between narcissism and non-narcissism—because there is no clean cut or divide between them. For both Kierkegaard and Derrida, undecidability is the condition of possibility of a decision: things do not fall ready-made into our lap; we must choose in the midst of darkness and non-knowledge, of fear and trembling.

But Derrida and Kierkegaard are not worrying about the same thing. For Derrida is addressing the non-programmability of a situation that requires judgment, not an algorithm, where decisions fall into *conflict* with each other (OH, 45–46), which is his reading of the *akedah,* a reading that differs noticeably from that in *Fear and Trembling.* Johannes de Silentio contends that Abraham's ethical duty to Isaac has been *suspended,* and the terror is that he must venture forth in silence in this land beyond the law where he is alone before God. But Derrida thinks that Abraham is caught between conflicting ethical duties, *both* of which are in play, *neither* of which has been suspended, moving not in silence but amid conflicting calls coming from two opposing directions at once. This conflict generates a paradox or an aporia that is paradigmatic of ethical choice in general: we are obligated to the *tout autre* who stands before us and lays claims to us *and* at the same time, in the same moment, to all the other others, too. Both–And and Either–Or. Thus what Derrida wants us to embrace, the aporia of the "conflict of duties," de Silentio would regard as a merely "tragic" conflict, the conflict between duties each of which makes sense. But on de Silentio's accounting Abraham is asked to head for Mount Moriah single-mindedly, with the full terror of a faith that the conflict, and hence the claim of Isaac, has been suspended. Derrida and Kierkegaard are trying to dispel different illusions. Derrida is concerned with the illusion that the conflict of ethical duties can be resolved in a formalizable and rule-governed way, while Kierkegaard is addressing the "ambiguity" of someone who wants to play at being Christian without the terror by striking up a bargain with the "world" and earning a good living off the Crucifixion.

According to the logic of undecidability, the binary distinction between the illusion of Christendom and the truth of Christianity, which is analogous to the distinction between what he would call an "economy" (in Christendom, his reverence earns a good living) and the "gift" (the "mad" economy of de Silentio), cannot be so clear; there can be no "pure cut" between the either and the or. A Christian must, in a mad moment of choice, decide to be a Christian, while *also* knowing full well that Christendom is all that exists, that the economy of Christendom will be the inevitable result, and so one must "risk entering its destructive circle" (GT, 30). For *there is no one Christendom*. There can only be "degrees of Christendom," ranging from the most hypocritical, illusory, and fraudulent up to the more earnest and heart-felt. A possible Derridean gloss on the distinction between Christianity and Christendom may be found, mutatis mutandis, in the interview "There is No *One* Narcissism," where Derrida is discussing the distinction between narcissism (read: Christendom) and non-narcissism (read: Christianity): "There is no [Christendom] and [Christianity]; there are [Christendoms] that are more or less comprehensive, generous, open, extended. What is called [Christianity] is in general but the economy of a much more welcoming, hospitable[Christendom], one that is much more open to the experience of the other as other" (*Points,* 199).

The position is not unlike Augustine's defense of the earthly Church as a *societas mixta* over and against the Donatists, who insisted on what Augustine considered a kind of inhuman purity; the Donatists had, by the way, an admiration for martyrdom quite like Kierkegaard's. Derrida is deeply suspicious of the very logic of purity and contamination that goes to the heart of Kierkegaard's view of the logic of Either–Or. For Derrida, there is a certain "double gesture" involved in every decision that will always, from Kierkegaard's point of view, look like double dealing, like the dreaded "to a certain degree." The *first* gesture is the "purity of heart," to affirm the pure and unconditional character of the gift, of hospitality, of forgiveness; for it is only in this unconditionality that the gift, the welcome, and forgiveness are to be found, if they are to be found, *s'il y en a*. But the *second* gesture is to acknowledge that they are never found and do not exist in just that way, with just that purity, for the gift, and hospitality, and justice, are to be entered among the existing economies, making the way possible for "a much more welcoming, hospitable" economy than would otherwise be found.

Where Climacus sets forth a "double reflection" aimed at inducing purity of heart, Derrida defends a "double gesture" that acknowledges there is no such purity. The *first* gesture is to *question* every economy, every compromise and negotiation with economic considerations, in the name of the pure and unconditional gift, which means to "know" all the ways in which the gift will annul itself; but that questioning is followed by a *second* moment, a second gesture, which is to *give* and in giving to give economy—or Christendom—a chance (GT, 30). For it would be a mistake to be taken in by the desire and the phantasm of the "proper," the "pure," and to try to rescue it from "contamination" (*Points,* 214), a mistake to be lured by the Donatist desire for purity, a desire from which, I would say, Kierkegaard is not free. So the second gesture is to make a deconstructive *movement within* the economy, to *intervene* in and open it up to possibilities to which it has hitherto been closed. The affirmation of the purity of the gift, which means that the gift, if there is such a thing, is always and structurally to come, is to be inserted within the text and the context of the existing economies, lest it have no existence at all. Justice, which is not the law, is always to come, but the idea is that there should be as many just laws in existence as possible. So, in between Kierkegaard's binary distinction between the present age and a revolutionary age Derrida would insert the moment of *intervention in* the present age so as to open it up to the future. It is not a question of beginning with a compromise, with accommodating oneself to the constraints of reality, and of "doing what one can" given the limits of the situation, which is denounced in the "Ultimatum." Rather, it is a question of *beginning by the impossible,* of going where one cannot go, of calling for the incoming of the unforeseeable, *and also,* at the same time, in a second movement, of knowing that the world is all in all, that the various economies are inescapable. The double injunction is: (1) know everything that is at work in giving and then give; and (2) in giving *give economy[Christendom] a chance* (GT, 30).

Thus when Kierkegaard says that "Christianity does not exist at all," he means that it does not exist *now* but it certainly *did* exist once, in the

Christianity of the New Testament, in the primitive or apostolic age, for *things are never so pure as they are in the beginning*. But Derrida rejects the logic of purity-and-contamination, of the pure beginning and the contamination process that follows (which is another idea that Heidegger seems to have borrowed from Kierkegaard). For Kierkegaard the idea that there are at least two different kinds of Christianity is a confusion put forth by Herr Pastor Fog. Christianity is not like butter, he says, which can be graded from extra prime to very good to good and to drippings that are almost as good as butter (TM, 560; not like beer: TM, 581). The thrust of the rhetoric of the Either–Or in Kierkegaard is to show not only that there is no third alternative—*tertium non datur*, unless that third be confusion (BA, 87)—but that there are not even two alternatives, not really and truly. There is only one demand, one thing necessary, which one is either *for or against*. But for Derrida there is always more than one (*plus qu'un*) and hence more than two. The Christianity that is not *one* is not Christianity at all. The notion that Christian purity of heart must sit down to table with the world, must make a compromise or two with the world, is not a *religious* consideration, Kierkegaard says, but a political one, where politics is the art of the possible, where half a loaf is better than none, where something is better than nothing, which is not true in the world of the spirit (TM, 521).

So for Derrida the exercise of decision and judgment takes place in a context where things never get so decisively and binarily clear. There is a logic of binarity and purity in the authorship that is systematically criticized in Derrida. For Derrida we never get to remove the mask; when we have decided, we do not know if we have decided or whether what we have decided is right. In Derrida's logic of undecidability, decision does not assume the binary dimension of a clear Either–Or where one of the alternatives is *clearly to be excluded;* when I respond to the other, all the *other others* cry out for help, others who are *no less* in need of my help, who *ought not to be excluded* from my choice with the sharp Abrahamic dagger of Either–Or. It is not a matter of *either this,* which can be exposed as fraudulent if only I am honest with myself, *or that,* which lays an uncompromising claim on me. Rather both this one and that one demand everything of me, *and* I must choose between them, even though they both lay equal claim on me. Isaac's hold on me is never suspended; it is always ringing in my ear. *Both* the *tout autre* and Isaac, *and* I must *choose between* them, as in *Sophie's Choice*. That is the *aporia,* the undecidability.

In Christian Socratism, to choose, really and honestly to choose, is really to choose or *will one thing* so that the choice is not divided against itself, as Kierkegaard himself explained in an edifying discourse of the same period as *Either–Or*. The one and only one thing that really can be chosen in an earnest purity of heart is the good, which is the only thing that is truly one, while the choice of evil is inevitably divided against itself.[6] But for Derrida the good is divided into conflicting goods, and a choice is really a choice pre-cisely when it is not pure in this sense, precisely when it passes through the aporia of being divided against itself, precisely when it has excluded some-thing that should not be excluded, which is his allegorical gloss on the story of Abraham and Isaac in *The Gift of Death,* which differs considerably from the argument of *Fear and Trembling.*

Two Concepts of Irony

But there is a second, and perhaps more overarching, difference between these two sublime pranksters. The pseudonyms and the upbuilding discourses put more stock in the concrete historical clothing that is given by the *Post-script* to the story of "the god" in *Philosophical Fragments* than Derrida ever would or could. For Derrida, "the god" can always and in principle *be determined otherwise,* while for Kierkegaard, the *determinate* name of Jesus— for "God gave him the name that is above every name, so that at the name of Jesus every knee should bend in heaven and on earth and under the earth" (Phil. 2 2.9–10)—and a *particular* "book called *The New Testament of Our Lord and Savior Jesus Christ*" (TM, 130) have a *non-ironic* status that it would be impossible for Derrida to attach to any name or text. For Derrida, a certain irony or meta-irony will always cling to any text, to any historical name, to any name, historical or not, to any belief or practice. The existence of a sacred name, the name of Jesus, and of a sacred scripture, the text of the New Testament, of a divine Word and of sacred words, give irony a bearing, orientation, and directedness in the authorship that it simply lacks in the Derridean corpus, where irony is a little more lost, indeed a little more like the irony of Socrates as he is portrayed in the dissertation *The Concept of Irony.*

For the Christian Socrates, irony and humor are strategies and incognitos, whereas for a more deconstructive Socrates irony is not a strategy but an inescapable condition, what Derrida calls a "necessity" (ON, 125–26) that undermines first-order distinctions between irony and direct communication, humor and seriousness, with the result that everything is submitted to a more deep-set, bottomless, second-order irony. In the *Point of View,* Kierkegaard said that he knows that Socrates "was no Christian" but that he cannot help believing that he "has become one" (POV, 54). The change of verb tense is the clue: he means that while "on earth" Socrates "was" (past tense) not a Christian; now, in heaven, he "has become" one (present perfect), since for Kierkegaard the vast illusion called Christendom, where millions and millions call themselves Christian, actually comes true in heaven, where everyone is in truth Christian in a Church triumphant. (That is why, he adds, he could also call Socrates his teacher, even though the Lord Jesus Christ is the only teacher.) But in Derrida's more open-ended nominalistic

Socratism, Socrates just goes on becoming, goes on and on asking questions, eventually appearing on a perplexing postcard in Oxford. For Socrates/ Jacques does not know who he is, or what justice is, or what the gift and forgiveness are. Deconstruction never "rests transparently in the power that established it," to use Anti-Climacus's words (SUD, 14, 49). That means that in deconstruction, matters can always be determined otherwise and that they never assume the sort of *historical determinacy* that they have for the pseu- donyms. We can never say that at the end of the day this Socrates "has become" anything, because there is no end of the day and *there is no one thing to become*—Christian or otherwise. So let us see if we can get to the bottom of the difference between these two Socrates, at least one of whom may be bottomless.

Christian Socratism is an exercise in irony and humor in order to awaken the God-relationship in a slumbering Christendom and this without defraud- ing God of the individual's God-relationship, without taking over for the individual the decision that each individual must make for himself before God. The individual must make the leap and, as Heidegger would say later on, we must not leap in for him (*Being and Time,* §26). So the method is Socratic, but in the sense of ironically inducing a conversion, *metanoia* (not a recollection), which is strictly a private matter between the individual and God, and in which the Socratic interlocutor steps aside. The idea is to be an author without authority while still having an effect. The whole "au- thorship" arises from an author who is not an author in the usual sense. The authorship obeys the strange logic of the *sans.* The Christian Socratic author, who is the author of the authors, who has authored many works on the text of existence, professes not to be an authority on the subject, which would of course ordinarily explain why someone has *not* authored several books on a subject. But the *sans* is not a simple negation, for there is all the difference between being the author of the authors who write several books on a subject *sans* assuming a position of authority and simply not writing anything at all.

He writes as a "poet," someone who paints a poetic portrait of existence *sans* presuming himself to be an authority on the subject of existence- relationships. He is a Socratic *poet* who does not presume to say how the reader may bring himself into relationship with the subject of existence. He is a Socratic *midwife,* even a kind of Christian Socratic "*matchmaker,*" intro- ducing the individual to God and then stepping aside, letting grace take over from there. The Christian Socratic roams the streets of old Europe trying to break up the nineteenth-century "sophistry" of "Christendom," which is the bourgeois illusion, the self-deception, the confusion, the fraudulence, of proclaiming oneself to be precisely what one is not, and this in virtue of that very self-proclamation. That means that everything in Christian Socratism turns on a decisive and well-determined distinction between the reality of

Christianity and the illusion, honesty and self-deception, good faith and bad faith, masking and unmasking, purity of heart and ambiguity, transparency and opacity, bargain-basement imitations and the real thing, which never comes cheap. In short, Christian Socratic irony turns on a relatively sharp and stable distinction between the ironic and non-ironic, between ironic strategies and the non-ironic ideal embodied in apostolic Christianity. Without presuming to say that any existing individual has ever met the standard of being Christian, has ever measured up to the evangelical ideal, Christian ironic discourse presupposes the normative and non-ironic status of the New Testament, which is itself rooted in the normative and non-ironic reality of the historical birth and life and the passion and death of Jesus Christ, of the name of Jesus, which is above every name. Christian Socratic irony plays on the difference between a difficult and sublime norm, which is all but impossible to achieve, and the fraudulence of the easy imitations, which are too numerous and commonplace to take seriously.

Christians in Christendom "play" at Christianity, "the way soldiers play at war on the parade grounds" (TM, 133). Christendom is a masquerade in which Christians don the various masks of Christianity. Christendom is a vast stage show, with all the props of Christianity—"churches, bells, organs, offering boxes, collection boxes, hymn boards, hearses, etc." (TM, 35)—all serving to produce the vast illusion of a Christian world. Like puppets in a puppet show (CUP, 1:244), Christendom is a "theatrical connivance, a theater marriage" (TM, 94). The movements it makes are no more real than the tender embraces of an actor and an actress on a stage express real love. Christendom is like an entire continent of sleepwalkers who do not want to wake up. Indeed, Christendom would be like an inverted version of *Truman's World,* where *only one* man, "Truman (true-man) Climacus," would know the truth, would know it is all a show, the true man and man of truth being the Christian Socratic Apostle, whom everyone would therefore consider mad, an offense, whose life would accordingly be in danger. In Christian Socratism there will come, in this life or the next, a midnight hour when every mask must be removed and we must stand before ourselves face to face. Sooner or later there will be a moment of "transparency," in which the mask is removed, when the Either–Or is clear as clear can be, and the decisive is demanded of us. In Christian Socratism, Socrates himself would eventually come to discover, in this life or the next, that he "has become" a Christian.

Thus, in order to decide, the present age must be led *into* genuine *undecidability;* it must be given undecidability as a gift—in just the way Socrates had to induce undecidability in the Athenians—in order *then* to decide what they have hitherto just taken as given. The truth is that there is something deeply *seductive* about both Socrates and the two Johanneses: when Johannes the Seducer manipulates Cordelia into thinking that she has broken the

engagement, that is but a dishonorable form of the honorable task that Soc-
rates/Johannes Climacus undertakes: to deceive Christendom into the truth
(POV, 53), since it is not a loss to be robbed of an illusion. The pseudonym
is to be the occasion of awakening an existential movement in the individual,
which means to break the illusion and *induce undecidability*. Like Socrates,
Climacus the Seducer is trying to induce, educe, seduce the thousands and
thousands into seeing that their faith is a fraud, which is the first step toward
making a genuine leap in the midst of objective uncertainty.

The genuine decision is blocked by the *lack* of undecidability, and the
undecidability is blocked by Christendom's illusion that it has already decided, so that the illusion must first be broken in order to let the undecidability awaken a genuine decision. But *what we must decide is well determined
and determinate*. One need only walk the streets of old Europe holding the
New Testament over one's head, saying *tolle, lege*. The whole question is
whether we will summon up the "earnestness" or whether we are content
to drift along with the comfort of an illusion. The authorship undertakes a
dialectic of indirection, irony, and humor in order to stir Christendom out
of the sleep of somnambulant Christian practices. Climacus, de Silentio, and
the author of *The Point of View for My Work as an Author* are not sure that
there *are* any Christians, themselves included, and they all can speak of Christians or Christianity, *s'il y en a,* in Derrida's sense, which they too regard as
the impossible in a Derridean sense. They would never say that Christianity
exists; they would even deny that it exists. But they can tell you (1) where
it does *not* exist, namely, in this masquerade ball in which they find themselves; (2) what it would be like were it to exist, namely, in the New Testament of our Lord and Savior Jesus Christ. The author of the "edifying
discourses" does not lack a determinate idea of what a Christian would be,
if there is one, namely, someone who freely confesses that before God a man
is always in the wrong, that one cannot so much as take a walk in the Deer
Park without God, that none is good but God, that all good and perfect
gifts are given by God and this precisely in virtue of the absurd. There may
or may not be an existing spirit whose soul is shaken by the terror of these
thoughts, whose life is marked by them all the way down, but be that as it
may that is what a Christian would be, *s'il y en a,* if one ever came strolling
along, de facto, looking for all the world like a tax collector. Everything
comes down to a certain radical honesty or self-transparency or self-
examination. The question is whether the existing spirit can ever be moti-
vated to take a close look within, but there is no doubt about exactly *what*
the individual would find if ever he could brave a look, if ever he would
dare remove the mask, or shake himself out of this dream and wake up. The
what is sitting there, all the while, patiently waiting for us if we could ever
muster the courage of the *how*. The first self is infinitely patient, waiting for
the second self to come home (EUD, 314).

If for Climacus the *what* must be converted into the existential coin of the *how* (CUP, 1:199), for Derrida there never was a what, no *determinate* content to a *what,* that must become a *how.* Consequently there is no comparably strong distinction between irony and non-irony, humor and seriousness, mask and unmasking, assumed disguise and genuine self, reality and illusion. There is a kind of open-ended indeterminacy and felicitous nominalism about the *what,* an objective uncertainty that really does not know what is what, that does not know the definition of anything.

In Christian Socratism there is a certain midnight hour when all masks are removed, an hour or an *Augenblick* when we see as we are seen, when we see what we have to do, when we can no longer take flight from ourselves, and it comes down not to seeing it or deliberating about it but to *doing* it. But for Derrida there is no midnight hour when the *mask of traces* is removed. We never quite reach a comparable state of trace-free transparency or lucidity or binarity; the call of conscience is never quite so sharp, because the choice never has the sort of determinacy attached to a proper name like Jesus Christ, to some determinate moment in history upon which the eternal pivots, someone who could actually *be* the way, the truth and the life, instead of being a substitutable emblem of them. For Derrida we do not know who we are or what we want to be, not in any *determinate* way; the *what* is endlessly determinable. We suffer not from a loss of the origin but from an origin that was never present, so that we are subject to an uncontrollable and uncircumventable play of simulacra and imitations without originals. That is why Derrida makes only limited use of pseudonyms and, in "Circumfession," which might pass as his own *Point of View for My Work as an Author,* confesses not that he is seeking to deceive us into the truth but that he is "cut off from the truth" (Circum, 314). Hence the distinction between the pseudonymous and veronymous is not in play because he does not propound a determinate truth that has been masked by an "illusion," or reduced to a bloodless "objectivity" that needs to be recharged by subjective passion. He does not really have a *determinate what,* and he does not, if I may say so, know what is *what.* His idea of truth is in a sense even more existential, more tilted to the *how* than the *what,* than Climacus's. He has the Augustinian idea of truth as *facere veritatem,* which is certainly what Climacus would call an "existential" truth, but one that has to do with what he calls the "secret," and lacks any objective *what,* any objective certainty or uncertainty, for we do not know *what* we are, so we are not even *tempted* to speculate it into an "objective" truth or offer historical proofs to back it up. Kierkegaard may or may not be a Christian (he said he is not: TM, 340); the pseudonyms may or may not be Christians (they say they are not); there may or may not be a way of Socratically communicating the task of becoming Christian that does not defraud God of the God-relationship; the two thousand years may or may not lend credibility to Christianity. But there is no doubt what a *Christian* is or what must be done to become one, *s'il y en a,* or what it is that one must become if there is ever to be one (again—after the passing of the apostolic age). If there is any doubt at all about what a Christian would be, then open the New Testament at any page you choose; *tolle, lege.*

Derrida's authorship is *neither* pseudonymous *nor* veronymous because it lacks the fulcrum, anchor, or Archimedean point that this distinction requires. Or perhaps we could say that it is *both.* His works are all pseudonymous inasmuch as we can hardly say who is saying what to whom—which is why all his "dialogues" are among unnamed voices, whose number, identity, and gender we are left to guess at. But by the same token, all his works are veronymous, in the sense of the Augustinian *facere veritatem.* They are all upbuilding or *religious,* with the religiousness not of religion A or B but of a religion *without* religion. But what religion is that? It is the religion of justice and the gift, of faith and friendship, of hospitality and forgiving, of deciding in the midst of undecidability, in the midst of a *khora* that does not go away. This is the religion that I have elsewhere argued should be described as a "pact with *the* impossible,"[7] which is the defining feature of the Knight of Faith for Kierkegaard (FT, 47), a covenant with the unconditional, an unconditional affirmation of the justice to come, or the democracy to come, which turns on our love of the name of "God," even though Derrida "rightly passes for an atheist" (Circum, 155–56).

The Khoral Socrates

We can encapsulate the difference between the determinacy of Christian Socratism and the open-ended nominalism of deconstructive Socratism in terms of two different figures of Socrates, the figure of the Christian ironist and humorist who is enacted in the Kierkegaardian authorship, and what I will call the "khoral" figure of Socrates, the one whom Derrida describes in a gloss on a text on the *khora* from the *Timaeus* that is currently receiving a lot of attention in French philosophy.[8] The Socratic ironist in general always stands between two worlds, occupying the place between the sophist, whom he wants to expose, and the philosopher, to whose ranks he dare not lay claim. In Kierkegaard, the interlocutive *place* of the ironist is *determinate* because he is negotiating the distance between two determinate places, Christendom and the Christianity of the New Testament. But in Derrida the Socratic place is described as a kind of indeterminate non-place. Derrida takes Socrates to be *himself* a "khoral" figure in the *Timaeus,* a third thing, who occupies a non-place in between the place of the sophist, the dissembler who is full of empty words, and the man of the truth, the true or truthman, who belongs to the *genos* of the philosophers. So Socrates steps aside and makes himself a receptacle for what Timaeus has to say (ON, 107–109).

The Christian figure of Socrates deploys irony and humor as strategies, as incognitos—and an incognito implies a *cognitum*—as points of passage, in order to negotiate the distance between two identifiable regions, *either* apostolic Christianity *or* bourgeois Christendom, whereas the khoral figure uses irony and humor in a domain where there are no such identifiable distinctions and we do not know who we are.

One way to see all this is that, for Derrida, "humor" and "irony" are not "border" phenomena or points of *passage,* but *points of undecidability.* Irony does not signify a "passage," a from/to movement, from aesthetics to ethics (or the reverse), but a movement of undecidability, the fluctuation back and forth between them. To describe them as "passages" or borders to be crossed is already to determine them, to submit them to a law from above that, speaking from a phenomenological point of view, is not already inscribed within them. The ironist as such is not on the way to ethics but suspended between a momentary pleasure and the moment of decision. To say that irony is "above" the pleasure but "below" the decision makes a rank-ordering that presupposes a non-ironic point of view, for irony as such is simply detached from both. Irony cannot be said to be "on the way" until *after* the decision and *from the point of view of* the decision. From the point of view of the aesthete, irony is not on the way but adrift, cut off from the pleasures of immediacy (unless of course there are interesting possibilities to be drained from occupying an ironic stance). So, too, with humor: to see the joke in the young man's complaint in *Repetition* that he was not consulted about being born as a transition to faith is already to occupy the standpoint of faith and to have moved beyond the humor (R, 200). To see Qoheleth's experience of vanity as a passage from idol to icon, from indifference to love, as Marion does, is to adopt love's point of view.[9] In themselves, irony, humor, and vanity tremble in undecidability and to undergo them is not to experience a passage, *eine Er-fahrung,* as if we are travelers passing through, en route to somewhere else, but to run up against an *aporia,* to be brought to a standstill, caught in a whirlwind, not knowing where to turn next or where to go. For we do not know who we are, we who are a question to ourselves. *Quaestio mihi factus sum.*

For Derrida *khora* is a "surname" for *différance* (ON, 126), another name for the nameless name of *différance,* which is itself the name for the irreducible "spacing" in which everything is inscribed, the irreducible abyss in which all binary pairs are inscribed. *Khora* pre-contains and destabilizes all of philosophy's most treasured distinctions—between the particular thing and the form, the sensible and the intelligible, the changing and the unchanging, time and eternity. In virtue of its radical "anachronism," *khora* is "older than" all these distinctions. We would not even be able to say that *khora* "is," or even that "*es gibt khora,*" for *khora* does not give; we might at best say *il y a khora. Khora* would even include and pre-contain the names that philosophy gives to *khora* herself in order to find a place for her within philosophy, names like "mother," "receptacle," "wet nurse," which it would in turn destabilize. Taken radically, *khora* resists all of these names, and so the khoral figure of Socrates is neither mother nor a midwife, neither a wet nurse nor a matchmaker, but a receptacle for a doctrine without a model and without a name.

For Derrida, all of the binary schemes upon which both the pseudonymous and the veronymous works depend—bourgeois Christendom and apostolic Christianity, illusory and authentic Christianity, masking and unmasking, time and eternity—are inscribed within *khora*. That includes of course that very distinction between aesthetic and edifying works because it includes the distinction between the ironic and the direct or non-ironic modes of communication. It even includes always having laughter on your side (EO, 1:43), because it would include *both* sides of this equation, both laughter and solemnity. That is because *khora* would never allow us the surefooting to distinguish the ironic and the non-ironic, in a determinate way, because nothing inscribed in *khora/différance* could ever enjoy a non-ironic standing, that is, would ever be immune from substitution.

Now to a certain extent, and this is what Michael Strawser argues in the insightful "Conclusion" of his work,[10] recognizing something like this belongs to any good reading of Kierkegaard. The aesthetic and religious always intermingle in a kind of chiasmic "both–and," if for no other reason than that the personal views of the living Kierkegaard are forever inaccessible so that even when he signs his own name what we have is a text, whose author is dead, structurally or in fact or both. That would apply, as Strawser says, even to *The Point of View for My Work as an Author,* which is sometimes treated as if it were outside the authorship, as if this too were not another text, as if Kierkegaard would somehow here be authorizing himself to step outside the play of *différance* and arrest its play, to settle the case about the authoritative interpretation of his texts, as if this were not still one more text for his readers to interpret. The very structure of writing insures an ironic distance between the text and the author, on both sides of the aesthetic/religious divide, so that his readers are always and as a structural matter on their own. In striking a pseudonymous and ironic posture as an author, Kierkegaard is only exaggerating a structure that is already built into writing, any writing, ironic or non-ironic. Furthermore, the "faith" that gives stability and "transparency" to life that is described by both the pseudonyms and the edifying discourses is hardly an "epistemic foundation." Faith is faith and something more than a bourgeois convenience only in virtue of the fear and trembling; to have faith is to understand that one is bobbing in a fragile craft over 20,000 fathoms. One never knows, one only believes, and the more unknowable things become, the more faith is required and the more faith is really faith.

To be sure. These are matters that I would myself want to emphasize in reading the Kierkegaardian corpus. But I am pointing to a certain structural limit of irony in Kierkegaard. In one sense, the irony is unbroken: we never know if there *are* any Christians, and even if there are, neither the pseudonyms nor Kierkegaard himself claim not to be one of them; so the reader is left to fend for himself. But if the irony is never arrested or broken, nonetheless it operates within structural limits, inasmuch as it is organized around a determinative text or sacred word to which a non-ironic status is ascribed, the New Testament, and this because it bears witness to a determinate historical figure, the God-man, and a determinate event, the historical entrance of the eternal Word of God in time, to which a non-ironic and normative status is ascribed. But for Derrida, no text or figure—Greek or Jew, Western or non-Western, aesthetical, ethical, or religious, theistic, atheistic, or polytheistic, faithful or infidel, masculine or feminine, divine or human, historical or non-historical—could ever assume an absolutely normative, non-ironic status. No one could ever *be* the way, the truth and the life. No name can ever be placed above every other name in some sort of unrevisable, unrepealable way. For Derrida, the distinction between ironic and non-ironic is always relative to a language game, always framed inside a determinate universe of discourse—like the one at work in the pseudonyms and upbuilding discourses—and hence overshadowed by a certain overarching meta-irony or second-order irony. There would never be any access to a name that can be used in an unconditionally non-ironic way, neither the name of God nor of the god, neither the name of the God-man nor of man.

To speak ironically is to use a word without using it, to use it but in such a way as to keep a certain distance from it, to use it in such a way that if push comes to shove one would be willing to recall it or repeal it. But for Derrida, there is no word in the language that we could ever deploy non-ironically and unconditionally that would ever be exempt from recall. Derrida does not merely mention the name of God, he uses it; but he uses it ironically, with the proviso that he could always substitute another name in another context and under other pressures. No word can escape the chain of substitutions, because a word gets to be a word by assuming its differential place within the chain of substitutions, by its spacing from other words. Any word that would seek an exemption from that condition would seek exemption from language itself. There is no *appeal* that can be formulated in terms that are not subject to *repeal*. That means for Derrida, *not that there is no unconditional responsibility,* but that (1) an unconditional responsibility, if there is such a thing, *can never be formulated in unconditional terms, in non-ironic language,* because there are no terms from which one would not want to keep a certain distance; (2) something unconditional does not belong to the order of "knowing" at all.

Spacing

For Derrida, Christianity is not simply a religion in which the eternal is *inscribed in time,* which is the offense and paradox that sends the head of Johannes Climacus spinning. For him, Christianity is inscribed in the *khora,* and along with Christianity the very distinction between time and eternity, which are the binary Platonic terms in which Climacus formulates the Absolute Paradox. For Derrida, "eternity" arises from its differential spacing (*différance*) from "time," and therefore the very idea of eternity itself is inscribed in *khora* (*différance*). That, if I may say so, poses an offense that would be even more disconcerting for Johannes Climacus than the one he poses, because everything in Kierkegaard and his pseudonyms depends upon the determinacy of this distinction, upon what Nietzsche calls a certain "faith in opposites," the faith that God and his eternity differ from and hence *escape this spacing.* But what if the very distinction between time and eternity were itself inscribed in *khora*? Then the question that Climacus asks would have to take an even more paradoxical form: can an eternal happiness be based upon a point of departure in the *khora*? Let us consider this more closely.

There is an important notion of "spacing" in the *Postscript,* and "existence" is its surname. For Johannes Climacus, "existence is the spacing that holds apart" (CUP, 1:118), that spaces being and thought and keeps them separate. But God, who is "outside existence," is untouched by this spacing, which is why the *name of God* has a non-ironic status and is not drawn into the chain of substitutions or play of undecidability, a non-ironic status that then is communicated to the God-man, as the place where the eternal makes its decisive and unique entrance into time. Spacing defines the space of existence, but God occupies a place (or a non-place) outside existence, so that God can view existence as a whole, which is why Climacus thinks that existence for God is a system.[11] That means that "spacing" for Climacus has a "regional" sense: spacing ranges over a limited or finite space, a created space, the space of creation. For Johannes Climacus, the fit between "reality" and "ideality," or between being and human thought, is never airtight. There is, one might well say, a structural or formal undecidability about the relation between anything ideal, anything that takes place in thought or language, and its counterpart in reality. Reality left to itself is the sphere of simple immediacy; ideality left to itself is the placid sphere of the self-identical thought. "Consciousness" is the disturbance that results when their wires are crossed, when they "collide," as it is put in *Johannes Climacus* (PF, 166–72). Consciousness is the friction or static that is produced when these heterogeneous elements come into contact. Something that exists in reality enjoys innocence and tranquility, but a disturbance is created when language, which is ideality, attempting to express that reality, inevitably ends up saying something *else,* something ideal. Consciousness is the *différance* between the two, the *relation* between the two, the comparison of the two, the attempt to negotiate the distance between the two, to bring the real to its ideal expression, to pin the ideal on the reality it expresses. Left to themselves, reality and ideality represent a hushed silence, like a newly fallen snow, untouched and unmarked, while consciousness is the jarring dissonance that results by bringing them into relation, like clanking gears that do not quite mesh. Ideality is a suit that is never cut to fit reality; it is too perfect, too unchanging, too sweeping, too universal for the facticity and actuality of what exists. To put it in Aristotelian terms, ideality seems always either to overshoot (*hyperbole*) or undershoot (*ellipsis*) the mark of actuality. The position, as has been pointed out,[12] is extremely close to Derrida's, for whom there is a structural gap between language, which belongs to the element of ideality (or repeatability) and singularity (or unrepeatability). The gap appears most famously in Derrida's well-known discussion, in *On the Name,* of the proper name, which, if it is to be proper, the name of just this one and no one else, must be unrepeatable, and if it is to be a name, a signifier, must be a repeatable—an "aporia" that Johannes Climacus would call a "collision" or "contradiction."

Consciousness, which arises from the collision and takes an interest in the relation, can *either* choose to leave the gap uncrossed, to withhold consent, and thus in the manner of the *epoche* of the Greek skeptics avoid error. *Or* it can engage existence, take the leap across the gap and *believe,* have faith, that the real and the ideal somehow or other meet up *in actu exercitu.* That would be true of faith in the ordinary sense, but it is true *eminentiore modo* of religious faith, faith to the second power (PF, 87–88). That is the leap par excellence from time to eternity, clutching to a line that stretches from time to eternity, which is also a line of force that charges the moment with eternal significance. In faith, Anti-Climacus says, the self "rests transparently in its source," which is God, who is outside existence and time and spacing. The self in time is anchored by faith in the "changelessness of God," linked to the eternity that gives the moment both urgency and what Anti-Climacus calls a certain "transparency." The voice of eternity is always hovering just off stage, like a producer who is liable at any moment to cancel the play, to make an entrance on stage and pronounce the words that fill us with fear and trembling: "this day your soul is required in eternity." So when Anti-Climacus speaks of "transparency," I understand a situation that has been drained of irony.

But because the effects of *khora* are not "regional" for Derrida but ubiquitous, and because its spacing spaces everything, including the space or distance that stretches from time to eternity, the "self" in deconstruction cannot rest "transparently" in an eternal source but is tossed about in *khora,* as is the very distinction between time and eternity. For Derrida everything—self and non-self, resting and restlessness, time and eternity, derivative and source, God and world, aesthetic, ethical, and religious—is inscribed in *khora*. Nothing is unmarked by its spacing, which means that none of these names can be drained entirely of irony. Accordingly, faith in Derrida has no such "transparency," no non-ironic anchor in the "changelessness of God," for eternity, like time itself, is inscribed in *khora*. Derrida's faith is the faith of an anchorite without an anchor, a faith marked not by "resting transparently in its source," but by a restless exposure to *khora,* which is neither temporal nor eternal but provides the place for both. *Khora* is the spacing of *différance,* in which everything is spaced, *including* the name of God. Even to say that God is "outside existence" is itself to invoke the spacing of *différance,* in virtue of which one is able to mark off the distance between what is inside existence and what is *"outside"* it, so that nothing escapes this spacing, including and especially anything "outside" existence. There is no outside-spacing: *il n'y a pas de hors-espacement.*

Let there be no misunderstanding. I am not saying that Kierkegaard did not have a lively sense of the darker side of the "abyss" of *khora,* which frequently shows up in the authorship. Who can forget his citation of *Richard III* in *Fear and Trembling,* when he says that Richard's monologue—"I that am rudely stamp'd, and want love's majesty/ To strut before a wanton ambling nymph"—"has more value than all the systems of morality, which have no intimation of the nightmares of existence or of their explanation" (FT, 105)? No one has faith who has not grasped "the horror of life," who does not realize that "a soldier standing alone with a loaded rifle at his post near a powder magazine on a stormy night thinks strange thoughts" (FT, 50), which is how and why faith comes to our rescue. Nothing is truly edifying without the terror of existence. The forgiveness of sins is edifying, but sin itself is the terror; healing pain is edifying, but the pain is the terror. The degree of the terrifying and the degree of the edifying correspond.[13] When, sitting all alone in Sæding, where his father tended sheep, in distant Jutland, thinking such abysmal and eternal thoughts, the thought comes over him that we are loved by God, loved by the father, which is, he says "the one single unshakable thing in life, the true Archimedean point" (JP, 5:5468). That changeless love of God, which is the subject of "The Changelessness of God," is the one bit of changelessness in our lives, and is our anchor, our fulcrum, for God, who is in eternity and outside existence, escapes its spacing. But for Derrida such faith is always faith inscribed within the *khora,* which means faith without faith, as hope is always hope against hope. For we do not know who we are, and we have no such determinate Archimedean point, for the name of God is endlessly substitutable. When Derrida returns, not to the Jutland heaths but to his Algerian home not far from the desert/khora, he is overtaken by the thought not only of the father's love and also of the mother's, of Monica/Georgette, but he also finds both inscribed within the *khora* and so finds himself "before," or face to face, with faceless *khora*—*coram khora*. For Derrida there is no way to sink anchor within *khora*, no place to sink anchor in an abyss, no way to swing free from it. Derrida is an an-chor-ite without an anchor.

In Place of a Conclusion

Well, then, the truth is out. The midnight hour has arrived and I have removed my mask. I have come full circle: the truth is that deconstruction is *not* an edifying discourse, and deconstructive Socratism is in truth a form of the sickness unto death after all, which takes the form of a certain *khoral* or anchoral despair, lost in a place-less, face-less abyss! The stern judges of deconstruction with whom I began were right after all! Is that not so? No, no, God forbid. I am not saying that there is nothing unconditional in deconstruction, no radical responsibility, no affirmation of the impossible, nothing "undeconstructible." On the contrary, I have labored mightily to demonstrate the prayers and tears of Jacques Derrida. But I am saying there are no terms in which this affirmation can be unconditionally expressed, no non-ironic way to express the faith, hope, and love of deconstructive praxis. For its *viens, oui, oui* belongs to a more indeterminate and endlessly determinable sphere, to a khoral space, where we do not know who or what we are, where we may very well rightly pass as atheists, where the *name* of God is the name of God's love for us, the name of someone who loves us, the name of love itself, the name of what we love, but the question persists, *what do I love when I love my God?*

Because the name of God is not outside existence and time but inscribed within the play of substitutions, because it is not outside the *khora* but inscribed within it, and because the *khora* is an abyssal place, a *mis en abîme,* the name of God is endlessly *translatable* for Derrida. That means that it is caught up in an undecidable fluctuation with justice and hospitality, the gift and forgiveness. That is not true in Christian Socratism, which is organized by a non-ironic word/Word. God is the author of every good gift and every gift comes from "above," from outside existence, from God "with whom there is no variation or shadow due to change" (James 1.17). But while it is true for Derrida that every good gift comes from God, it is *no less true* that the name of God is forged in *différance,* with the result that the name of God is one of the names we give to the gift, that every God comes from good gifts, that the gift is the author of every good God. That is also true; there is no Either–Or here, no question of choosing between the two. There is no way to arrest the fluctuation between the undecidability of God and the gift, no way to stop God and the gift from *trading places* (ON, 76). In Kierkegaard, the Christian ironist and humorist negotiates the distance between two relatively determinate places, urging a decision Either–Or; in Derrida, these places keep trading places undecidably.

It is not that deconstruction is not up-building, but that there is no way to know *what* we are building up in Derrida's up-building discourse, no non-ironic Archimedean point. Deconstruction is building up, not building down, as its name might suggest, but it is building without a plan, constituting an upbuilding discourse in which we cannot say what is under construction, building in "view" of an absolutely unforeseeable future, without the aid or benefit of a normative text or normative life and death, of anything or anyone who could provide the pattern for the way of the truth and the life to come. Of this absolute future we can only say that it is to come, that we are "hoping, sighing, dreaming" of its coming (Circum, 314), as we dream of the Messiah (who never quite shows up). That is because what we are building belongs to the structure of desire (*inquietum est cor nostrum*), which requires a horizon of unforeseeability, a "to come" (*à venir, l'avenir*), which renders every historical name, however holy, revisable and in principle subject to obsolescence, so that no one name can be given that is above every other name in an unrevisable way. That includes presently privileged names like democracy, justice, and the gift, which are but the least bad names we have now for what is to come, but which remain names that we are prepared to recall in the name of something to come, I know not what.

Because for Derrida *khora* represents an uncontainable receptacle and an implacable "necessity" (ON, 125–26), the effects of undecidability cannot be regionally contained. Undecidability cannot be resolved by transparency, by removing the mask and facing up to the truth that we are living an illusion, that we are not what we say we are, that our lives are steeped in two-headed ambiguity, in *Zweideutigkeit*, because there would never be any non-ironic way to say who we really are or what we should be. For the khoral figure of Socrates, *undecidability* is more radical than *ambiguity*, more many-headed, more unmanageably Medusan, even as its second-order irony or "meta-irony" is more bottomless than an irony or humor that is strategic, the incognito of a *cognitum*, which means of a determinate something that is in some way accessed or affirmed by faith. Undecidability runs deeper than ambiguity because undecidability lies in not knowing who we are, or *what* we are, in keeping that an open Socratic question, in a medium that Derrida once described as *sans voir, sans avoir, sans savoir*.[14] In virtue of its notion of undecidability, deconstruction drifts in the direction not of a sure-footed Socrates who knows his place but of a Socrates who occupies a non-place, perhaps a little more like the Socrates of *The Concept of Irony*, whose irony is an "infinite absolute negativity," a completely negative power (CI, 40). Or perhaps a "circumcised" Socrates, who roots out illusion, not in order to deceive us into the truth, but who is "cut off from the truth," (Circum, 314), who is accordingly the greatest among the sophists because he is the most radical and consistent sophist (CI, 138–39).

To be sure, deconstruction could never make do with "infinite absolute negativity" alone. For its higher-order irony goes hand in hand with a higher affirmation of the impossible, a more radical desire for what is to come, which requires that we keep a certain ironic distance from anything that is present, past present, or determinately foreseeably future-present, like a historical Messiah who has already come and promises to come again. But this has nothing to do with despair; for this is all said in order to keep hope alive, to keep the future unconditionally open to the messianic itself, *s'il y en a,* so that it is always necessary to hope and sigh and dream, to say and pray, *viens, oui, oui.*

Notes

1. Although such critics are legion, for a recent criticism of Derrida as an aesthete, devoid of hope and lost in a bad infinite, see Graham Ward, "Questioning God," in *Questioning God,* ed. John D. Caputo, Mark Dooley, and Michael J. Scanlon (Bloomington: Indiana University Press, 2001), 274–90; see also C. Stephen Evans, "Realism and Antirealism in Kierkegaard's *Concluding Unscientific Postscript,*" in *The Cambridge Companion to Kierkegaard,* ed. Alastair Hannay and Gordon D. Marino (Cambridge: Cambridge University Press, 1998), 154–76.

2. I use the following abbreviations of the works of Derrida:
Circum: "Circumfession: Fifty-nine Periods and Periphrases," in Geoffrey Bennington and Jacques Derrida, *Jacques Derrida* (Chicago: University of Chicago Press, 1993);
DP: *Deconstruction and Pragmatism: Simon Critchley, Jacques Derrida, Ernesto Laclau, and Richard Rorty,* ed. Chantal Mouffe (London: Routledge, 1996);
FL: "The Force of Law: 'The Mystical Foundation of Authority,'" trans. Mary Quantaince, in *Deconstruction and the Possibility of Justice,* ed. Drucilla Cornell et al. (New York: Routledge, 1992);
GD: *The Gift of Death,* trans. David Wills (Chicago: University of Chicago Press, 1995);
GT: *Given Time, I: Counterfeit Money,* trans. Peggy Kamuf (Chicago: University of Chicago Press, 1991);
OH: *The Other Heading: Reflections on Today's Europe,* trans. Pascale-Anne Brault and Michael Naas (Bloomington: Indiana University Press, 1992);
ON: *On the Name,* ed. Thomas Dutoit (Stanford, Calif.: Stanford University Press, 1995);
Points: Points . . . Interviews, 1974–94, ed. Elisabeth Weber, trans. Peggy Kamuf (Stanford, Calif.: Stanford University Press, 1995);
WD: *Writing and Difference,* trans. Alan Bass (Chicago: University of Chicago Press, 1978).

3. I have argued for an interpretation of Derrida as a certain Jewish Augustine in *The Prayers and Tears of Jacques Derrida: Religion without Religion* (Bloomington: Indiana University Press, 1997); see sec. VI, "Confession." See also Gideon Ofrat, *The Jewish Derrida,* trans. Peretz Kidron (Syracuse, N.Y.: Syracuse University Press, 2001).

4. For Anti-Climacus, to be oneself, to be alone with oneself, is not to be alone at all but to be before God, *coram deo,* with all the "prodigious strenuousness" and "prodigious responsibility" this requires (SUD, 5). In Derrida, the "structure" of the "before God" is repeated—even though he quite rightly passes for an atheist—a certain "before God or death," for he will often juxtapose the two. The "name of God" for Derrida is the name of the future and of expectation, of a hope in a justice to come, or a democracy to come, which keeps the future open and which holds the present up against the white light of messianic expectation. It does not succumb in despair to what Anti-Climacus calls settling for the finite, the possible, but keeps hope alive for the impossible, the infinite, the *à venir.* Thus just as the self for Kierkegaard must stand in the absolute white light of the *coram deo,* the self for Derrida must keep itself open and exposed to the *à venir.* By the same token, there is in deconstruction no despair of infinitude, no empty dreaming of an impossible justice, but rather justice is demanded here and now, and justice deferred is justice denied. *The* impossible, the justice *to come,* is always deferred, *and* justice deferred is justice denied. The aporia posed by holding both these positions defines the situation in which decisions are made, providing its conditions of (im)possibility. See FL, 22–29.

5. Michael Strawser, *Both/And: Reading Kierkegaard from Irony to Edification* (New York: Fordham University Press, 1997). Hereafter BA.

6. While there might seem to be a formal purity of will in consistently willing evil, such a choice is actually divided against itself by the bite of conscience; for however long and deeply one desires evil, one will just as long and just as deeply be gnawed at and disturbed by the good that one *also* wills, that one cannot help but will, that one wills without wanting to will, while the evil that one wills one knows one also does not will; this we know, if not full well, at least in some subterranean recess in our souls. Kierkegaardian undecidability is Pauline and Augustinian: it is willing what one wills not and willing not what one wills. See "Purity of Heart Is to Will One Thing," in UDVS.

7. Caputo, *Prayers and Tears,* xx.

8. I have tried to spell out more carefully the role of *khora* in Derrida in *Deconstruction in a Nutshell: A Conversation with Jacques Derrida,* ed. John D. Caputo (New York: Fordham University Press, 1997), ch. 3.

9. Jean-Luc Marion, *God without Being,* trans. Thomas Carlson (Chicago: University of Chicago Press, 1991), 119–26; see the discussion of the "inanity of Being" in *Idol and Distance,* trans. Thomas Carlson (New York: Fordham University Press, 2001), 233–53.

10. Strawser, *Both/And,* "Conclusion," 227–49.

11. When Climacus says that an existential system is possible for God, one would have to qualify that: it is possible for God only insofar as God is "outside existence" (CUP, 1:118), so that God is able to *see* all things in time in a single sweep. God is not subjected to the "spacing that holds apart," by which existence spaces being and thought (ibid.). But this must not be construed to mean that the choices of existing individuals belong to a deductive system and hence are necessitated by the system in a way that is known only by God and not by us. For that would mean that they are objectively certain and logically necessary,

although the existing individual is ignorant of their necessity, which would mean that the abyss of freedom, possibility, and the leap are all optical illusions created by being trapped inside existence, by living in time.

12. See Strawser, *Both/And,* 71–81, for an excellent discussion of this line of argument from *Johannes Climacus.*

13. See ibid., citing CD, 102.

14. Derrida, *Parages* (Paris: Galilée, 1986), 25.

2

R E A D I N G *E I T H E R – O R* F O R T H E
V E R Y F I R S T T I M E

Roger Poole

DEAR *SYMPARANEKROMENOI,* this is a very important occasion. We are all aware that this is no ordinary gathering. We have not been blown together from the four corners of the earth as delegates to such gatherings usually are, coming at random for a variety of reasons. No, we know that we are not here by chance. A process of selection has gone on, over quite a few years, such that, inexorably, bit by bit, as publications have come out and we have read reviews of each other's work, we have marked each other's names out as "interesting," then "significant," then "essential" in the plan of our own reading and writing. Indeed, would it be too much to say that over the years we have become friends?

We, the *Symparanekromenoi,* the fellowship of buried lives, first of all fell under the incantatory influence of Søren Kierkegaard, and then some of us fell a second time, fell under the influence of those many subtly dissonant and jarring literary identities that are all officially attributed to one man, called Jacques Derrida. In an act of what Harold Bloom would call *apophrades,* the dismal days on which the mighty dead return to haunt us with their voices, we began to read Kierkegaard's texts in Derrida's and Derrida's in Kierkegaard's. A strange kind of dialogue was set up between them, and we began to hear Derrida adopting an unusually old-fashioned Danish accent, while Kierkegaard seemed suddenly to have taken on a French sophistication that we had never noticed in him before.

And we, the delegates to this conference, the *Symparanekromenoi,* picked up this strange dialogue on the acoustic intertextual airwaves. Each locked away in some dim corner of the house that we call euphemistically our "study," ignored by the entire academic world, and especially ignored by the utterly sane members of our family, who could never work out what it was we were doing in the first place, we became party to this intriguing dialogue on the philosophical airwaves, the dialogue that only the *Symparanekromenoi* can hear—or overhear. We fell under its spell. We turned down the CD player with its blaring discords from Mahler's symphonies, and then, eventually, we turned it off altogether. We needed silence, in order to listen.

So we are here because we listen. We hear things. We pay attention. That is, I suppose, what the anonymous after-dinner lecturer in *Either–Or* who addresses his friends, the *Symparanekromenoi*, mainly assumes about them—that they pay attention, that they notice things, that they reflect, that they are independent minds, free spirits, and above all, that they are mentally pretty sharp. No slouches they, no sluggards. That after-dinner speaker knows full well, as he talks about his modern Antigone or about how all men are bores, that he is talking to people who have a very low tolerance for boredom. They are witty, sharp people, people who notice things. They are so naturally, for it is a characteristic of the *Symparanekromenoi* that they have given up on the flashier and gaudier pleasures of life. They are not deceived by outward appearances. They want the real thing. And so they listen attentively, and the lecturer is on his mettle not to be either boring or predictable.

And so, it is with some apprehension that I am undertaking to talk today about reading *Either–Or* "for the very first time." When we were crossing the bridge out of Frederiksborg Castle last spring, Joakim Garff asked me about my title for today and when I told him that it was "reading *Either–Or* for the very first time," he laughed out loud. And indeed others have laughed too at my title. Even more so when I tell them that it is taken from a famous song of Madonna's, "Like a Virgin." "Like a virgin, for the very first time" she croons in her overfamiliar way. Another individual who heard that line and thought he could profit from it was Sir Richard Branson, the richest multimillionaire in England. He decided to found a new transatlantic airline, which would do something "for the very first time," and that would be to ferry passengers across the Atlantic for almost nothing (if only they would agree to sit for hours and wait for a seat in the departure lounge and also have the forethought to bring their own sandwiches with them). The idea flourished and made him the fourth or fifth of his fortunes. He founded Virgin Airlines. Just because he listened, just because he heard, the potential of Madonna's line, he seems to me to have elected himself as an honorary member of the *Symparanekromenoi*. In fact, he is the wealthiest of our members, and I for one am delighted to have this amount of financial backing for our after-dinner society.

But, whatever it may be that Sir Richard Branson made of Madonna's line, what use do I propose to make of it? It seems to me that the essence of good reading is to read each literary work, as soon as we set ourselves to re-read it, for the very first time. The philosopher never dares to believe that he knows something for sure, for certain, for ever. Every text from Kierkegaard's hand is an attempt to get us to read, not through the spectacles of custom and convention, but for the very first time.

No work of Kierkegaard's has suffered more from the reading of custom and convention than *Either–Or*. In one of David Lodge's novels, there is an amusing dinner-party scene in which all the dinner guests are put on their honor to name a famous book that they have not read. One guest is so naïve as to admit that he has never actually sat down and read *Hamlet*. At this, there is a general swell of revulsion against the poor man, because, of course, *not one* of the dinner guests has actually *read Hamlet*. It is so famous that one somehow assumes one has read it, without actually bothering to do so. *Either–Or* comes into this category. And *Either–Or* is, it must be admitted, very difficult to read, from end to end. There are terrible lacunae of boredom, which belong to its genre, the Danish belles lettres of the 1830s and 1840s. But some sections are so sharp—the preface, the "Diapsalmata," the essay on Mozart, "The Rotation Method," for instance—that one feels refreshed in the way that one does when listening to a brilliant conversationalist at a party. And its *mood*—its mood is so generous, so unbuttoned, so entirely relaxed, that it is hard to find anything that resembles it: sections of Shakespeare's Falstaff, perhaps; sections of Laurence Sterne's *Tristram Shandy;* passages from *Pickwick Papers;* passages from Joyce's *Ulysses.*

But of course, the suggestion that we could ever read *Either–Or* "for the very first time" is an irony. Only by reading everything we possibly can, can we ever read well enough to read for the very first time. But as we read and re-read, we also have to do a certain amount of un-reading, for we now have to read *against the commentaries* as well as *for the text.* The reason there is so much unhelpful commentary about *Either–Or* is that its *genre* has never been taken sufficiently into account. That is perhaps understandable and even forgivable, in view of the difficulties of classification. *Either–Or* is in fact sui generis.

First we read it through Walter Lowrie's biography and saw it as a text about a broken engagement. Then we read it in the translation by David Swenson and Lillian Swenson (vol. 1) and Walter Lowrie (vol. 2) of 1944, which was the received text for forty years. This translation is a kind of Edwardian Olde Englishe Tea-Shoppe, with its oldy-worldy tradition of "ayes" and "forsooths" and pretty little Danish maidens tripping along "East Street" and being seduced by passionate aesthetes. Most readers, I suspect, gave up halfway through when it came to reading the long and turgid letters of Judge Wilhelm, and I also unkindly suspect that few ever actually got round to reading the sermon from the vicar on the Jutland heath with which *Or* concludes.

Then in 1988 it was turned into something that very much resembles an academic treatise, through the stately translation from Howard and Edna Hong. Unfortunately, and I say this with regret, the *tone* of *Either–Or* has been lost in this new translation. Hence, as a direct result, the *genre* of *Either–Or* too has been changed out of recognition by the new translation. Originally an irreverent, devil-may-care potpourri of exuberant essays flung together by a young man madly in love with writing, it has become indistinguishable from a textbook, whose serious tone seems to aim at instructing, rather than amusing, its audience. Now, whatever else it may set itself as an aim, *Either–Or* does not set out to instruct: rather it places the reader in front of a series of choices and decisions, all of which demand *reader participation*. It is what Roland Barthes would call a "scriptible" (as opposed to a "lisible") text.

Meanwhile, in *After Virtue* we had been dragooned into reading it through Alasdair MacIntyre's[1] eyes and been instructed that it was a fatally flawed example of modern slapdash thinking, which so betrays the great tradition that Aristotle had founded that it was little less than actually pernicious (one chapter actually proposes an either-or of its own in the form of "Nietzsche or Aristotle?"). Since then, we have had a reformulation of his own position from Alasdair MacIntyre, plus a host of accompanying critical essays on that, in a volume called *Kierkegaard after MacIntyre*.[2]

And so it goes. One tradition of reading occludes another, and always we are always failing because we fail to take the first correct step. The first correct step is to define the kinds of difficulty we are in. We have to start here because (of necessity) we cannot define the *genre* of *Either–Or*. And this is what I see as the importance of this conference. We are here to re-state the reading-problem of *Either–Or*, we are here to set the readerly "horizon of expectation" *back* a century and a half, and in doing that we propose to start our object of scrutiny on its *modern* career. We are here to read it "for the very first time," and that means *accurately*.

So, what "is" *Either–Or*?

The very first thing to note about it is that it is a literary work. This may be stunningly obvious, but in fact the great tradition of what I call "blunt reading" has never taken account of that. The first green shoot that sprouted was Louis Mackey's *Kierkegaard: A Kind of Poet* in 1971.[3] The implications appear to have lain quite unappreciated for fifteen years. Apparently undeterred, Louis Mackey expanded his own line of thought in a new study, which managed to incorporate some of the best insights of deconstruction, *Points of View: Readings of Kierkegaard* (1986).[4]

Due to the entrepreneurial activity of Mark C. Taylor, who issued that volume in a new series called *Kierkegaard and Postmodernism*, it was accompanied by a breakthrough comparative essay by John Vignaux Smyth entitled *A Question of Eros: Irony in Sterne, Kierkegaard, and Barthes*.[5] The coordinates offered in the subtitle show that something finally was afoot. In 1987, Pat Bigelow's remarkable study *Kierkegaard and the Problem of Writing*[6] finally linked *Either–Or* up with Husserl, Heidegger, Derrida, and the acoustic world of Joyce's *Finnegans Wake*. One might have thought that Louis Mackey's basic contention—that Kierkegaard is and remains "a kind of poet"—was now at last safely launched. But alas, that happy moment of

1986–87 seems a kind of lost paradise, which has, over the last fifteen years, given way to an ever greater Alexandrianism, an unfettered self-indulgence in interpretation and commentary. The essential *aim* of *Either–Or,* that is to say, has got lost. The work has been so over-interpreted that it has become uninterpretable.

So, I return to my question: what "is" *Either–Or?*

The very first thing to notice about it is that it is a literary work *first and foremost,* not a philosophical treatise or a series of lectures, as it appears to be in the new Princeton translation. During the first three months of 2000, I had the honor of being a research fellow at the Søren Kierkegaard Research Center in Copenhagen, and it fell to me as part of my duties to deliver three seminars. I delivered, then, three seminars on various works of Kierkegaard— *Fear and Trembling, Either–Or, The Concept of Dread, The Sickness unto Death.* I presented these works as artifacts that were *first and foremost* literary works. These works were literary constructions, I insisted, *before* any form of philosophical or theological "meaning" could be extracted from them, and any philosophical and theological "meaning" was in fact inextricably bound up with their literary form and could not be presented in any way that was independent of their literary form. I got a friendly, well-disposed, and tolerant reception, but I could see that my learned colleagues entertained a very great deal of skepticism. *First and foremost* literary works? *No* "meaning" that would be independent of literary form?[7]

Since I was arguing that *Either–Or* is first and foremost a literary work, let me tell you how I presented it on that occasion. Given the fact of pseudonymity, which places the work firmly in the tradition of German belles lettres of the earlier nineteenth century, I suggested that we needed what I called a "filter" to put over our lens, in order to give the sort of reading that was appropriate to that convention. The convention is an intertextual one. *Either–Or* is a continuous play upon preceding literary works in the Romantic canon, and the amount of intelligibility we can derive from any given essay in *Either–Or* depends upon the *significant distance, the literary distance, that the essay sets up from its original.* This significant distance is decided by its relation to the foregoing work in one or more of four ways: genre, style, intention, or mood.

It follows from this that if we are to read *Either–Or* for the very first time, we have to read each and every essay in it as *a departure from* some other text that the young Kierkegaard of 1841–43 may have had in his mind as part of his recent reading. In other words, the reading of the individual essays in *Either–Or* is quite literally an exercise in Derridean "difference." In charting the ways in which the copy is calculated to give a different "meaning" from its original, in charting the ways in which an original can be ironically mishandled to give it a quite new sharpness and point, Kierkegaard obliges us to identify what Harold Bloom calls the "ratio of defense" that is *apo-*

phrades. We have to read, with Derrida, for "difference," and in particular for that form of it that Barbara Johnson calls, in a superbly focused study of Poe, Freud, and Lacan, "the critical difference."

Thus reading *Either–Or* "for the very first time" can only be done once you have read it twenty times before, and not only it, but all the first-, second-, and third-rate Danish and German literature upon which the young Kierkegaard may have grazed during his impressionable student years, years in which he did little else but read voraciously. From this "differential" reading, one can derive a first, preliminary layer of authorial intentionality, shorn (so far) of any actual context. It is for the reader to find a context. It is here that the work of decipherment involves intertextuality. For *into what context* is the reader to set these essays?

That the essays are not set out as a choice in philosophical ethics as such must surely be clear, yet the reading that is in fact traditionally imposed on *Either–Or* is a crude and violent one. It is usually put in these terms: *either* one chooses the aesthetic life *or* one chooses the ethical life. But this is an impossibly "blunt" formulation, and that for textual reasons. The whole structure of the book is aesthetic and *both* the offers made within it are aesthetic offers. "Blunt reading" refuses to recognize this obvious fact. The whole "novel" is aesthetic through and through. For that is what it is—"a kind of novel," just as Kierkegaard is "a kind of poet."

The whole novel is aesthetic through and through. It is curious to have to assert this about a novel, for who would ever have thought otherwise? But the tradition of "blunt reading" (which in this case starts with the Danes themselves, from Brandes and Høffding to Thulstrup and Løgstrup) has always read the work as if it were an essay on ethics, with a stark choice presented to the reader, and a demand that he or she should *choose* and thus amend his or her life accordingly. Of no other novel in existence could or would such a demand be made.

I have settled to the conviction that *Either–Or* is modeled much more closely upon *Wilhelm Meister* than I had thought before. In the Copenhagen seminars, I laid out a variety of possible literary models, *Wilhelm Meister* among them, but I now think that the forms in *Either–Or* are based upon the forms in Goethe's novel, both *Wilhelm Meisters Lehrjarhe* of 1794–96 and *Wilhelm Meisters Wanderjahre* (1821–29). The intelligibility *Either–Or* has, in any specific section, is directly derived from an appreciation of the distance it has taken from Goethe's original. Intelligibility is thus literally a function of Derridean difference.

The suggestion that *Either–Or* was modeled on *Wilhelm Meister* was first made by F. J. Billeskov Jansen in his book *Kierkegaard's Literary Art* in 1951. It was repeated by Louis Mackey in his book of 1971, but with a considerable sophistication. Mackey agreed that *Either–Or* was a *Bildungsroman* like Goethe's, and was indeed modeled upon it.

> But when Kierkegaard set about writing a *Bildungsroman*, there had to be
> some changes made. His view of human nature and in particular of human
> freedom necessitated a parodic imitation. For if each stage on life's way rep-
> resents a radical self-choice from which there is no exit save by way of
> another equally radical choice of a radically different self, then it follows that
> there is no necessary continuity in human personality. And this breach of
> continuity—the transition from aesthetic to ethical, ethical to religious, or
> vice versa—cannot be represented unambiguously in fiction. The free elec-
> tion of an existential *possibility* cannot be exhibited without distortion in a
> fictional mode committed to the principle of the natural evolution of human
> *potentialities*. It must therefore be left out.[8]

"It must therefore be left out." I take my hat off before criticism of this
order. For it deduces a philosophical position from literary form as such.
This is the opposite of "blunt reading." The invention, too, of the new
genre-category of "parodic imitation" is interesting. If "parody" is normally
a pastiche for its own sake (for fun) and if "imitation" is a serious literary
endeavor (such as Spenser's "overgoing" of Ariosto and Tasso), then "parodic
imitation" (Louis Mackey's term) is slightly oxymoronic. It implies a parody,
yes, but one that is not content with merely guying the original text, but
that seriously intends to substitute a new meaning for the one that has been
ironized or ridiculed. *Don Quixote* would be an excellent example.

> There is no narrative resolution of the stretto among A, Judge Wilhelm, the
> priest from Jutland, and all the real or putative others. Each is stuck fast in
> his own categories, by his own choice; none of them develops; their actions
> merely reiterate their choices. The novel in which they live is a *Bildungsro-
> man,* but without *Bildung.* Kierkegaard has exaggerated the technical variety
> of the universal novel in such a way as to prevent its unity.[9]

"The novel in which they live is a *Bildungsroman,* but without *Bildung.*"
Again the incisive insight. And again the invention of new genre-categories:
exaggeration, technical variety, universal novel, prevention of unity—without being able, so rapidly is he thinking, to come up with exactly the terms
he needs. Louis Mackey has left the proper naming and sorting of these new
genre-categories for us to establish.

Now, possibly, we have begun on our way toward reading *Either–Or* "for
the very first time," and that is because we are reading it through the filter
I proposed in the Copenhagen seminars, a "filter" that picks up differential
distance from an unstated original text. We are reading for difference. F. J.
Billeskov Jansen[10] had pointed out, as early as 1951, that *Wilhelm Meisters
Wanderjahre* established the following literary conventions: the exchange of
letters, inset narratives that are read aloud, the diary form, a collection of
aphorisms, and scattered observations taken from an archive. He further notes
that Goethe's novel set the fashion in German fiction for thirty years, by
inventing the fashion for anonymity, in whole or in part, and for what he

calls "Navneskjulet," the hiding of names. German writers who imitated *Wilhelm Meister* were Ludwig Tieck, in *Franz Sternbalds Wanderungen* (1798); Frederick Schlegel with *Lucinde* (1799); Jean Paul with *Titan* (1800–1803); and Novalis with *Heinrich von Ofterdingen* (published posthumously in 1802). But then he adds a throwaway line, the significance of which I had not seen until recently:

> *Either–Or* and *Stages on Life's Way* are part of this line of descent. The German Romantics, from whom Kierkegaard had assimilated so much, gave his own novels about life-views a multicoloured playfulness in style, an interplay of irony and pathos, *which was foreign to Goethe*[*som Goethe ikke kendte*].[11] (my emphasis)

So, it was through the sentimental, excessive, Romantic, fantastic, self-indulgent copies of *Wilhelm Meister* made by this "second eleven" of German Romanticism that Kierkegaard learned how to modify the austerity and didactic formality of Goethe himself. In other words, if Goethe had given him the model of a *Bildungsroman* that could be shorn of *Bildung,* then Tieck, Schlegel, Jean Paul, and Novalis had been ransacked for technical devices by which the aesthetic elements of the novel could be made much more intriguing to a reading public that might well have found Goethe tedious or even incomprehensible. (That *is* possible, even today!)

Add to this that it was Schleiermacher's *Vertraute Briefe uber die Lucinde* that in 1835 introduced to Kierkegaard the very idea he was looking for. Schleiermacher, instead of offering a single coherent reasoned view of *Lucinde,* invents the device of having a variety of letter writers offering personal (and also seriously conflicting) views of this scandalous novel, all under a single pair of covers and issued anonymously. Well! The basic formal structure of *Either–Or* was delivered to the young Kierkegaard on a plate: a central idea, position, philosophy, or text discussed by a variety of personages under the covers of a single book, and that book published by a mere editor! Writing in his Journal in 1835 Kierkegaard gives high praise to this device:

> These letters are written about a book *Lucinde* published at one time by F. Schlegel. It is not known for sure whether or not this book is by Schl.(eiermacher), but Gutzkow puts the burden upon everyone to prove that it is not by him. . . . It is probably a model review and also an example of how such a thing can be most productive, in that he constructs a host of personalities out of the book itself and through them illuminates the work *and also illuminates their individuality,* so that instead of being faced by the reviewer with various points of view, we get instead *many personalities who represent these various points of view. But they are complete beings,* so that it is possible to get a glance into the individuality of the single individual and through numerous and yet merely relatively true judgments to draw up our own final judgment. Thus it is a true work of art [*et sandt Kunstværk*]. (PAP I C 69)

Schleiermacher, the theologian, has written (surprisingly enough) "a true work of art" (*"et sandt Kunstværk"*). It was "a true work of art" that Kierkegaard was to reflect upon for three years before, in the period of 1841–42, he began to sketch out the views and opinions of the many characters who set up their debate in *Either–Or.*

We are now starting out toward reading *Either–Or* "for the very first time," because we are reading it in the literary context in which it was conceived, and bringing to bear, by the correct use of the "filter," exactly those intertextual factors that we need to be aware of if we are ever to attempt to establish "meanings."

But as well as *Wilhelm Meister,* as a matrix of forms, there is *Faust* itself. For, shorn of all its metaphysical armature, what does Goethe's *Faust* portray? It is a sketch of a subjectivity that has reached the limits of what might be called objective knowledge. Faust's intelligence has outstripped all the academic systems of his day. There is a kind of divine impatience with the world, an ethical impatience. When he makes the mistake of trying to suppress or forget this impatience by losing himself in an ordinary love affair, he ruins his victim and brings his own intelligence down to a mere parody of itself.

Goethe's *Faust* absolutely haunted the young Kierkegaard. *Faust* and readings of *Faust* take up five columns of entries in the index to his Journals. *Faust* suggested itself irresistibly as a model for *Either–Or.* Margarethe in Goethe's *Faust* is of course one of the three heroines in "Shadowgraphs" who cannot cross the bounds between inner grief and outward expression.

> The source of Faust's fascination for Margaret, according to Goethe also, is not the seductiveness of a Don Juan but his tremendous superiority. Hence she simply cannot understand, as she herself says so lovably, what it is that Faust sees in her to love. . . . What Goethe has somewhere said about Hamlet, that in relation to his body his soul was an acorn planted in a flowerpot which at last breaks the container, is also true of Margaret's love. Faust is too great for her, and her love must finally break her soul in pieces.[12]

Well. Modesty was never his strong suit. "One does not forget my side glance so easily."[13]

But then "The Seducer's Diary" is an extension of "Shadowgraphs," showing what can be done when the seducer does not descend to the body for his seduction, but carries it out entirely at the level of suggestion, innuendo, implication, and the whole arsenal of mere words, both spoken and written. But the seductiveness of suggestion, innuendo, implication, both spoken and written, had been given brilliant notoriety by Schlegel in *Lucinde,* in whose rhetoric and tone we find the exact acoustic ancestor for much of "The Seducer's Diary." If we listen as well as read, we shall *hear* Schlegel while *reading* Goethe. The result—the acoustic-literary result—is the tone of "The Seducer's Diary."

We therefore need two filters to read this part of *Either–Or*, one for Goethe (to do with anxiety and form); and one for the Romantic (to do with decadence and acoustic tone).

But even so, why does all this matter? I have said that *Either–Or* is not set up like an ethical choice as Alasdair MacIntyre believes, but that it is a priori an aesthetic construction. But then, where does the ethical dimension emerge, if we are to read *Either–Or* "for the very first time"?

It emerges in the realization that in *Either–Or*, Kierkegaard has developed a new *genre,* one that has melded the subjectivity of Goethe and the Romantic extravagance of his successors, and created a form in which each and every essay presents a form of existential subjectivity. Each and every essay "tries on" a form of subjectivity, a style of subjectivity, in order to test and examine its implications. To return to the idea of critical difference, it might be useful to recall that Oscar Wilde built *The Picture of Dorian Gray* on that "little yellow book," Huysmans's *A Rebours,* inverted its significance, and established his own "meaning" by the distance he takes from Huysmans's original.

In *Either,* the world of A is a world without others in it. It is the world of a subjectivity either afraid of, or able to do without, communication with others in a *Mitwelt.* For this reason A retreats to the world of the aesthetic. In the preface, with his brilliant little fable of smashing the writing desk, Victor Eremita sets out a program for a continuous pastiche of Hegel's philosophy; A imitates the Fragments of Schlegel in the "Diapsalmata" by setting up a world of solipsistic boredom whose only flashes of illumination come from witty cynicism; it is no doubt simply to pass the time, too, that he writes the brilliant essay on Mozart, and this leads him on, in "Shadowgraphs," to derive some satisfaction from the inability of mishandled women like Donna Elvira and Goethe's Gretchen to give expression to their pain; it is not surprising then, that this suite of essays about the mishandling of women should end up in the found manuscript, the lonely, sadistic, and repressed fantasy of "The Seducer's Diary." Over all the essays hovers the spirit of one of the "Diapsalmata": "How terrible tedium is—terribly tedious. . . . Even pain has lost its refreshment for me. . . . But my soul's poisonous doubt is all-consuming. My soul is like the Dead Sea, over which no bird can fly; when it has flown midway, then it sinks down to death and destruction" (EO, 1:36). In the volume called *Or,* however, the long essays called "The Aesthetic Validity of Marriage" and "Equilibrium between the Aesthetic and the Ethical in the Composition of Personality" propose a quite different experience of time as a subjective reality.

In another (perhaps more surprising) example of *apophrades,* we might find in Marcel Proust the modern development of Kierkegaard's theme of the boring and enervating reality of aesthetic time. *Either–Or* presents two phenomenological descriptions of lived time, both of which are set up by, and constituted by, a certain attitude toward life itself. In the terms in which Husserl put it in his *Lectures on Internal Time Consciousness* (1905–10), it is a matter of intentionality. If the intentionality shown toward the world is that it is an external and hostile space, inhabited by "Others," all of whom are a danger to privacy and safety, and with whom as little as possible communication is to be entered into, then the kind of time experienced will correspond to that, and a failure to desire the very existence of a *Mitwelt,* a world-with-others, will mean that there will be a failure in the flow of time. Such, at least, would seem to be the case of A in *Either.* The aesthete is bored stiff by the passage of time. However much he tries to vary his pleasures, he finds that time never gets a move on. Like des Esseintes in Huysmans's *A Rebours,* the aesthete A takes extreme care with his surroundings, the colors and decorations of his rooms, his food, his amusements, and his erotic obsessions. The aesthetic life turns out to be made up of pleasure and pain in almost equal quantities. "The Seducer's Diary" is, evidently, first and foremost a device for whiling away time. There is no seduction carried out, of course, only the thought of one, and in this act of organized repression the aesthete seeks to kill time. But time persists in flowing ever more slowly. Since aesthetic time is time from which all concepts of the *Mitwelt,* the "we," have been driven out, time begins to drag because there is no new act of self-indulgence or perversity that is interesting enough to develop. Only with the acknowledgment that we share time with others would it be possible to break out of the timelessness of neurotic solipsism.

If, on the other hand, the intentionality shown toward the world is that of a common ethical space, inhabited by *others,* some of (or even most of) whom present a potential for friendship, and with whom daily communication is a very necessity, then the creation of a *Mitwelt* will be automatic, and time will cease to terrify. Time then is not a menace for the ethical individual. The worst that time can do is to flow a bit too slowly. This is an irritation, no doubt, but it is not life threatening. When time flows too slowly, the Judge studies his wife as she moves around in the house, or others as they pass in the street below. He relates to others to improve the flow of time. Being anchored in a communal life, sharing a time scheme through the day with others, a time scheme involving daily tasks and duties as well as pleasures, time is controlled and shared. It is not, as it is for the aesthete, demonic or sudden. Ethical time is communal time, historical time.

The concluding essay, the sermon from the pastor on the Jutland heath, is a formal ending, but the closing lines of *Either–Or* sum up the thrust of the whole: "[Be] convinced that what you have known belongs to you, that no power can take it from you; for only the truth which edifies is truth for you." With that deliberately chosen use of the word "edifies," *opbygger* (deliberately chosen, yes, and also artfully chosen, because technically that which "edifies" belongs to *another* stream of the authorship, that of the *Edifying*

Discourses), we hear the echo of the famous Journal entry at Gilleleje of August 1, 1835: "The thing is to understand myself, to see what God really wishes *me* to do; the thing is to find a truth which is true *for me,* to find *the idea for which I can live and die*" (PAP I A 7:53–60).

Now, while all of these essays in *Either–Or* present styles of subjectivity, some of them seem to us today to be hopelessly rooted in the literary conventions of the day, while others stand out as essays with a striking relevance for our time. And these latter essays are the ones that propose authentic forms of existential subjectivity. The most relevant of these, in our time, may well turn out to be the essays in *Or* rather than those in *Either.* These are the essays about a possible or achievable security of the self in a sea of impressionism and terror that postmodernism has imposed upon the modern world. They tend forward to the major discussion of "Truth Is Subjectivity" in the *Postscript* and are sketches for it.

But *all* the essays in *Either–Or* belong to the aesthetic, and insofar as they raise ethical issues, they do so from an aesthetic point of view. But some of these essays do in fact have a very strongly marked ethical *bearing or attitude,* even if they are not proposed as ethical positions one could or should take up oneself. Indeed, it is a part of any aesthetic consciousness that it should have an ethical consciousness. This is the sophisticated and ironic wisdom of *The Picture of Dorian Gray.* Insofar as Kierkegaard is arguing that we have a right to our own subjective reality, he is making a case of the utmost contemporary importance. He places himself beyond postmodernism. Indeed, the very survival of philosophy itself may well depend on our taking his proposal seriously, the proposal, that is, that each and every one of us has a right to his or her own *subjective* experience. This was what the existential psychiatrist R. D. Laing derived from his study of Kierkegaard: the right to trust one's own experience.

If one takes the essays in *Or* more seriously than those in *Either,* what is the new ethical discussion that *Either–Or* opens up for us? It demands a return to subjectivity, very much in the manner of the *Postscript* that will follow it only three years later—indeed, the two texts are seamlessly joined. The return to subjectivity means some sort of reflection on the self as an entity that is "self choosing." Now in an era when determinism of the old nineteenth-century sort is being reinforced massively by the discoveries of biochemistry and of the Genome Project, we stand in danger of being told (assured) that we actually do NOT possess an inner self, a subjectivity, an "I," a recognizable "self" at all, and this not in the old benign Humean sense, but in a deadly serious modern version in which all recourse to ethical norms is going to be subtracted from us as just so much "idealist" "essentialism."

So, I would see the importance of *Either–Or* and the *Postscript* as insisting upon my right to enter and to identify with and to trust my own subjectivity, and to claim its existence as real, something that can survive the implied threat of biochemistry and the Genome Project. In fact, we have to regard the doctrine of subjectivity as something that we have to use *proactively,* in order to defend ourselves from silent and gradual annihilation at the hands of a postmodern "objectivity" or a Nietzschean nihilism that dare not say its name.

Kierkegaard, as Harold Bloom would say,[14] has given us the texts that enable us to continue the inner dialogue with ourselves. I do not sense the presence of any other philosopher around us now who is offering to be so helpful. It is not surprising that Kierkegaard has emerged recently as a philosopher who is central to a modern discussion of ethics. The way that John Caputo in *Against Ethics*[15] demoted "ethics" to "obligation," and thus managed to make of Levinas a philosopher with whom we could do business anew, was a helpful opening up of the ethical dimension. In an interesting temporal overlap, Derrida himself, in 1992, had brought out *The Gift of Death,*[16] and chose to place his discussion of Kierkegaard's *Fear and Trembling* in an explicitly political context, by starting his book with an essay on Jan Patocka. His opening chapter is called (significantly enough, in that it explicitly recalls Husserl's great theme) "Secrets of European Responsibility." This in its turn was helpful, in that ethical debate was suddenly put into an everyday political and culturally specific framework. Ethical discussion was summoned down from Abraham's absolute duty to God and Levinas's "absolute Other" to a world in which relative choices have to be made, and in which responsibilities are chosen, arbitrarily, toward certain people and this necessarily at the expense of others.

But John Caputo's contention that we can dispense with "ethics" and simply substitute "obligation" raises a matter of fundamental importance. Can we actually do this? According to a very interesting school of thought emerging from the University of Virginia, there can be no such thing as a theory of "best practice" without the presence of endorsing positives. James Davison Hunter, in a book called *The Death of Character* (and even more significantly subtitled *Moral Education in an Age without Good or Evil*),[17] argues that all contemporary research into the moral behavior of young people today tends to suggest that young people will not do what is right just because it fits in with what society teaches, or what political correctness or "best practice" suggests, but that they tend to ask, at a basic level, the question *"Why* should I obey these injunctions?" In other words, they do not recognize the binding power of moral injunctions unless an endorsing or underwriting positive is given to them as a ground for such belief—and John Caputo has asserted, at a volume's length, that such endorsing and underwriting positives (God, the Moral Law, the Absolute, Good and Evil, Ethics itself) are too "expensive" for us, in our impoverished postmodern condition, to be any longer able to afford.

But here is James Davison Hunter:

We say we want a renewal of character in our day, but we don't really know what we ask for. To have a renewal of character is to have a renewal of a creedal order that constrains, limits, binds, obligates and compels. The price is too high for us to pay. We want character but without unyielding conviction; we want strong morality but without the emotional burden of guilt or shame; we want virtue but without particular moral justifications that invariably offend; we want good without having to name evil; we want decency without the authority to insist upon it; we want moral community without any limitations to personal freedom. In short, we want what we cannot possibly have on the terms that we want it.[18]

This passage seems to address John Caputo's *Against Ethics* directly and in terms, and to say, in effect: the demotion of "ethics" to "obligation" may make philosophical sense but it won't work. It can't be done. It is a fantasy. And John Caputo seems to sense the danger:

But we who have had the impiousness to take our stand against Ethics, which means to take a stand between Nietzsche and Ethics, between Evil and the Innocence of Becoming, we must confess to having no cosmic backups for our condemnation of Auschwitz. That is our embarrassment and scandal.[19]

This does indeed seem to be, at the philosophical level, an extraordinarily exposed admission. It is true that, in the eighth and last of the pseudonymous "discourses" earlier in the book, a certain "Felix Sineculpa," who may be taken to represent Nietzsche in his most blustering atheist mood, does advance such outrageous propositions as

Auschwitz is not Evil, not Absolute Evil. . . . Auschwitz is not a fact but a perspective. . . . Disasters are not Evil. Nothing is Evil. . . . Auschwitz is a part of the whole, a piece of the fate that belongs to the whole. . . . Auschwitz is what it is, a piece of fate, a constellation of base, cruel forces. But there is no one or nothing to blame, no subject that can be separated from its predicates, no doer separable from its deed. . . . There is no Evil here, just stronger and weaker forces, noble and ignoble forces, hostile and peace-loving forces. There is no 'obligation' here.[20]

But these expressions of "Felix Sineculpa," the cosmic Overman, like the views expressed in the preceding discourses by "Johanna de Silentio," "Magdalena de la Cruz," and "Rebecca Morgenstern," are of course only offered as "essais," try-ons, possible points of view, "thought-experiments," in Kierkegaard's own pseudonymous manner, and are not to be taken as representing John Caputo's own view.

Nevertheless, the passage first quoted on the previous page is not pseudonymous. In fact, along with the whole of the tenth chapter, "Otherwise than Ethics, or Why We Too Are Still Impious," it seems to argue for a moral defeatism that is indeed personally meant. Its basic philosophy is summed up in the oft-repeated "*Il y a. Es Gibt.* It happens."[21]

It is true that one of the forms of "*Es Gibt*" is: "*Es gibt,* there is, obligation. That is all."[22] Yet, in the end, *Against Ethics* insists on being understood as a work that sees no alternative to abrogating philosophical reflection as such, and substituting for it a kind of *poetics of helplessness in the face of evil*. The beautiful "discourse" by "Rebecca Morgenstern," which invokes Paul Celan's *Todesfuge* with such passionate élan, is surely the mode in which this kind of poetics of helplessness works best? And for this very reason, for the reason that the discourse of "Rebecca Morgenstern" gets to the heart of the matter so effectively, it may be that in the end *"Il y a"* and *"Es Gibt"* may be helpful preliminaries to philosophical reflection, even though they cannot replace it?

So James Davison Hunter's important study is a re-statement, but in reverse, of John Caputo's case in *Against Ethics*. James Hunter is bringing to the theoretical-philosophical debate a piece of researched empirical evidence, to the effect that, in fact, in practical empirical reality, *we just can't have* "obligation" without the endorsement of universalist principles based on religion or "ethics" or both. And since Hunter and Caputo are saying directly opposed things, it will be up to them to argue it out.

James Davison Hunter heads up a new outfit at the University of Virginia called the Institute of Advanced Studies in Culture. Its journal is called the *Hedgehog Review,* after the famous saying of Archilocus, "The fox knows many things, but the hedgehog knows one big thing." It is sometimes useful to take an implication literally. What is the "one big thing" that the *Hedgehog Review* knows? It is surely the importance of asking fundamental ethical questions at five minutes before "that midnight hour when everyone has to take off his mask."

One of the 11:55 P.M. questions that the *Hedgehog Review* decided to tackle head on is the theme of Evil.[23] One of the most striking essays in the issue on Evil is by Richard Kearney. Kearney re-instates Evil, both as concept and as word, into the discourse of Ethics. Tackling the problem of evil partly from the point of view of Derrida's essay *De l'Hospitalité,*[24] he finds himself obliged to make distinctions between the alien as friend and the alien as enemy. Indeed, he argues that Derrida's theory of hospitality (as a duty that in general principle I owe to all and sundry) must be to some extent revised. "To be absolutely hospitable is to suspend all criteria of ethical or juridical discrimination. . . . One must also be careful to discern, in some provisional fashion at least, between good and evil."[25] In the real world, that is, we have to distinguish the friendly alien from one with murderous intentions.

John Caputo wittily remarks, "The Other is absolutely infinite—up to a point. You have to be sensible. There are limits. For example, if the Other is shooting at you, then we say, that is not the Other."[26] This I think of as John Caputo's "Gaza Strip" passage. Kearney agrees with Caputo in being wary of the absolutism of both Levinas and of Derrida, insisting that we need "an ethics of judgment," a hermeneutic that allows us to make distinctions. "The genuine struggle against evil presupposes a critical

hermeneutic of suspicion."[27] Kearney's point is that we need a phenomenology of ethical analysis of the Other's place in the world—both of his
place in *his* world *and* his place in *mine*. So he engages with the problem of
the unknowability of the intentions of the Other by adding to his "hermeneutic of suspicion" a "working-through the experience of evil" that is
"central to a hermeneutics of action." "The hermeneutics of action offers,
I submit, an answer (if not a solution) to the challenge of evil."[28]

No, just being wary of the Other is indeed not a solution. If we need
"a conditional openness to otherness based upon the need for some hermeneutic discernment between good and evil," then how are we going to
construct that hermeneutics? What models do we need? And (whatever
models we *do* begin to work with) will they not necessarily be investigations
into subjectivity, into subjective states? Will these models not necessarily
involve a phenomenology for studying subjective "intentionality"? We
would join up here once again with the brave and lonely analyses that Husserl was carrying out in Part Two of that remarkably prescient series of studies
we know as *The Crisis of European Sciences*.

And so, we rejoin our original task: to read *Either–Or* for the very first
time, though now in a much wider ethical context than the one we originally started from. How should we attempt to develop this thinking? I think
there is one major conceptual task that we Kierkegaardians have to start in
on, and that is to discover, retrieve, and describe exactly what Kierkegaard's
philosophy of subjectivity (as opposed to his phenomenology of religion)
actually *is*. Have those philosophers who have derided him as a mere "ir-
rationalist" for so long been right or not? If (as I believe) they have not,
then is there not a major conceptual job for us to do in retrieving what is
original and what is valid in the philosophy of subjectivity from Kierkegaard's
work, and setting it out in a way that could contribute new resources to
current ethical debate?

We need these new resources. In the face of ever more powerful "Objectivity" ("Objectivity" quantified and quantifying—"Objectivity" deprived of any sense of teleology), these resources may mean—for the Self as
ethical subjectivity—survival as such.

Notes

1. Alasdair MacIntyre, *After Virtue* (London: Gerald Duckworth, 1981).
2. *Kierkegaard after MacIntyre,* ed. John Davenport and Anthony Rudd (Chicago: Open Court, 2001).
3. Louis Mackey, *Kierkegaard: A Kind of Poet* (Philadelphia: University of
Pennsylvania Press, 1971).
4. Louis Mackey, *Points of View: Readings of Kierkegaard* (Tallahassee: University Presses of Florida, 1986).
5. John Vignaux Smyth, *A Question of Eros: Irony in Sterne, Kierkegaard, and
Barthes* (Tallahassee: Florida State University Press, 1986).

6. Pat Bigelow, *Kierkegaard and the Problem of Writing* (Tallahassee: Florida State University Press, 1987).

7. The three seminars have since been published as "Towards a Theory of Responsible Reading: How to Read and Why," in *Kierkegaard Studies: Yearbook 2002* (Berlin: Walter de Gruyter); and a complementary study, "Dizziness, fall . . . Oh (dear)! . . . Reading *Begrebet Angest* for the very first time," may be found in *Kierkegaard Studies: Yearbook 2001*. A suggestion for a hermeneutic principle that would allow us efficiently to differentiate between "light" and "heavy" usage of certain "oscillating" terms used by the pseudonyms, an essay entitled " 'My wish, my prayer': Keeping the Pseudonyms Apart," also belongs in this group, and may be found in *Kierkegaard Revisited*, Kierkegaard Studies, Monograph Series, 1 (Berlin: Walter de Gruyter, 1997). In the near future, these essays will be collected and published by the University Press of Virginia.

8. Mackey, *Kierkegaard: A Kind of Poet*, 273–74.

9. Ibid., 274.

10. F. J. Billeskov Jansen, *Studier i Søren Kierkegaards litterære Kunst* (Copenhagen: Rosenkilde og Bagger, 1951).

11. Ibid., 23.

12. Søren Kierkegaard, *Either/Or*, trans. David F. Swenson and Lillian Marvin Swenson, Anchor Books edition (Garden City, N.Y.: Doubleday, 1959), 208–209. Hereafter EO.

13. Ibid., 312.

14. Harold Bloom, *Wallace Stevens: The Poems of Our Climate* (Ithaca, N.Y.: Cornell University Press, 1976), 387.

15. John D. Caputo, *Against Ethics* (Bloomington: Indiana University Press, 1993).

16. Jacques Derrida, *The Gift of Death*, trans. David Wills (Chicago: University of Chicago Press, 1996).

17. James Davison Hunter, *The Death of Character* (New York: Basic Books, 1999).

18. Ibid., xv.

19. Caputo, *Against Ethics*, 236.

20. Ibid., 186–89.

21. Ibid., 226.

22. Ibid., 237.

23. *Hedgehog Review* 2, no. 2 (summer 2000).

24. Derrida, *De l'Hospitalité* (Paris: Calmann-Lévy, 1997); trans. Rachel Bowlby under the title *Of Hospitality* (Stanford, Calif.: Stanford University Press, 2000).

25. Richard Kearney, "Evil and Others," *Hedgehog Review* 2, no. 2 (summer 2000): 71.

26. Caputo, *After Ethics*, 123.

27. Kearney, "Evil and Others," 76.

28. Ibid., 77.

3

"THE ESTHETIC IS ABOVE ALL MY ELEMENT"

Joakim Garff
Translated by Stacey E. Ake

A AND B KNOW EACH OTHER. A is a young man. B is seven years his elder. A is an aesthete and, therefore, unhappy. B, however, is not, because he is married. For this reason, B writes a letter to A, in which he holds forth in great detail about marriage and its esthetic validity. This, however, makes no impression upon A, who neither in writing nor in discussion responds to B's heartfelt letter. Despite or perhaps because of this, B writes an essay examining the balance between the esthetic and the ethical in a personality's constitution. But A does not respond to this letter either, which is actually strange since A seems to stay quite regularly in B's home. After this snub, nobody could blame B if he lost patience with A, but this he does not do. Instead, B simply sends another letter that seems to be a sermon that he himself once received from a priest living on the moors of Jutland. The sermon dwells upon the edification that can be garnered from the thought that we are always in the wrong in relation to God. But about whether A has actually been edified, the story imparts nothing, for A maintains his silence.

In this way, one might briefly sketch the basic structure in the second half of *Either–Or*. But unfortunately things are not what they seem to be. Following a sort of inner logic, the second half appears to be a continuation of the first half; but it is actually doubtful how familiar B is with A's papers. In addition, the second half presents the difficulty that B evidently perceives his inquiries as contributions to a discussion about a correct life-view, and A does not.

Thus, one must ask the simple question of what *Either–Or*, as a work, is really after. With its complex foreword, it seems to point so emphatically to its own literariness that the reader is almost compelled to read the work as pure fiction, but the work wants to be something else, something more. It also wishes to be a representation of two differing spirit-types and as such to create a mirror in which the reader has the possibility of recognizing an image of himself.

One can say that *Either–Or*, from the viewpoint of genre, is a both/and, both fiction and nonfiction. Where one begins and the other ends is to some extent the problem. But there can hardly be any doubt about the work's own inner priority: the fiction can be assigned to A, the nonfiction to B.

Historicity as His-story

Kierkegaard's designation as the father of existentialism is due not least to the character B (better known as Judge Wilhelm). It is he who, with his comprehensive treatment of the subject's responsibility to choose oneself or take possession of oneself, produces the material from which French existentialism has received its nourishment and enjoyment. I will not tire anyone with a course in French existentialism, even less so since Kierkegaard cannot at all be reduced to that position. "Kierkegaard, existentialism's father?" Ricoeur asked in 1963. He continued: "We saw Kierkegaard as the progenitor to a whole family in which Gabriel Marcel, Karl Jaspers, Heidegger, and Sartre were supposed to be cousins. Now it has become clear for everyone that this grouping has been dismantled, if it ever did exist anywhere other than in handbooks."[1] Ricoeur here presents a philosophical genealogy that hardly anyone would question today, but at the same time, it also makes it questionable whether Kierkegaard can be placed anywhere at all, that is, anywhere besides "outside" the family just mentioned.

If we then turn our attention to Judge Wilhelm in order to pinpoint the character of his philosophical activity, it is obvious that regardless of *how* pragmatic his existential thinking may be, it cannot, under any circumstances, be detected from the outside. The fundamental distinction before and after is unobservable. There is no objective correlate that signals a change between Wilhelm the First and Wilhelm the Second, because Wilhelm is from first to last the same. According to Wilhelm a human being does not just accidentally *have* a history but substantially *is* his story, a story that becomes mine, whenever I, in my appropriation of it, make it into my own:

> A human being's eternal dignity lies precisely in this, that he can gain a history. The divine in him lies in this, that he himself, if he so chooses, can give this history continuity, because it gains that, not when it is the summary of what has taken place or has happened to me, but only when it is my personal deed in such a way, that even that which has *happened* to me, is transformed and transferred from necessity to freedom. (EO, 2:250)

One of several consequences of this is that one's relationship with God does not create a caesura in one's already existing history; on the contrary, it is precisely in virtue of God that the single individual's history succeeds in maintaining its continuity. God does not add new epic material to Wilhelm's history, nor does Wilhelm become another though being written into an/other('s) history.

> "If I wanted to be clever," he writes, "I could say here that the individual knows himself in a way similar to the way Adam knew Eve, as it says in the Old Testament. Through the individual's intercourse with himself the individual is made pregnant by himself and gives birth to himself. . . . Only within himself can the individual become enlightened about himself." (EO, 2:259)

Wilhelm is not just being clever here; he is also disclosing the source from whence he acquired the impulse to his history, namely from "himself."

Aesthete A

Allow me to take a leap, not in Kierkegaard's categorical sense, but a leap within his text. More specifically, a leap back to A. Concerning those papers that belonged to A, Victor Eremita acknowledged in his foreword that he kept them in the original order in which he found them, as he could provide no information about whether A had composed his texts before or after he had received Wilhelm's letters (see EO, 1:14). But the order Victor has chosen suggests that he considers the former situation the more likely.

It is no small wonder Victor should be in doubt, because whenever one reads the published papers, A's section shows as little regard for B as B's section obviously shows that he is corresponding to A. And yet. B appeals often enough to A, but to an A who is one of B's circle of acquaintances and not the author whom the reader has gotten to know through reading A's papers. The *person* who visits B and tells of his powerful performances in the province of the erotic is difficult for the reader to identify as the *author* of the first half of the book.

When one inspects the papers A left behind, one finds, in addition to "The Seducer's Diary," the following: a collection of aphorisms gathered under the rubric "Diapsalmata"; a longer treatise about Mozart and the "musical-erotic" in his treatment of Don Juan; an analysis of Scribe's one-act comedy titled "The First Love"; a little burlesque piece called "Rotation of Crops," with cheerful advice for those who would rather die laughing than be bored to death; and finally, a lecture written for a gloomy society of so-called *symparanekromenoi,* along with three small essays dealing with the encounters of various female characters with the men who deceived them and thus sealed their fates forever.

As one can see, this is extremely complex material reflecting an equally complicated psychological type. Thus, if one were to follow the work's explicit assertions, accepting the person to whom Wilhelm appeals as identical with the author of the first part of the work, then Wilhelm's basic characterization of the esthetic seems to be so oversimplified as practically to miss its mark. For example, somewhere Wilhelm asks, "What is the esthetic in a person, and what is the ethical?" (EO, 2:178) and answers himself, saying that "the esthetic in a person is that by which he spontaneously and immediately is what he is; the ethical is that by which he becomes what he becomes. The person who lives in and by and from and for the esthetic that is in him, that person lives esthetically" (EO, 2:178). With this tautological definition Wilhelm accuses the esthetic of being an immediate or pre-reflective position, something that lies in clear opposition to the definition of the esthetic that one finds woven throughout A's papers. The finely crafted portraits of Marie Beaumarchais, Donna Elvira, and Faust's Margarethe (see EO, 1:165ff.) in themselves bear witness to the presence of an extremely reflective and anything but immediate subject. But add to this an analysis of both original or "hereditary sin" (see EO, 1:154) and that ambivalence that is always felt as soon as a human being has anything to do with "anxiety" (EO, 1:155), and it would seem that A is not merely competing with Wilhelm in the category of psychological perceptiveness but also anticipating some of the points for which Vigilius Haufniensis would later be acclaimed.

Yet there can be little doubt that Wilhelm has offered up the right diagnosis of A as being a person in despair; it is, however, more doubtful whether he has read the symptoms within the right context. The symptoms are not limited to an individual psychological type à la A, but extend and include an entire era: the modern. Had Wilhelm studied A's treatise "The Tragic in Ancient Drama Reflected in the Tragic in Modern Drama," he would have been able to convince himself that the problem of authenticity seen therein was viewed as a problem specific to modernity, which neither the individual's self-usurpation nor that individual's ever so many happy marriages can overcome. "Our age," as it is so accurately termed, "has lost all the substantial categories of family, state, kindred; it must turn the single individual over to himself completely in such a way that, strictly speaking, he becomes his own creator" (EO, 1:149).

Precisely because modernity has lost both its substantiality and its formerly fixed references to a transcendental signifier, the subject has become burdened with the titanic task of procuring its own existential substance. In an era, notes A, where "the power in religion that insisted upon the invisible [has] been weakened and destroyed" (EO, 1:141), "the subjects' doubt," of which despair is the psychological equivalent, is helplessly released. Therefore, despair is not, in and of itself, a sickness but an expression of a healthy reaction to "the [dissolution] of the age" (ibid.). It is not the observer who is imaginarily ill; rather, it is the observed who are imaginarily healthy inasmuch as those who are imaginarily healthy have not yet realized that the subject's self-definition also disappeared when the age lost its own substantial definitions.

A's problem, moreover, is *not* that he does *not* want, as Wilhelm wrongly supposes, to be a self. Rather, the problem is his consciousness of exactly how problematic it is to become a self in an era in which the human being has been handed over to a system of contingent signs that have no regard for anything other than themselves and furthermore never represent, but only simulate, the presence of significance.

A's criticism is far from simple destruction, for behind the contemporary criticism he formulates, there lies a concept of the subject in ancient tragedy, a concept of subjectivity that declares genuine authenticity. It is through this that the imaginarily healthy individual can be reminded of his sickness and perhaps led on to the hope of recovery. A explains:

> In the tragic there is implicit a sadness and a healing that one indeed must not disdain, and when someone wishes to gain himself in the superhuman way our age tries to do it, he loses himself and becomes comic. Every individual, however original he is, is still a child of God, of his age, of his nation, of his family, of his friends, and only in them does he have his truth. If he wants to be the absolute in all this, his relativity, then he becomes ridiculous. (EO, 1:145)

It is here, I maintain, that A points out the critical point of Wilhelm's ethical theory. Surely Wilhelm is in no way ridiculous, but his project depends upon the transhistorical condition that the individual can choose "the absolute" and thereby obtain "eternal validity" (see EO, 2:214). And it is this condition that A problematizes by revealing the transhistorical as an illusion that dangles before the individual the possibility of being able to repossess his own origin, an origin definitively lost in interpersonal and sociocultural relations. Therefore, whenever Wilhelm argues about that repossessed origin in which the "personality appears as the absolute that has its teleology in itself" (EO, 2:263), A justly objects that Wilhelm has himself become the victim of that very desire for authenticity and transparency that modernity has awakened but that it cannot succeed in satisfying. This is a case that A argues in terms of the following transformation, namely that "when the age loses the tragic, it gains despair" (EO, 1:145). To want to endow his own history with continuity and meaning by choosing himself in his eternal validity consequently becomes the modern's compensation for the loss of the significance that tragedy engendered by showing that the individual was not the source of the tale but had, in fact, fallen into the hands of another.

As directly reacting to Wilhelm's long-winded treatises, A settles the question by pointing out to him the following:

> In a certain sense, therefore, it is a very appropriate discretion on the part of the age to want to make the individual responsible for everything; the trouble is that it does not do it profoundly and inwardly enough, and hence it half-

measures. It is conceited enough to disdain the tears of tragedy, but it is also conceited enough to want to do without mercy. And what, after all, is human life, the human race, when these two things are taken away? Either the sadness of the tragic or the profound sorrow and profound joy of religion. (EO, 1:146)

This is A's either–or, and it clearly exposes the difference between A's position and Wilhelm's critique thereof. While Wilhelm reconciles the tension between the esthetic and the ethical in matrimonial equilibrium, A maintains the difference between the "tragic" and "religion," between the esthetic and the religious.

As in the master's dissertation, the concept of reconciliation is just as cardinal here as it is problematic. The two figures are completely and explicitly thematized as types representing the difference between the beautiful and the sublime, between harmony and catastrophe, joy and terror, continuity and eruption. And with an almost paradigmatic formulation of the difference, Wilhelm, with regard to A, bluntly declares: "For you, a turbulent sea is a symbol of life; for me it is the quiet, deep water" (EO, 2:144). Such a difference seems almost to have been taken verbatim from Immanuel Kant's *Critique of Judgment,* a book in which Wilhelm would be found in the section titled "Analytic of the Beautiful," while one would meet up with A in the "Analytic of the Sublime." This latter is the section wherein Kant is dedicated to the so-called dynamically sublime and is the place where the wild sea's foam is said to exemplify the sublime and its ability to disturb the harmonic contemplation of the beautiful. What A desires is his own concentration within the essence of the sublime and not the triviality of extension. A wants to reconstruct the sublime. And, as the ultimate compensation for the absence of the sublime, he wants to reconstruct it through seduction. "To entertain your mind; you shoot it all off in a brilliant firework display" (EO, 2:199) observes Wilhelm, who has cause to worry. "There is," he writes, "an absolute contradiction between us that can never be canceled. I cannot live within esthetic categories; I feel that what is most sacred in my life will perish. I require a higher expression, and the ethical provides me with that" (EO, 2:237).

Here Wilhelm emphasizes an absolute contradiction between himself and A, and if in this way he is just about to cancel the actual possibility of a choice, it is because of his understanding that the sublime cannot be lived but resists "everyday life" because it violates social and individual continuity and thus undermines all theology with its sudden revelation of the Other.

It is quite otherwise with A. He insists, as Wilhelm has so rightly noted, that something should send "a shudder through the consciousness" (EO, 2: 133). Therefore, he stands in relation to the tragic and attempts to re-play the pathos of myth. And what the esthetic represents for the sublime qua the Other corresponds narratologically with the storyteller as the Other.

When, in this manner, A can conclude his famous lament over his uncouth age's want of passion by recognizing that his soul always returns to the Old Testament and to Shakespeare because there it can meet real human beings who can be said to hate, to love, and to sin (see EO, 1:28), it is not simply a pretty rhetorical gesture. Rather, it is an expression of the fact that the individual's identity does not "as with Wilhelm" rest upon *his identifying with his own history,* but rather upon his *identification with a stranger's storytelling.*

A desires a storyteller, but his desire is unhappy because it is attended by knowledge of the fact that modernity has smashed the mythic and destroyed tragic history's previously fixed form. Given this, the lecture for the dead about the reflection of the ancients in the moderns has thus been well provided for with its subtitle of "A Venture in Fragmentary Endeavor" (EO, 1: 137). That the absence of meaning in many places is formulated into semioticized allegories (see EO, 1:36) wherein the text's letters disintegrate in abortive signs without the ability to organize their own significance does not merely indicate that ancient and Old Testament texts have been superseded by modern fragmentary writing. It also implies that the narrative, the story told, has itself lost any immediate connection to its storyteller. For this reason, a human being is now regarded as being the responsible, and hence final, editor of his own history.

Not Serious about the Serious

With the inquiry about the genuine storyteller we are brought back to Victor Eremita's foreword, where the authors disappeared into the "boxes in a Chinese puzzle" (EO, 1:9). Who they were, these disappeared ones, is of less importance. The crucial point is the fact *that* they disappeared. This shows that *Either–Or* by way of both composition and structure is actually an unfolding of the consciousness that occasions A's conflict. The very mystification is repeated in the techniques A employs to regratify that existence that has lost its natural gratitude. The preface's casting of disappeared authors is moreover a reflection of A's own consciousness of the storyteller's absence. And the preface, like the work itself, remains a fragmentary endeavor— something that becomes even more obvious when A juxtaposes the fragmentary with the "art of writing posthumous papers" (EO, 1:152).

That the work is a repetition or an extension of the preface's esthetic plot renders somewhat natural the suspicion that "Victor Eremita" is a name for *the implicit storyteller's hidden victory within the text.* In other words, the text establishes a priority between its two tellers and merely simulates a choice that has already been made—and moreover made in favor of the aesthete. This means that Wilhelm is not the complete master of his own work; actually he seems to be a parody of representation by an implicit storyteller, who obviously knows better than Wilhelm.

The implicit narrator's presence in the text can be documented with a host of examples. One could also just make the story short and cite what Kierkegaard wrote to Emil Boesen when he spoke of the creation of *Either–Or*. He explains his own position in relation to the work with the following, pregnant formulation: "The esthetic is above all my element." Since biographical arguments have, strangely enough, never carried much weight with regard to the great philosophers, I will instead exemplify my claim about the subtle presence of the implicit narrator by turning my attention to the most marginal figure in Judge Wilhelm's enormous ego-(*centric*) epic: his wife. It is with her, I would like to suggest, that the implicit narrator plays his most subtle game with Wilhelm. This requires an explanation.

The ABCs of the Erotic

The woman to whom Wilhelm is married essentially appears to be a principle rather than a person; she does not even have a name—so at least Cordelia did. And she does not seem to have much of a body, either, for in one of the few places where Wilhelm presents her to the reader, she is described as peeking through a windowpane into his private office, "in such a way that one could believe that the head did not belong to any body" (EO, 2:83).

But closer examination reveals a strange eroticizing to be at play in Wilhelm's writing. The eroticizing does not bear directly upon Wilhelm's relations with his wife, since on such ticklish points as these he is rather tight-lipped, but by contrast upon the connection between Wilhelm and the Aesthete A, whose erotic escapades Wilhelm strongly condemns. Yet Wilhelm nonetheless often repeats these escapades at great length in his own writings (see EO, 2:7) in which erotic situations either are accompanied by ardent monologues (see EO, 2:90–92, 276) or the stage becomes set by the experienced seducer's capacity to awaken and then seize the first love.

On that score Wilhelm gets around. One minute he is with "an understanding little seamstress" (EO, 2:32), and the next with a "young peasant girl," sighing in her bed and thinking with "a sweet, pleasant restlessness" about her wedding night (EO, 2:44–45). Then he is to be found with a "good-natured and reliable cook," and, finally, he also knows "a handy maid who is so clever that she can be used for everything" (EO, 2:77). All these excursions, which look remarkably like those *actiones in distans* with which Johannes the Seducer filled his diary, somewhat disorder Wilhelm, so that after a visit to one of these handy housemaids, he must once again bring the text into order with a remark about how he is now returning to the case in question, namely the institution of marriage (see EO, 2:8, 25, 45 et passim).

This does not sound overly convincing and seems to indicate that

Wilhelm himself partakes in the very game of seduction for which he criticizes A. And this he also does, but indeed, not as the master of the game, rather as its victim. It becomes clear when one presents the case as follows— where for the sake of clarity I continue the letter-practice introduced by Victor Eremita with A and B by calling the nameless wife C.

Those times that C emancipates herself from the principle and becomes a being of flesh and blood, it becomes apparent that it is not B, but A, who is the real occasion. Thus, B can write to A about himself and C:

> You have known me for many years; you have known my wife for five. You consider her rather beautiful, exceptionally charming, which I do, too. I know very well, however, that she is not as beautiful in the morning as in the evening, that a certain touch of sadness, almost of ailment, disappears only later in the day, and that it is forgotten by evening when she can truly claim to be appealing. (EO, 2:9)

The remark reveals that B knows how good C looks to A's eyes: beautiful, exceptionally charming; in short, she is a true attraction for any seducer. For the same reason, B's friendly relations with A, who besides being the letter's recipient is also a frequent guest in the letter writer's bourgeois home, are obviously dependent upon a complete confidence regarding A's real intentions.

But it is precisely this confidence that A has abused (see EO, 2:326), since B has himself noted certain irregularities, some ambiguous "traces" that seem to reveal that A just like another "Zeus" is taking "the wrong path" (EO, 2:8). What traces B has in mind are not directly evident, but one senses their direction when he, in relation to a remark about his own three-year-old daughter, mentions his own apprehensions about the seducer's behavior and therefore, with regard to A, finds himself obliged to set his mind at ease by observing that "you do not open your telegraphic communication with girls that young" (EO, 2:78).

One can well understand that B is worried, so worried in fact, that his acquaintanceship with A has almost become a burden, because when A comes sailing in, only to take his seat in B's favorite easy chair and then recount all the news from his suspicious activities, such amusement can sometimes make it difficult for B to find the right attitude. "How often have you entertained me—yes, I do admit it—but how often you also tormented me with your stories of how you had stolen your way into the confidence of one and then another married man. . . . You are really very gifted at slipping in with people; that I will not deny" (EO, 2:8).

And certainly C would not either. But in contrast to B, she seems to be well satisfied with A's sneakiness. Is this what B is now comprehending and what, despite all of A's repeated assurances to the contrary, is about to make him "jealous" (EO, 2:324) and thus fill him with that very "fear" that he has so often very high-mindedly asserted he has never in the least entertained (see EO, 2:78)? And why does he say that he cannot understand what C fills her time with (see EO, 2:308), and why, "late at night," does he light his lamp and "tiptoe softly into her bedroom to see if she is really sleeping"— what else would she be doing? And why must we be told that C knows the exact ring of the doorbell (see EO, 2:83) that announces B's homecoming, and why does this information give occasion to the parenthetical exclamation that "(we poor bureaucrats are so handicapped in this way that we are unable to surprise our wives)" (EO, 2:83)? What particular incidents are encased in these particular parentheses? Perhaps it has been filled by A who, while B has, for the last fortnight, diligently used his "evenings" (EO, 2:154) to write about the validity of marriage, has taken advantage of C's claim to be truly appealing in the evening?

Whether there is an erotic liaison between A and C will remain forever uncertain, but there are many details that give that impression, indeed suspicion, which definitely does not diminish when B, immediately after his first "deposition" (EO, 2:324), must submit a new one, which reads:

> Recently I have often spoken about you with my wife. She is really very fond of you, but no doubt I scarcely need to say this, because you have many capacities for being appealing if you so desire. . . . Her feeling for you has my full approval. I do not become jealous easily. . . . I have no fears. In that respect, I think I may venture to say that *Scribe* himself would despair over our prosaic marriage, because I believe that even for him it would be impossible to make it poetic. (EO, 2:324–25)

One must say that B has really taken to learning his Scribe. Not only does he resemble another—sleepless—police informer, who also began by sneaking into a woman's bedchamber to see if she was sleeping, he has also become aware that even the most devoted wife's chastity can be a mere fake. That the marriage is despairingly prosaic might just be reason enough for the judge's wife to try and add a little clandestine poetry.

Bringing these suspicions together with the fact that B introduces his text with a declaration of love to A, whom he loves "as a son, as a brother, as a friend" despite all his "bizarre qualities" and "with an esthetic love" (EO, 2:6), and yet closes the text with a rather chilly remark about the friendship no longer being what it once was (see EO, 2:332–33), it is almost just to conclude that what presented itself, in the beginning, as a marital apology showed itself, one might say between the lines, as containing all the elements necessary for a three-sided drama of the most classic kind: A is a friend of B who is married to C who is in love with A. So, in an attempt to escape the dilemma and resolve the moral conflict, B exhorts the penetratingly perceptive A to get married.

Deconstructive Divertimento

Has *Either–Or* now been definitively deconstructed? Hardly. Have I read *Either–Or* for the very *last* time? I hope not. But if deconstruction has done nothing other than to make visible the textual complexity of this work, it has nevertheless fulfilled one of its most essential heuristic claims.

It is a fact that the deconstructive reading has led to a paradigm shift in research: the supposed father of existentialism has been lifted free of the jargon of authenticity and reinserted into the labyrinth of his own writings. Viewed historically, one can speak of deconstruction as a reaction against the synthesizing interpretive tradition in which the Kierkegaardian system—including the theory of stages—has been repeated so often that the theory has become a lumped cliché. With a deconstructive reading, Kierkegaard is no longer perceived as an oracle for existentialism but read as an author who explicates problems that branch out into the most diverse regions of modernity.

It goes without saying that deconstruction is not an unequivocal discipline, and from time to time it transforms itself into a kind of jargon of inauthenticity, an infinite sophism. But *good* deconstruction has, in my view, led to a sharpening of a focus on the text as text, or on the textuality of the text itself. The inner contradictions, blind spots, rhetorical games, narratives, metaphors, and allegories of the text are made into a kind of hermeneutic of suspicion that believes just as little in the innocence of a text as in the trustworthiness of the author. Not on moral grounds, but ontological.

To deconstruct Kierkegaard (to read Kierkegaard with Kierkegaard and against Kierkegaard) is, in my view, to read him adequately, since his texts are already and in advance in one way or another potentially deconstructive. This is not only due to their striking intertextuality; no, the deconstructive reading is just as much written into the entire enterprise of the literature. Thus deconstruction becomes important every time a new pseudonym makes his entry and implicitly or explicitly begins to commentate one of his predecessors and thereby lets the earlier unity break down and reappear. As we have seen in *Either–Or*.

This plurality of voices, pens, positions, and literary jokers—which *are also present* in the most philosophical parts of the work (the *Fragments* and *Postscript*)—necessitates a never resting attentiveness on the part of the reader. The reader must have a dual view, which not only grasps *what* Kierkegaard writes, but also *how* he writes what he writes. And if one could wish for a future reading of Kierkegaard, I would wish for a less reverent, more flippant reading than in earlier generations. A reading that delivers a type of restrained affection or a "sympathetic antipathy"—to say it along with Vigilius Haufniensis. A reading that makes use of the rhetorical discipline and irony that the authorship itself prefers, but at the same time turns irony upon itself in order to counteract itself. A reading that does not fall for a reductionist theory of stages, and is not blind to the existential progression and conceptual development throughout the authorship. A reading that does not naively lead the work back to the author behind it, but that is aware of the complex and dramatic connection between life and writing. A reading that mixes blood and ink with a science of cheerfulness, and thus, in praxis, shows that cheerfulness can be a part of science, and that seriousness is never necessarily found where it seems most obvious. A reading with a sense for rhetoric—a sense that rhetoric is not merely decoration and exterior ornamentation, but is essentially written into the discourse and is thus inextricable from both epistemology and edification. And finally, a reading that bears witness to the fact that the seemingly most useless parts of the Kierkegaardian corpus—everything in the margins and all the fragmentary material—is in reality the most indispensable, since it opposes every attempt to instrumentalize the texts and thereby be done with them. And if one asks why such a sense is important, the answer is simple: the indispensability of the useless corresponds to—in fact, is repeated in—the most fundamental existential phenomena that the authorship captures and illuminates both negatively and positively: phenomena like anxiety, despair, trust, devotion, faith, and forgiveness—which also are just as useless and indispensable.

May a sense for the indispensability of the useless therefore be an edifying pulse in every deconstructive reading of Kierkegaard.

Note

1. Paul Ricoeur, *Denne slyngelagtige eftertid: Tekster om Søren Kierkegaard,* bd. 1, ed. Finn Frandsen and Ole Morsing (Aarhus, Denmark: Slagmark, 1995), 69f.

4

Elsebet Jegstrup

> Skulle jeg ønske mig Noget, da vilde jeg ikk ønske
> mig Rigdom eller Magt, men Mulighedens Lidenskab,
> det Øje, der overalt evigt ungt, evigt brændende, seer
> Muligheden. Nydelsen skuffer, Muligheden ikke. Og
> hvilken Viin er saa skummende, hvilken saa duftende,
> hvilken saa berusende!

> If I were to wish for something, I would wish not for
> wealth or power but for the passion of possibility, for the
> eye, eternally young, eternally ardent, that sees possibility
> everywhere. Pleasure disappoints; possibility does not.
> And what wine is so sparkling, so fragrant, so
> intoxicating!
>
> —EO, 1:41[1]

THOSE LINES ARE FROM THE "Diapsalmata," the fragments of life that form the introduction to the beginning of a most peculiar authorship that throughout is focused on existence and hence on possibility—which never disappoints. This possibility that desires existential decision but is confronted by undecidability, this passion that lives for im/possibility, for the theme of Either–Or, this philosophical questioning that has its ground in a wonder that disrupts our ordinary world and discloses the unknown, this awakening to otherness—all this permeates an authorship that posits an understanding of existence, but does so with such methodological complexity as to almost refuse reading. It is this methodological complexity, which is not a methodology at all, that shall be the focus of this investigation. Taking the aporetic characteristics of Kierkegaard's authorship into consideration, one hopes to disclose for oneself a certain wisdom that recognizes that the distance between our questioning of these texts and their originary intent is non-traversable, that they lend themselves only to the arduous task of self-discovery.

Kierkegaard's use of pseudonyms, subtexts, and other ironic approaches to writing render this labyrinthian authorship an entanglement of textual difference embroiling the reader in the turmoil of the movement between direct and indirect communications. This turmoil characterizes the aporias of his writing, the possibility of which, as Sylviane Agacinski suggests, "is also the possibility of irony."[2] Kierkegaard makes full use of this possibility. Self-disclosure is not something communicable to an other, as we know well; self-disclosure is just that, something singularity must endure by itself and is the very aim of this phenomenology of existence, or so we are told. The reader is present precisely as one who cannot be (directly) addressed, but who, nevertheless, is the addressee. The immediate text gently, and sometimes not so gently, nudges the reader toward a subtext revealed only by solicitation. The best the immediate text can do is make the reader take notice. As Kierkegaard writes in *The Point of View,*

> The situation is like that of the fisherman when he sees the float move— maybe it means a bite, maybe it is due to the motion of the water. But the fisherman says: I will not pull up the line; if I do, I indicate that I have surrendered this possibility; perhaps it will happen again and prove to be a bite. (PAP X³ A 413; POV, 249)

And so he continues to write. If the reader bites, the indirect communication is being solicited, and, as Kierkegaard may hope, this reader may become aware and achieve self-disclosure (SV, 18:102; POV, 51). The reader therefore has to be careful not to see these aporias as obstacles to the "truth" of Kierkegaard's writings, something, we want to argue, Kierkegaard never posited, at least not directly. On the contrary, the pseudonyms, subtexts, and other ironies, these aporias, are precisely the clue to reading Kierkegaard. If this is correct, then an examination of these aporias will not only go a long way toward describing Kierkegaard's entire authorship in all its peculiarity, but will also show that the site of the Kierkegaardian text is both modern and postmodern.

But why all these obfuscations? Two things come to mind. First, I want to suggest that Kierkegaard realized that as wonderers, if that is what we are, we do break through to the beyond, but we do so only by becoming aware that its quality is indeed beyond us—transcending what is knowable in a way that will for ever more prevent us from equating it with what is knowable.[3] Recognizing what is beyond us as unknowable and indeed as unsayable, Kierkegaard was compelled to adopt an approach so as not to say too much and thereby fall into a system that Roger Poole has so wittily dubbed "Hegelian Lego." Still, he had to make the serious reader take notice, gain courage in the face of such dread, and rather than attempt to overcome it, try "to be open to it and even willing to be devastated by it."[4] Second, the *only* way to get behind modern thinking's fortifications is by subterfuge, by trickery, by play. Only as such can it reveal the character of existence as Kierkegaard understands it, existence stripped of the cognitive accretions that make it invisible to itself. The text becomes pretext and the real communication takes place entirely behind the reader's preconceptions. That is, after all, what irony is about.

So it is tough to read Kierkegaard. As the cartoon on my office door tells my students, "Thank you for pretending to understand Kierkegaard." One student of mine refers to his authorship as a minefield. The question is, shouldn't such a complexity make it more interesting to read Kierkegaard? Apparently not. His name is all too often casually dropped in the most bizarre places, such as Richard Rhodes's best-seller *The Making of the Atomic Bomb,* where it appears no fewer than five times.[5] Often it is casually dropped without his works ever having been read. Then there are those who begin to read him seriously and run dead up against the aporias of the text and consciously or unconsciously remain satisfied with reading the immediate text bluntly.[6] They all but ignore the aporias, ignore the particular role of the pseudonyms that Kierkegaard himself emphasizes both in the *Postscript* and in his Journals. They also ignore the intent of the subtext, which announces itself only upon solicitation, and at all cost they ignore the generosity of the ironic that explosively interrupts any serious reading of the immediate text, nullifies the "total-view" (*Total-Anskuelse*),[7] and urges toward that *other* text.

None of this came as a big surprise to Kierkegaard, I suspect. We may even suggest he would have been disappointed had this not been the case. His writings were aimed at that singular reader (*den enkelte læser*) who was able and willing to slowly crawl through the minefield, listen, and one by one discover the mines, mark them, appropriate them, and, finally, walk upright through the reading, bracketing the immediate text, incorporating the aporias, and *experiencing* that other text that addresses only singularity. Here there can be no substitution. Thus Kierkegaard's writings are not about positing doctrines that fit all; they are not about providing *one* meaningful way, they are not a command. It is about singularity simply—to be disclosed beyond what is bracketed by the reader attuned to the *other* of Kierkegaard's text. As he says in his Journals, what counts is that freedom gives existence the elasticity required for transforming the corruptible into the incorruptible:

> Everything must have an end by which is meant that the free individual [*individ*] comes to assist existence or anticipate it, and by righteously providing an end to the matter, saves herself from eternity's unnatural death [*Straaddød*] or its parodic metamorphosis. (PAP IV B 59:211)

★   ★   ★

The first aporia to examine would be Kierkegaard's use of pseudonyms, which he also refers to in his Journals as a polyonymity (PAP VII[1] B 76). The way Kierkegaard uses pseudonyms is intriguing, for, as it turns out, they all have different perspectives—that is their role—and they embody this perspective entirely, meaning that is all they are: perspectives that speak. There are eleven different pseudonyms that speak—Pat Bigelow would insist there are twelve, counting S. Kierkegaard as a pseudonym as well, and I would not be inclined to disagree with him—but at least eleven, some of whom author more than one writing. But we also have the occasion of the non-pseudonym, or better, the non-author, meaning we have at least one case where there is no author at all, namely *Either–Or*. At the same time we should not forget that alongside the pseudonymous authorship, Kierkegaard published a large number of what he calls discourses, upbuilding and otherwise, all written under the name S. Kierkegaard. We tend to forget these, but as Hermann Deuser reminds us, it is in these writings that we discover the "textual narrative's ability to 'make present'" and the human proximity to what we seek most of all expressed in wonder, immediacy's sense of the unknown.[8]

My understanding of Kierkegaard's pseudonymity comes mostly from his Journals. In an 1845 article in *Berlingske Tidende,* the daily Copenhagen newspaper, in which Kierkegaard is responding to a review that attempts to place his authorship, we are told that the pseudonymity of his writings is to be understood as "a divorce [*Skilsmisse*] between the author and what he, the pseudonymous author, has given presence [*hans Frembringelse*]" (PAP VI B 184:255, 259). That is to say, Kierkegaard differentiates between the pseudonyms and their productions. He concedes that he created the pseudonyms, but what they put forth is theirs, not his. A divorce is more serious than the claim of distance that Louis Mackey has suggested. A divorce between author and text implies disagreement, indeed rejection, a falling out (of love in the Platonic sense, perhaps) or away from the particular perspective presented by the pseudonym. A divorce implies the end of conversation, "the *fact* of marriage," as Stanley Cavell writes, reading John Milton.[9] A divorce is not a temporary condition. There is no intent to reconcile either now or later. There are no regrets. It is a negation of ownership of the words of the pseudonyms, and hence, we want to argue, the polyonymity constitutes a form of alienation toward the writings by the pseudonymous authors. Heidegger might suggest Kierkegaard is homeless within this authorship. Kierkegaard himself insists, "There is not a single word by me" (SV, 10:286; CUP, 1:[626]). "I am only an unknown person who is the author of the authors . . . not in an eminent sense as the extraordinary, but in a philosophical sense as the foundation that founders [*Grunden der gaar til Grunde*]" (PAP VII¹ B 75). He is the author who disappears as his creations become creative. He is the *souffleur* or the prompter who has "poetically produced the *authors,* whose prefaces in turn are their productions, as are their *names*" (SV, 10:286; CUP, 1:[626]). The pseudonymous writers are strangers in Kierkegaard's world, if we can say even that much.

The perspectives of these pseudonymous authors are suggested by their names: Johannes *de silentio,*[10] the poet, who is unable to speak about the unfathomable; Johannes Climacus, the rationalist, who is always climbing but never arriving; and Anti-Climacus, the idealist, who has always already arrived. The names belong to the creative pseudonyms as do their texts. The pseudonymity is not accidental but essential in the authorship itself, and as Kierkegaard again insists, "It is my wish, my prayer, that he [the reader] will do me the kindness of citing the respective pseudonymous author's name, not mine" (SV, 10:287; CUP, 1:[627]).

But what does it mean to use a pseudonym? Kierkegaard cannot have been unfamiliar with the Greek origin of the words ψευδω and ψευδωμαι, which in Homer meant "to lie," "to speak false," "play false," and later in Plato "to say that which is untrue." Other uses suggest "to deceive," "to be mistaken," "to be perjured or forsworn." The *OED* adds some intriguing meanings to the use(r) of pseudonyms, such as "counterfeit," "a false person," "a pretender." Kierkegaard's approach seems to fit any and all of these meanings, and we must ask whether in allowing the pseudonyms to speak, he simultaneously rejects what they say. That would make sense of how he understands his own use of pseudonyms. In a rather convoluted manner he explains the complexity of this approach. He concedes that the ideal expressed in the reality of the pseudonyms, which causes this ideality to be heard in mundane reality, indeed belongs to him precisely because he is the author of the authors, "though not of their writings" (PAP VII[1] A 108:57). By giving the pseudonyms a particular voice, he causes them to be heard, whatever they write. Is it possible that Kierkegaard has created a dialogical event between the different viewpoints, including his own? He seems to have paid the respect to each that Plato calls for—except, perhaps, to his own. However, he does seem to have fulfilled the requirements for philosophical dialogue. If this is true, has he not opened the possibility for thinking (experiencing) truth, a truth he has to withdraw from to allow discovery, that is, the reader's self-discovery? A poetic bringing forth of the idea(l) (in a philosophical sense) would not be possible if every word were to be hooked unto the poet himself, he says. As we are reminded in a later Journal note, "My personal actuality in relation to the pseudonymous books is actuality's burden which they [the readers] best wish away" (PAP VII[1] B 78). The poet's actuality gets in the way of his words, gets in the way of unconcealing meaning, gets in the way of self-disclosure—therefore the pseudonyms. The point is, the perspective of each pseudonym has to be seriously approached, independently of other texts, in order for the subtext to emerge and perhaps negate the direct communication, a maneuver that has been forgotten, overlooked, in the "blunt" reading of the text. The reading of each of these texts thus oscillates between the direct and the indirect communication, maintaining the tension of the existential dialectic.

A good example of the problematic of Kierkegaard's use of pseudonyms

is Johannes *de silentio,* the poet and author of *Fear and Trembling,* who claims
to have a secret and therefore keeps silent. What is the secret "one must"
remain silent about? Well, maybe he is not as silent about it as his name
suggests. As Derrida proposes, "[t]he nature of this 'one must' is significant . . . : it inscribes the injunction to silence into the order or the promise
of a 'one must speak,' 'one must—not avoid speaking'; or rather, 'it is necessary that there be a trace.'"[11] Thus *de silentio* speaks, admitting that he can
only admire, love, and delight in the hero, who, as we know, is not, could
not be, Abraham. The secret, the unsayable, leaves a trace; *de silentio* is unable
to relate Abraham's experience, not even phenomenologically, although as a
poet he is supposed to address the impossible, as we are told in the *Postscript*
(SV, 10:83; CUP, 1:388). By his speaking he leaves a trace when he insists:
"I *think* myself *into* the hero; I cannot think myself into Abraham" (SV, 5:
32; FT, 33). Abraham's experience is a "second immediacy," and as we shall
see in the either of *Either–Or,* the immediate in any form cannot be spoken
about; it is only open to experience. "Yet [Johannes] too is happy—no less
than that one [Abraham], for the hero is, so to speak, his better nature,"
presumably meaning what Johannes aspires to become, a better nature, "with
which he is enamored—yet happy that the other is not himself, that his love
can be admiration" (SV, 5:17; FT, 15).

By speaking denials, *de silentio* appears to suggest that it is better to admire
(and to aspire?) than to be; he is the poet whose task it is to give presence
to the hero, someone who is happier in the possibility of possibility than in
actual accomplishment, which is only for the few. *De silentio* is not Abraham,
could not be Abraham, for Abraham was the chosen one, the only one, the
founder, and to claim to engage in a repetition of his act would be to reduce
the other to the same. *De silentio* is not Abraham, and neither is the reader.
No, Johannes *de silentio* is happy that he is *not* the other, happy that he is
not the hero (SV, 5:17; FT, 16), and certainly not the hero for whom this
category is entirely inappropriate. Abraham's experience is one thing, radically other and hence extraordinary, while *de silentio*'s experience is quite
ordinary and quite explainable.

So who is Johannes *de silentio*? Well, first and foremost he is Kierkegaard's
first *writing* pseudonym, a writer who withdraws in silence yet with a certain
persistence speaks denials and thus communicates the trace of the unsayable.
In addition, he presents the many obstacles, internal and external, to Abraham's achievement, which, nevertheless, remains unfathomable. Joakim Garff
in *"Den Søvnløse" Kierkegaard læst æstetisk-biografisk ("The Sleepless")* suggests
that inasmuch as we already know the story of Abraham and, as Kant proposes, there is no real danger, we as readers are not likely to comprehend
the experience of fear and trembling that filled Abraham's journey. Therefore
Johannes *de silentio* rhetorically dramatizes Abraham's journey to Mount
Moriah, extends its time, so to speak, and meticulously describes the tools

required for a slaughter, in such a way that underway Abraham is accompanied by a script that invests its energy into reproducing the real presence or autopsy on which the terror of the idea rests. In some sense, then, Johannes *de silentio* can have it both ways, for as Garff continues:

> If the sublime is able to avoid any and all representation, it simultaneously raises a conception about a world outside human understanding. The fear of the different is, in other words, accompanied by an awe of reason's reconciling capacity to distance itself from the chaos the sensual world can unexpectedly demonstrate.

And Garff goes on:

> If the imperative of the work is anti-aesthetic inasmuch as the terror of the idea opposes all explicitness, the imperative can nevertheless only be accomplished in aesthetic practice that reestablishes the medium of the actual explicitness. The paradox, then, is not merely that Johannes de silentio writes what cannot be written about and therefore ought to be silent; the paradox is also that only by rhetorizing silence is it possible to reinstall Abraham in the temporality wherein his fear and trembling belong. Autopsy is the point; time is the threat the text has to prevent.[12]

Johannes has been drawn into the text of this narrative speaking denials but always already in the voice of the poet, and hence the question lingers: is this a poetic production, merely a rash anticipation, or is it the moment of appropriation when the power of the ethical recedes, when what is generally the case withdraws and only one existence sphere extends its gracious welcome? Is this, perhaps, the hour of decision when "only the one who draws the knife gets Isaac?" (SV, 5:27; FT, 27).

★ ★ ★

Either–Or precedes *Fear and Trembling* by only a few months. It is pseudonymously *edited* by one Victor Eremita and also published in 1843. It is a work that quite literally has no author and thus introduces a kind of writing that engages in the highest form of irony. *Either–Or* is about the unsayable. That is why I am not really here talking about *Either–Or*—it belongs entirely to immediate experience, which "is altogether impossible to express," "is too immediate to be contained in words" (SV, 2:78; EO, 1:81). I am not speaking! The here is the unsayable; it has no language of its own. The here is the unsayable, *but,* it is *not* a secret, it is *not* something concealed or in hiding. This unsayable does not withdraw from language per se, yet language betrays it. Of course, our senses are limited too, betray us too, inasmuch as autonomous Reality is filtered by our very biology. My dog hears and smells what I cannot, yet he cannot see what I can see; his biological filter is also limited.[13] But it is not a secret; it is not the wholly Other of which I speak. I opine about this unsayable all the time—I have to—but *it* withdraws from my opining. I can experience this unsayable; I do not need language or discourse to find pleasure. What I experience, however, be it ever so limited, is wholly mine, mine alone, and this is equally true of that other unsayable that is wholly Other, that is a secret, that does hide from language, the unsayable we meet in *Fear and Trembling*—what Johannes *de silentio* refers to as a "second immediacy" (SV, 5:75; FT, 82). My experience of this other unsayable also withdraws from language, for it is a secret, a secret that is also mine, mine alone. Neither language nor discourse can share either experience—the unsayable belongs solely to singularity. It is this characteristic of singularity that interests Kierkegaard and is the reason he makes *den Enkelte,* or singularity, the focus of his authorship.

So, I am not here, I am not speaking of *Either–Or,* but were I, I would have to say, as suggested elsewhere, *Either–Or* is a phenomenology of what is not that is presented, not written. Thus Kierkegaard presents the possibility of writing deconstructively, which is the ironic, and

> is creatively used in *Either–Or* where there is an ambiguous attempt to dis/involve the reader in the apparent text, a dis/involvement that aims at the indirect communication concealed within the apparent text. The reader is . . . doubly misled: the manuscript was found; there is no author, and in a double sense, the text as a whole is absently present.[14]

So, first we have a pseudonym that neither writes nor says anything except to explain the discovery of his treasure. What are we to make of this peculiar circumstance of the lack of an author? Here I think it important to understand that Kierkegaard would not be caught dead being called a philosopher; so what better than to start out with no claims of authorship, no claims of philosophical propositions, no claims of authority. *Either–Or,* of course, is his first publication. The reader is literally thrown out into the proverbial 70,000 fathoms of water of what the non-author understands as aesthetic experience, and the indirect communication is that we quite literally start swimming! Later we shall examine what it could possibly mean "to start swimming" and hence why there is no author of *Either–Or.*

Second, we get a pseudonym who finds himself unable to portray the saying in the said apparently because he is not privy to the saying, but this is an impossibility anyway, as Levinas cautions. Nevertheless, there is an anticipation in Johannes *de silentio,* who both is and is not a poet, both is and is not a philosopher, for although both the imagination and the dialectic can engage in phenomenology, neither can accurately account for the experience of the unsayable, Abraham's experience. And yet, for Johannes *de silentio* it is better to admire (and perhaps to aspire?) than to be. Abraham loves God, Johannes loves his own admiration of Abraham's love of God. And still there is an anticipation. That is precisely how Johannes Climacus, who *can* speak, recalls this prior work by *de silentio,* whose portrayal of the knight of faith he considers as only a rash anticipation,

> and the illusion was gained by depicting him in a state of completeness, and hence in a false medium, instead of in the existence medium, and the beginning was made by ignoring the contradiction—how an observer could become at all *aware* of him in such a way that he could place himself, admiring, outside and admire that there is nothing, nothing whatever, to *notice,* unless Johannes *de silentio* would say that the knight of faith is his own poetic production. (SV, 10:178 n; CUP, 1:500 n)

Not the accident of discovery, not the poetic art of writing, not even the thinker could do what Abraham did, and all were resigned to this lesser position—that is, until we come to the much later pseudonym, the author of *The Sickness Unto Death:* Anti-Climacus. He is the non-climber, the one who has always already arrived, the one who like Abraham is able to say: "Here am I." It is in him we find an explanation for Johannes *de silentio's* admiration. Anti-Climacus defines admiration as "happy self-surrender" (*lykkelig Selvfortabelse*) (SV, 15:139; SUD, 86), a condition of the theological self, we are told, someone animated by possibility. But elsewhere, in *Practice in Christianity,* Anti-Climacus, the idealist, comes down hard upon the admirer.

> When it comes to the moral, to want to admire instead of to imitate is not an invention by bad people—no, it is the spineless invention by those who must be called the better but also the weak people, whereby they seek to keep themselves detached. They are related to the admired one only through the imagination; to them he is like a theatrical play, except that he, since this is in actuality, has a somewhat stronger effect. But for their part, they make the same demands that are made in the theater: to sit safe and calm oneself, detached from any actual relation to danger, while they still put it down in their favor that they admire him, whereby they presumably think to share in his merits of truth and right—in a rather convenient, cheap way that is also almost sensual. (SV, 16:227; PC, 244)

One could easily think that Anti-Climacus's stern words were directed at Johannes *de silentio,* who himself concedes:

> I do not believe; this courage I lack. To me God's love . . . is incommensurable with the whole of actuality. . . . My immense resignation would be a substitute for faith. I would not be able to do more than make the infinite movement in order to find myself and again rest in myself. Neither would I have loved . . . as Abraham loved. . . . I can easily walk upside down in existence, but I cannot make the next movement, for the marvelous I cannot do—I can only be amazed at it. (SV, 5:33–35; FT, 34–36; trans. amended)

Roy Martinez has suggested Johannes *de silentio* has to observe silence so as to hear the word.[15] That is certainly possible, but Johannes's constant emphasis on Abraham as the chosen one, the only one, the founder, might also suggest that in spite of Anti-Climacus's harsh words, the best the rest of us can do, and that would include Johannes *de silentio* himself, is to admire, to strive, to ground our love in admiration, and thereby and like Johannes also be transfigured. Perhaps it is his own words he must be silent to hear. It is, after all, better to admire than to be!

★   ★   ★

Let us now move to the discourse signed by one S. Kierkegaard, namely *Works of Love,* to try and understand the further implication of Kierkegaard's aporetic writings. This discourse is a chapter all of its own. Traditionally it has been read as a direct communication, but when it comes to this discourse, not only do we get a direct communication as explicitly related by this S. Kierkegaard, but, just like the (other) pseudonymous works, it too contains an indirect communication concealed by the confusion of the direct text that is purposely misleading. If the following is correct, then this discourse is also pseudonymous, making S. Kierkegaard the twelfth pseudonym.

Traditionally, *Works of Love* has been understood as a substantial thesis on Christian ethics. However, more attention to the preface and the introductory chapter reveals that this text does not represent an ethic at all. Rather it is a text about secrets, about the unknowable, indeed about the unsayable, or, more correctly, about the origin of love and the love of the unsayable (SV, 12:18; WL, 13). It is a love that makes no demands, that asks no questions, a love without a why. Although it resembles the other pseudonymous texts in its approach and, to a large degree, parallels *Fear and Trembling, Works of Love* represents a dramatic change inasmuch as here singularity is historicized, is situated within a context that raises the appropriate question: how to speak about the unsayable. Obviously, the unsayable does not itself speak or it would no longer be unsayable. So how in the economy of everydayness to speak about the unsayable? How to speak denials? The unsayable can easily be betrayed, as we are all too often confronted with; it can easily be brought into the light of day; indeed, as Jason Wirth has commented, "one can make the infinite finite and the nothing something and God a mortal."[16] Or one can let the unsayable be what it is, unsayable, secret. One can let the unsayable speak without betraying itself, without demanding that by announcing itself it must lose its unsayableness. While ordinary or direct communication always betrays the unsayable, as Climacus has already warned, only subjective thinking has secrets, secrets that only indirectly can speak for themselves without self-betrayal. To awaken to such secretive communication, to render the unsayable audible in its very unsayableness, to hear what has no sound, is love of the unsayable. *Works of Love* is a text on the love of the unsayable.

Works of Love is thus a discourse on the gifts of love, gifts that are "totally

present everywhere and *essentially* cannot be described" (SV, 12:9; WL, 3).
It is a text, therefore, not about love but about the gifts of love whose source
is always more originary, hidden, and impossible to articulate. The gifts of
love can be revealed only in love's performative act. "The life of thought is
hidden; the utterings of speech [are] the unconcealing [*det Aabenbarende*]"
(SV, 12:14; WL, 8). But its origin remains a secret, leading Kierkegaard to
ask:

> Where does love come from, where does it have its origin and its source,
> where is the place in which it has its dwelling and from where it originates?
> Yes, this place is hidden [*skjult*] or is in hiding [*i det Skjulte*]. There is a place
> in singularity's innermost being; from this place originates the life of love . . .
> but you cannot see this place; no matter how deeply you penetrate into it,
> its origin eludes you in remoteness and hiddenness; even when you have
> penetrated furthest in, its origin is always already [*endnu bestandig*] still like a
> bit further in. (SV, 12:14; WL, 8–9; trans. amended)

What is always already a bit further in is the infinite dimension of existence, hidden and inaccessible except through the gifts of love. If love/
existence cannot be seen, then it is at least possible to see the gifts of love,
though not necessarily so. Kierkegaard is not talking about expressions of
love or platitudes. "[T]he word and the phrase and the inventions of language may be a mark of love, but that is uncertain" (SV, 12:17; WL, 11).
As Glaucon notes with some distress in Plato's *Politeia,* it is impossible to
determine whether justice is truly present;[17] so Kierkegaard insists we cannot
know that genuine love is present in the other. Love hides as do the gifts of
love. Instead we must look to the *how* [*hvorledes*] of the gift of love, that
love may reveal itself. It is in the *how* love is expressed, it is in *how* singularity
comports itself that the gifts of love may become visible, not to sense perception but to the minds' eye, not as cognition but as *noetic* experience, if we
may borrow from Plato.[18] If this is correct, then *Works of Love* is not a theory
of love or even a theory of the works of love, and that would mean it is
not an ethic. It is, rather, a deconstructive phenomenology of singularity's
being-in-the-world *as* love, a love that has a vertical direction but whose
horizontal connection to existence, we are told, is "unfathomable" [*uudg-
rundelig*] (SV, 12:15; WL, 9).

This is a radical claim that no doubt is disturbing, but, if it is correct, it
goes a long way to explain how this reading of Kierkegaard's texts sees his
entire authorship. While in the pseudonymous works, reading is about *knowing* and hence epistemological in content, in the discourses, upbuilding or
otherwise, reading is about *being,* and hence ontological in content, and only
indirectly, as Joakim Garff has suggested, if I have understood him properly,
about doing or acting.[19] It is a leap from depth to surface, from cognition
to resolve, from knowing to experience, from transcendence to immanence.

It is a leap to what precedes all knowledge, a leap to origins, all of which the indirect communication of these texts reveals only through solicitation that in itself constitutes an existential appropriation of the text.

Moreover, and to strengthen this reading, Kierkegaard presents singularity (*den Enkelte*) for the first time not in the non-authored writings of *Either–Or*, but when it is needed, in the first upbuilding discourse, indeed, in the preface to the first upbuilding discourse to follow *Either–Or*, a discourse entitled "The Expectancy of Faith: New Year's Day," and dated May 5, 1843, Kierkegaard's thirtieth birthday. There he says:

> It [*Two Upbuilding Discourses*] finally met that singularity [*hiin Enkelte*] whom I with joy and gratitude call *my* reader, that singularity whom it seeks, to whom, so to speak, it stretches out its arms, that singularity who is favorably enough disposed to let himself be found, favorably enough disposed to receive it, whether at the time of the encounter it finds him joyful and confident or weary and pensive. (SV, 4:13; EUD, 5)

It is the text that finds singularity, it is the text that seeks out the solicitation that allows its unconcealing, it is the text that seeks the other and to whom it empties itself regardless of her mood. But why now? Why not earlier? Why not later?

Inasmuch as *Either–Or* (impossibly) represents immediate experience, it does not require a positing of singularity. This is true for volume 2 as well, since Assessor Wilhelm's ethic is merely aesthetic, grounded in external measures to which immediate experience becomes habituated, dare I say, obsessively so. But Kierkegaard's following productions, the *Upbuilding Discourses* and the pseudonymous *Fear and Trembling* and *Repetition*, necessarily call for subjectivity inasmuch as experience has now moved beyond the immediate, beyond finite being to transcendent experience, to existence grounded in the reflective and hence to a phenomenology of infinite being. It has moved inside; singularity has attained another dimension. Thus the discourse on "The Expectancy of Faith," and we should note the language of this title: expectancy of a birth, a re-birth, a new beginning, which immediately throws singularity into its first test: prayer, and in *Fear and Trembling* into a so-called second immediacy relevant only to the command for an *absolute* responsibility that, as Derrida reads, necessarily renders Abraham *relatively* irresponsible.[20] That is to say, once interiority announces itself, the dialectic of singularity comes into play. Now the external and its obligations withdraw in a non-contextualized study of being's utmost possibilities. Now for the first time we are presented with obligation without ethics, hence the need for singularity, for pseudonymity, for indirect communication. Now we have learned from Kierkegaard's complex presentation that singularity means responsibility, that singularity does not respond to some external (arbitrary) value but seeks to draw on its own ontological characteristic as responsible being. If this is true, then we can say that for Kierkegaard singularity means responsibility.

This hermeneutical exploration of Kierkegaard's texts goes a long way to explain the *why* of the pseudonymous authorship that is simultaneously accompanied by a number of upbuilding and other types of discourses written under the name of one S. Kierkegaard. I want to suggest that Kierkegaard had both Parmenides and Plato in mind when he thought out the *how* of his authorship in consideration of what he was trying to communicate. In the *Postscript* there is a crucial clue to Kierkegaard's thinking. Climacus argues: "A human being thinks and exists, and existence [*Existents*] separates thinking and being, holds them apart from each other in succession" (SV, 10:36; CUP, 1:332).[21] To separate thinking and being by completely changing the approach from one text to the next is certainly to emphasize the in-between, the *inter-esse* of existence, responsibility as such. It also makes sense of this peculiar authorship where the author maintains more than a distance from his communications, leaving it to the readers to disclose the unsayable for themselves. Moreover, it was the only way to communicate what could not be communicated except in some Socratic maieutic way. It was the only way to communicate the *in-between,* the stuff of existence, as it reverberates between, holds apart, being and thinking, thus correcting Hegel's over-ambitious neglect of existence as such. It follows that direct communication *is* impossible, because what we desire to communicate is unsayable.[22]

★ ★ ★

Finally, we want to return once more to *Either–Or* to understand what it means for a text to have no author, as was suggested earlier. As you know, the manuscript was supposedly found by the editor, Victor Eremita, who left it in the order in which it was found. How this mysterious editor found it is a hilarious story of a fight with his reluctant writing desk. The description of this fight with a thing is significant to our understanding of the lack of an author. What emerges with this lack is a subtext, but before we begin to unravel this mystery, we should ask, *why* is there no author? The fragmentary introduction to *Either–Or,* which collectively is called "Diapsalmata," has tentatively been interpreted as "Mellemspil" by the Danish editors. I wonder if we might think of these fragments as "middle voices."

The first thing we have to understand is that either–or is *not* a title, it is an *activity,* or better, a disposition, a comportment. As the reader is told by Victor Eremita in Kierkegaard's Journals,

> The book had no author; since the honored unknowns [Don Giovanni, etc.] are to me what they were to me and presumably to the reader as well— unknown; therefore it should have no title either. Its title, therefore, does not point outwardly but inwardly toward the work itself. The one who says:

the book is called either-or, he says absolutely nothing; the one, however, who says the work *is* an either-or, he himself produces the title. This is obviously something every single reader can do as well as the editor. (PAP IV B 59)

The reader is, quite literally, invited to engage in the performative act together with the text, invited to start swimming. It is likewise with this editor whose name, Victor Eremita, the solitary victor, was also directed inward, not outward. But in fact, the editor himself tells us, there ought not be an editor either. To identify a title, an author, or even an editor is to objectify the text and hence to approach it under the subject-object paradigm that implies the text can be cognitively known. This is not so in the case of *Either–Or*, nor, incidentally, in the case of any other Kierkegaard text. No, the text of *Either–Or* is intended to float, so to speak, to avoid standing in a *conclusive* relationship to singularity. It is not a book with a message, not outwardly, anyway. It does not render any truths or information that can be categorized as factual truth, in which case it would need a name. No, this is pure experience as Kierkegaard understands it. The essay on Mozart's *Don Giovanni,* or "Don Juan," as the text says, is a fine example of what the non-author has in mind. It is experience that is uncommunicable, constituted only in the performative act. The book is but for a single reader who under the name of Victor Eremita produces the book, brings it forth every time it is seriously appropriated. That is to say, she who reads it, really reads it, brings it forth, appropriates it, *becomes* its editor. This reader becomes the witness presencing herself; the performance erases the pseudonym, Victor Eremita withdraws.

In his very first book, then, Kierkegaard uses all the tricks available to him to make the reader take notice of what is most immediate in her own experience and hence what is most familiar and, ironically, utterly unknowable. It is a most scandalous use of the maieutic approach. As the Journal note suggests, the book was bought, not read, meaning not understood. How could it be understood? All people at that time had to go by was theory, dialectical in the Hegelian style or otherwise. All they knew was doctrine; all they understood was pure reason and the rule of logic. All they comprehended was Knowledge with a capital K. Never before had they been presented with a deconstruction of theory. Never before had they been confronted with the aporias of traditional epistemology. Never before had their reading been so disrupted by the interruptions of Kierkegaard's biting irony. But that is precisely what he offers the reader in his first book, and he does so to make the reader take notice: that philosophy is about the significance of *how* the reader relates *to* experience, not what theories we can produce *about* experience. The lesson has begun: *how* to philosophize, as in wondering in an unrestricted manner, shattering the knowable world, removing us from the familiar preoccupations of everydayness and disclosing an unlimited horizon, disclosing possibility and even im/possibility, the unsayable, and allowing ourselves to be devastated. The aim here is acceptance, not violence. It all seems very plausible, but before concluding, a question needs to be asked. Is it possible the contemporary reader may indeed have been deprived of this capacity *to be lost*?

While Kierkegaard's irony, his way of deconstructing existence, may make us take notice and read with more care, it may also make us discard these aporias of writing, in which case the reader suffers a lack of loss. Reading Kierkegaard is a serious challenge; the payoff is discovering something about ourselves. But is there a problem here? As a reader of Kierkegaard, I am both the focus of the text and the ignored other. I have no author who takes responsibility for effecting the communication of the text. I am, in fact, left entirely alone; I have been abandoned. Is this still the case today, however? Are we really reading Kierkegaard in this way? Is this feeling of being abandoned perhaps hidden for us today because the corpus left by commentators has usurped the position given the non-author by Kierkegaard and has even supplanted Kierkegaard himself? Do we, as Pat Bigelow once asked, still possess the capacity for the inwardness necessary for appropriation? This body of interpretive text certainly serves a necessary purpose, but it also shields us from some of the unease that we would have felt had we been truly abandoned, as Kierkegaard perhaps intended. In other words, the works may no longer be pseudonymous, and the suspended undecidability may no longer urge an individual response. And yet, can we not still find the surprise that awakens us, makes us wonder, catches us unawares and enables us once more *to be lost*?

Awakening comes with the essay with the strange title "Rotation of Crops." Here is much to wonder about. The subject of the essay is idleness. In its pedestrian misperception, modernity claims idleness to be the root of all evil. But the text insists that idleness is a genuine good, for it allows for authentic being, it allows for thinking existence. Idleness is not the evil, the text insists; indeed, it may be said that everyone who lacks a sense for it thereby shows that she has not raised herself to the human level. Here, of course, is the clue to the importance of this essay with the strange title. There is an indefatigable activity in the economy of everydayness, it says, an activity so obsessive that it excludes thinking proper and places the human in a class with the animals, who, instinctively, must always be in motion (SV, 2:267; EO, 1:289). But what does this have to do with crop rotation? Idleness is customarily associated with boredom, which *is* the root of evil according to the text. The infinity of change implied by crop rotation *is* boredom expressed by restlessness. Presumably crops are continually rotated because boredom has set in, but, of course, also to gain better crops. For those of you who are unfamiliar with traditional farming, crop rotation was the old-fashioned way of fertilizing. But proper fertilization of the earth requires

more than crop rotation; it also requires that a field every so often be left
fallow or idle, left to be receptive to whatever falls from the sky or whatever
the wind brings, left to receive the unexpected, left to once again be creative
and productive, and hence left to be confronted with existence.

Creativity and decision can emerge only within possibility, and possibility
presences itself only upon solicitation. Hope is useless, for it desires the impossible, desires what is limitless (SV, 2:270; EO, 1:292), and hence is not
the way to proceed, says the text. Only during an idle year can the field
recover, regain its strength. Only during an idle year can thinking restore
itself to its originary occupation: to think the in-between, think existence.
This is the time when mental weeds take over. This is the time when "the
accidental outside a person corresponds to the arbitrariness within" (SV, 2:
277; EO, 1:300). Idleness is the time to become prepared for whatever
emerges out of the ground, be it a plant, a worm, a grasshopper, all of which
I can experience, all of which needs no cultivation, yet they nourish the
field for next year's productivity. Imagine all the cropping up with no order,
no obvious purpose, no demands, no whys. Like wild flowers, these crop-
pings are just *there,* interrupting the economy of everydayness; they are just
there to be received in their fragmented natural state that speaks to us of the
arbitrariness of existence. We can leave them be, take pleasure in their aesthetic beauty. We can cut them, take the metaphysical route, and arrange
them according to some preordained order. Or we can feed them into disparate vessels (or thoughts) and *let them be* to make their own statement.
Through this interruption, this aporia, thinking can once again become creative and productive, can once again think existence. As the text argues,
when "one enjoys something totally accidental, one considers the whole of
existence [*Tilværelsen*] from this standpoint; one lets its reality *run aground* on
this" (SV, 2:276; EO, 1:299). The aporia of idleness awakens and lets us
wonder as the subtext discloses and seeds; it blooms in the mind of its
receptive addressee; and what is revealed by the non-author is the condition
for the possibility of the performative act if, once in a while, allowed to be
idle. Dis-covering *this* is self-disclosure, nothing more—nothing less.

Notes

1. I wish at this point to express my discontent regarding the Hong translation of the title of this first publication of Kierkegaard's, which in the original
Enten–Eller contains the all-important dash, which, in the Danish, is *tankestreg*—
translation: "thought line." Nothing could be more important than the admonition *to think* when confronted by decision and, ultimately, by *undecidability.*

2. Sylviane Agacinski, *Aparté: Conceptions and Deaths of Søren Kierkegaard,*
trans. Kevin Newmark (Tallahassee: Florida State University Press, 1988), 78.

3. Jerome A. Miller, *In the Throe of Wonder: Intimations of the Sacred in a Post-
Modern World* (Albany: State University of New York Press, 1992), 3–4.

4. Ibid., 8.

5. Richard Rhodes, *The Making of the Atomic Bomb* (New York: Simon and Schuster, 1986), 60–61, 63–64, 75, 76–77, 131.

6. Roger Poole, "The Unknown Kierkegaard: Twentieth-Century Receptions," in *The Cambridge Companion to Kierkegaard,* ed. Alastair Hannay and Gordon D. Marino (Cambridge: Cambridge University Press, 1998), 60.

7. Michael Strawser, *Both/And: Reading Kierkegaard from Irony to Edification* (New York: Fordham University Press, 1997), 34.

8. Hermann Deuser, "Religious Dialectics and Christology," *Cambridge Companion to Kierkegaard,* 381, 392.

9. Stanley Cavell, "Naughty Orators: Negation of Voice in *Gaslight,*" in *Languages of the Unsayable,* ed. Sanford Budick and Wolfgang Iser (Stanford, Calif.: Stanford University Press, 1987), 342.

10. I write the name of Kierkegaard's pseudonymous author of *Fear and Trembling* without capitalization and in italics inasmuch as this is the manner in which it always appears in the original text.

11. Jacques Derrida, "How to Avoid Speaking: Denials," in *Languages of the Unsayable,* 11.

12. Joakim Garff, *"Den Søvnløse": Kierkegaard læstæstetisk-biografisk* (Copenhagen: C. A. Reitzels Forlag, 1995), 162–63 (my trans.).

13. See Richard Lewontin, *The Triple Helix: Gene, Organism and Environment* (Cambridge: Harvard University Press, 1998), especially ch. 2.

14. Elsebet Jegstrup, "Kierkegaard on Tragedy: The Aporias of Interpretation," *Philosophy Today* 40, no. 2 (summer 1996): 292.

15. Roy Martinez, "Poetic Self-Expression and the Self-Reference of Silence in Kierkegaard's *Fear and Trembling*" (paper presented at the annual meeting of the Georgia Continental Philosophy Circle, Mercer University, Atlanta, March 1998). I am grateful to Jason Wirth for his illuminating reading of a prior version of this essay at this meeting and indebted to him for the next few lines of the text.

16. For more on this reading of *Works of Love,* see Elsebet Jegstrup, "Text and the Performative Act: Kierkegaard's (Im/possible) Direct Communications," *Philosophy Today* 45, no. 2 (summer 2001): 121–31.

17. Plato, *The Republic of Plato,* trans. Allan Bloom (New York: Basic Books, 1968), 361B–E.

18. Borrowing from Plato here is not inappropriate inasmuch as the text in this introductory chapter to *Works of Love* to a large degree reflects Plato's cave allegory.

19. Garff, *"Den Søvnløse,"* 265.

20. Jacques Derrida, *The Gift of Death,* trans. David Wills (Chicago: University of Chicago Press, 1995), 60–61.

21. See also CUP, 1:123, 189–91, 196–98, 302–308, 328–35, on the relationship of thinking and being.

22. As Johannes Climacus insists, thinking's passion is to think the unthinkable (SV, 6:38; PF, 37).

5

On the Borderline of Madness

John Llewelyn

But a borderline is precisely a torment for passion.[1]

The Higher Madness

ONE OF KIERKEGAARD'S MOST COMMON ways of issuing a warning against commonnness is to say that it would drive you mad. Yet to say that someone is mad is one of his most common ways of distinguishing someone's uncommonness. Under the heading "Literary Quicksilver," he declares that what he is to say under it may be described as "A Venture in the Higher Madness with *Lucida Intervalla*."[2] He then cites as an epigraph a couplet from Oehlenschlæger's *Dina*:

> I will not sing along in harmony
> But grate as a strange dissonance.

Strange dissonance indeed, strange absurdity, because the very first paragraph of the text that begins after this quotation states that it will be difficult to distinguish the venture in the higher madness from the intervals of lucidity. They will be found to stand alongside each other peacefully, he says. Apparently, then, there will be a harmony, albeit a strange one, as though the two were on the point of suddenly coalescing into one, communicating with each other like two drops of quicksilver, like mercury, which gets its name from or gives its name to the god of communication between heaven and earth. The so-called higher madness is evidently a deep madness, deeper, 17,000 fathoms deeper, than the level at which one opposes peace of mind and mental derangement. That this is so, that here the higher is in one sense—though, as we shall discover, not in another sense—the lower, is suggested by entries in Kierkegaard's *Journals and Papers* dating from some time in 1839 stating that the higher madness is "the most concrete of all categories, the fullest, since it is closest to life and does not have its truth in a beyond, the supraterrestrial, but in a subterranean below, and thus, if it were a hypothesis, the most grandiose empirical proof of its truth could be made."[3] We are then told that it is by this category that the transition is

made from abstract madness to concrete madness; on the one hand it may
be expressed in the formula "the unity of madness [*Galskab*] in the duality
of all creation [*Alskab*]," borrowed from the work by the poet Jens Baggesen
ominously entitled "The Abracadabra of the Untimeliness of the Ass" [*Asen-
utidens Abracadabra*]. On the other hand, this category of the higher madness
may be expressed speculatively (and speculative idealism is what is here being
mocked) in the formula "the unity of all creation in the duality of madness."
These formulae are written in entries of the *Journals and Papers* that relate to
the book attributed to Nicolaus Notabene entitled *Prefaces,* which consists
of eight prefaces followed by a very brief postscript. Is this an allusion to the
prefatory and introductory parts of the works of Hegel in which comments
are made about the anomalous status of prefaces and their relation to the
texts that follow them? That this is an allusion to the speculative system is
confirmed by the *Writing Sampler,* attributed to A. B. C. D. E. F. Godhaab,
which is printed after *Prefaces* in the same volume of *Kierkegaard's Writings*
and contains only a preface to eight more prefaces followed by a postscript
that repeats (backward) almost verbatim the first sentence of the first preface:
"Finally, please read the following preface, because it contains things of the
utmost importance." This is a riverrun repetition (forward) to the broken
circularity of another speculation on the Speculative system, Derrida's guying
and gaying of Hegel in generative and degenerative chiasmus with Genet in
Glas.[4]

But what of the chiasmus of the two formulae cited above? We can only
speculate as to how that might work. Perhaps creation is both unity and
duality because it is the whole of what is created and implies a creator. This
duality of the creator and the created is at the same time a multiplicity insofar
as, to speak with Leibniz, the goodness of the creator implies the greatest
possible variety and difference in his creation. To speak with Kierkegaard,
all creation implies multiplicity, that is, whatever you wish, "*Quodlibet* or the
loonier the better."

The duality of the higher madness is implied in its being a "pathos–filled
transition—a dialectical transition,"[5] from abstract madness to concrete madness, these being not disconnected insanities, but species falling under a genus
that is the unity of higher madness.[6] It so happens that the entry in which
these distinctions are made is followed immediately in the English edition
of the *Journals and Papers* by one dating from three years later in which
reference is made to the *Meditations* of Descartes. This is a happy accident.
For madness is at stake in these *Meditations.* Furthermore, it is the treatment
of madness in them on which turns the debate between Derrida and Foucault
concerning the history of madness in the age of reason and whether madness is deeply embedded in reason and philosophy. Derrida acknowledges
Kierkegaard as another contributor to this debate when he takes as an epigraph for his discussion of Foucault the assertion of Johannes Climacus in

Philosophical Fragments that "the moment of decision is *folly,*" "Afgjørelsens
Øieblik er en *Daarskab.*"[7] What Kierkegaard contributes to this discussion
of reason and philosophy and history cannot be appraised independently of
his response to Hegel, as the terms "reason," "philosophy," and "history"
announce. Before reminding ourselves of where Hegel stands on some of
these questions, let us quickly take note of some of the distinctions made by
the philosopher to whom Hegel in his turn is responding, "the honest Kant"
who anticipates Kierkegaard by denying reason in order to make room for
faith and of whom Kierkegaard says that he declares the relationship to God
to be a mental derangement.[8]

The Limits of Reason

Hegel is discontented with the way Kant draws a line between understanding
(*Verstand*) and reason (*Vernunft*). Because Kierkegaard is ultimately concerned
with what he contrasts with both reason (Danish *Fornuft*) and understanding,
no serious misunderstanding may result from translating his word *Forstanden*
by "reason," as in the Swenson version of the paragraphs of the *Philosophical
Fragments,* which is changed in the Hong and Hong translation to "understanding."[9] At issue with Kierkegaard is the question of philosophical translation from understanding or reason to religion regarded as exceeding both,
as madness or folly or foolishness, where the second and third of these are
the translations of *Daarskab* given respectively by Swenson and the Hongs.
But Hegel's difference with Kant turns on the prior question of whether,
like drops of quicksilver—or indeed water (*Critique of Pure Reason* B319)—
understanding flows into reason or whether it remains discrete. It turns also
therefore on this discretion, on how a *discrimen,* a borderline, is to be conceived, on what it is to be on a border or at a limit or frontier. And here
this philosophical question of translatability across a line brings us up against
a question of textual translation that cannot be as easily passed over as the
question of textual translation raised above in connection with Kierkegaard.

At B322 of the *Critique of Pure Reason,* Kant writes, in Kemp Smith's
translation, "as regards things in general unlimited reality was viewed [by
former logicians] as the matter of all possibility, and its limitation (negation
[*Negation*]) as being the form by which one thing is distinguished from others
according to transcendental concepts."[10] Kemp Smith's words "unlimited reality" translate *unbegrenzte Realität,* and his word "limitation" translates *Ein-
schränkung.* Although in B322 Kant is speaking of pre-Critical logicians, and
it is arguable therefore that an ambiguity is tolerable in this context, he
himself does not use one and the same root word. To do so would be to
blur a distinction made at B789, B795, and in §57 of the *Prolegomena* between
what, following Kemp Smith's translation of the *Critique,* would have to be
called a bound, a *Schranke,* and what, following that translation, would have

to be called a limit, a *Grenze*. In P. G. Lucas's translation of the *Prolegomena* the terms are reversed.[11] Provided they are employed consistently, it does not much matter which pairing we prefer. I follow Lucas because, as we shall soon see, it enables us to maintain a continuity of usage from Kant to Hegel. Postponing the question of whether this enables us to maintain a continuity of usage from both of them to Kierkegaard, and postponing a question raised by Kant's repetition of the word or particle *gleich*, let us consider the distinction made in §57 of the *Prolegomena*.

> Boundaries [*Grenzen*] (in extended beings) always presuppose a space which is come across outside a certain determined place and encloses it; limits [*Schranken*] do not need any such thing [*dergleichen*], rather are they mere negations [*Verneinungen*] which affect a magnitude in so far as it does not have absolute completeness. But our reason sees as it were [*gleichsam*] around it a space for knowledge of things in themselves, although it [*ob sie gleich*] can never have determined concepts [*bestimmte Begriffe*] of them and is limited merely to appearance.

Thus, as Kant goes on to explain in the sentence immediately following this paragraph: "As long as knowledge by reason is homogeneous [*gleichartig*]," as in mathematics and the natural sciences, we have mere *Schranken*, limits, with the ever-open possibility of knowledge being extended beyond a particular point it has reached. But, he observes in the sentence immediately preceding the paragraph just cited, "although [*obgleich*] it cannot be refuted" or grounded in intuition, the idea of a being that somewhere serves as a *Grenze*, a bound, to this infinite or indefinite extendibility of mathematical and physical knowledge is demanded by reason. However, he goes on to say a few paragraphs after the one just cited, this demand of reason can lead only, as it were (*gleichsam*) to the contact of filled space (phenomenal experience) with empty space (the noumenal, the unknowable). The "as it were" signals that the connection between filled and empty space is being invoked only as an analogy to illustrate the difference between the sheer negativity of a limit, a *Schranke*, and the positivity of a boundary, a *Grenze*. A surface is the boundary of a three-dimensional physical volume, but it is still spatial; a line is the boundary of a surface, but is still spatial; a point is the boundary of line, but is still spatial. Here what is beyond each boundary is homogeneous (*gleichartig*) with the boundary. Kant's geometrical analogy illuminates Hegel's account of reason better than it illustrates Kant's own. For although Kant says that a boundary belongs to both sides of what it bounds, on one side are the concepts that have a constitutive use only over indefinitely extendible experience of the spatio-temporal, whereas on the other side are the ideas of reason whose legitimate use is not constitutive but regulative. For Hegel reason is constitutive on both sides of a given bound. That is to say, what Kant calls a *Schranke*, a limit, and contrasts with a boundary, is assimilated to a boundary by Hegel. Hence, according to Hegel, understanding and reason have between them a boundary, not a limit, which they have according to Kant's definitions. If a boundary is positive in the sense that it participates in what lies on both sides of it, then so too is a limit according to Hegel's redefinition. A limit is not merely negative. It is not to be compared with a wall. It is to be compared instead with a passageway—however narrow, aporetic, or difficult. And that is what the etymological derivation of the word "limit" from Latin *limes* would lead us to think.

To say with Hegel that there is a limit between understanding and reason is to say that they are not utterly heterogeneous. Reason, Hegel argues, is the truth of what Kant calls understanding. Understanding finds that it is not opposed to reason, but is an immature form of it. In the supplement to §386 of the *Philosophy of Mind* Hegel writes:

> We make ourselves finite by receiving an Other into our consciousness; but in the very fact of our knowing this Other we have transcended this limit [*Schranke*]. Only he who does not know is limited [*beschränkt*]; whereas he who knows the limit knows it not as a limit of his knowing, but as something known, as something belonging [*Gehörenden*] to his knowledge; only the unknown would be a limit of his knowledge, whereas the known limit on the contrary is not; therefore to know one's limit means to know of one's unlimitedness [*Unbeschränktheit*]. But when we pronounce mind to be unlimited, truly infinite [*unendlich*], this does not mean that mind is free from any limit whatsoever; on the contrary, we must recognize that mind must determine itself [*sich bestimmen*] and so make itself finite, limit [*beschränken*] itself. But the abstract understanding [*Verstand*] is wrong in treating this finitude as something inflexible, in holding the difference between the limit and the infinitude to be absolutely fixed [*fest*], and accordingly maintaining that mind is *either* limited *or* unlimited. Finitude, truly comprehended, is as we have said, contained in infinitude, the limit in the unlimited. Mind is therefore *both* infinite *and* finite, and *neither* merely the one *nor* the other; in making itself finite it remains infinite, for it reduces-raises [*aufhebt*] the finitude within it to what is merely ideal, merely appearing [*nur Erscheinendes*].[12]

It reduces-raises it to what is a merely appearing moment, one could say, in order to give notice of the violent reinterpretation which that term will undergo when with Kierkegaard it becomes the *Øieblik* that resists the reduction of the either-or to the both-and. For Kierkegaard the Critical Kantian case for resisting the both-and is not violent enough. It relies on the distinction between the constitutive and the regulative uses of reason, from which it follows, according to Kant, that his notion of the borderline (*Grenze*) can be used only as a sensuous and therefore not unmisleading picture (*Sinnbild*) in his attempt, as he puts it at the beginning of §59 of the *Prolegomena,* to fix the limits (*Schranken*) of reason in respect of its appropriate use. The proper use is non-constitutive, regulative, practical, analogical, symbolic: thinking or faith rather than theoretical knowledge. Therefore reference to a highest being would tell us nothing about the being. It would tell us only something about the relationship of that being to the world of which we have phenomenal knowledge, so that we regard the latter as if it related to a highest being in the way that a clock relates to its maker.

Hegel's response to this is that Kant the philosopher is obliged to admit that he knows the appropriate use of reason unrestricted by the forms of sensibility and understanding to be regulative: "he who knows the limit knows it not as a limit of his knowing, but as something known, as something belonging to his knowledge." So the content of Kant's claims is in conflict with his making it. He has failed to take account of his own use of speculative reason as a philosopher.

Here, then, the question of the limits of reason is one with the question of the limits of philosophy. And the question of frontiers within philosophical reason, whether they be borders or limits, flows into the question whether the apparent others of philosophical reason are ultimately other than it. Either-or or both-and or either-or and both-and? *Aut-aut* or *vel?*

Of the many others that might be suggested as candidates for being the other of philosophical reason, let us now consider one, madness, bearing in mind Kierkegaard's references to lunacy, insanity, and folly or foolishness cited in the first section of our discussion. We shall find it necessary to be more precise about some of these expressions if certain misconceptions of Kierkegaard's maniology are to be avoided. We return to this question in due course via a remark made in the section of *Anthropology from a Pragmatic Point of View* in which Kant classifies the different kinds of what he refers to generally as *Verrückung*, or, as I shall provisionally and usually say, madness.

Madness

Madness, Kant notes, is a *Versetzung,* a distancing and displacement, that is to say, a change of place: a *kinêsis,* to use the term Kierkegaard transports to the psychological sphere from Aristotle's *Physics.* Note too that the provisional translation of *Verrückung* and *Verrücktheit* by "madness" is supported by the fact that the term "mad" comes from *mutare,* to change. It is thus more informative than the privative term "insanity" and less questionably theory-laden than the term "lunacy." "Folly," it may be remarked in anticipation, straddles mental deficiency, in the form of foolishness or stupidity, and mental illness. It may be a deficiency of theoretical or practical knowledge, or it may be a non-cognitive deficiency of mind. The latter kind of deficiency may be such as to leave room only for causal explanation. The former kind of deficiency may take on a moral tinge, as when it is asked rhetorically in the Koran, "who turns away from the religion of Abraham except they who debase their souls with folly [befool themselves, *safeha*]?" (Sûrah II, 130). In the *Philosophy of Mind,* also under the heading "Anthropology," Hegel gives his own classification of the different varieties of madness, uses the terms *Verrückung* or *Verrücktheit* for the genus, and underlines the notion of distancing conveyed by it when he writes that in madness the mind is divided in itself, *in sich selber entzweiten* (§402, *Zusatz*).

Hegel prescribes a talking cure for this splitting. We must humor the patient, appeal to his or her reason and prudence; in general patients may deserve considerate treatment (*rücksichtvolle Behandlung*) because their rational and moral nature is not entirely destroyed. If someone believes he is Mahomet, tell him he will not be confined provided he promises not to abuse his freedom by being a nuisance to others. Or appeal to the insane person's practical reason. For instance, if he believes he has fragile glass feet, get him to think he is being attacked by robbers. That way he'll very soon find how useful his feet are for running away. Hegel, like Kant, observes that madness may have either a psychological or a physical cause. Where the cause is physical the cure may be physical too, as when someone is cured by falling on his head. But generally the most effective treatment is the talking cure, in which an appeal is made to the patient's reason. Presumably that is what Hegel would prescribe for the madman of Descartes's First Meditation who believes he has a head made of earthenware or glass.

Does this mean that Hegel's philosophy does not exclude madness from reason or from the full blossoming of reason known as philosophy? Or does it point rather to the apparently opposite conclusion that Hegel does exclude madness from reason and philosophy by refusing to face the full blossoming of madness? Answers to these questions can be approached by reflection on the difference between Derrida's and Foucault's readings of the First Meditation.[12]

Why does Descartes put aside the hypothesis or pseudo-hypothesis that he, Descartes the philosopher, might be as mad as the madman who thinks his head and feet are made of glass? Descartes does this, Derrida says, because he believes that it is not the philosopher but the man in the street or the field who cannot contemplate the possibility that he himself might be mad. Descartes himself only reserves the hypothesis that he might be mad until the hypothesis of the evil genius makes it relevant to bring it back into play in order to show that, although the evil genius could be instrumental in making me think in particular that I am sane when I am in fact insane, the possibility of that deception (like the possibility of the hypothesis that I am always dreaming) is included within the possibility of a general deception contrived by the evil genius. The scope of the systematic deception contrived by the evil genius is wider because it brings into doubt not only beliefs based apparently on sensory experience and the imagination, but also beliefs based apparently on the intellect, for instance the propositions of arithmetic. This increase in scope of the range of beliefs is matched by an increase in force of the thought that whether my feelings or thoughts are all placed in me by a deceiving trickster, I *am* feeling or thinking, and that while doing so I can be quite certain that I exist. What I still cannot be certain of is that I can count on the truths of arithmetic and rules of inference when I am not thinking about them, when they are written down for the benefit of others and for myself at some later moment. In order that they may be able, in Hegel's phrase, to stand the test of time, to sustain the possibility of rigorous science, they need the support of a valid argument from my existence to the existence of a non-deceiving God. It is only at this stage, Derrida says, that Descartes turns his back on madness as manifested in the hypothesis that I am always dreaming and in the even madder hypothesis that I am always being systematically deceived by an evil genius. However mad I am, while I think that I think, I exist. So Descartes does not need to discount madness. Philosophy as such cannot discount it. So Hegel's philosophy of philosophy cannot. It cannot exclude it even by the talking cure, by appealing to the madman's reason. For reason has its own moment of madness. Before moving to the question of the nature of this moment, we must return to the two questions posed above about Hegel in order to ask what answer we should expect Foucault to give to them on the basis of his reading of the First Meditation of Descartes. Would he say that Hegel's philosophy includes madness in reason and in the full blossoming of reason known as philosophy, or would he say that Hegel excludes madness from reason and philosophy by refusing to face the full blossoming of madness?

There is some evidence for concluding that Foucault would emulate Hegel by drawing both of these seemingly opposite conclusions. For, on the one hand, he seems to express a Romantic Rousseauistic nostalgia for a pure *esprit sauvage* of madness reminiscent of Lévi-Strauss's invocation of alternative concrete logics to account for the behavior of Bororo and other so-called primitive tribes.[13] On the other hand, Foucault refers precisely to the discussion in Hegel's *Phenomenology of Mind* of Rousseauistic sentimentalism in order to applaud Hegel for returning madness to the fold of philosophy from which, Foucault argues, it had been expelled by Descartes. Where Derrida takes Descartes to be saying that it is the vulgar who would find the hypothesis of madness untenable and for that reason drops it, but only temporarily, from consideration, Foucault maintains that in the First Meditation it is Descartes the philosopher himself who refuses to allow that the madman can think. Neither skepticism nor its refutation can be grounded on the thought that the insane take themselves to have heads made of pottery or glass, for once I entertain that thought I shall inevitably discover myself supposing that I myself might be mad. Does not Descartes write, "I should not be any the less insane were I to follow examples so extravagant"? Following examples so extravagant would mean that I could not think, whether to argue for skepticism or for its refutation—or indeed be able to know that I was following these examples. That is why, according to Foucault,

Descartes turns his back on this self-refuting hypothesis in order to consider the hypothesis that I might always be dreaming. So, in contrast with Montaigne, Descartes does in philosophy what was done by the political and social powers in the seventeenth century, namely, exile the insane in asylums from which, as far as philosophy is concerned, they await liberation by Hegel. The passage in the *Phenomenology of Mind* of which Foucault must be thinking in telling this story is one that has a similar content and dialectical pattern to that of many other passages in the *Phenomenology* and *Encyclopaedia*—for example, the paragraph cited above from the *Philosophy of Mind*. Like this paragraph from the *Philosophy of Mind,* the passage in the *Phenomenology of Mind* makes explicit reference to madness, but there are more unexplicit allusions to forms of madness in the *Phenomenology* and the *Encyclopaedia* than readers usually acknowledge. It is arguable that madness is a key to the reading of these works.[14]

It is also arguable that madness is a key to the reading of the works of Kierkegaard and his pseudonymous and anonymous authors, provided we allow for a displacement of madness, a displacement of displacement, a derangement of derangement, as we move from Hegel to Kierkegaard. This movement from one movement to another, from one *kinêsis* to another, from one moment to another, can be traced only if we take time to read Hegel very closely.

The context of Hegel's explicit references to madness in the *Phenomenology* is a treatment of the figure of consciousness that purports to see the law of the heart as the only way to the welfare of humankind. Hegel's treatment has reached the stage of declaring his diagnosis when, under the heading "The Law of the Heart and the Frenzy [*Wahnsinn*] of Self-Conceit," he writes:

> The heart-throb for the welfare of humanity therefore passes into the ravings of an insane self-conceit [*das Toben des verrückten Eigendünkels*], into the fury [*Wut*] of consciousness to preserve itself from destruction; and it does this by expelling from itself the perversion [*Verkehrtheit*] which it is itself, and by striving to look on it and expressing it as something else. It therefore speaks of the universal order as a perversion of the law of the heart and of its happiness, a perversion invented by fanatical priests, gluttonous despots and their minions, who compensate themselves for their own degradation by degrading and oppressing others, a perversion which has led to the nameless misery of deluded humanity. In this its derangement [*Verrücktheit*], consciousness declares its individuality [*Individualität*] to be the source of this derangement and perversion, but one that is alien [*fremde*] and accidental [*zufällige*]. It is the heart, however, or the singularity [*Einzelheit*] of consciousness, that would be immediately universal, that is itself the source of this derangement, and the outcome of its action is merely that *its* consciousness becomes aware of this contradiction. For the True is for it the law of the heart—something

merely *intended* [*Gemeintes*] which, unlike the established order, has *not stood the test of time,* but rather, when tested, is overthrown. This its law ought to have reality; the law, then, is for it *qua* reality, *qua* valid ordinance, its own name and essential nature; but reality, that very law *qua valid ordinance,* is on the contrary immediately for it something which is not valid. Similarly, its *own* reality, the heart *itself* as singularity of consciousness, is for it its essence; but its purpose is to establish that particular singularity as a *being* [*seiend*]. Thus it is rather itself as *not* singular that is immediately for it its essence, or its purpose has the form of a law, hence the form of a universality, which it is for its own consciousness. This its Concept becomes by its own action its object; thus the heart learns rather that its self is not real, and that its reality is an unreality. It is therefore not an accidental and alien individuality, but just this heart, which in all its aspects is, in its own self, perverted and perverting.[15]

Thus the heart learns that it has to take the step of becoming a head. One wonders whether that step might have to be made on feet at least one of which is made of glass, and whether the head itself or at least one of its eyes may be glass too. For is it not possible that the figure of madness outlined in this part of the *Phenomenology of Mind* is a metaphor for the moments of destruction, going under, breakdown, sacrifice, and meta-phorization that the mind is called to endure patiently in some or all the other crises of alienation and recuperation or cure of the phenomenology of going out of one's mind or of the mind's going out of itself along with a therapy for this? That would be in a very old tradition, a tradition as old as Plato, as old as philosophy itself, the tradition to which Derrida maintains that Descartes belongs, notwithstanding Foucault's attempt to exile Descartes from it, to commit him to an asylum as though he were mad—which would be one way, against Foucault's own intentions, of bringing Descartes back into the philosophical fold if not only the phenomenology of mind but philosophy itself is a philosophy of psychosis, a psychopathology.

And that is what it is according to the moral Derrida draws from his meditation on Descartes's First Meditation and from what Foucault writes about that First Meditation and about the history of madness (for despite their different readings of that First Meditation, Derrida concludes that "Michel Foucault teaches us to think that there are crises of reason in strange complicity with what the world calls crises of madness").[17] "Philosophy," Derrida writes, "is perhaps the reassurance given against the anguish of being mad at the point of greatest proximity to madness. This silent and specific moment could be called *pathetic*" (59), a "first passion" (62). On the other hand, Derrida refers to "[d]anger as the movement of reason menaced by its own security" (62), and maintains that it is *pathos* that secures *logos,* reason and philosophy, from this danger. Is this then a reaffirmation of the law of the heart that Hegel says is mad, *verrückt,* because it claims self-contradictorily both that it is immediacy and that it is an objective (*seiend*) reality? Derrida seeks to avoid such a reaffirmation by affirming that the moment of *pathos* in question is silent. But doesn't this formulation of the difficulty only underline the difficulty raised by Hegel for the proponent of the law of the heart? It is the difficulty that Foucault himself raises for his project of an archaeology—a *logos*—of the silence of madness. Is the only way out of this difficulty, Derrida asks, "to follow the madman down the road of his exile"? Or could one

> perhaps say that the resolution of this difficulty is *practical* rather than *formulated*. By necessity. I mean that the silence of madness is not *said*, cannot be said in the logos of this [Foucault's] book, but is indirectly, metaphorically, made present by its *pathos*—taking this word in its best sense. A new and radical praise of folly whose intentions cannot be admitted because the *praise* (*éloge*) of silence always takes place *within logos*, the language of objectification. (37)

The language of objectification is the stumbling block the defender of the law of the heart places in his own path when he maintains that the immediacy of feeling is an objective reality. It is to be heard already in the gloss Hegel puts on the term "individuality" used of the one who experiences the allegedly immediate feeling. For it gets its sense, like all linguistic sense, from the universality to which it is opposed. The individual is posed or posited, and thereby deposed and deposited, in the same dimension of reality as the universal to which it is opposed. So is a new Erasmus seeking to write a *Praise of Folly* bound to discover that he has written instead a *Praise of Sanity*? If Hegel's psychopathology seems to entail this, so too already does that of Kant if it insists that "[t]he one universal characteristic of madness [*Verrücktheit*] is loss of *common sense* (*sensus communis*) and substitution of *logical private sense* [*Eigensinn*] (*sensus privatus*)."[18] It becomes clear at once from the example of madness Kant gives—the case of someone seeing or hearing something no one else does—that the privacy he intends is a privacy that is only contingently private and that in principle can and should be made public. As with Hegel, no matter how resistant the madman's stubbornness (*Eigensinn*), his claims must be put to the test of time, that is to say, to the test of corroboration. As with Hegel, the sense of this private sense is still logical and the logic is the logic of representation. The privacy and silence of the *pathos* to which Derrida alludes would be on the borderline of that logic, a disturbing nonsense on the threshold (*limen*) of sense that endangers that sense and causes *logos* to tremble. We can expect to learn more on the alternative geometry of that line and what it is to be on it when, from what he says about the *pathos* and silence of madness in connection with Foucault and the *cogito* of Descartes on madness, Derrida turns to the fear and trembling of Johannes de silentio and that author's author.

Imprudence

That author's author writes in an entry in his *Journals and Papers:* "They say that experience [*Erfaring*] makes a man wise. This is very unreasonable talk. If there were nothing higher than experience, experience would drive a man mad [*gal*]."[19] That craziness would be a lower madness in comparison with what we may call, borrowing the phrase from an entry cited at the beginning of this essay, the higher madness. The higher madness would be that madness of which Kierkegaard speaks in connection with the Apostle Paul.

> It is easy enough to defend the use of prudence in achieving something by appealing to Paul, who, after all, also used prudence. Well, let's take that. A life which has qualitatively and totally secured its own heterogeneity as madness (something, in fact, achieved by acting in total opposition to prudence), such a life can use prudence without any danger. But it is dangerous for a person not so distinguished to act prudentially, for then prudence makes capital of him *in toto.* Such a person has not secured for himself any heterogeneity (which, relative to Paul, is achieved only by acting decisively against reason at some time). Religious people do not think this. Religious persons undistinguished in this way religiously defend acting prudentially by appealing to Paul, without noticing or wanting to notice that the "total madness" [*"totale Galskab"*] of Paul's life, that is, its dissimilarity with prudence, adequately safeguarded him, while their crumb of religiosity drowns in the total prudence [*totale Klogskab*] of the world and the secular mentality.[20]

Applying to this Derrida's reference to "[d]anger as the movement of reason menaced by its own security," one could say that Paul is protected from the menace of the security of his prudence by the danger of the heterogeneity he has secured through his madness. The theoretical counterpart to practical total prudence would be ancient Greek contemplation or modern Germano-Greek absolute knowing, the *sagesse* or *savoir absolu* of which the author of *Glas* (*Glasskab?*) is no great friend.[21] Paul took it for his first mission to preach to those for whom the basis of his teaching is described as an offense or a stumbling block. As Johannes Climacus, the pseudonymous author of the *Philosophical Fragments,* observes in a footnote, the Greek expression for this is *skandalizesthai,* in the middle voice. On the one side (the side of the "melancholy" Dane), the offense is a suffering. "Christianity is really all too joyous, and therefore really to stick to Christianity a man must be brought to madness [*Afsindighed*] by suffering."[22] We say "He is offended." But the passive voice of this expression is crossed by the active voice of the equally apt expression "He takes offence." This equivocity is manifested also in the words "passion" and *pathos.* A passion may be regarded either as passive or active. It is this equivocity that gives rise to what Climacus calls an acoustic illusion. This is the illusion that the offense has its source in the understanding, and not in the paradox. The activity indicated by the fact that we say of someone that he takes offense leads us to mistake the under-standing, perhaps the understanding and reason of the philosopher, for the origin of the activity, whereas the initiative is with the paradox itself. In a paragraph of complex and convoluted etymological resonances that prefigure such paragraphs in Heidegger and that reveal the comedian within the so-called melancholy Dane, the words "moment" (*Øieblik*) and "wonder" (*Under*) are pronounced, words that Heidegger will adopt. But when Heidegger adopts the second of these words, it translates Greek *thaumazein*. That that is the wonder in which philosophy begins is what we are told by the Greeks. That is the moment that Socrates can know, if what he knows at that moment is only that he knows nothing. And when he begins to teach that we know nothing, Socrates is opening the way for another beginning, a begin-ning in the moment of decision that remains foolishness to the Greeks—for instance, those Corinthians to whom Paul directed his message after it had become a stumbling block for the Jews.

The Jews were offended, but their memory of the story of Abraham and Isaac on the chosen land of Mount Moriah meant that the story of the incarnation and sacrifice of Christ would not be foolishness to them, not *môria* (1 Cor. 1.23), meaning, as in its derivative "moron," the kind of dementia that is less a mental derangement than a lack of understanding or of reason. That is a typically Greek category, notwithstanding the Platonic acknowledgment that the love in the love of wisdom, in philosophy, is a god-inspired *mania*. For, whatever may be said about this *mania* under the name *furor*, when the degrees of madness described in the *Symposium* are harnessed via Plotinus to Christianity by, for example, Ficino, knowledge of the universal continues to be the end that Platonism seeks. What Plato calls *mania* stands to *thaumazein* as what Paul calls *môria* stands to intellectual *stupor*, the stupidity that is a moment of the moment of wonder, an *Øieblik* of the *Øieblik* of *Under*. The Jews have already learned that there are things that surpass understanding. They have had to accept that the categories of knowl-edge have been shaken by the category of paradox. But for them the paradox of the incarnation is a paradox too far, one that affronts not just their un-derstanding but their religious faith. Except for the one among them named Saul and renamed Paul, the one whose shortness of stature is not an occasion for puffing himself up unless put under pressure by the Corinthians. The folly he tries but fails to avoid—compare verse 6 and verse 11 of 2 Corin-thians 12—is *aphrôn*, the mindless excess of self-glorification. For although he takes second place to no one in apostolic authority, he cannot forget the thorn in his flesh, and the infirmities, reproaches, necessities, persecutions, and distresses he is called to suffer for Christ's sake.

This description matches that which Kierkegaard gives of himself, except that he never pretends that he is an apostle and often questions whether he dare call himself a Christian. Only by adopting a position he calls "armed neutrality,"[23] denying that he is a Christian and that he has had a revelation, can he deceive another into an awareness of the truth of Christianity. Let us not be deceived about deception. It is required by the indirect communication that is the only kind of communication that Socrates found was appropriate for him and that Kierkegaard finds necessary to his aesthetic and poetic mode of addressing the person who is confused over the difference between the religious and the aesthetic.[24] Kierkegaard humors this person, rather as the madman is humored by Hegel.

Nor will Kierkegaard and many of his pseudonymous writers go so far as to claim for themselves the title of religious genius. The religious genius has in common with the apostle that he is put under pressure and that he is mad. Of genius generally, Kierkegaard writes, citing Seneca, *De tranquillitate,* 17, 10:

> *Nullum unquam exstitit magnum ingenium sine aliqua dementia.* The explanation
> is very simple. In order truly to be a great genius a man must be the excep-
> tion. But in order that there shall be seriousness [*Alvor*] in being the excep-
> tion, he must himself be unfree, forced into it. Herein lies the significance
> of his *dementia.* There is a fixed point at which he suffers; he cannot ever
> run with the crowd. This is his anguish. His *dementia* perhaps has nothing at
> all to do with his real genius, but it is the pain by which he is tormented
> into isolation—and he must be in isolation if he is to be great, and no man
> is able freely to hold himself in isolation; he must be constrained if he is to
> be serious.[25]

The great genius is driven out of his mind because he is driven out of society. He must be driven out of society if he is to be driven out of his mind. This is because the mutation that madness implies also implies muteness; it prohibits at least direct communication. It is true that one way of maintaining an inner secrecy is constantly to indulge in talk. Kierkegaard cites Talleyrand's remark to this effect.[26] He refers to Talleyrand also, however, as an instance of a man of genius who might have become a great religious genius if he had not devoted himself to a career in the public world. Perhaps his clubfoot was a divine sign of this, comparable to Paul's shortness of stature and the thorn in his flesh—comparable also to what Kierkegaard called the thorn in his own flesh and to the spindly legs that protruded so far below his trousers that they provoked taunts from the burghers of Copenhagen. The spindly legs are but the outward physical sign of the inward spiritual splinter.

> A genius equipped with all possible capacities, with power to dominate all
> existence and to make men obey him, discovers in his consciousness one
> little sticking point, one bit of madness [*Galskab*]. He becomes so indignant

over it that he decides to kill himself, for to him this one little point is not an externality (for example, being lame, one eyed, ugly, etc.; such would not concern him) but has an element of spirit and thus would seem capable of being removed in freedom—therefore it goads him.[27]

When, in the entry in the *Journals and Papers* reproduced before this last one, Kierkegaard writes of the great genius, it is the religious genius that he means. That this is so is made clear when he writes elsewhere of the sentence cited from Seneca that it is "the secular expression for the religious thesis: one whom God blesses religiously he *eo ipso* execrates in a secular way. So it must be: the first has its basis in the boundaries [*Grændse*] of existence [*Tilværelse*] and the second in the doubleness [*Duplicitet*] of existence [*Tilværelsens*]."[28] Here we come back to the notion of boundary (*Grenze*), Kant's definition of which was compared with Hegel's definition of limit (*Schranke*) in the second section of our discussion. We discovered there that while Kant defines a limit as a negative barrier, and a boundary as positing a continuity from one side to the other, Hegel questions Kant's treatment of the line between understanding and reason as a negative barrier. Hegel maintains that this limit is much more like what, speaking of mathematics, Kant calls a boundary. When we come to the line between, on the one hand, understanding and reason and, on the other hand, what Kierkegaard means by religion, religion is no longer what it remained at its furthest development for both Kant and Hegel, within the boundaries of reason alone, where Passion is the history of the suffering of reason. With Kierkegaard the passion of religion must remain the suffering of the existing singular individual. Not any suffering whatsoever. Not the pain of toothache or of disappointed desire for worldly good fortune. The passion of religion, specifically of *imitatio Christi,* is the suffering of the doubleness of existence.[29] That doubleness or duplicity is described when, in a note mentioning that he has introduced the new pseudonym Anti-Climacus, he writes that "this is precisely the intimation of a halt; that is, the dialectical way of making a halt: you point to something higher which critically forces you back within your boundaries [*Grændse*]."[30] The intimation of a halt is not the arrival at a halt. The dialectical way of making a halt is what Kierkegaard sometimes means when he uses the word "interesting" as a border category (*Grændsekategori*) or *confinium.* The latter is a word he frequently uses because, like the "inter" of "interesting," its first syllable indicates a duplicity. So that the dialectical way of making a halt is always the *dia-,* the *via,* the through and thoroughfare of a turning point on life's way, ultimately the life of a singular individual, therefore in a concrete historical situation, *in discrimine rerum.*[31] This brings us to another turning point in our discussion, a return to Derrida's analysis of Foucault's *History of Madness,* a concluding postscriptural either-or on the Kierkegaardian confines of the scriptural and postscriptural.

Passion

Derrida argues that a history of madness calls for a history of history, and a history of history and of madness cannot assume that what historicity is goes without saying. An account of historicity is called for, a *logos* of it, a philosophy of it. We have seen that Derrida argues too that such an account reveals that from the beginning philosophy is not simply contaminated by madness, but is quasi-conditioned by it. That is to say, madness, meaninglessness, is what makes philosophy and meaning and language possible, though at the same time it makes them impossible if philosophy and language are conceived as a systematic totality of pure sense, pure science, and pure reason. If this is so, it requires to be asked, as Foucault does not, whether the "classical," Cartesian moment at which Foucault maintains madness is excluded is at best an example in the sense of a sample, rather than an example in the sense of an exemplar and paradigm.

Kierkegaard is alive to the difference between objective historiography and existential historicity. The latter is the transfiguration of the temporal by the eternal. It is therefore neither pure factuality nor pure eternity. Its history is not to be understood retroactively as, say, "Pagans before Christianity."[32] Although and because he stresses this difference, a question similar to the one Derrida puts to Foucault must be put to Kierkegaard. He writes that "the possibility of offense is the dialectically decisive factor, is the 'borderline' ['*Grændse*'] between paganism, Judaism-Christianity,"[33] where, as always punctilious on matters of punctuation,[34] instead of using a conjunctive "and" Kierkegaard prefers to use a comma to stand for the decisive factor: *komma* comes from *koptô*, "to cut." An implication of his not being primarily concerned with the chronological sequence of "Pagans before Christianity" is that he does not limit paganism to what precedes Judaism-Christianity historiographically—say the *Weltanschauung* of the ancient Greeks, of which he sees Socrates to be one of the earliest critics. Rife in his contemporary Denmark was what he calls Christian paganism. Perhaps that is why in the sentence just reproduced he writes "borderline" in inverted commas. This may be in order to mark a less decisive cut such as would be marked by "and," where Judaism-Christianity could be mentioned in the same breath as paganism, or as Mohammedanism or as Hinduism or as Buddhism and so on. Alternatively, the relation between any one of these and Judaism-Christianity might be marked, as in the cited sentence, by a decisive comma, or by a hyphen (grammatically intermediate in force between the comma and the "and") such as marks the discontinuity in the continuity of Judaism-Christianity. We do not have to question Kierkegaard's right to opt his own options. Nor do we have to deny that in saying this we are speaking, as he would say, aesthetically. But he himself and his pseudonymous authors demand that an account of the stages of life's way be given that is dialectical

in the sense of reflective but not dialectical in the sense of the System of
Hegel. Now Heidegger's thinking of the epochs of being is another way of
challenging Hegel. It may be said, as Levinas says, that this is still too close
to Hegel for comfort, too close to comfort, because it springs from *thaumazein* (*thauma-sein?*) understood as wonder at the being of there being anything at all. We might instead, taking as our point of departure what Heidegger writes about *Ereignis,* explore with Derrida the chance that both
systematic philosophy or metaphysics and the thinking of being have always
been on the borderline of madness or of what Levinas goes as far as to call
psychotic obsession by, possession by, and persecution by the human or other
other—an astonishing eventuality Kierkegaard touches on when in *The Book
on Adler* he writes that religion is not something one has, but something one
is had by.[35] But religion is something one may be had by in the sense that
it may be that by which one is taken in. This possibility is necessary for
religion. Religion is necessarily on the borderline of madness. It is always
exposed to the chance that its God or its god can be explained away either
in the language of rational justification, for instance the rationality of Hegel
that talks the madman out of his madness, or in the language of causal
explanation, or in both of these languages, as is the case with a feature of
sentences reproduced in the second section of this essay from §57 of Kant's
Prolegomena to which we promised to come back. In the compass of a few
sentences Kant has recourse again and again to the word *gleich*. It is as though
the sound of the word is dictating its use, as though he has lost control of
his senses. Do we have here then a phenomenon for which only a causal
explanation can be given? Not if his sentences make sense. And they do
make sense, even though a purely causal theory ("echolalia"?) may have to
be invoked to explain why Kant expresses this sense precisely in this seemingly obsessive way. As Kant's own philosophical theory maintains, accounts
in terms of reasons and accounts in terms of causal explanations are not
incompatible. But both types of account are objective. Therefore to give
either kind of account of what Kierkegaard calls his inward subjective passion
is to miss the point, what one of his titles calls "the point of view of my
work as an author." He may well agree with Kant that the relationship to
God is a kind of mental derangement (*Sindssvaghed*),[36] but the subjectivity
of this derangement places it as far beyond the range of all rational or causal
accounting as the singular, according to Aristotle, is beyond scientific knowledge. Subjective passion is unaccountable, being ultimately the condition of
accountability. The madness of subjective passion is the madness of the idiot
in the etymological sense of the term *idios,* the singular and solitary individual
Kierkegaard calls *den Enkelte,* hence for him first of all the author who signs
himself "S. K."

There is both an enormous risk and an enormous security about this
subjective passion. It is the passion of choosing myself absolutely. And the

absolution here is ab-solution, that is to say, separation. It is the unbinding of myself in my binding myself to myself. What I unbind myself from is this and that, what Eckhart and Angelus Silesius call "things." These things are things of the world. Moreover, these things include what we call God, insofar as God is regarded as a thing, albeit a highest thing. In the archaic script of Silesius's *Cherubinischer Wandersmann* God's name is written *GOtt*. There is a God or a god that must go. This is that God that exists—or does not. And the risk of the non-existence of this God is the chance of S. K.'s eternal salvation. Not a duration in time, but an endurance in eternity, Kierkegaard's eternal salvation is not contingent upon the contingent or necessary existence of God. "By itself, to have a genuine concern for one's eternal salvation (as Christianity requires), this alone is an enormous weight compared to the manner of living that leaves the eternal an open question."[37] That question ceases to be open when I choose the absolute. "And what is the absolute? It is I myself in my eternal validity."[38] This validity is not undermined by the non-existence of God. My idiocy saves me from the madness by which I might be said to be gripped if I persisted in believing I heard a voice (as Abraham believed he heard God's voice bidding him take Isaac into the land of Moriah and then, on Moriah, the voice of an angel of the Lord bidding him not to lay his hand on the lad) when there was no one there to speak (as "there was no voice, nor any that answered" when on Carmel at Elijah's behest the people called upon Baal [1 Kings 18.26, 29]).[39] My choice of my eternal validity is self-validating. This does not mean that its validity is independent of how I comport myself toward others. The faith in which the choice of myself is made is what saves ethical works from the pure universality of Kantian *Moralität* and the mere public custom of Hegelian *Sittlichkeit*.

In this way Kierkegaard's choice of himself does what in Levinas's teaching on the ethical is performed by my being elected by the other. In Levinas's writings the other may be the human other or God, yet the metaphysical or empirical existence of the other as God is as beside the point for Levinas as it is for Kierkegaard. What Levinas calls psychosis, like what we have called the idiocy of the Kierkegaardian subject, is immune from exposure to the sort of madness we might diagnose in the case of someone who persists in believing that he is being addressed when there is no one there to address him. Now the doctrines that Kierkegaard and Levinas propose are not doctrines that hold only for themselves. As Derrida asks rhetorically, when Levinas writes in reference to the system of Hegel, "It is not I who do not accept the system, as Kierkegaard thought, it is the other": "Can one not wager that Kierkegaard would have been deaf to the distinction?"[40] That is to say, Kierkegaard does not deny that there are other subjects capable of passionate subjectivity like himself. Kierkegaard is speaking of subjectivity in general. He knows, to quote Derrida again, that "[t]he name of a philosophical subject, when he says *I*, is always, in a certain way, a pseudonym."

Derrida again: "The other is not myself—and whoever has ever maintained that it is?—but it is *an* Ego, as Levinas must suppose in order to maintain his own discourse."

Nevertheless, there remains a difference between Levinas's and Kierkegaard's conceptions of the ego. What Levinas calls the psychism of the ego, mine or another's, is its being addressed by another. The self owes itself to its being addressed, even accused and persecuted by another, and primarily by another human being, where it is only through the other human being that one can make sense of the word "God." It is by the other that the self's egoity becomes ethical, and this holds too for the other. The psychism of the others is psychotic, being chosen and possessed by yet another. With Kierkegaard, however, the self chooses itself. It remains egological, if not egoistic. With Kierkegaard selfhood is affect or passion. With Levinas it is the affect of affect, the passion of passion before the face of another. In the first place this face is the face of another human being. The other is my center of gravity. Kierkegaard's stress on subjectivity and inwardness makes it difficult to see how for him the center of gravity could be other than myself. Where he does say things suggesting that my choice of myself is also my being chosen, as when he writes "I can say that I choose the absolute which chooses me,"[41] the absolute that chooses me may be God, but it is not the other human being. Where for Levinas the move to God is made through the other human being, the human being comes after and through God for Kierkegaard. Now although I may be wrong in supposing that the call of this human being is more urgent than the call of that one, there is no room for mistake as to whether another human being calls. My ethical responsibility is unconditional. Not so according to the doctrine of Kierkegaard, not if by the ethical we mean not purely universal morality or public custom, but the religiously ethical that is moved by passionate choice of the self. For if the choice of the self is response to the voice of God, we are back with the risk that I am imagining that voice, imadgining it [*sic*], someone might say. I am on a borderline not only of the madness from which, according to Hegel and Kant, I may be turned by reasoning. I am on the borderline not just of the psychosis that, according to Levinas's humanism of the other human being, is both passion and the rationality of rationality. I am on the borderline not simply of the idiocy of excommunication implied by Kierkegaard's notion of the singular individual, the borderline of the *dementia* that "perhaps . . . is the pain by which he is tormented into isolation." All three of these madnesses are in their different ways conditions of ethicality. But ethicality is under threat once I find myself on the borderline of the madness of fancying I hear someone who is not there. This is not a reassertion of the thought that for ethics to grow up it must pass through the test of being suspended. After the test of which Abraham's decision to sacrifice his son is a paradigm, ethics is given back transfigured. There is a transfiguration of ethicality, too, when its universality is interrupted by the singularity of one's being faced by another human being. In this humanistic transfiguration of the ethical, there is a transfiguration also of the metaphysical. The metaphysical becomes the ethical. But the metaphysical retains its traditional sense when it posits God as a being, albeit highest being, believed in on the basis of experience. To recite Kierkegaard's words: "They say that experience makes a man wise. This is very unreasonable talk. If there were nothing higher than experience, experience would drive a man mad."[42] If to base belief in God on belief of the objectively historical facts of Christianity is to court a lower madness, the higher madness is to choose to believe in God in a way that is independent of the objectively historical facts, because in the passionately subjective choice of oneself made in this choice to believe in God the historical is the contemporary. The choice is a choice against objectivity for subjectivity, against the crowd for isolation, for passion, for suffering: "really to stick to Christianity a man must be brought to madness [*Afsindighed*] by suffering."[43] And this brings us back finally to the peaceful coexistence of madness and lucidity referred to in the first section of this essay on the borderline of madness. We have treated of madness at some length. We have spoken only indirectly of the *lucida intervalla*. Where lies the borderline between madness and lucidity?

A man is already brought to suffering as soon as he is brought to isolation, for isolation is contrary to the urge toward direct communication that is natural to the human being. Direct communication is the propounding of propositions, the declaration of beliefs and opinions, *doxa*. But "really to stick to Christianity" is to be struck by the paradox of the God-man, to be offended by it. Christianity is not a belief, a teaching. A teaching or a doctrine is such as a Greek may find foolish, a contradiction in terms, even a madness, but only a lower, because abstract, madness. The madness of Christianity begins to become concrete when the Jew, for instance Peter, is scandalized by the thought of God become man; as we have already observed, according to Kierkegaard "the possibility of offense is the dialectically decisive factor, is the 'borderline' [*'Grændsen'*] between paganism, Judaism-Christianity."[44] To this scandalous offense to reason the Christian responds with belief that is not the overcoming of intellectual and therefore abstract doubt, but a passage through a suffering of the paradox.[45] Why a suffering of the paradox? Why does the paradox of the God-man bring pain? Because this paradox is not an abstract formal contradiction, but the suffering willingly accepted when God becomes abased as a suffering servant. And because Christianity is concrete this-worldly *imitatio Christi*. That is what it means for Christ to be one's contemporary. It means that the Christian is patient in the passion that, in his human way and "confirming at every moment the chasmic abyss between the single individual and the God-man over which faith and faith alone reaches,"[46] he shares with the passion of the God-man.

And the passion is a passing. It is a passing through madness. The higher madness is a transition. To what is it a transition? Not to the lucidity in which one recognizes that what seemed to be madness was not madness at all. That would be a return to the lucidity of the purely universal and to the possibility of communicating it directly. That would be a return to Hegel and to Greece. The transition of the higher madness is rather a transition to grace. It is a transition to the space in which direct communication is bent through ninety degrees by irony and humor. Kierkegaard tells of Lucretius, "a Roman poet who was mad but had his more lucid moments and devoted these very moments to his poem *De rerum natura.*"[47] Lucretius was a heathen. This may explain why he could not do what the poet of Christianity can do, write "both in and out of season," both in his intervals of madness and in his intervals of lucidity, so that "it will be hard to distinguish the one from the other." It will be hard to distinguish the one from the other because the intervals of lucidity are intervals in madness and the intervals of madness are intervals in lucidity, as the movement of a blink or a wink (*Øieblik*) is a moment both of darkness and light. Lucidity here is the lucidity of madness, madness's lucidity. Madness here is the madness of lucidity, lucidity's madness. Here the borderline of madness is neither simply a *Grenze* nor simply a *Schranke,* neither as defined by Kant nor as defined by Hegel in the passages reproduced in the second section of this essay. For although in the transition across this line lucidity is not left behind, any more than spatiality is left behind by the line that is the border of a square, the lucidity to which one moves is not like that to which reasoning would bring the madman according to the cure prescribed by Hegel. If the lucidity to which humoring brings the madman is still a madness, it is only what in the first section of this essay we decided to call a lower madness. When the transition is made not by humoring but by humor, *logos* is crossed with *pathos.* The *Logos is* the Passion, the Word is existed as suffering, is lived as death on the Cross. The line of the borderline of madness that is crossed in becoming a Christian is never finally crossed. The Cross remains an eternal crossing. This eternal crossing of the Cross that saves is eternal salvation. The suffering without end, without point, without *telos* and without pause, period, or stop [*Standsning*], is the eternal rest.[48] The line between eternal suffering and eternal salvation is invisible. This is why a reader of Kierkegaard can write of a *pathos* of "feeling *absolutely* safe. I mean the state of mind in which one is inclined to say 'I am safe, nothing can injure me whatever happens.'"[49]

The reader of Kierkegaard just alluded to writes also that some things one is inclined to say must be consigned to the secrecy of silence. And those servants of the secrecy of silence who bear the name Søren Kierkegaard or pseudonyms like Johannes de silentio would affirm with their countersignatures that the higher madness is in danger of being reduced to the lower if whatever is written on the borderline of madness is said directly, without a serious sense of irony and humor.

Notes

I thank Alastair McKinnon and Eileen Dickson for giving me access to the former's invaluable Kierkegaard Computer Workshop CD. For helping me with the technological facilities at the Søren Kierkegaard Research Center at Copenhagen, I thank Joakim Garff. I thank James Giles for pointing out to me various oversights in a draft of this essay.

1. Søren Kierkegaard, *Philosophical Fragments; or A Fragment of Philosophy, by Johannes Climacus,* trans. David F. Swenson, rev. Howard V. Hong (Princeton, N.J.: Princeton University Press, 1936), 55. Søren Kierkegaard, *Philosophical Fragments; Johannes Climacus,* ed. and trans. Howard V. Hong and Edna H. Hong (Princeton, N.J.: Princeton University Press, 1985), 44.

2. Kierkegaard, *The Corsair Affair and Articles Related to the Writings,* 73–75 (COR).

3. *Søren Kierkegaards Papirer* (English trans.: *Søren Kierkegaard's Journals and Papers*), II A 808 (1581). Hereafter PAP + number (JP + number).

4. Jacques Derrida, *Glas* (Paris: Galilée, 1974), trans. John P. Leavey Jr. and Richard Rand (Lincoln: University of Nebraska Press, 1986).

5. PAP IV C 94 (JP, 4:4420).

6. PAP II A 808 (JP, 2:1581).

7. PF, 52. See 1 Cor. 1.23.

8. PAP VIII¹ A 358 (JP, 2:2236).

9. Kierkegaard, *Philosophical Fragments,* trans. Swenson, 64.

10. Immanuel Kant, *Critique of Pure Reason,* trans. Norman Kemp Smith (London: Macmillan, 1968), 280.

11. Kant, *Prolegomena to Any Future Metaphysics,* trans. P. G. Lucas (Manchester, England: Manchester University Press, 1953).

12. G.W.F. Hegel, *Philosophy of Mind,* trans. William Wallace (Oxford: Clarendon Press, 1971), 24.

13. Jacques Derrida, "Cogito and the History of Madness," in *Writing and Difference,* trans. Alan Bass (Chicago: University of Chicago Press, 1978); Michel Foucault, *Madness and Civilization: A History of Insanity in the Age of Reason,* trans. Richard Howard (New York: Pantheon, 1965).

14. Claude Lévi-Strauss, *The Savage Mind* (London: Weidenfeld and Nicolson, 1966).

15. See Daniel Berthold-Bond, *Hegel's Theory of Madness* (Albany: State University of New York Press, 1995).

16. G.W.F. Hegel, *Phenomenology of Spirit,* trans. A. V. Miller (Oxford: Clarendon Press, 1977), 226.

17. Derrida, *Writing and Difference,* 63.

18. Kant, *Anthropology from a Pragmatic Point of View,* trans. Mary J. Gregor (The Hague: Nijhoff, 1974), 88.

19. PAP IV A 46 (JP, 1:1070).

20. PAP X² A 441 (JP, 3:3198).

21. But on friendliness, see Jacques Derrida, *Politiques de l' amitié* (Paris: Galilée, 1994).

22. PAP IX A 360 (JP, 1:491).

23. Kierkegaard, *The Point of View for My Work as an Author*, 129–41 (POV).

24. Ibid., 50–56.

25. PAP X³ A 499 (JP, 2:1300). Compare "If my genius can be said to be connected with anything, it is with being in the minority" (PAP IX A 307 [JP, 6:6260]), and the observation that he would have been "regarded as a genius of the first rank" in any other country, but "by being born in a demoralized provincial town quite logically turned out to be a sort of Mad Meyer" (PAP X¹ A 247 [JP, 6:6382]). Of Mad Meyer the editors of PAP note: "Presumably Edvard Meyer (1813–80), journalist, founder of the humor paper *Kjøbenhavns Morskabsblad* (1842), a competitor of Goldschmidt's *Corsaren*. Meyer himself and his activities had something of a comical cast, and he was the object of jokes by students and others. See *Corsaren*, 407, July 7, 1848, col. 11."

26. Kierkegaard, *The Concept of Anxiety: A Simple Psychologically Orienting Deliberation on the Dogmatic Issue of Hereditary Sin*, 108 (CA); PAP V A 19 (JP, 1:623).

27. PAP IV A 154 (JP, 5:5695).

28. PAP IV A 148 (JP, 1:1029).

29. For a discussion of difficulties concerning the connection between what Kierkegaard says about suffering in the context of Christianity and his account of anxiety, see James Giles, "Kierkegaard's Leap: Anxiety and Freedom," in *Kierkegaard and Freedom*, ed. James Giles (Basingstoke, England: Palgrave, 2000).

30. PAP X⁵ B 206 (JP, 6:6518).

31. Kierkegaard, *Fear and Trembling*, 82–83 (FT).

32. PAP V B 6:16; *Philosophical Fragments*, trans. Swenson, 99ff.

33. PAP X² A 389 (JP, 3:3035).

34. PAP VIII¹ A 33 (JP, 5:5981); VIII¹ A 35–38 (JP, 5:5983–5986).

35. Kierkegaard, *The Book on Adler*, 107 (BA). *The Book on Adler* is also a book on Hegel, whether or not with Derrida we pronounce the German's name as the French do and thereby assimilate it to *aigle* or "eagle," that is to say, Adler.

36. PAP VIII¹ A 358 (JP, 2:2236).

37. PAP X² A 617 (JP, 1:844).

38. Kierkegaard, *Either/Or: A Fragment of Life*, trans. Walter Lowrie (London: Oxford University Press, 1946), 2:179.

39. I thank Jacques Derrida for drawing my attention to this text.

40. Derrida, "Violence and Metaphysics," in *Writing and Difference*, 110.

41. Kierkegaard, *Either/Or*, trans. Lowrie, 2:179.

42. PAP IV A 46 (JP, 1:1070).

43. PAP IX A 360 (JP, 1:491).

44. PAP X² A 389 (JP, 3:3035).

45. Kierkegaard, *Practice in Christianity*, 81 n (PC).

46. Ibid., 139.

47. COR, 74.

48. PC, 23–68.

49. Ludwig Wittgenstein, "A Lecture on Ethics," *Philosophical Review* LXXIV, no. 1 (January 1965): 8. Cited by D. Z. Phillips, "Self-Deception and Freedom in Kierkegaard's *Purity of Heart*," in Giles, *Kierkegaard and Freedom*, 168. In this essay Phillips argues that the distinction between morality and immorality does not coincide with the distinction between single-mindedness and double-mindedness. His citation from Wittgenstein is followed by one from Kierkegaard: "How wonderful, here is a borderline [*Grændse*], a borderline that is invisible, like a line that is easy to overlook with the senses, but one that has the strength of eternity in resisting any infringement" (*Purity of Heart Is to Will One Thing*, trans. Douglas Steere [New York: Harper, 1958], 97). Referring apparently both to what Kierkegaard says and to what Wittgenstein says, Phillips writes: "All seem to testify to a freedom in the midst of affliction." Need descriptions of moral situations where freedom seems not to survive affliction undermine Wittgenstein's avowal of a feeling, or Kierkegaard's oblique references to first-personal passion? And, as we have noted, according to Kierkegaard the paradox of the higher freedom that goes with the higher madness is that one reaches it only by being unfree. "In order truly to be a great genius a man must be the exception. But in order that there shall be seriousness in being the exception, he must himself be unfree, forced into it. Herein lies the significance of his dementia" (PAP X³ A 499 [JP, 2:1300]).

6

REVOCATED TRIALS: ON THE
INDIRECT COMMUNICATION
IN TWO OF KIERKEGAARD'S EARLY
RELIGIOUS DISCOURSES

Jacob Bøggild

ACCORDING TO KIERKEGAARD HIMSELF, he practices what he terms "indirect communication," which means that his works are not written in a straight-forward manner. They are, as he puts it, "revocated" (*tilbagekaldte*). In rela-tion to the pseudonymous works, the so-called aesthetic part of his author-ship, we may think we know what is meant by revocation in the Kierkegaardian sense. Kierkegaard distanced himself from the fictive authors he invented, like Johannes de silentio, and we are warned that we should not read them as if they express anything that he would subscribe to himself. Kierkegaard's wish and prayer is that we respect that the pseudonymous works are signed with a signature other than his own.

However, the religious part of his authorship, which mainly consists of religious and Christian discourses, is also stated to be revocated, even though these works carry Kierkegaard's own signature. The usual explanation is that Kierkegaard disclaimed his own authority as a religious teacher and that he accordingly wanted to point out that his discourses are not sermons in any traditional sense. In the following, my aim will be to demonstrate that there is far more to the equation than can be explained in this fashion. It is, I hope to show, Kierkegaard's understanding of human language that makes indirect communication a matter of exigency regardless of, but of course related to, the questions of signature and authority.

I shall base my argument upon rhetorical readings of two of Kierkegaard's early religious discourses,[1] "The Lord gave and the Lord hath taken away, blessed be the name of the Lord" from 1843 and "The Thorn in the Flesh" from 1844. I have chosen these two discourses not just because they are illuminating but also because they correspond in interesting ways. The first discourse deals with Job in his time of trial, as is clear from its title, while the latter is about the trial of Paul when he is confronted with his thorn in the flesh. I begin with the one on Job.

Job's Trinitarian Metalepsis

What initially strikes one about this text is the way it demonstrates Kier-kegaard's awareness of what we in the wake of J. L. Austin's *How to Do Things with Words*[2] understand to be the performative dimension of language. At the very beginning it is stated that the significance of Job "is by no means due to what he said but to what he did."[3] Immediately afterward we are told that what Job did he did by means of what he said. It is emphasized that his utterance was an act: "he acted in asserting it, so that the expression itself was the action" (67). Furthermore, the significance of Job's utterance depends on the context in which it is carried out: "The expression itself is truly beautiful and worthy of consideration, but if another had used it, or if Job had been different, or if he had uttered it under different circumstances, then the word itself would have become something different" (67–68).

The dependence of the performative utterance, the speech act, on the context in which it is uttered is indeed one of the fundamental insights of Austin. If I sentence a man I accidentally meet on the street to twenty years of prison, I carry out an act that is absurd in the context, because I am in no way authorized to do such a thing and because we are not situated in a court of law. In Austin's idiosyncratic terminology, my speech act "misfires" in such a case. A minor excursus on Austin's theory will be helpful at this stage.

Austin starts off by discriminating between performative utterances and constative ones, the latter being utterances that state whether something is the case or not. He does, however, quickly come up against some severe difficulties. He is, by his own scientific integrity, forced to acknowledge that the performativity of a speech act cannot be grasped merely by means of grammatical analysis. First of all, a performative utterance need not contain a performative verb (ask, promise, sentence, etc.). Secondly, an utterance that grammatically speaking must be said to be constative might well have a performative dimension. If I enter a crowded room where the window is open, I might say, "it is quite cold in here," thereby asking any person near the window to close it. Austin must then make it clear that when you analyze a constative utterance, you disregard its potential performative dimension, and vice versa.

Having made this clear, he can then identify three aspects or levels of the performative act. The first one is its *locutionary* aspect, which is defined purely and simply as the act of uttering something. The second one is its *illocutionary* aspect, which is defined as the specific act carried out by means of the utterance (a question is asked, a promise made, etc.). The third is its *perlo-cutionary* aspect, defined as the further action the speech act might effect (a question is answered, an order is carried out, etc.). End of excursus.

As mentioned, our text indicates that none of this would come as a surprise to Kierkegaard. For example, the text on Job says: "Since he had thus surrendered himself to sorrow, not in despair but stirred by human emotion, he was swift to judge between God and himself, and the words of his judgment are these: 'Naked I came forth from my mother's womb, and naked shall I return thither'" (74). This utterance of Job's appears to be constative; he intimates the state he was in when born and that he will die in one that is no different. However, Kierkegaard, like an adept student of Austin, notes that this speech act has a performative dimension, that it is in fact the passing of a judgment. It is quite disturbing that he does this, though, since he lets Job pass this judgment between himself and God. Surely, a Christian, as Kierkegaard understands such a person, is not entitled to pass judgment when it comes to his relationship to God. Is it because we are dealing with a text from the Old Testament that Kierkegaard ignores this fact? Certainly, the Christianity that Kierkegaard advocates is "the Christianity of the New Testament," but does that mean that he reads the Old Testament as a collection of Jewish myths that one can treat as one sees fit? Only a close reading of the discourse on Job can indicate to what extent this is the case. My reading will in fact show that a blasphemous thread, so to speak, runs all the way through it. I shall follow this thread, which will prove to be the key to the way in which language makes indirect communication a necessity in this discourse.

As my reading will further demonstrate, Kierkegaard orchestrates a subtle play on the power of the speaking subject as an agent in and of language. This play is structured by the rhetorical figure, or trope, *metalepsis*. Like numerous other tropes of classical rhetoric, metalepsis is a figure of *substitution*.[4] More specifically, an immanent effect is ascribed to a distant cause, which thus replaces a closer one.[5] Therefore, the deviation or turn of the trope of metalepsis can coincide with a manipulation of the agent, in the grammatical sense, of any given speech act.[6] Though it is not one of the well-known tropes, like metaphor, metalepsis might then be a highly relevant figure in any context where human language is being discussed. Do we speak language or does it speak us? Are we the causes or the effects of language and subsequently of linguistic acts? I will let these questions linger and focus on the metaleptic play in our discourse.

This play is centered around Job's utterance: "The Lord gave, and the Lord hath taken away, blessed be the name of the Lord." Let us, as a starting point, analyze the utterance in the light of Austin's theory. At a first glance, only the third part could be considered a performative, more specifically a short eulogy or panegyric that bestows praise upon the Lord. The first two parts are both constatives—though perhaps not of the verifiable kind.

According to Kierkegaard, however, the whole utterance is a performative. In fact, he points out that all three parts of it are distinct performatives, distinct illocutionary acts. He underlines the importance of the fact that Job *first* says "the Lord gave." In saying this, Job first of all rejoices in all that he received even though he has now lost it. Job thus expresses his gratitude, says Kierkegaard, which is obviously a performative act. With the second part of his utterance, Job is resigned to what has happened to him, and, according to Kierkegaard, he thereby overcomes the world in the sense that he radically parts with it.[7] And overcoming the world in this way is clearly not a constative, but an act. Still, this moment of victory is dangerous because it is in itself a temptation. One can take pride in one's victory over the world and thus relapse into vanity. Kierkegaard momentarily parts with the context of the Old Testament and refers to Paul, who explicitly expresses the wish that his congregation will resist this temptation.[8] By means of his "blessed be the name of the Lord," however, Job demonstrates that he can resist the temptation, that he can sustain his victory, so to speak. The short eulogy or panegyric thus carries an additional performative dimension as Kierkegaard reads it. Until now, nothing apart from Job's passing of judgment has appeared disturbing at all. But when certain passages of the discourse are read closely, several even more disturbing aspects cannot be ignored.

For example, the following passage addresses the first part of Job's utterance:

> While thankfulness rested in his soul with its quiet sadness, he bade a gentle and friendly farewell to everything at once, and in this farewell everything disappeared like a beautiful memory; moreover, *it seemed as if it were not the Lord who took it, but Job who gave it back to Him.* (76, my emphasis)

Here, a certain reversal takes place: it is as if it is not God who takes, but Job who gives. This reversal provides the *first* metalepsis of the text. Of course, it is only "as if" Job gives back to the Lord what the Lord took away from him. But again Kierkegaard is on the verge of making his version of Job indulge in blasphemy: can Job legitimately make himself the agent of an action performed by the Lord?

At least this example indicates that my idea that the text is structured by the figure of metalepsis is not too far-fetched. And indeed, as my next example will show, Kierkegaard almost defines the figure in the discourse when discussing the second part of Job's utterance, "the Lord hath taken away," making the following comment: "Did Job not say something other than the truth, did he not use a more distant [*et fjernere*] expression in order to designate what should be designated with a nearer one [*et nærmere*]?" (79, trans. modified). The linguistic *substitution* that Kierkegaard makes Job perform in this question coincides neatly with the definition of metalepsis given above. Kierkegaard goes on to ask—rhetorically?—whether it was not the Sabeans who attacked Job's herds, if it was not lightning that consumed his sheep and shepherds, and if it was not a windstorm that made his house collapse and buried his children? We might reply that it probably was, but Job

substituted these immediate causes for the disastrous effects of a more distant
one: "Yet Job said, 'The Lord took'; in the very moment of receiving the
message, he realized that it was the Lord who had taken everything" (80).
This provides us with the *second metalepsis*. And along with it another disturbing "as if" looms in the discourse. Is it not almost as if Job with his
synthesizing metalepsis creates the Lord, invents a more distant cause for his
losses? If it is, then this metalepsis acts like a sublime metaphor. But such a
reversal, where Job creates the Lord instead of the other way round, borders
on the height of blasphemy.[9] It is, to coin a phrase, quite a meta-*lapsus*.[10]
Therefore, it is little wonder—but perhaps slightly hypocritical since he is
commenting upon his own rhetorical plot—that Kierkegaard raises the question whether Job is justified in performing this synthesizing metalepsis:

> Who told Job this? Or was it a sign of his fear of God that thus shifted
> everything over to the Lord,[11] or who permitted him to do it, and are we
> not more devout [*ere vi ikke frommere*], we who sometimes hesitate a long
> time to speak thus? (80, trans. modified)

Of course, Kierkegaard can now do nothing but offer an apology for Job,
and he does so. What justifies Job is the fact that his synthesizing metalepsis
has a therapeutic effect as it delivers him from the snare of reflection:

> Perhaps there was a man who had lost everything in the world. Then he set
> out to consider how it had happened. But everything was inexplicable and
> obscure to him. His happiness had vanished like a dream, and its memory
> haunted him like a nightmare, but how he had been cast off from the glory
> of the one into the wretchedness of the other, he was unable to understand.
> It was not the Lord who had taken it—it was an accident. (80)

It is no use trying to untangle the web of causes and effects in our worldly
existence since nothing can be established for sure by those living in the
midst of it. Any attempt to do so can only lead to anxiety or even despair:

> He [the man from the quote above] understood quite well how it had hap-
> pened, and the more immediate [*den nærmere*] explanation was that those
> men had done it, and the more distant [*den fjernere*] one was that men are
> evil and their hearts corrupted. He understood that men are neighbors [*hans
> Nærmeste*] to his injury; maybe he would have understood it likewise if they
> had benefited him; but that the Lord, who dwells far away in heaven [*der
> boer fjernt i Himlen*] (a), should be nearer [*nærmere*] (b) to him than the person
> closest [*nærmest*] (b) to him . . . such an idea was remote from his thought
> [*fra en saadan Forestilling var hans Tanke saare fjernet*] (a). (80, trans. modified)

Note how masterfully Kierkegaard plays on the metaleptic manipulation
of nearness and distance here in order to illustrate how one will inevitably
lose one's way if one tries to master the ambiguous interaction between
causes and effects by means of thought and reflection. As the a's and b's in

the quotation indicate, the metaleptic play is in the latter part of the quotation governed by the chiasmus.[12] In other words, metalepsis as a synthesizing metaphor can cure the ills that might result from chiastic metalepsis! But the fact that you need the Lord as a synthesizing entity hardly justifies Job in inventing him. Or rather: it hardly justifies Kierkegaard in making Job do that. Let us proceed with our reading.

As mentioned, Kierkegaard interprets the third part of Job's utterance, "blessed be the name of the Lord," as proof of his not falling prey to the temptation of taking pride in overcoming the world. What he writes in relation to this is no less disturbing than my former examples:

> Hence the Lord remained the same and ought He not to be praised as always? Or had the Lord really changed? Or did not the Lord remain the same, as did Job? (23)

Whether these are Kierkegaard's own questions, or whether they paraphrase what Kierkegaard thinks Job might have thought in his time of trial, or whether they are put on behalf of the reader, is not clear. Nevertheless they suggest that there might be a causal relationship between Job's resisting the temptation constituted by his victory over the world and the permanence of the Lord. Did Job not only invent the Lord with his synthesizing metalepsis, but also ensure the Lord's permanence by sustaining his victory over the world? We are, in short, confronted with the *third metalepsis* of the discourse. And because of its perlocutionary effect, the fact that the permanence of the Lord is secured, it is no less of a meta-lapsus than the former one. In a Kierkegaardian context it might even be the most shocking.

This shocking effect is due to the fact that a number of Kierkegaard's early upbuilding discourses find their point of departure in the Letter of James, in which tribute is paid to "the Father of lights, with whom is no variableness, nor shadow of turning."[13] The Letter of James is in fact one of the texts in the Bible that meant the most to Kierkegaard, as is clear from his final discourse from 1855 on the unchangeability of God. To let Job ensure the permanence of the unchangeable God is thus especially provocative in the context of Kierkegaard's own writings. It is therefore pertinent to ask, which purpose or purposes might these blasphemous metalepses serve? Perhaps they warn us against believing that we are in control of the language we speak.

Such a warning might well be implicit in an admonition the discourse offers as a kind of conclusion:

> Then look you to it that you, as little as any man, do not become enslaved by some tribulation, and above all learn from Job to be sincere with yourself, so that you may not delude yourself by an imagined strength, through which you experience imaginary victories in an imaginary conflict. (24)

The latter part of this admonition warns against imagining that one can do as well as Job when undergoing a trial like his. A narcissistic identification like that is just as vain as it is phantasmagoric. And it is language that enables—and perhaps tempts—us to make projections like that. We can make mental projections and identify with idealized images of ourselves only because we are speaking beings. But according to Kierkegaard we are capable of nothing at all without the aid of God, wherefore it is a relapse into vanity whenever one takes pride in whatever one might have accomplished or thinks one will accomplish. Rather than congratulating oneself on one's strength of character in imaginary situations, one should trust that God will be of assistance in any time of trial one might find oneself in. Be humble, the discourse advises its reader, because "no man knows the time and the hour when the messages will come to him, each one more terrifying than the last" (86, trans. modified). We can now specify that Kierkegaard's admonition means as much as the following: do not let language lead you to believe that you are capable of anything at all without the aid of God; do not make yourself guilty of committing meta-lapsus; do not let the performativity inherent in language make you confuse yourself with God. This piece of advice is addressed to the Christian believer or would-be believer. It is communicated indirectly—not by the *what* of the discourse, by what is said straightforwardly in it, but by its *how,* its rhetoric. Thus, a character from the Old Testament, Job, is indirectly made an agent of a plot that is designed in accordance with "the Christianity of the New Testament."[14] We might then safely conclude that "Kierkegaard called, Kierkegaard revocated, blessed be the name of Kierkegaard."

The Apostle in the Guise of a Modern Antigone

I shall now go on with a reading of "The Thorn in the Flesh." This discourse comments upon the passage from Paul's Second Letter to the Corinthians[15] where the apostle tells the story of his excursion to the third heaven, where he heard unsayable words, only to be fetched down to earth again by an angel of Satan, who hit him on the mouth to make sure that he would not pride himself on his privileged experience. This angel is a metaphor for what Paul calls his "thorn in the flesh," which is in itself a metaphor for something not identified for us.

Kierkegaard emphasizes the fact that the higher one has risen, the deeper is the fall. Paul thus experiences a lapsus of the most disagreeable kind. Like Job he is certainly being tried. And like Job he must prove that the trial will not make him despair. This he does, when he declares that it was beneficial to him to be dragged down from the exaltation he had been granted. Kierkegaard makes the following comment: "How simple, how plain, how gentle, is not this speech! After having mentioned the most blissful and the hardest experiences, after having won and lost, then to be so calm!"[16] The lord gave, and the Lord hath taken away, blessed be the name of the Lord, we might add!

However, the discourse begins with some considerations of a more general kind. The practice of snatching a phrase from its biblical context in order to circulate it in everyday speech is criticized:

> But sometimes in the daily and worldly speech we also hear a scriptural expression which has strayed away from its sacred context out into the world—strayed away, for the way in which it is used is sufficient proof that it has not voluntarily forsaken its home, and is now associated with men's worldly thoughts and aspirations for the sake of gain, but it shows that it has been abducted. (327)

A scriptural phrase that has been robbed in this fashion is of course the expression "a thorn in the flesh." One could counter Kierkegaard's disapproval of such a practice by pointing out that a certain poet carrying his name has written quite a lot about his own thorn in the flesh—without specifying what this metaphor refers to.[17] Instead, the famous—or infamous—"secret note" that maybe would clarify this has been torn from this poet's diary and destroyed. And indeed the version of Paul of the discourse resembles the aforementioned poet in several ways. Nor is he able to communicate directly:

> But an apostle—he speaks in the strongest terms about a thorn in the flesh, about a messenger of Satan, who smites him on the mouth [*slaaer ham paa Munden*] and thus prevents him from asserting that unspeakable happiness. (328, trans. modified)

But there is more to be learned from this passage. If phrases from the sacred text can be abducted and used out of context, it seems that common phrases can in their turn invade the holy scripture. "To strike oneself on the mouth" (*at slå sig selv på munden*) was a common phrase in Kierkegaard's time and is still in use. It is used about a person who contradicts himself without acknowledging it. In fact this phrase is common to several European languages, which normally indicates a biblical origin. But this is not the case in this instance. The phrase does not come from the Bible and thus not from the passage in the Second Letter to the Corinthians.[18] The phrase stems from a widespread custom in earlier times. If a person had said something sufficiently offensive or stupid, he would have to strike himself on the mouth in public in order to take it back. Now, all that remains of this custom is the phrase in question, which of necessity reverberates in the passage from Paul where the apostle is called back from heavenly bliss, and especially in a context where revocation is involved! Words and phrases do not patiently await being abducted; they actively invade other contexts.[19]

Another point of convergence between the apostle and the poet can be found in the discourse. Consider the following remark about the communicative difficulties of the apostle:

> But this expression about being carried up into the third heaven, of participating in lofty revelation, of feeling an unspeakable happiness—this he cannot use. He has not used it about that beautiful joy he shared with others, for that unspeakable happiness he could not utter. Alas, to prevent this, there was given him a thorn in the flesh. (334, trans. modified)[20]

This is uncannily reminiscent of a remark made about the poet in general in Johannes de silentio's *Fear and Trembling:*

> For a poet acquires this power of words in order to give expression to the heavy secrets [*tunge Hemmeligheder*] of others only at the cost of a tiny secret he cannot express [namely his own], and a poet is no apostle, he only exorcises devils by the power of the Devil. (FT, 61, trans. modified)

Why does this strange convergence occur in the discourse? Maybe because the one who is writing the discourse can easily identify with the communicative difficulties experienced by (his version of) the apostle, since the former has to be ever so careful when writing in a language that so easily leads one astray. And maybe also because the discourse occupies itself with "heavy secrets," thorns in the flesh that might tempt curiosity more than is sound. Let us first consider how language operates in the discourse. A fine example is the following statement, which is manifestly false:

> *In the world of the spirit* [*i Aandens Verden*] *there is no jest* [*Spøg*] *and no ghosts* [*Spøgelser*]; there fortune and chance do not make one man a king, the other a beggar; one beautiful as the queen of the East, another more wretched than Lazarus. (335, trans. modified, my emphasis)

In writing this, Kierkegaard is contradicted by nothing less than the language he is writing in. In Danish, to be witty is to have *ånd,* while one word for a ghost is *ånd.*[21] It is therefore entirely wrong that jest and ghosts are alien to the world of the spirit [*åndens verden*]. Language strikes the writer of the discourse on the mouth when he makes the statement just quoted! Why this blatant contradiction, unless Kierkegaard is again indirectly pointing out that language is beyond our control even though it tempts us to believe that we are in control of it?

Let us now see how the discourse deals with the secrets it addresses. Kierkegaard begins by disapproving of those interpreters whose curiosity is tempted by such secrets:

> Who would ever finish if he tried to mention all the ingenuity and foolishness which has been expended in explaining or trying to explain this passage, which, ever since it got the reputation of being a riddle, seems to have

afforded an uncommonly favorable opportunity for everyone to become an interpreter of the Bible. (329, trans. modified)

A riddle is of course always a temptation. But in the case of Paul's secret, his thorn in the flesh, it is a temptation to be resisted. And it was, by the way, never Paul's intention to tempt anyone:

> But an apostle is also the last person in the world to write riddles that no one can guess, which at most only hinder those who try to guess them. An apostle who seeks to be all things for all men, is certainly the last one to wish to be something so special that he thus becomes nothing at all for anyone. Let us therefore renounce all inquisitiveness which is judged without even knowing it; for its judgment is that either it cannot understand it, or that it will be able to understand it; and its sin is that it either neglects the lesser matters in order to immerse itself in thinking about the mysterious, or that it craftily employs its powers in making it unintelligible, and hypocritically pretends that this was an earnest endeavor to explain. (335, trans. modified)

Whoever is curious about what Paul's thorn in the flesh refers to is hereby condemned! The question is whether the one writing the discourse can resist the temptation—though he certainly should be able to do that when he says that "there is no superhuman temptation" (55). Perhaps we should first of all specify what kind of temptation we are talking about.

As far as I can see, it is a temptation linked to *Das Interessante*, "the interesting." This is a category designed in the aesthetic theories of early Romanticism where it was adopted to characterize modern tragedy as compared to ancient tragedy. In the latter the hero is a type, a character who embodies something general. In modern tragedy the hero is a specific individual with singular traits, often of an obscure or unfathomable kind. It is these individual traits that make him interesting and thus awaken our curiosity. When one's aesthetic experience is governed by *Das Interessante*, one does not identify narcissistically, at least not in any immediate sense. One distances oneself from the interesting character suffering whatever he suffers; one is situated at a safe distance of contemplation and reflection. Narcissistic gratification derives from a negative identification in such a case.

In fact, Kierkegaard has written a text that thematizes *Das Interessante*, namely the essay on ancient and modern tragedy from the first part of *Either–Or*. This text is allegedly a lecture given by A to an audience consisting of people who are both aesthetes and aestheticians. A and his fictive audience all belong to a society named the *symparanekromenoi*, which means a fellowship of the dead.

A starts out with an analysis of ancient tragedy that comments upon Sophocles' *Antigone*. Then he addresses his audience directly in order to discuss whether his lecture lives up to the requirements of their society. To his great relief he can conclude that it does. The requirements of the society seem to stem from the early Romanticism of Jena, since its striving must be fragmentary and its tendency is to write posthumous papers.[22] Such papers tempt one to fantasize about the personality of the person who wrote them, and therefore they are of particular interest.[23]

Having discussed the stylistic appropriateness of his lecture, A goes on to sketch a modern version of the tragedy of *Antigone*. He emphasizes that the heroine of this modern version is indeed interesting:

> So, my dear *symparanekromenoi,* come closer to me, form a circle around me as I send my tragic heroine out into the world, as I give the daughter of sorrow a dowry of pain as her outfit. She is my work, but still her outline is so indistinct, her form so nebulous, that each and every one of you can fall in love [*forliebe sig*] with her and be able to love her in your own way. (EO, 1:153)[24]

But what is the painful secret of this modern Antigone? What is her thorn in the flesh? Well, in A's little piece of fiction she is the only one who knows about the crime that her father, Oedipus, committed. The people still pay tribute to his memory, and Antigone guards her secret like it was a treasure. She falls in love, however, and she will have to reveal her secret to her lover if they are to establish a truthful relationship. But this is the one thing that she cannot do. She is caught in a conflict that only her death can resolve. As A so sympathetically (and fiendishly!) puts it: "Antigone is in love, and I say it with pain—Antigone is mortally in love [*er dødeligt forelsket*]" (EO, 1: 162, trans. modified). Thereupon he adds in a more cold-blooded manner: "The focus of *interest* here [*Det, hvorom Interessen drejer sig*], then, is to extort her secret from her" (EO, 1:164, my emphasis). He must surely have a firm grip on his audience!

A curious aspect of this modern version is that it probably cannot be performed well on stage. When Antigone is unwilling to speak, when she will not and cannot divulge her secret, how, unless by means of more or less clumsy monologues, can the audience learn what the conflict is about? The point of A's version is that in modernity, in the era when subjectivity holds center stage, it is on the inner scene that tragedy is performed. And this scene is the site of anxiety as far as A is concerned. He explicitly defines anxiety in the following terms:

> That anxiety is a reflection category is shown by language itself, for I always say that I am anxious about something, and I thereby distinguish between the anxiety and that about which I am anxious. . . .
>
> Furthermore, anxiety always contains a reflection on time, for I cannot be anxious about the present but only about something belonging to the past [*det Forbigange*] or the future [*det Tilkommende*]. (EO, 1:155, trans. modified)

In a way, the lecture on ancient and modern tragedy is thus a draft for Vigilius Haufniensis's *The Concept of Anxiety*. There, Haufniensis demon-

strates that antiquity is permeated by ambiguity because it hovers in an in-
determinable zone between the psychic and the somatic. A is quite in agreement with Haufniensis, which is clear from this further definition of anxiety,
where anxiety as a psychic phenomenon is described by means of images
that derive from the somatic life of the body:

> Anxiety has a double function; in part it is the exploring *movement* that
> continually *makes contact* and by this *groping* discovers sorrow as it *circles* around
> it. (EO, 1:155, my emphasis)

The tragedy of the modern Antigone is therefore an ambiguous affair that
is played out on her inner scene.

Astonishingly, the version of Paul in "The Thorn in the Flesh" appears
to be a similar case:

> You who know whereof we speak, what shall I say to you? But you who
> do not know of what we are talking, to you it may be said that we are
> speaking about how impatience suddenly awakened in gigantic strength, and
> by its anxiety [*Angest*] changed the little into much, the brief time into an
> eternity, the little distance into a yawning chasm, the one difficulty into the
> decisive thing, the one lack into the loss of everything. We are speaking
> about how power degenerated into impotence, how mistrust frightened away
> all assistance, how despondency abandoned every hope, how the past [*det
> Forbigangne*], from which the soul believed it had redeemed itself, again stood
> there with its demand, not like a memory, but more terrible than ever before,
> through having entered into a conspiracy with the future [*det Tilkommende*].
> We are speaking about—the thorn in the flesh. (344, trans. modified)

And this can be complemented with a later passage:

> the fear [*Angesten*] of the relapse, when it suddenly awakens, even if it is only
> a momentary relapse, knows how to use it in making everything so imme-
> diately present—not as a memory but as a future event [*en Tilkommelse*].
> (345, trans. modified)

Both passages echo A's definition of anxiety quoted above. In short, Paul is
staged in the guise of a modern Antigone in the discourse. But while A
explained to us what provoked Antigone's anxiety, we still do not know
what the apostle's thorn in the flesh was. However, the one who is writing
the discourse is able to enlighten us regarding this:

> Paul's life had been very eventful, and as the apostle's unceasing activity had
> gathered for him many, many joyful memories, so had his earlier activities,
> when with all his might he kicked against the pricks, wounded him for the
> rest of his life with a memory [*en Erindring*] *which tormented him like a thorn
> in the flesh, which like an angel of Satan struck him dumb.*[25] (340, trans. modified,
> my emphasis)

Alas, he could not resist the temptation; he could not help delving into the secret of the apostle and reveal it to us, wherefore he, since he condemned such behavior right at the outset of the discourse, ought to deal himself a severe blow on a certain part of his face.

Well, Paul's secret is something from the past, a memory or recollection, just like that of the modern Antigone. Paul is haunted by the recollection of the time before a certain episode on the road to Damascus when he did not spread the Gospel, but persecuted the Christians, and where the recollection of Antigone was fatal to her:

> To take her secret away—this is what the lover must struggle to do, and yet it is also her certain death. At whose hand does she fall, then? At the hand of the living or the dead? In a certain sense, at the hand of the dead . . . , inasmuch as the cause of her death is the recollection of her father; in another sense, at the hand of the living, inasmuch as her unhappy love is the occasion for the recollection [*Erindringen*] to slay her. (EO, 1:164)

Paul is assisted by his belief, and therefore he can conquer anxiety and even sustain his victory:

> The man is returned to himself. No longer is he happy in being saved from himself for himself, and in being transfigured in God, so he is no longer judged by the past, because the self-accusation is softened, forgotten in the understanding of the unfathomable wisdom of providence, in the blessed instruction of the atonement; so the eternal fears no future [*Tilkommelse*], moreover, hopes for no future, but love possesses all things without ceasing, and there is no shadow of turning. (338)[26]

Still, faith cannot conquer anxiety once and for all. There is no exit from the snare of reflection that might not lead back into it. This side of eternity, faith is a perennial crisis to Kierkegaard. Every time Paul's recollection enters the stage, "the chase of anxiety begins again" (344, trans. modified). What first and foremost provokes anxiety is anxiety itself, which, of course, is a frightening thought. But it is also an *upbuilding* one: "For woe to him who would edify without knowing the terror; he surely does not know what he himself does!" (ibid.). But, we must now ask, does the one writing the discourse know whether he is writing about the trial of the apostle or the plight of one who is forced to communicate indirectly? Does he know if one snatches a word or is being snatched by it? Does he, after all, know what he is *doing*?

> *We have not been particularly concerned in fathoming what Paul may have especially intended by his expression;* least of all have we wished to ask about it in the same way that someone might ask whether Paul was large or small of stature, beautiful of countenance, and other such irrelevancies. *We do not particularly seek to indicate that which is perhaps accidental, perhaps insignificant, that which to the individual may be his thorn in the flesh.* Perhaps the description might

captivate a reader . . . ; but that would indeed be contemptible, if by so doing the speaker would nullify the edification. (346, trans. modified, my emphasis)

Hypocrite auteur! You have just sent Paul back and forth to the third heaven in the guise of a modern Antigone, and that was a whole lot more interesting than if you had told us how tall or small he was or what he looked like! And do not pretend you are not aware of that!

Like the discourse on Job, the one on the thorn in the flesh involves its reader in a fearful *performance* by means of its rhetoric. Both discourses communicate indirectly by performatively illustrating how one risks being controlled by what one thinks one is in control of—not hesitating to turn blasphemy and self-contradiction into upbuilding agents. Both discourses point out how reflection and recollection are snares that turn back on the recollecting and reflecting subject, because these phenomena depend on the language that tempts us to think we are autonomous subjects while it splits our being.[27] But there is one marked difference between the two discourses. The one on Job addresses a text from the Old Testament, and anxiety, which is linked to the modern concept of subjectivity, is only hinted at in the passage on trying to entangle the web of causes and effects by means of thought and reflection. The one on the thorn in the flesh, on the other hand, finds its subject matter in a specifically Christian text, one from the New Testament, and accordingly it deals explicitly with anxiety. And in addition to this it plays on the temptation that might be hailed as *the* temptation of modernity: the temptation that emanates from *Das Interessante.*

Notes

1. The discourses from 1843–44, along with *Three Discourses on Imagined Occasions,* are normally referred to as the early ones.

2. J. L. Austin, *How to Do Things with Words* (New York: Oxford University Press, 1976).

3. "The Lord gave and the Lord hath taken away, blessed be the name of the Lord," in *Edifying Discourses,* vol. 1, trans. David F. Swenson and Lillian M. Swenson (Minneapolis: Augsburg Publishing House, 1943–46). All quotations from this text will be from this translation.

4. Perhaps I should add that Kierkegaard was well versed in classical rhetoric; it was, in fact, an integral part of his education.

5. A good example can be found in Shakespeare's *Measure for Measure:* "There spake my brother; there my father's grave did utter forth a voice" (3.1.84–85). The subject that speaks, the brother, is not represented as the cause of the utterance; the grave of the father is.

6. The term "trope" literally means turn. A trope deviates from the normal usage of language—if any usage of language can indeed be deemed normal.

7. This is the first explicitly Christian motif in the discourse. In Kierkegaard's interpretation of Christianity, a genuine Christian believer must be dead to the

world, which requires an act of will. In order to be dead to the world, one must actively die away from it [*afdø fra verden*]. That it is not possible to do this once and for all I will discuss later.

8. Cf. Eph. 6.13.

9. Especially when you consider the way that God introduces himself as the creator of all creatures in the Book of Job.

10. It is not considered witty to explain a pun, but maybe I'd better comment upon this one. *Lapsus* in Latin means fall or collapse, and theologically the word is associated with the Fall (think of the term postlapsarian, denoting the time after the Fall). In the present context it is perhaps noteworthy that a *lapsus linguae* is a slip of the tongue.

11. Another specifically Christian motif in the discourse. It is recommended that one does this in 1 Peter 5.7.

12. A rhetorical figure in which the order *ab* is reversed to become *ba*. Kierkegaard's dialectic is permeated by this figure, which Vigilius Haufniensis's definition of anxiety bears witness to. According to Haufniensis, anxiety is "sympathetic antipathy and antipathetic sympathy." I might add that Kierkegaard's dialectic is chiastic because it is negative; it does not strive to abstract from the ambiguity of our existence as speaking beings but to confront it.

13. James 1.17.

14. As also indicated by the presence of a couple of specifically Christian motifs in the discourse.

15. 2 Cor. 12.7.

16. "The Thorn in the Flesh," in *Edifying Discourses,* 4:62. Again, all quotations will be from the Swenson translation.

17. For example, in *The Point of View for My Work as an Author:* "Now Governance really had me shackled: perhaps like a dubious character I have been kept on a very restricted regimen. I am accustomed to living in such a way that at most I believe I have only one year left and at times, nor rarely, when things are tightened up, I live on a one-week, yes, a one-day prospect. Governance had curbed me in every respect. As for the esthetic production, I could not leave it understood in such a way that it ended with my having my life in the esthetic. Even if the religious had not been in the background, that 'thorn in the flesh' would still have kept me from it" (quoted from POV, 86). What is interesting about such a mystification I shall discuss later.

18. The passage is clearly difficult to translate. In newer Danish translations the apostle is no longer hit on the mouth but in the face.

19. Kierkegaard is most likely well aware of this; what we today understand to be the implications of the iterability and quotability of language would hardly be news to him.

20. This is obviously a paradox: why do you need a thorn in the flesh in order to keep you from expressing what is unspeakable, inexpressible? But this paradox cannot be found in the text of Paul; he does not lament the fact that he cannot give expression to the unsayable. Thus the paradox alludes to the situation of a certain poet who communicates indirectly rather than to that of the apostle.

21. Thus, *Ånd* behaves very much like the word *Geist* in German.

22. Irony and fragmentation were the main aesthetic strategies of the Jena Romanticists, among whom were the Schlegel brothers and Novalis. The word "tendency" is a keyword in the writings of Friedrich Schlegel. Schlegel also defines irony as a permanent parabasis, a permanent interruption. A's discussion of the stylistic legitimacy of his lecture is in effect such an interruption.

23. It is just as interesting that Kierkegaard, whose fictions often present themselves as posthumous papers, in this way designs a trap for the biographically oriented reader—A's fiction about a modern Antigone even contains a crisis in a love affair and a problematic relationship to a father! Kierkegaard is an expert in making himself interesting to us only to trap us, as the quotation from *Point of View,* note 17 above, bears witness to. For more on this, see my article "The Fine Art of Writing Posthumous Papers: On the Dubious Role of the Romantic Fragment in the First Part of *Either/Or,*" in *Kierkegaardiana 19* (Copenhagen: C. A. Reitzels Forlag, 1998), 95–112.

24. All quotations from the essay on ancient and modern tragedy will be from EO, 1.

25. The metaphorical status of the thorn in the flesh and the angel of Satan is underscored here.

26. Cf. what I wrote about the Letter of James above.

27. As analyzed in depth by Vigilius Haufniensis.

7

THE FIRST KISS: TALES OF INNOCENCE AND EXPERIENCE

David Wood

An old proverb fetched from the outward and visible
world says: Only the man that works gets the bread.
Strangely enough that proverb does not aptly apply in
that world to which it expressly applies. For the outward
world is subjected to the law of imperfection. . . . It is
different in the world of spirit.

—FT[1], 38[1]

When you say the first kiss is the most beautiful, the
sweetest, you insult the loved one, for what gives the kiss
absolute value here is time and what pertains to that.

—EO[1], 454

But healthy love has a quite different worth; it works
itself out in time, and is therefore also capable of
rejuvenating itself through these outward signs; and—
what for me is the main point—it has quite another idea
of time and of the meaning of repetition.

—EO[1], 465

WHETHER WE DO SOMETHING for the first time, or repeat what we have done
before, the significance of such events, and hence the fate of innocence or
experience, is tied up with the ways we inhabit time, and how we count.
The philosophical interest in pursuing the "economy" of a thought rests on
the supposition that how we count ultimately determines "what counts."

In *Either–Or*, one of his most celebrated books, Kierkegaard seems to
pose for us a choice between two ways of life—the aesthetic and the ethical—and makes the question of repetition central to this choice. I argue here
that when it comes to choosing between the aesthetic and the ethical, it is
not possible to choose between the forms of repetition each enjoins. Rather,
what is called for is a grasp of the ineluctable tension between the two.
Kierkegaard helps us to see the bare choice as problematic at the very point
at which he seems to be recommending the ethical. Is there a spiritual accountancy?

The Question of Number

Throughout Kierkegaard's writings we find him toying with number, typically illuminating unexpected dimensions of a dialectical movement from first to second, in which what is often at stake is the economy of loss amid progress, the aporias of old and new. And he will play off the whole world of measurement and calculation against that of spirituality, only to reverse the opposition at a critical juncture. In one place,[2] Kierkegaard alludes to magic with the Danish expression 1,2,3 *Kokolorum*, an analogue of our *abracadabra*. And I will use this as a point of entry for a consideration of the significance of number.

Even within mathematics, it is not hard to see that the apparent simplicity of counting 1, 2, 3, and so on is home to numerous puzzles. For example, there is the question of negative numbers, the question of zero, and the question of the first number. The first two issues emerge early on in the practical sphere of accountancy. (Imagine owing someone more cows than you possess.) And it is not difficult to see how these concepts could have aroused passions, as numbers take on a life of their own. Uncanny feelings must have accompanied the development of credit—sentiments that still linger. These associations suggest that to the extent that arithmetic is tied to the practice of counting, it will inherit the developing social significance attached to counting and accounting. And it would not be a wholly original claim to suggest that the strangeness associated with these concepts might be tied to the mercantile social transformations they heralded. But what about the third question we posed, that of the first number? Aristotle is said to have declared that "2" is the first number. And we can imagine various arguments against "1": because it is exhausted by its ontological significance as unity, singularity, because until there is a second number, the first cannot be the first, because first means first of a series. On this argument, the first number is "2," which then retrospectively confers that status on "1."

Small numbers—1, 2, 3—seem to appear even before arithmetic, as fundamental to biology (think of symmetry, cell division), physical sciences (bilateral symmetry), to simple human interactions (conflict, gift, exchange, recognition, intercourse), to systems of justice (law of the talon, restitution), religion (monotheism, the mystery of the Trinity, Manichaeism), cosmology (the war of opposites, struggle of good and evil), and so on.[3] And when we say that two's company and three's a crowd, *c'est mieux avec deux,* or talk of looking after number one—or more reflectively, when we think of Levinas's insistence on the importance of the third or Peirce's distinction between firstness, secondness, and thirdness—we can see that the significance of small numbers is deeply embedded in our grasp of the primitive structures of human relationality and of relationality in general.

By enumerating these various domains in which the play of unity, duality, and thirdness is so all-pervasive, it is hard not to notice that number seems here to operate prior to its extension into arithmetic, into counting or into abstract seriality, and it is hard not to wonder whether there are not at least some common principles in play, common issues that arise, common solutions and dilemmas.

Those who have studied the Pre-Socratics, pursued the dialectic through Hegel, Kierkegaard, Marx, and Sartre, and even followed its twists and turns in contemporary philosophies of difference (Derrida and Deleuze) may think that these issues have been sufficiently clarified and resolved. And yet the thought that they may have been resolved suggests, not least to Kierkegaard, that it is in the very idea of resolution that the danger lies. So let us rehearse just a little what is at stake.

The binary choice captured by the title *Either–Or* could be said to reflect an opposition between two ways of understanding time and repetition—one we could call external, and the other internal. The external way understands temporal succession in terms of an outer sequentiality, while the internal account not only proposes an inner connectedness, it believes that the external view itself can be taken up as a moment in the development of that internal perspective. And Kierkegaard seems to suggest that it's only on this latter view that various of the normative conditions we imagine to govern the external view are actually realized. Thus, the idea that those who work get the bread suggests that there is some sort of natural causality and justice in the ordinary world. In fact, says Kierkegaard, in the real world this principle is often mocked, while in the spiritual world it really is true. "Here an eternal divine order prevails" (FT[1], 38). For Kierkegaard spiritual work has a direct connection to results, one not mediated by fallible external circumstances subject to a law of indifference. Though it has to be said that the significance of faith does not suggest that if you make the right spiritual moves you will get the right results, for that would reduce spiritual life to a calculable activity, leaving no room for grace. Rather, as Hegel said, there is no royal road to truth, even if spiritual work is a necessary condition for self-transformation. Whether it is sufficient is another story.

The Phenomenology of the First Kiss

Kierkegaard often ruminates on the significance of the first kiss. Why is it so difficult to think this through on the ethical plane? The argument rests surely on the phenomenology of the first kiss, by which I mean not necessarily the very first kiss, or even the first "romantic" kiss. There are kisses one gives and receives as a child from parents and ancient aunts that just don't count. And even romantic kisses can be exploratory, imitative, learning how to do it, what it feels like. By the first kiss, I mean a kiss that inaugurates a relationship. It is not enough to say that it does so intentionally, for it may precisely be the occasion for the formation of such an intention, and it may happen precisely on the understanding that it not inaugurate a relationship. For the sake of our discussion, I would describe the first kiss as the experience of the opening of a possibility, as a trembling on the brink of something inchoate but momentous, the experience of the realignment of boundaries. Space and time, self and other, activity and passivity, certainty and uncertainty are all thrown into the air, and caught again, differently. I will not decide here whether one is being kissed or doing the kissing, or whether there is some ideal mutuality. Whatever the general shape, the first kiss solicits the tenderness of a response, a visceral recognition of the desire of the other. But it also asks a mute question, a question every bit as important as "What is the meaning of Being?"

For Kierkegaard's aesthetic seducer, the first kiss, coupled with the subsequent conquest, presages the end of all interest. A kiss always has a distinct character. "Sometimes," he writes, "it is clicking, sometimes hissing, sometimes smacking, sometimes popping, sometimes rumbling, sometimes resonant, sometimes hollow, sometimes like calico, and so on" (EO[1], 350). But this sonorous classification pales into insignificance compared to the spiritual and subsequently erotic levels of intensity that Johannes seeks to develop in his Cordelia. The first kiss, he writes, is indifferent not just to sound but also "to touch, [and] time in general" (EO[1], 351).

A little later, Johannes begins to be troubled that it might occur to her at some moment to consider the future:

> So far this hasn't happened; I have been too good at drugging her aesthetically. Nothing less erotic is imaginable than this talk of the future, the reason for which is basically that people have nothing with which to fill the present. When I'm there I have no fear of that either, for I can make her forget both time and eternity. (EO[1], 373)

Finally, we recall how it ends:

> Once a girl has given away everything, she is weak, she had lost everything. . . . I will not take leave of her; nothing disgusts me more than a woman's tears and a woman's prayers. . . . If I were a god I would do for her what Neptune did for a nymph: change her into a man . . . now it is over and I want never to see her again. (EO[1], 376)

Judge Wilhelm's aim in part II of *Either–Or* is to show that we do not have to jettison the intensity of the first kiss in marriage. It is not necessary for a woman to "exchange maidenly yearning for marital yawning" (as Johannes Climacus puts it in the *Concluding Unscientific Postscript*). On Johannes's aesthetic model, thinking about the future is a distraction from the intensity of the present. And this is easy to understand. It is hard to listen to a fugue while wondering about how to meet the mortgage payments. The aesthetic

intensity of the present may be thought to rest precisely on its exclusion of
the outside world, of time and space. I am reminded of John Donne's poem
"The Good-Morrow":

> I wonder by my troth, what thou, and I
> Did, till we lov'd? were we not wean'd till then?
>
> . . . .
>
> For love, all love of other sights controules,
> And makes one little roome an every where.[4]

The claim that the First Kiss is indifferent to time, that it is important
that she "forget" time, and that thinking of the future ruins everything, and
so on, may be more complicated than it seems, even before we turn to Judge
Wilhelm's response. Leaving aside the manipulative unpleasantness of "The
Seducer's Diary," it is simply not clear that Johannes and Cordelia actually
have the kind of encounter that could count as a First Kiss. It is surely not
sufficient that Cordelia have no thought of the future. For a true First Kiss,
even in aesthetic terms, I would think it necessary that Johannes too be
"controuled" by love. In fact, he is not really occupying their "little roome."
The whole action is contained within a calculative temporal and spatial
framework. She may not know this, but he certainly does. Moreover, even
if Johannes were fully participating in the first kiss, which I claim he is not,
the idea that we "forget" time in these moments seems too simple. It does
not, for example, preclude the possibility that time is operating as one of the
grounds of the intensity of the experience.[5] It may well be that time is not
being represented, or that a certain linear understanding of time is suspended.
But that does not mean that time is absent.[6]

There are many philosophers, and I am thinking specifically of Heidegger
and Irigaray, who argue that it is precisely through our reversion to, or a
transformation into, a more "original" inhabiting of space and time that new
possibilities of thinking and being arise. The experience of the opening of
love may not be alone in convincing us of the plausibility of this thought,
but it is certainly a powerful source. If it is not the experience of unity, of
the dissolution of boundaries (as it is often poetically expressed), it surely
involves a dramatic disturbance, or mobilization and interrogation of boundaries—bodily, emotional, and social. It is in this sense that love truly makes
us tremble. And this trembling occurs in part because what is at stake is
utterly inseparable from time. The feeling of safety, the sense that she is the
one you have always been looking for, the sense that whatever this leads to
will be good—the tension between the ecstatic exhilaration and the anxiety
that this will not last—these are all surely part of the experience of the First
Kiss, and of first intimacy in general. It is not that time is banished. It is
rather transformed, put into play, renewed. And at the level of fantasy, time
operates forcibly whenever we feel or say "forever."

Clearly, any sense we give to the First Kiss is an idealization of some sort. I am arguing for the First Kiss as the event of opening of love, which has a projective and destabilizing dimension, one in which the destabilizing reveals the schematizing parameters of our standardly individuated existence. And it is one that sets in motion powerful desires for connection, and re-connection, desires that themselves almost certainly have archaic origins. As I see it, this account is a corrective of Johannes's sketch of the aesthetic take on the First Kiss in two respects: (1) It is no longer wedded to the distortedly one-sided formulation that the manipulative seducer sets up. Once we have genuine mutuality, then a cycle of growing recognition and tenderness is set in motion, which cannot happen in a seduction framed even by altruistic manipulation. (2) Time is not banished at all. Rather, it enters in more profound ways.

The Ethical Transformation

The revisionary thesis about first love in part II has many aspects, and it seems important to know if they can be separated. For the sake of speed and clarity, I will list some of them:

1. Judge Wilhelm expresses extreme gratitude that his eventual wife was his first love. This makes first love into only love. But is this claim necessary? And if he thinks it is, does not that point to a limitation in his whole account of how first love develops?

2. Judge Wilhelm is clearly seeking to impress on the aesthete that there are dimensions of relationality (in love) that only something like long-term unconditional commitment makes possible. This seems to be a central claim, and an important truth to which a certain kind of aesthete is indeed blind.

3. The aesthete might respond: But there are equally dimensions of hell that only open up under these circumstances. Marriage, he suggests, can be like living in a prison cell. Judge Wilhelm boldly affirms that these people are betraying marriage and so on. And he explicitly does not attack divorcees, who at least have courage.

4. We might understand Kierkegaard as arguing for the constitutive role of long-term commitment, or for the constitutive role of an absolute commitment. He is ambivalent precisely because an absolute commitment by one party, even by both parties, does not guarantee constant renewal, which seems at least to be the justification of marriage over a life of mere repetition. In fact, one might argue, it is a condition of the possibility of renewal of the significance of First Love (constant rejuvenation), not that one simply occupies the space it opens onto, but that one enacts and re-enacts the anxious movement, the trepidation, of opening onto that space, and that one allows the boundaries to be put in play. And in extremis, one risks the possibility of the failure of this repetition. The logic here is that of the faith of an

Abraham—it is only in being prepared to risk all that one can possibly continue to renew the promise of the First Kiss. Anything less than risking the
loss of the whole guarantees the loss of the whole. You can win only by
being willing to lose everything. And that loss must not only be possible, it
must from time to time happen. (Which is one reason why the Abraham
story is problematic, because the story is only allowed to have one outcome,
even though Kierkegaard offers various glosses. This leaves open the destructive thought that faith is a sufficient condition for success. But if that were
true, and known to be true, it would self-destruct, because it could be relied
on, and hence no longer function as faith.)

Let us work this through a little more slowly. The blindness of the aesthete's view of the First Kiss is that it understands thinking about the future
only as a distraction from the intensity of the moment, and it fails to recognize that an unconditional commitment to a future life together is necessary for the realization of certain values and virtues. One thinks of loyalty,
mutual understanding, true recognition, a shared context of meaning—
everything that is possible only as part of family life. The aesthete focuses
on the boredom of a life that falls into habit and routine. The champion of
the ethical life argues not just that certain values presuppose unconditional
commitment, but that we do not need to think of our commemoration of
the First Kiss in terms of nostalgia for a lost past. We can find new ways of
re-opening the space of mutual desire, excitement, and significance. Kierkegaard will call this unconditional commitment the eternal. It is what is
missing, he suggests, from the intentional horizon of the contractual five-
year marriage.

I have already suggested that we need my reworked account of the First
Kiss for this story to work, one that would preclude the seducer's kiss, a kiss
that is far from excluding time. What is reworked, I claim, is precisely the
essential ambiguity and tension about the relationship between present and
future, self and other, and so on. The aesthetic, in other words, is already
more than the aesthetic; it is, rather, constructed by the repression of time
and the other. And the same can be said, in its own way, of the ethical. Here
I am on the side of paganism. Suppose we agree that certain human virtues
are possible only on the basis of unconditional commitment—giving oneself,
one's life, to another. Kierkegaard is surely right about this.

The problem is that unconditional commitment is "actually" and essentially conditional, for all promises and conditions are framed. This blind spot
is usually highlighted in the marriage ceremony in the singular form of death:
" 'Til death do us part." However, this is ambiguous, because one can clearly
continue in some sense to love (and even honor and obey) someone who
is dead. But there is something strange lurking in this whole structure of
double promising. In the typical case of a marriage, whether legally sanctified
or not, we find something like a mutual commitment. Each party publicly

or privately commits himself or herself to the other, in the context at least of the other's reciprocal commitment. Now we can imagine a mediating device (such as the institution of marriage) that would contain, guarantee, and distribute all the benefits of such a declaration. And the supposition of such a device may itself make possible consequences that would not flow without such a fiction. If you believe the streets are being policed, you can walk in areas you would otherwise be afraid to walk in. Even if the police are all at home asleep. The belief that one's own commitment or vow is unconditional and that the other intends his or hers in the same way may make possible all kinds of decisions that facilitate the development of the relationship—like moving to a different city, changing a job, having children—which would not make sense without those assurances. Death, we say, will part us. But in truth, there are many ways in which relationships "die," the avoidance of which constitutes the tacit conditions of unconditional commitments. The briefest possible way of putting this would be to say that the breakdown of a couple's capacity to re-enact the play space opened up by the first kiss would constitute a breach in the conditioned unconditionality of marriage. The basis of this breakdown may be utterly unpredictable, and uncontrollable such that it is not at all possible or meaningful to assign blame. After all, in some sense, this capacity for rejuvenation has to remain a spontaneity, which can of course be cultivated, but cannot be guaranteed.

It is perhaps worth referring here to Kierkegaard's own comments on the whole question of the importance of keeping the habituality of certainty at bay. He first mentions this in the context of explaining the alliance between indirect communication, and uncertainty and becoming, and illustrates this danger by alluding to "the woman who wants to settle herself in legal security as a spouse." If she "lets go of the Idea," she is as unfaithful as if she had found another lover. What this means, however, is that the ethical advance on the aesthetic does not merely continue to feast on the aesthetic in the sense that it repeats and reaffirms the First Kiss, rather than consigning it to the innocence of youth. It also draws on what is arguably the fundamental limitation of the aesthetic—its being embroiled in appearance and illusion. We make unconditional promises we are in no position to make. And yet, in trying to keep them, we make possible things that would not have been possible without them. This, we might say, is a miracle, a paradox. If we supposed that it was important not to say this, for this to remain secret, then we would have generated an explanation for the language of eternity, the god, and so on. It would be the language that concealed the ineliminability of (aesthetic) illusion from the ethical. But in so doing, it would introduce a further illusion.

I am wary of offering these comments as a critique of Kierkegaard. For that to be possible, I would first have to offer a definitive reading of

Either–Or, resolving the relationship between the aesthetic and ethical per-spectives, and then drawing in the question of the religious. Instead, I have treated the two halves as themselves lips that are kissing—whether each other or another I cannot tell (compare here Kierkegaard suggesting that Either and Or may be treated as an internal debate within one person). On analogy with my revision of the aesthetic understanding of the First Kiss, I would add that for the kiss to be a real one, there has to be both confidence and uncertainty about the relationship, and neither party can be allowed to be manipulating the response of the other. This is not just to say that the verdict of whether *Either* or *Or* wins is to be left open—far from it. I am saying that it is in our repeating their First Kiss that this book continues to be rejuvenated.

5. Kierkegaard is also clear that one of the other key dimensions in which repetition operates in an importantly complex way is that of generational transmission. First, he says that it is only by having a son that a father can understand his own childhood. Second, he suggests that children inherit and have to work through the sins of their fathers, as the Bible says—to three and four generations. "There's something pleasing about a son's repenting his father's sins—it is only in this way that he can choose himself" (EO[1], 519). Third, he says that the sense in which we come to "know" ourselves is analogous to carnal knowledge—in which one begets oneself, and gives birth to oneself (EO[1], 549). And again, "the only saving thing, is that always, in relation to his own life, a man is not his uncle but his father" (EO[1], 556). Here paternity is being understood curiously as a phase in self-discovery, and salvation. In this way, having children is drawn into the heart of the sphere of meaning rather than being relegated to a biological or prac-tical matter (such as support in old age). (Compare Nietzsche's "For woman, every problem has one solution: the child.") Understanding paternity this way is also strangely limited, suggesting that what is distinctive about the "ethical" perspective is still contained within a temporally extended narcis-sism. And curiously, at least in the account in *Stages on Life's Way,* Kierkegaard understands the value of marriage for a woman in similar terms. For marriage opens the possibility of motherhood, which transforms a woman from a girl, a "phantom," to the reality of woman. "This is a metamorphosis which has no analogy in the man—a woman's development is not complete until she is a mother, only then does she exist . . . in all her beauty."[7] What this sug-gests, however, is that it is the child who does this for the woman; the man is just a means.

6. Something of what Kierkegaard says about the first kiss is true of any inaugural event. Such events open up a future, but this will have happened only if that future is welcomed and preserved. This reference to the future makes it clear that while the excitement of the first kiss may be restricted to the present, its significance lies in the historical possibilities of development

that it sets up. A similar event structure can be found in Heidegger's "The Origin of the Work of Art," in which the work of art is said to open and preserve the strife between earth and world.[8] Heidegger, too, insists on the need for preservers. The parallel deepens remarkably when we notice how Heidegger interprets the shoes as the shoes of a peasant woman, who through her labor is connected to the earth, but who also occupies a world. The connection is this: where Kierkegaard speaks of the woman supplying finitude to the man's infinity, Heidegger speaks of the peasant woman's shoes as indicating her groundedness in the earth, and animating the relation to world. In each case, it is woman who supplies the grounding corrective. There is perhaps a further parallel with the residual privilege Hegel attributes to the slave whose relation to the earth gives him a kind of intimacy with things that the master lacks.

Kierkegaard's account of generational transference seems wholly patrilineal. This makes sense if it is only men who (insofar as they are essentially cut off from their natures) suffer the pathologies of the infinite, and need to have that connection restored by their relation to a woman. But we might wonder whether there is not some connection between the role being set aside for women in this model and the absence of the mother in the generational succession story. The young aesthete who luxuriates in the pleasures of seduction and then moves on to a new conquest could be said to be actually engaged in an internal repetition of an infantile scene, while never allowing the significance of the event to blossom. But the melancholic recollection that can only seek the repetition of the first kiss itself needs its story to be filled out. It is noteworthy that Kierkegaard's most striking accounts of the role of the mother occur in the analogical commentaries he gives to the four variant replays of the Abraham/Isaac story in *Fear and Trembling*. In each case what is at stake is a different strategy of weaning, of facilitating the separation of the child from the mother, different ways of coping with loss: by deception, displacement, shared mourning, and substitution. Put very crudely, we might wonder whether the schematic role Kierkegaard offers women in love is not connected to the absence of any account of the relation to the mother, and the absence of any account of the historical relationship of love as a two-way street, as dialogically developing. This is a complex issue. Clearly the terms in which Kierkegaard understands the relationship between men and women—infinite and finite (women grounding men)—are problematic, even if they are quite capable of supplying the rhythmic background for the narrative development of a relationship. The description he gives of the wife whose husband doesn't come down to dinner because he is entranced by an orthographic eccentricity on one of the manuscript pages he is poring over is very amusing. The dot on which all attention is focused turns out to be a particle of snuff that his wife just blows away, bringing him down to earth. But this positioning of woman seems to many readers like a blind spot on Kierkegaard's page that we struggle to blow away without success.[9]

Obviously we could read *Either–Or* as an extended working through of the distinction he makes in *Repetition* between recollection and repetition. He explicitly ties recollection to Platonism, and to what Freud will call mourning, while repeating forward is very close to what Nietzsche will call affirmation. Each could be said to relate to a First Kiss, a founding event. But the former repeatedly, tragically, and impossibly attempts to recapture an imaginary past. While the latter recognizes the distinctive virtues of narrative continuity, of marriage as a kind of co-authorship (with a metaphysical script, e.g., finite and infinite), and the possibility of a continuous re-enactment of the founding event—its preservation as Heidegger would put it.

I have argued that the phenomenology of firstness would rescue an adequate account of the aesthetic from both one-way manipulation and recollective mourning. I have further argued that the religious dimension that brings the framework of eternity and unconditionality into marriage renders the ethical dependent on illusion and aporia. This suggests that the aesthetic and the ethical are interwoven in ways that would make the development from one to the other inherently problematic. And the conditionality of marriage that Kierkegaard clearly acknowledges suggests that as well as there being an essential ambiguity between aesthetic and ethical, the truly ethical dimension is one in touch with its own fundamental uncertainty and hesitation.

Conclusion

The girl who would be a "phantom" until married, until she became a mother, the scholar who would be studying imaginary punctuation until it is blown away as dust by his wife—these examples testify to what I would call the economic flow that characterizes Kierkegaard's thought. It is a flow that returns us from appearance to reality, from the secondary to the primary, the derived to the original, from 2 to 1. The aesthete's understanding of the first kiss is a serial nostalgia—a philandering repetition that gets nowhere, that merely repeats the exhilaration of a timeless moment. The force of Judge Wilhelm's comment is to release us from servitude to this empty seriality, and open us to the unity of a shared life. The primary effect of marriage on each partner is separate fulfillment, elimination of the shadow side, with some acknowledgment of co-authorship of a joint project.

The initial contrast we cited between the real world, in which there is no necessary justice, no balance between effort and rewards, and the spiritual world, where such justice does reign, is precarious. Hard work is neither a sufficient nor a necessary condition for worldly rewards, and yet while it is necessary for spiritual completeness, it is not sufficient either, for there is still grace, good fortune, and so on. As for marriage: if the success of that relationship depends on the continuing capacity to recreate, rejuvenate the delights of the first kiss, then despite the symmetry of the agency of spiritual completion that each can perform for the other, the unity of a shared life will depend precisely on the irreducible duality, twoness, of the relationship. It is not just, as Levinas once said, *mieux avec deux*. It is impossible *sans deux*. Kierkegaard admits the possibility of failure of marriage. He favorably compares the courage of those who divorce with the unfaithfulness of those who linger trapped in their cells. And as much as he seeks for married life the stamp of eternity, and the exorcism of doubt, the logic of both the continuous recreation of the first kiss, and the possibility of faith, is that a certain uncertainty must remain, and a certain resistance must continue to the economic reduction of plurality to unity. It is essential to the eventuating excitement of the first kiss that it cannot ever wholly anticipate what it will open up. *Either–Or* begins with the whimsical thought that it could just as well be read as the conversation one might have with oneself, which immediately renders the externality of the dialogue into something of an artifice. For all these reasons, *Either–Or* does not actually enjoin an absolute choice at all. Not only does it open the way to recognizing the interpenetration of the ethical and the aesthetic, it also problematizes the very terms of the connection between individual and shared fulfillment.

Notes

I would like to thank Jonathan Rée and Jane Chamberlain for their helpful input on this essay.

1. Abbreviations are employed in this paper as follows: EO[1] = *Either/Or*, trans. Alastair Hannay (New York: Penguin, 1992); FT[1] = *Fear and Trembling*, trans. Alastair Hannay (New York: Penguin, 1985).

2. *Concluding Unscientific Postscript*, ed. and trans. Howard V. Hong and Edna H. Hong (Princeton, N.J.: Princeton University Press, 1992), 117.

3. I recommend for further reading "The Lore of Number," by Julian Barit, in *From Five Fingers to Infinity*, ed. Frank Swetz (Peru, Ill.: Open Court, 1994).

4. *John Donne*, ed. John Hayward (New York: Penguin Books, 1964), 23.

5. This forces philosophers to a critical re-examination of Herman Hupfeld's lyrics in the theme song "As Time Goes By" in *Casablanca* (1942). In a world in which so much is changing, his argument goes, some "fundamental things" can be relied on: "A kiss is still a kiss." Notwithstanding his creative deployment of what Erasmus Schäfer (discussing Heidegger) called "tautology as *figura etymologica*," Hupfeld's brilliant inversion of the more common sense of the fleetingness of love is nonetheless defective in failing to grasp the inherent fragile projective temporality of the kiss.

6. It is illuminating to note that the same sort of remark can also be made in

response to Freud's claim that the processes of the unconscious have no reference to time. The apparent insulation of primary processes from the passage of time, time as it "goes by," only conceals the most powerful drive to master our mortal immersion in time.

7. *Stages on Life's Way*, trans. Walter Lowrie (Princeton, N.J.: Princeton University Press, 1992), 134.

8. In *Martin Heidegger: Basic Writings*, ed. D. F. Krell (New York: Routledge, 1978).

9. Without in any way wanting to reduce Kierkegaard's complex view of women to his own relation to his mother, a relation complicated by his father's later confessions of impropriety toward his mother (and probably worse), and by Kierkegaard's struggle to deal with the psychic inheritance of his father, the complexity and intensity of life in the Kierkegaard family does give us a powerful example of the extreme circumstances under which some thinkers have had to construct their fundamental images of self, identity, gender, the other, women, and so on. Such circumstances, however, may be closer to being the normal state "writ large" than we might think. It is for this last reason that a biographical reductionism is almost always naive.

8

I or You: The Dash of Ethics

Robert Gibbs

WHY ARE WE POSTMODERNS reading Kierkegaard? There are of course various reasons, but what would count as a good reason to read his works? Let me sharpen that question: Why am I reading Kierkegaard texts with you in these pages? You might suppose that I was doing it for one more line on a CV or because I had promised the organizers, or simply because I was curious for myself about what Kierkegaard says. But a better reason would take me deeper into both the texts of Kierkegaard and into the relations I allow to happen here between you and me and the texts of Kierkegaard. To approach that ultimate question, I will need to discern in Kierkegaard not only what he claims for the relation of I and you (that it should be love of the neighbor), but also how he can articulate that claim, and indeed, not only how he makes the claim but how to write about the responsibility to love the neighbor. Such written reflection on writing and on its ethical dimensions is not foreign to Kierkegaard—on the contrary, few authors have taken more seriously the complex relation between the performance of writing and the claims advanced in that writing. My task, in order to present the best reasons for reading Kierkegaard, by asking you to read Kierkegaard together with my own reading of Kierkegaard, is to move through his account of the problems of writing toward our questions about reading. We will move still further to reflect upon my act of setting you to read, which is the task of commentary. This commenting itself performs an ethical task.

The immediate complication for me is that I delivered this essay as a paper at a gathering, and made my audience listen to me read Kierkegaard, and asked them to read along with me on an overhead screen. I held them hostage in a performance. One might think that any attempt to repeat that act would somehow fall short of the immediacy of the hour we shared—under my direction. But, of course, the written text of my lecture, and indeed the pretexts by Kierkegaard were indeed written out. Moreover, the dynamics of commentary are best experienced in reading and not in listening—hence this essay will better allow you, the readers, to examine both Kierkegaard's pretexts and the relation I set up between my commentary and those pretexts. Hence the second version, on these pages, is both prior to the first (since I wrote a version that I thereafter read) and offers a richer and even more ethical version of the oral one—with consequently a bit less drama. I have, however, not completely eliminated the traces of orality in the essay, and I hope that you can imaginatively bridge some of the gap from the first to the second version.

I had intended to compose each page with different text blocks. Kierkegaard would be inset on the left, and some biblical texts inset on the right, texts that Kierkegaard cites and alludes to. That framework was developed more fully in my recent *Why Ethics? Signs of Responsibilities,* and there I also offered a fuller justification of the need for commentary. Instead, you will have a more familiar page, where the texts of Kierkegaard and the Bible are indented. Still more important than the page is the need for commentary, but for the present purposes commentary arises as a way of taking responsibility for another's text. The density of Kierkegaard's texts will be juxtaposed by a set of comments that are, I hope, more accessible. The ordering of the pretexts is my own, following a set of issues that control the essay. The texts are numbered consecutively (1, 2, 3). Kierkegaard's texts are then parceled out in short chunks (2a, 2b, 2c, 3a, 3b . . .). All texts are from *Works of Love.*[1] I have made a few alterations (deleting the "false" dashes, etc.) from the 1995 Hong and Hong translation, assisted by Tim Stock. I cite or paraphrase phrases and sentences from Kierkegaard in my commentary in SMALL CAPS, but the *italics* in his text are his own. The biblical texts are assigned letters (A, B, . . .), and the translations are my own from the Greek or the Hebrew and based on the Revised Standard Version and the new Jewish Publications Society.

Given the vastness of the general question about why we should read, and indeed, comment upon Kierkegaard, that is, how he would account for that responsibility, I have opted to focus on a very narrow compass: two small words and one punctuation mark. The method is pragmatics, the study of meaning that arises in the relation of signer and sign. This is really much like a pragrammatology, the pragmatics of writing, borrowing an occasional usage of Derrida. I have picked a set of five texts, each of which will contribute to an interpretation of the ethical task of interpreting love of the neighbor. I underscore ethical, again, in order to distinguish both the content and the method of this reading from speculative, aesthetic, or even dogmatic kinds of tasks. Or perhaps, if I said that all tasks arise from ethical responsibilities, then this is the responsibility about responsibility. Most of the most famous dialectics and moods of Kierkegaard's works appear here in the arena of ethics, precisely to articulate the responsibility to love the neighbor. The focus of the pragmatics, in any case, is the address or alternatively the "to" of signification: for a sign means something *to* someone. That address finds me both as the addressee, called or commanded to love, and as addresser, as the one who speaks, writes, comments to you. In that doubled directionality

I have different responsibilities, and the "I" and the "you" will help us articulate just what the differences are. The dash (—), however, takes us more deeply into the responsibility to give without reducing the recipient as depending on the gift. By exploring the dash, we will also be able to turn from the why of writing to why we read.

Kierkegaard's ethics appears most of all in a large work of 1847, *Works of Love,* published under his own name. Despite what many readers think, based on their reading *Either–Or,* or other pseudonymous works, like *Concluding Unscientific Postscript* or *Fear and Trembling,* beyond the universal rational ethics on the way to religion, there is for Kierkegaard a second ethics: a Christian ethics, which has as its center the command to love the neighbor. Such a commanded love, commanded by God, is rigorously particular and asymmetric: You shall love your neighbor (who is not everyone but anyone, and that anyone is not qualified as a rational being or a virtuous being, or as clever, or as Christian—just anyone). That love is not to depend on the other's reaction to me. I am commanded even were she dead, even were she a stranger or my sister. My own particularity develops precisely in loving the neighbor through God's love.

Such an ethics is much richer than the ethical themes from Kierkegaard more familiar to us. What Kierkegaard most resembles here is Levinas with his account of responsibility for the other. This is not an altogether novel insight, but it raises questions beyond my range today. Only Merold Westphal and the important commentary by Jamie Ferreira on *Works of Love* have explored this important connection.[2] In the second part of this essay, we will seem to be thinking in the middle of Derrida's reflections on the gift, both *Given Time* with its questioning of the gift economy and *The Gift of Death,* with the account of secrecy.[3] Adding Derrida, we find more reflection on Kierkegaard's ethics, and John Caputo's work clearly stands out,[4] but again, the focus here is on the ethical practices of reading and commenting where the work of Elsebet Jegstrup[5] stands out, particularly in relation to *Works of Love.* In this essay as a whole we will focus on my own practices here, as commenting on specific texts of Kierkegaard.

Section One: I or You

Like von Humboldt and Feuerbach, Kierkegaard discovers the significance of the word "you." "You" is a term of invocation, an address to another that solicits response. The "you" is the addressee of discourse, and to be a "you" is to be called to respond. To be an "I," however, is to speak and to make a claim upon another. The first part of my title, then, raises the question of whether love of the neighbor is found in the "I" or the "You"—is it a matter of speaking to someone or of being spoken to?

We turn now to our first text from *Works of Love,* to get started properly:

It is a text about "you," and distinguishes sharply between a love that goes to an other "I" and one that goes to a "you." The former, for Kierkegaard, represents self-love; the latter, love of the neighbor. He often accuses the former of being selfish—even when the beloved is my sweetheart or even my friend. So long as I can count on some preference and reciprocity of my special feelings, I am not loving the neighbor (although I can love even my mother or wife as my neighbor).

> 1a) [57–58] In the beloved and the friend, it of course is not the neighbor who is loved, but the *other I,* or the first *I* once again, but more intensely.

It is not the neighbor in these loves that is loved, but it is an OTHER I. We have here an interesting mirroring of myself in my beloved. I love myself: I love THE FIRST I, and not another person. But through this diversion through another, I love myself MORE INTENSELY. In the one whom I prefer, my love rests on my own preference, but now separated from my will (objectified, if you want), and still my own. A self-alienation consummated by a return to self. That is not love of the neighbor (although it is a Hegelian motion of spirit). And the return to self makes my self-love more intense.

> 1b) Even though self-love is reprehensible, it frequently seems as if a person does not have the strength to be alone in his self-love; thus it does not really manifest itself until the other *I* is found and the one *I* and the *other I* in this alliance find the strength for the self-esteem of self-love.

SELF-LOVE, however, is weak. To use myself, to honor myself, to enjoy myself is often not passionate enough. But really to love myself, I require another person, someone who in loving my own image of myself, can allow me to assert my own sense of myself. Here is a remarkable presage of Lacan. I join my own I with the other I—making "I" so much stronger and manifest. Here is no true "we," but still an "I" that develops its self-love with its partner. This relation may even be reciprocal: that even as my pride in the virtues or beauty of my beloved or my friend augments and expresses my own self-love, so for the other, I might be a way to strengthen SELF-LOVE, too. Together we do not love each other as neighbors, but we each are able to be more self-loving. But even that self-love was commanded, was it not?

> 1c) . . . But does he not love the beloved *as himself,* as the commandment that speaks of the neighbor commands? Certainly he does, but the beloved he loves *as himself* is not the neighbor: the beloved is the *other I.* Whether we speak of the *first I* or of the *other I,* we do not come a step nearer to the neighbor, because the neighbor is the *first you.*

If one has self-love through another, then one does love the other as one loves oneself—but not as the neighbor. For the beloved is just a paired self, an alter ego, a second "I." But the neighbor is not an "I," he is THE FIRST "YOU." Kierkegaard here breaks boldly into a moment of linguistic reflection. The neighbor is a "you": a "you" is an other who can speak, and to whom I must address myself. All of the otherness and disinterestedness that Kierkegaard has been struggling to contrast with self-love concentrates into this pronoun. For my beloved is either a "you" or an other "I"—and it is not that he is a subjectivity, a paired other self who also has egoity—on the contrary, the assimilation of the neighbor into an other "I" is what marks the intensification of self-love through or with another. No, the other, the neighbor, is a "you"—who creates address and not just self-consciousness. And the neighbor is THE FIRST "YOU" because only in love of the neighbor is that otherness discovered—that another person is not *for me* but is beyond my self-recovery, as one *to* whom I speak.

> 1d) The one whom self-love, in the strictest sense, loves is basically the *other I*, because the *other I* is he himself. Yet this certainly is still self-love.

Thus Kierkegaard can identify self-love with love of THE OTHER I, a second "I." And here a plasticity of pronouns repeats: that second "I" becomes a "he" in self-love. Not only is the other person assimilated to another I, but the "I" itself becomes a mere "he" in this detour of self-love through another. An appropriating self is not a true "I," for a true "I" is in relation to a "you"—I only appears as "I" when it loves the neighbor, and not when it loves itself. The passion of self-love destroys the "I," even as it intensifies its relation to itself through another.

But for Kierkegaard's Christian ethics, the "you" of love of the neighbor requires also a love for God that breaks up the relation of the "I" with its other I's and makes a "you" possible. To those who are entangled in the webs of the pseudonymous works, it will seem odd to see how easily Kierkegaard can natter away about a relation with God, and indeed, can base an ethics on love for God, but the more familiar anxiety and trembling and even despair will arise in this ethics, too, but not before the dash. In any case, this passage continues by clarifying, simply and brilliantly, the foundation of ethics in love for God.

> 1e) . . . Ultimately, love for God is the decisive factor; from this originates love for the neighbor—but paganism has no inkling of this. It left out God, made erotic love and friendship into love, and abhorred self-love. But the Christian love commandment commands loving God above all else, and then loving the neighbor.

PAGANISM, and that includes Socrates and Plato, does not know that one must love God in order to love the neighbor. Indeed, it seems quite doubtful that they know to love the neighbor at all. Love one's friend—ah, but that is the self-love we have already bundled up with love of the erotic lover.

A) Matthew 22.37–40: And he said to him, " 'You shall love the Lord your God with all your heart, and with all your soul, and with all your mind.' This is the great and first commandment. And a second is like it, 'You shall love your neighbor as yourself.' On these two commandments depend all the law and the prophets."

But it is not so subtle to bring Jesus' recitation of the love commandments forward here. Of course, the whole book is a form of commentary on this text (A), but Kierkegaard's point is that love of the neighbor is the second command. ABOVE ALL ELSE is a familiar, if somewhat limited paraphrase, but each term of the second command finds its own lengthy commentary in *Works of Love*. I will neglect the obvious task of seeking the Jewish roots of both the two commandments (which are indeed citations from Torah), and also the parallel rabbinic discussions of which commandments are the "essence," or the condition for all the other commandments. These are CHRISTIAN commandments because they were Jewish, and because Jesus is a kind of Jew—the kind who loves and cites, and indeed recites in order to command the commands of Jewish text and life. But Kierkegaard also dwells strongly upon how as commandments they COMMAND. Love is commanded, and only from love for God arises the love for the neighbor.

1f) In erotic love and friendship, preferential love is the middle term; in love for the neighbor, God is the middle term. Love God above all else; then you also love the neighbor and in the neighbor every human being.

Kierkegaard treats the opposition as a question of MIDDLE TERMS—the term that allows the relation between the "I" and its other. Despite the limited otherness of the other "I," the "I" comes into relation with the other "I" through its love of love—that is, through its desire for its own desire, for and through its self-love. The love that loves love here is precisely the relation that comes back to myself, that grounds me through another. The relationship even to my friend is mediated by my self-love, and so by a desire toward myself. But in love of the neighbor, I must go through God in order to reach my neighbor. The alterity of that "you" is mediated by God (by the Other par excellence), who is lovable. God commands love to God; God loves by commanding love. To love another person through this love to God is to love through a love that is not self-love. God's love for another commands love, and makes me able to love a "you" and not just myself. And from the love for the unique God, I can love then anyone, and in loving anyone love every other, EVERY HUMAN BEING. The lack of self-interest in all three loves here (the love to God, to the neighbor, and to everyone) moves against the self-interest and self-constitution of love to another "I."

"You" is not merely a topic in *Works of Love;* it is also a term of address in the text. Significantly, we can turn to a text where "you" is addressed with a question, where the reader is sought and a question gestures a need to respond, a need for a reader to answer to a "you" in the text. I take as my text, moreover, one that claims that to love the neighbor requires that I assume that my neighbor also loves. Such love looks for love and discovers the loving in the neighbor. Such a presumption in the favor of the neighbor means that Kierkegaard will also need to presume love in his reader, presume that the neighbor (you, his reader, or is it me, his reader?) is already loving and so can be built up.

> 2a) [222–23] *Love builds up by presupposing that love is present.* Have you not experienced this yourself, my listener? If anyone has ever spoken to you in such a way or treated you in such a way that you really felt built up, this was because you very vividly perceived how he presupposed love to be in you.

The paragraph begins in italics in a description that the work of love (building up) occurs by PRESUPPOSING love. This third-person claim is then turned toward the reader in the second person (HAVE YOU NOT EXPERI-ENCED?) in a question. Kierkegaard situates us as the beloved, not as the lover, shifting away from the agent to the one who is passive. To be built up by love, you must also see that another trusts you, that that other pre-supposes love in you. Kierkegaard calls upon our VERY VIVID PERCEPTION of having love presupposed of "you." But what about these "you"s? Do they alter the text from a discussion that continued in the third person? Well, of course. They put you, the reader, on the spot, but notice that that spot is not as the one commanded (as it was in the earlier discussion), but as the beloved, as the one who is to appear as already loving, and so is loved by appearing as loving. Maybe the point is not just to collar the reader, but precisely to locate the "you" in the neighbor position (and not the lover position), to see what being loved is like, in order to be better able to love. *For to be loved, at the end of the day, seems to be more significant than the love— because the beloved must be discerned as already loving.*

> 2b) Or what kind of person do you think one would be who could truly build you up? It is true that you would desire him to have insight and knowledge and talent and experience, but you still would not consider that it depended crucially on this but rather on his being a trustworthy, loving person, that is truly a loving person. Therefore you consider that to build up depends crucially and essentially upon being loving or having love to such a degree that one can rely upon it.

From the perspective of the beloved, the central characteristic of the lover is not insight or skill, but BEING A LOVING person. Just as you know you are loved when your lover presupposes that you already love, so you recognize the love in the lover as a TRUSTWORTHINESS. The issue for us, moreover, is that for the one who would love another, the key is to presuppose it (and that we can see when Kierkegaard puts us in the addressed position by asking "you"). To ask, in this way, is also to question us about whether Kierkegaard himself seems to be able to build us up by his discourse. What do we require of Kierkegaard—except that he be trustworthy and loving? We sense that he regards us as already loving, and able to be built up, but does his writing portray a steadfastness in love TO SUCH A DEGREE THAT ONE CAN RELY UPON IT?

To love is to presuppose love in my beloved. I can build up only when I presume he already is loving. And the author? Does the author not love, then, when the author presupposes love in the reader? Is this presupposition a presupposition that can be expressed in the "you"? Can Kierkegaard write, *I presuppose that you, my reader, are already loving the neighbor, and all I want is to build up that love*? Can we generalize this move? (An author, a reader?) Does it work for a reader—that a reader must also presuppose that an author is already loving, and then is a reader building up the author in reading? Reading then is a way of making the best one can out of the text, following a hermeneutics of charity. And reading on these pages, as I comment to you, I should presuppose love in Kierkegaard. And in you, my readers.

But Kierkegaard can also not say "you," can write about you where the "you" is only implicit, but is revealed *as* implicit. The first text was about the place of you in love of the neighbor, but the third is about the absence of the word "you" in a Gospel text, a text that commands you but does not need to say "you." Is the Gospel the model for Kierkegaard's own writing? The text is from Luke, and Kierkegaard interprets it at some length.

> 3a) [14] It does not read in the Gospel, as sagacious talk would say, "You are or one is to know the tree by its fruits," but it reads "The Tree is to be known by its fruits": The interpretation is that you who read these words of the Gospel, you are the tree.

The question is how does the Gospel command? How does it find its addressee? The first hypothesis is that a statement could direct a reader (you or one) to be the knower. The second hypothesis is that the Gospel describes events in which the reader is neither knower nor known. The third hypothesis is that the one known, the object, is the role established for the reader. The text from Luke does not help very much:

> B) Luke 6.43–44: "For no good tree bears rotten fruit, nor again does a rotten tree bear good fruit; for each tree *is known by its own fruit*. For figs are not gathered from thorns, nor are the grapes picked from a bramble bush."

The discourse is unambiguously third person. Jesus is speaking, indeed, speaking the Sermon on the Mount, and indeed the beatitudes are full of the word "you"; the sermon continues with phrases like "I say to you" (Luke 6.27), and an abundance of imperatives ("Judge not . . ." 6.37). But not in these two verses. The Gospel seems to take a breath, to slip into pure third-person discourse, to loosen the binding direct command and interrogation of the reader. (And a contrast with Matthew 7.15–20 would only make Kierkegaard's point weaker.)

But let us look again at Kierkegaard's opening comment:

> 3a) [14] It does not read in the Gospel, as sagacious talk would say, "You are or one is to know the tree by its fruits," but it reads "The Tree is to be known by its fruits": The interpretation is that you who read these words of the Gospel, you are the tree.

Kierkegaard has had to extract a rare text in the Sermon on the Mount, rare precisely in its reluctance to say "you." Kierkegaard, still, has his own interest. The Gospel, according to Kierkegaard, is not coming to command us to be cagey and good connoisseurs of others' fruitfulness. We are not the knowers but the known (hypothesis #3). The tree is the role for YOU WHO READ these words. The reader should find himself under judgment, known by others, by God. But the point of the statement is to recognize that whatever we think or say about ourselves, we will be known by how we do, by whether our love is fruitful. Kierkegaard is not troubled by his own use of the word "you" to displace the reader from the knower to the tree.

> 3b) The Gospel does not need to add what the prophet Nathan added to his parable, "You are the man," since it is already contained in the form of the statement, and insofar as it is a word of the Gospel.

There is a contrast then with the prophet Nathan, who taught David by a parable to recognize himself in the wrong. Unlike the parables in the same chapter of Luke, and unlike Nathan's parable, this one parable of the trees and fruits needs no "you." Please reconsider the confrontation of David by Nathan:

> C) 2 Samuel 11.27–12.7: And when the mourning was over, David sent and gathered her to his house and she became his wife and she bore him a son, but the thing that David did was evil in the eyes of the Lord. And the Lord sent Nathan to David, and he came to him and said to him: "There were two men in one city: one was rich and the other poor. The rich one had very many flocks and herds; and the poor had nothing at all, except one little lamb, which he had bought and kept alive and raised with him and with his sons together. It ate from his bread and drank from his cup and lay in his bosom and it was like a daughter to him. And a traveler came to the rich man, and he spared to take from his own flock or his own herd, in order to prepare for the one who came, but he took the lamb of the poor man, and prepared it for the one who had come to him." And David's anger burned hot against the man and he said to Nathan, "As the Lord lives, that man who did is like a dead man: he shall restore the lamb fourfold for he did this thing and he had no pity." And Nathan said to David, "You are the man. Thus says the Lord, God of Israel. I anointed you King over Israel and I delivered you from the hand of Saul."

David abused his authority to acquire Bathsheba. Nathan, sent by God, does not directly confront David, but tells a story. It snares David, until his anger raged against the fictional character. Then Nathan slams the trap—for David is the man. David needed to be told, after the parable, that "you are the man." The direct address is as blunt as possible, so that he recognizes himself as the one known (and not find himself in the position of the knower). Kierkegaard notices that Nathan uses the word "you," and the Gospel can omit the punch line of the image (not saying "you are the fruits"). Why? Because the statement bears this meaning within it and it is the very nature of A WORD OF THE GOSPEL. The Gospel comes with a built-in "you," but not an explicit one. Because it is Gospel it does not need a vocative pronoun—it calls us to attention at every moment.

> 3c) The divine authority of the Gospel does not speak to one person about another, does not speak to you, my listener, about me, or to me about you; no, when the Gospel speaks, it speaks to the single individual. It does not speak *about* us human beings, you and me, but speaks *to* us human beings, to you and me, and what it speaks about is that love is to be known by its fruits.

And so Kierkegaard can speak about DIVINE AUTHORITY, which would be then the authority in a text that always singles me out. It has no need to say *Shma,* listen up, because it is always saying it. Its discourse is recognizably a discourse *to* and not a discourse *about.* Or let me rephrase that: whatever it is about (and in this case it is that the tree is known by its fruits), it is *to* you or *to* me. And here is the interesting point: not about me to you or about you to me, but about me to me and about you to you. How can it do that? Because its *to* governs its claim. The address, the interlocution, determines the content or meaning. Now that property is, for Kierkegaard, what defines the authority of the Gospel, defines it as God's word, as a word written for each individual, for anyone, and only insofar as it is for anyone is it for everyone.

Of course, the question is whether Kierkegaard's text can speak thus. Or rather, whether a citation in Kierkegaard's text of the Gospel will itself speak to me about me and to you about you. And really, let's be a little more ruthless: the point is that it does speak to you (Kierkegaard's listener). The command you shall love makes the "you" explicit, but not in such a way that it is about the "you," but only when it becomes a word that speaks *to* you. This is not unusual for Kierkegaard. Yet in this passage we do run into the Gospel directly, and to the pragrammatics, the way that a written text can single out an individual. It does it, in this case, not by saying "you," but by placing you in the position of the one who is known by his fruits.

The fourth kind of "you," and the climax of this part, is not the topic, nor the interrogated, nor the elided, but the commanded "you." The set of discourses that set out the main discussion of the commandment to love are "You *Shall* Love," "You Shall Love *the Neighbor,*" and "*You* Shall Love the Neighbor," and the text regularly slips into the imperative. How are we to understand the text—does it find us as a "you"? Kierkegaard himself struggles with the question of direct ethical discourse many times in his works—and so it won't surprise any reader to find sustained and complex reflection on the pronouns. Kierkegaard confronts his own relation to us, and so to the impossibility of commanding us to love our neighbor.

> 4a) [90] But when a person in the infinite transformation himself discovers the eternal so close to life that there is not the distance of one single claim, of one single evasion, of one single moment of time from what *he* in this instant, in this second, in this holy moment *shall* do: then he is on the way to becoming a Christian.

The text starts in the third person. Here is the decisive moment rendered ethical, for the present here is the urgency of the *shall,* the obligation to love the neighbor. And Kierkegaard describes a dissolution of the distance that puts off the moment when I have to start loving, when I am turned toward the other. This destruction of the evasions and the obstacles reaches the "he." He is on the way—and at just that moment, Kierkegaard pauses and is struck not by the shall, which has been the topic, but by the pronoun, by the voicing of his own discourse. He winds his way to that question by making a biography of pronouns.

> 4b) It is a mark of childishness to say: *Me wants, me-me;* a mark of adolescence to say, "*I*—and *I*—and *I.*"

As a CHILD, one understands one's desires only as the object of them. One is addressed and has not learned how to choose for oneself, how to integrate desire and speech into self-determination. But ADOLESCENCE sees the emergence of the "I." Independence and authority exercised in my own name. I assert not only I, but also AND *I,* a gap marked here by a dash, that opens and then closes a motion to others. I and you? No. I and her? No. Only an aggression of more I in the place that the first I opened up. Ethics of the autonomous self, the first ethics, is then signed by the mark of adolescence.

> 4c) [T]he sign of maturity and the devotion of the eternal is to will to understand that this *I* has no significance unless it becomes the *you,* to whom eternity incessantly speaks and says: You shall, *you* shall, *you* shall.

A relation not to myself but to God, depends on a relation to you, but now not as a question of want or as naked assertion, but of *you* under the pulsing *shall.* Maturity arises, for an adult lives through obligations, understands himself not as the accusative of want (the child), but as the nominative of commandments. Kierkegaard gently marks the slipping from the emphasis on the shall, which requires a quotation marked "you," where the point is that the imperative needs a "you," to the italicizing of the "you"—picking out the "you," picking out you. Repeated, because you are obliged again and again, and the address, just like the Gospel, does not wander off to tell you about how I shall or about how he shall, but the address sticks to you.

> 4d) Youthfulness want to be the only I in the whole world; maturity is to understand this you as about yourself, even if it were not addressed to a single other person. *You* shall: *you* shall love your neighbor. O, my listener, it is not to *you* to whom *I* speak; it is to *me,* to whom eternity says: *You* shall.

This summary has then turned against itself. To be I with no one else, to be THE ONLY one who has discovered the secret inner life, the one who is able to relate to myself. The singularity of the adolescent, however, has this wondrous benefit: When the "you shall" breaks in, and adulthood begins, the solitude now lets the "you" be alone. My duty to love is solitary in this key sense—it depends on no one else's duties. The commandment singles me out for loving others. Then Kierkegaard must confront the problem: If he is obliged without us, then is his written text a compromise of that obligation? Does his attempt to write that "you shall" imply that only if others are obliged is he obliged? Of course not! He is addressed independent of his address to us. And so he withdraws his address, and in some important ways, all of his address. He is not speaking to me but only to himself; or rather, in his speech he announces that he is addressed as a "you" by eternity. God speaks to him, and he is simply repeating to us what he was told, in quotation marks. That is, God did not say, *tell them "You shall love";* rather God says *you shall love,* and Kierkegaard then tells us *God says to me "you shall love."* This moment then is not a direct imperative to the reader. It is a citation of a direct imperative to the author.

Is this the same indirectness as the Gospel? Or its inverse? The Gospel, recall, omitted citing the "you," because the "you" was implicit in the Gospel text itself. It singled the reader out. Is Kierkegaard's text direct about the "you," in order to single out the author and *not* the reader? Is Kierkegaard writing to you (to me and to us) in order to testify only of his own being commanded? Or is it not a delicate balance that he is striving for, to testify without losing his keen sense of his own unique obligation—that even were we *not* commanded, he still would be? Finally, can the displacement of one line, granted in an important context, undo the pragmatic force of reading you, you, you for hundreds of pages? I often feel this is like making us eat crow and then having it himself, too.

And let me then translate this problem more generally. If the discourse of ethical theory intends to communicate our being commanded, then must it lecture others about what you ought to do? Or if it is not imperatives, how will it instruct its readers? Is my commanding love a way of presupposing love in the other? Or is it better to talk about the command to love, or perhaps as Kierkegaard indicates here, to cite my own being commanded to love? Thus at this point I can make the first half of the title more clear. I or You is the difference between an address that presents the evidence of consciousness and one that commands the addressee. Can ethics perform commanding and remain ethical? And were it to cease to command, to oblige, would it still be ethics, or would it have become merely another adolescent or speculative theory? Somehow, the ethical writing must build up and also not simply command. The presupposition of love in the addressee may open a different way of interpreting the relation of writer and reader. But perhaps we can be clearer if we look at the dash.

Section Two: The Dash of Ethics

We have been reading texts that explore writing about ethics *to* another, to a "you." But now we are going to jump off into a long discussion of a punctuation mark, something that is not even a word and barely audible at all. The context is a deliberation from the second set, "Love seeks not its own," and the key introductory thought is expressed as

> 5a) [274–79] *Love does not seek its own; it rather gives in such a way that the gift looks as if it were the recipient's property.*

This is italicized in Kierkegaard and is the "maxim" of the deliberation. The challenge is linked to a long discussion about the gift, and the idea that all true gifts are not merely dispossessions but must also seek to appear as mere restitution might be of some value in the contemporary discussion. That is, the unreciprocated gift, the impossible gift, must also appear in the incognito of an economic gift, and that to appear as a purely generous donation would be to burden the recipient, to bind the one to whom I give in a duty of gratitude—which would ruin my gift. To write a text, then, so that the reader will see its reading as coming not from me, an other, but only from herself takes us far into a hermeneutics of reception. As a reader am I not one who learns not from the other, the author, but only through my own reading of this book, from my own interaction with the text? Is there any clearer orientation to Kierkegaard's own expressed position on reading? That whatever he might give us, it will have to appear to us as though it were merely our own discovery or our own insight—for he hides himself and disclaims any role as giver? To be a giver so that there is only the gift and the recipient while the giver disappears—that is the theory of love of the neighbor. But in order to explain this maxim, Kierkegaard proceeds to a six-page discussion of a declaration that one would tell oneself, as giver, in achieving such a giving. We don't have enough time, but I will take you through a few interpretations of that declaration, and dwell on the dash that lies at its heart. The gift is now translated as helping a person to be independent, to stand on his own. Can I help someone to do that?

> 5b) . . . If I say, "this person is standing by himself through my help" and what I say is true, have I then done the highest for him? Let us see! What am I saying by this? I am saying, "He stands simply and solely through my help"—but then, of course, he is not standing by himself, then he has indeed not become his own master; then, after all, it is to my help that he owes all this—and he is aware of it.

The first hypothesis is the declaration of a simple prepositional claim ("HE STANDS SIMPLY AND SOLELY THROUGH MY HELP"): my help is that *through* which he has become independent. That means that he is dependent on me; indeed without me, he would be nothing. This cannot work, for he may now stand, but not BY HIMSELF. The debt is absolute (HE OWES it ALL to me), and to give in order to underscore his dependence is not to give (and to help in such a way is not to help). Indeed, the key seems to be that he is made AWARE of my help. That undermines his own independence.

> 5c) . . . [T]he greatest benefaction, therefore, cannot be done in such a way that the recipient comes to know that it is to me that he owes it, because if he comes to know that, then it simply is not the greatest beneficence. On the other hand, if someone says, "This person is standing by himself— through my help" and what he says is true, well, then he has done for this person the highest that one human being can do for another, has made him free, independent, himself, his own master, and just by hiding his help has helped him to stand by himself. Therefore: to stand by oneself—through another's help!

In the second hypothesis we add a dash, and the declaration changes its shape. What motivates the addition of the dash is a matter of not knowing. Kierkegaard requires an incognito in the giver, or the one who receives will have a lesser benefit. The key is that by HIDING HIS HELP he has helped the other to stand by himself. But also we have a signal shift from declaration, complete with quotation marks ("THIS PERSON IS STANDING BY HIMSELF— THROUGH MY HELP") to a description (TO STAND BY ONESELF—THROUGH AN- OTHER'S HELP). In the first instance, I speak and refer to another person, whom I have helped but who does not know it, but in the second case there is a third-person description of someone standing through another's help. What Kierkegaard does not discuss is a spoken claim that I stand through another's help—for that is a contradiction. I cannot receive the greatest beneficence and know it. The general description, moreover, does not serve Kierkegaard as well as the declaration, where the "I" is located as the one who has helped and hidden.

5d) . . . [A] dash has truly never been used more significantly and never can be used more significantly than in this little sentence—if used, note well, by someone who has accomplished it, if there is such a person: because in this little sentence infinity's thought is contained in a most ingenious way, and the greatest contradiction surmounted. He is standing by himself—that is the highest; he is standing by himself—more you do not see. You see no help or support, no awkward bungler's hand holding on to him, any more than it occurs to the person himself that someone has helped him. No, he is standing by himself—through another's help. But this other person's help is hidden from him, . . . that is hidden behind the dash.

We have here the familiar Kierkegaardian vocabulary of INFINITY in the finite, the overcoming of CONTRADICTION—all in a dash, not even a word made flesh, but a mark on the page that itself is capable of holding everything together. I was discussing this essay with my daughter, Ariel, and she immediately responded: Why, that is a paradox, the paradox of everything. Kierkegaard's claim is that the dash itself makes the help invisible (MORE YOU DO NOT SEE), it marks the limit of knowing, in order that the gift lack a representation of the giver. He plays with the visibility of the helper and of his help, all HIDDEN BEHIND THE DASH. Behind another visible mark, a mask for the help. And also our expression "behind the dash": what follows the dash. What is behind the dash is exactly "through my help," legible but hidden from the one helped. And even obscured in relation to the reader. The reader sees the occlusion in the dash that interrupts the first declaration. And so we see dashes accumulate in Kierkegaard's own text. Here are two in a row that elide the phrase "through my help" in order to show us how we retain the missing phrase, although it is invisible. And again the text slides off into third-person description (HE IS STANDING BY HIMSELF). The first person in hiding (THROUGH MY HELP) simply disappears.

5e) . . . This noble rogue had understood in the profound sense that the highest one human being can do for another is to make him free, help him to stand by himself—and he had also understood himself in understanding this, that is, he had understood that if this is to be done the helper must be able to make himself anonymous, must magnanimously will to annihilate himself. . . . In this way he worked; and when the work was completed, he said very softly to himself: Now this individual is standing by himself. But then we come to the dash, and with the dash a smile comes upon the lips of that noble, yet roguish one, and he says, "Now this individual is standing by himself—through my help." He keeps to himself the secret of this indescribable smile . . . the smile, that is still the self-consciousness of ingenuity.

Kierkegaard then proceeds to describe the highest noble wisdom of a human, philosophy, in the un-named guise of Socrates. He, too, in a third hypothesis seems capable of the declaration with the dash, for important ethical and philosophical reasons. Here is the language of the *Philosophical*

Fragments again, doing THE HIGHEST ONE CAN DO FOR ANOTHER, and now it is compressed in the dash. The self-consciousness of Socrates carries with it the recognition that help must be ANONYMOUS. The will to help another is doubled as a will TO ANNIHILATE HIMSELF. Thus Socrates can make it all the way to the dash (not like our first dash-less and witless declaration). It is a dash with a smile of self-consciousness. "NOW THIS INDIVIDUAL IS STANDING BY HIMSELF—THROUGH MY HELP." Socrates earns his "I" (MY HELP), the relation to another (THIS INDIVIDUAL IS STANDING), negotiated by an "I" that is hidden, leaving only his smile.

> 5f) It is different with the one who loves. He also says: now this individual is standing by himself. Then comes the dash. Oh, but for the loving person this dash means something different from a smile; however noble and magnanimous and unselfish that rogue was, he still did not in the sense of concern love the one he wanted to help. Whereas that rogue makes himself infinitely light precisely in the cunning of the dash, and just this is the art to have been able to do everything for the other person and pretend as if one had done nothing at all, then for the loving person the dash, even though in the sense of thought an infinite lightness, in another sense (but please note that it is not noticeable), is like a heavy breath, almost like a deep sigh. In this dash are hidden the sleeplessness of anxiety, the night watch of work, and the almost desperate exertion; in this dash is hidden a fear and trembling that has never found any expression and for that very reason is all the more terrible.

But Socrates is NOT ONE WHO LOVES. When the Socratic delights in the art and in self-consciousness, a certain kind of aesthetic ethics emerges here. It bears a resemblance to some postmoderns, whose concern with the other is muffled precisely because of the need for a subtle dialectics. But the religious ethics is more complex than those dialectics. The dash hides more than the help given and the helper—it hides not only the infinity of self-relation, but also the anxiety of relation with God. All of the familiar existential moods return here, in contrast to Socrates: DESPAIR, FEAR AND TREMBLING, ANXIETY, THE SLEEPLESSNESS of relation with God. But all of that is hidden in the dash, or one can begin to see that even the dash is doubly hiding. Hiding first the relation to the other, and then the intense relation with God about the relation with the other. Moreover, unlike Socrates' smile, there is no possible expression for these relations with God. For some, the relation with the other person should be the place where the difficult and inexpressible relations with God are expressed, but for Kierkegaard there is no expression possible, only a trace in a dash. I import the term *trace* because I want the non-relation of the mark on the page to what can never become perceptible. Thus hidden in the dash are not only what needs to be veiled from the knower, but even that which exceeds knowledge altogether. Thus the dash points not only to help hidden, but to the source of my own ability to help, to a relation with God.

5g) The one who loves has understood that it truly is the greatest, the only beneficence one human being can do for another, to help him to stand by himself, to become himself, to become his own master; but he has also understood the danger and the suffering in the midst of the work, and above all the terribleness of the responsibility. Therefore, giving thanks to God, he declares: Now this individual is standing by himself—through my help. But there is no self-satisfaction in the last phrase, because the loving one has understood that essentially every human being indeed stands by himself—through God's help and that the loving one's self-annihilation is really in order not to hinder the other person's God-relationship, so that all the loving one's help infinitely vanishes in the God-relationship.

Here is THE TERRIBLENESS OF THE RESPONSIBILITY, THE DANGER AND THE SUFFERING of helping another and hiding that help. The extremity of the dash is clearer now. And so Kierkegaard then introduces God directly. And the irony is now clearer: a fourth hypothesis and another declaration is needed. EVERY HUMAN BEING INDEED STANDS BY HIMSELF—THROUGH GOD'S HELP. The vagueness of the shifting from first to third person in the earlier forms is now revealed to depend on the more primordial declaration. And the problem of hiding is made much more direct, for in my loving the other, God loves the other, and so one's own loving automatically disappears, insofar as I have helped the other come into a clearer relationship with God. The goal of independence is now supplanted with the goal of God-supported existence. The relationship has now three terms, and the middle term is again God. Through my help it becomes God's help, I help the other to stand in her relationship with God, to stand with God's help. The stakes are higher, but notice how different they have become from Socrates. His goal is self-consciousness and independence for the other. The goal in love of the neighbor is a pair of relationships.

Even the description of God's help requires the dash, and indeed, the place where God's help comes in is precisely: behind the dash. God can enter writing only through the sign of something that cannot be represented, a sign that does offer God as a topic, but precisely as that which is hidden *behind* the hiding of the help I give to another. The dash, it seems, hides a hiding, or is like a dash on top of itself. For Socrates the dash only hid his help, but for the lover of the neighbor, it hides both her love and the love from God that made it possible to love and to hide. Were I clever I might say that it was a doubled dash, a cross, or that the first dash was only a hyphen, which belongs in *Works of Love* to the question of incompleteness and the fragmentary, but I think we can see that a dash, which does not strike through another word, bears within it the possibility of not only hiding love, but the higher possibility of hiding God in hiding love.

5h) . . . In a way he can pack his whole life into a dash. He can say: I have worked as much as anyone, worked early and late, but what have I accomplished—a dash! (That is, if what he had accomplished could be seen directly, he would have worked less lovingly.) I have suffered as heavily as anyone, as deeply as only love can suffer, but what have I gained—a dash! I have proclaimed the truth as clearly and well thought through as anyone but who has appropriated it—a dash! In other words, if he had not been one who loves, he would have loudly and directly proclaimed the truth, less well thought through, and promptly had adherents who would have appropriated the truth—and hailed him as master.

The lover now PACKS HIS WHOLE LIFE INTO A DASH—which turns him willy-nilly into a writer, for a speaker does not "use" dashes. If the ethical form packed infinity into the dash, then what is more obvious than that this could be rendered existential. A life hidden behind the dash. The work is hard when it is made hidden. The suffering is heavier when hidden. Each sentence broken by a dash, preceding A DASH! Those first two dashes are a kind of literalization, reminiscent of when Victor Borge in his comedy routine transformed punctuation marks into sounds; or since they are not letters, a kind of marking up the text with the text's own thought. A doubling that is humorous, because it makes explicit what should be hidden—the drama of hiding and of hiding the hiding. The written dash is the revealing of the hiding. But the third one goes further, because proclaiming that truth depends on a hiding. The fruit of the labor is appropriated not by the neighbor, nor by himself, but by the sign of hiding, the dash. It all bundles in, behind the door of the safe house, to hide from the accolades of the adherents. Even here the—A DASH—is humorous, but now we are turning back to the key problem for this talk.

We now have the questions of how well Kierkegaard has hidden himself and settled for only a dash. If we HAIL HIM AS A MASTER, at least of typography, then are we giving the lie to his well-thought-through words? How can he disappear and help us to understand love? The declaration that we stand on our own—through his help—is not one of his hypotheses.

First, why does he write? If that is not bad enough, if I have helped you at all to understand better the task of giving and not appearing, the way that the second ethics transforms the series of issues on the stages of the pseudonymous authors, then I shall also need a dash to hide behind. Writing about these things requires a lot of dashes.

Second, then why do we read his texts?

An answer to the first is obvious, Kierkegaard *has* hidden more than any author since Plato. He has taught all of us that we do not meet the author in the text. He performs the dash continuously, and to do so, he writes. A mark on the page is the place where one can hide one's help to the other. It is all dashes: I mean that as the dashes start to clutter this last paragraph, we suddenly see that the written page is itself a set of dashes, a way of hiding from us the help given *to* us, as well as hiding the helper. And in a religious voice, we can say that God's writing is a further mode of occlusion. The Hebrew alphabet is filled with marks that are like dashes (reoriented vertically), especially the name of God itself. Love of the neighbor, in order to seek not its own, takes up the pen.

But the second question is harder to negotiate, for we have been reading Kierkegaard together. To read is a way of presupposing the love from the author, but never to find the author. From Kierkegaard's perspective, the highest reading would be one that first brought me into relation with God (our highest author). And even God hides in the dash—much more so the human writer. We would read to see the dash as an interruption of what seems too present, so accessible to us, revealing to us both the eclipse of the author and the more profound unpresentableness of our own relation to God. Not to discern what Kierkegaard thinks, or even what is the case in the world, but to be awakened to a love that marks but hides.

But still higher than such a reading would be one that heard the commandment to love the neighbor, and sought to love another, precisely in relation to the dash. Such a reading would become some sort of citation and commentary. Like Kierkegaard's citation of the tree that will be known by its fruits, the citation strives to find you, my fellow readers, addressed by the command that addresses me. And to comment, not to tell you what Gibbs thinks of Kierkegaard, or even what Kierkegaard said, but rather to re-open the dash, where our helpers hide, and where the infinite can reveal but cannot become present. A receptive act of reading, in the privacy of my own room, might be the way of receiving the gift, but if the gift given is love of the neighbor and understanding what we can of it, then it must be given on. Not reading, not writing, but commentary then combines the work of love in performing the marking of the dash.

Notes

1. *Works of Love,* trans. Howard V. Hong and Edna H. Hong (Princeton, N.J.: Princeton University Press, 1995).

2. M. Jamie Ferreira, *Love's Grateful Striving: A Commentary on Kierkegaard's "Works of Love"* (Oxford: Oxford University Press, 2001); see esp. ch. 8 and 15. Merold Westphal, "Commanded Love and Divine Transcendence in Levinas and Kierkegaard," in *The Face of the Other and the Trace of God: Essays on the Philosophy of Emmanuel Levinas,* ed. Jeff Bloechl (New York: Fordham University Press, 2000).

3. Jacques Derrida, *Given Time: 1. Counterfeit Money,* trans. Peggy Kamuf (Chicago: University of Chicago Press, 1992), and *The Gift of Death,* trans. David Wills (Chicago: University of Chicago Press, 1992).

4. John D. Caputo, *The Prayers and Tears of Jacques Derrida* (Bloomington: Indiana University Press, 1997).

5. Elsebet Jegstrup, "Text and the Performative Act: Kierkegaard's (Im/possible) Direct Communications," *Philosophy Today* 45, no. 2 (summer 2001): 121–31.

9

Love and Difference: The Christian Ideal in Kierkegaard's Works of Love

Vanessa Rumble

All of them . . . constructed at infinite cost to themselves
these Maginot Lines against the enemy they thought they
saw across the frontier, this enemy who never attacked
that way—if he ever attacked at all; if he was indeed the
enemy.

—John Knowles, *A Separate Peace*

I WOULD LIKE TO address Kierkegaard's concept of Christian love as he describes it in *Works of Love,* and to attend particularly to the devices by which he signals the alterity and unattainability of such love. In contrast to Kant, for whom ought implies can, in Kierkegaard's writing the command to love is directed toward humans who have forfeited the sine qua non for so doing. *Either–Or, Fear and Trembling, Repetition,* and *The Concept of Anxiety* all portray the ethical as shipwrecked on the fact of sin. Though they sometimes do so elliptically, these texts point to the eclipse of the subject by sin. Abraham, for example, is praised as the father of faith in *Fear and Trembling,* capable of fulfilling and therefore justified in surpassing the ethical, but when discussion of the effects of sin makes its appearance in Problema III, it becomes clear Abraham is a paradigm without exemplar, with the rest of humanity relegated to the status of mermen and mermaids who can never mount a claim to have met the dictates of ethics. The notion of the teleological suspension of the ethical allows the reader to discriminate in theory but never in practice between faith and immediate inclination. The other early works issue in a similar deadlock, leaving the reader like a beached merman, in the old Pauline predicament: too much enamored of the good to love the evil that we do. Barring the intervention of the transcendent, would-be knights of faith, would-be candidates for religious repetition, would-be practitioners of Christian love, never get further than to an awareness of separation from the ideal. Faces pressed to the glass, the ideal of a second immediacy recedes into the distance and is replaced by what Vigilius Haufniensis designates in *The Concept of Anxiety* as the task of second (post shipwreck) ethics, namely "the penetrating consciousness of [the] actuality . . . of sin."[1]

These seemingly Calvinist pronouncements on the severity of sin are not merely a bit of edifying indirection aimed either at aesthetes who regard freedom, death, and subjectivity as distant relatives or at ethicists like Wilhelm caught up in the myth of their own autonomy. The uncompromising distinction between the human and the specifically Christian is salient in the writings of Anti-Climacus[2] and unmistakable, too, in signed works, such as *Works of Love*.[3] Louis Mackey saw, in Kierkegaard's pronouncements on sin, an anticipation of Derrida's dissemination of the intentional subject, an insight elaborated in his "A Ram in the Afternoon: Kierkegaard's Discourse of the Other," among other pieces.[4] Those who contest such an equation, those who would dispute the existence of such sympathy between Kierkegaard and Derrida, tend to point to the upbuilding discourses or to *Works of Love* as proof that (1) Kierkegaard has an ethics and (2) where there is an ethics there must be a subject. It is in response to this line of thinking that I offer a deconstructive reading of *Works of Love*, illustrating a displacement of the conscious subject in this work similar to that effected in earlier pseudonymous writings. My first aim in what follows, then, is to bring to light Kierkegaard's anticipation of Derridean insights and maneuvers.

Following this reading of *Works of Love*, with its overview of provisional likenesses between the writings of Kierkegaard and Derrida, I turn to Derrida's own reading of Kierkegaard's *Fear and Trembling* in *The Gift of Death*. There Derrida underlines the manner in which our finitude qualifies ethical existence (the manner in which our moral experience makes our finitude inescapable). While his remarks on this subject seem to me importantly true in their portrait of what it means to be an existing individual obligated to others, emphasizing as they do our limitations in fulfilling our obligations as well as the uncertainty surrounding our status as agents, I am nevertheless left with the sense that Derrida's reading of Kierkegaard does not do justice to the nature of the affinity between his own thought and that of Kierkegaard's. In concluding, I argue that the very religious concepts that are minimized in most postmodern readings of Kierkegaard are precisely those best suited to establishing the similarity of Kierkegaard's and Derrida's most pronounced philosophical leanings. I focus in particular on the manner in which the concept of sin shapes Kierkegaard's "anti-humanism" and his relation to Derrida.

Wise as Serpents and Innocent as Doves: Consciousness of Difference in Works of Love

Works of Love is, on first reading, an attempt to reiterate the boundary between preferential love and Christian love, between friendship and erotic love (*Elskov*), on the one hand, and the spirit's love of the neighbor (*Kjerlighed*) on the other. Kierkegaard's insistence on the dethronement of "the love based on drives and inclination" (WL, 44) is so clearly spelled out and so passionately defended that the pseudonymous texts, with their rich ambiguities, seem far removed. With Kantian rigor, *Works of Love* contrasts the earthly lover's partiality for the beloved with *Kjerlighed's* indifference to earthly distinctions. The transformation of erotic love by duty is extolled, as is the manner in which Christian love encompasses and supercedes the claims of preference. The distinction between eros and agape, between nature and duty, is of great concern to any Christian, Kierkegaard tells us. The Christian "must understand everything differently than the non-Christian does, must be conscious that he knows how to make distinctions" (WL, 47).[5] This painstaking drawing of distinctions is of more than passing importance. Even "in eternity . . . we will talk simply and solely about mercifulness, and simply and solely about the distinction merciful—not merciful" (WL, 327). As with the earlier dichotomy between preference and impartial love, the disjunction merciful—unmerciful signals the disparity between the merely human, that is, self-enclosed, and the Christian.

This distinction, however, is subsequently seen to be *at best* one of theory rather than practice, and at worst a dangerous distraction from the one thing needful. The reader is enjoined from viewing the neighbor or himself through this harshly "objective" lens. We are warned that "comparison . . . loses the moment, the moment that ought to have been filled with an expression of love's life. . . . The moment of comparison is, namely, a selfish moment, a moment that wants to be for itself; this is the break, is the fall" (WL, 183). Finite love, preferential love, always dwells (*dvæle*) on comparison; such self-consciousness, such *dvælen*, in Kierkegaard's eyes, is tantamount to the work of the devil (*djævelen*). Kierkegaard's own dwelling on the comparison of the two forms of love, a pastime that we were initially assured was shared by the Christian, now seems wholly removed from Christian consciousness. The division between preference and agape that founded the text is now revealed as a potential obstacle to practicing agape in actuality. Slowly, *Works of Love* aligns itself with the conflict that pervades the earlier pseudonymous writings,[6] inasmuch as the author's preoccupations (in this case with mapping the boundary between the human and Christian) are separated by a chasm from the desired state of being.[7] What began as a theoretical distinction has resurfaced as a split within the narrative voice and presumably its author.

Agapic love dwells neither on itself and its distinction from the non-Christian, nor on an objective evaluation of the beloved. The beloved must exist for the Christian *only* as the beloved if the Christian is to fulfill the duty of loving the person she sees. No "duality" must enter the relationship with the beloved. If it does,

it is as if you had two ears in the sense that you do not, as is normal, hear
one thing with both ears but hear one thing with one and something else
with the other. With the one ear you hear what he says and whether it is
wise and correct and penetrating and brilliant etc., and, alas, only with the
other ear do you hear that it is the beloved's voice. With the one eye you
look at him, testing, searching, criticizing, and, alas, only with the other eye
do you see that he is that beloved. Ah, but to divide in this way is not to
love the person one sees. (WL, 165)

One cannot, Kierkegaard tells us, exist in loving relation to the beloved
while at the same time evaluating the beloved from a disengaged standpoint.
But is this reflective potential not rooted in consciousness itself? Kierkegaard
sets the Christian standard so high that no human work could attain it and
no human consciousness really wish it, so high that *Works of Love* disinte-
grates into the paired roles of so many pseudonymous texts, the observer/
poet caught up in submissive wonder before the inaccessible hero of immediacy. Kierkegaard, like his reader, can only observe agape's self-forgetful
movements, and this self-forgetful Christian "consciousness" exhibits an elu-
siveness similar to Rousseau's longed for state of nature, as described by
Derrida in *Of Grammatology*.[8] The ideal (of an unpolluted nature, or in Kierkegaard's case, a restored purity of will) is expressible only through a language
(or a consciousness) that precludes its fulfillment. (The only mystery remains
how the ideal arose in the first place.) Nor is this tension between a desired
second immediacy and the narrator's state of mind restricted to the pseudonymous works. Throughout the later authorship, statements concerning
love and the Christian requirement call into question the extent to which
Kierkegaard's writing, or his own activity as a writer, can fulfill the ethic he
is concerned to depict.[9] Undermining the authority and coherence of the
narrative voice, then, is a tactic common to both pseudonymous and veronymous works. If the narrator of *Works of Love* is of a divided mind with
regard to the value of the distinction between the loving and the unloving,
does the distinction itself maintain its legitimacy?

The sharp antithesis between the natural and the Christian in the First
Series of *Works of Love* is set in relief by the opening lines of the Second
Series, which point to the necessity of metaphor in expressing matters of the
spirit. Hope revives that after several hundred pages of Kantian denigration
of earthly love, the discussion of metaphor will indicate the intimate inter-
relatedness of preferential and agapic love, as well as some pathway from the
former to the latter. Kierkegaard's opening remarks are promising in this
regard: "all human speech, even the divine speech of Holy Scripture, about
the spiritual is essentially metaphorical [*overført*, carried over] speech. And
this is quite in order . . . since a human being, even if from the moment of
birth he is spirit, still does not become conscious of himself as spirit until
later" (WL, 209). Human existence invariably requires a bridging of the

realms of nature and spirit, inclination and duty. Metaphor, we are told, has its genesis when the first part of life, lived in "sensate-psychical" categories, is "taken over" by the spirit. The spirit must express itself in a language used initially to refer to physical or psychical, hence finite, realities.

The promise of mediation, however, is short lived. Though Kierkegaard acknowledges that the language of finitude and its longings must also be capable of expressing those of the spirit, he goes out of his way to underline the discontinuity between literal and metaphorical meaning:

> [Y]et there is an infinite difference, since[life within sensate-psychical categories] has no intimation of the secret of the metaphorical words although it uses the same words, but not in their metaphorical sense. There is a world of difference between the two; the one has made the transition [*Overgang*] or let itself be carried over [*føre over*] to the other side, while the other remains on this side. . . . Just as the spirit is invisible, so is its language a secret. (Ibid.)

Literal and metaphorical meaning are to be understood as simply disparate; no analogy draws us from the one to the other. Not only are the psychical and spiritual "roots" of metaphor posited as unrelated to one another, an unlikely position dismissed by Owen Barfield,[10] I. A. Richards, and others, but the power of metaphor to simultaneously reveal two disparate realms is denied to those lacking prior acquaintance with the spiritual. Spiritual meaning is said to be metaphor's hidden secret. But metaphoricity itself is then hidden, suppressed, unrecognizable to all except the initiates of the spirit, and the binary opposition between nature and spirit is reinforced. At the same time, *Works of Love* maintains, just as Climacus does in *Philosophical Fragments,* that a human language "too self-loving" to dream of Christ's intervention in human history nevertheless proclaims this event.[11] By virtue of its multivalence, language is capable of expressing many sorts of love, agapic love of other as well as self-enclosed love of one's own, but an understanding of the former is vouchsafed only to those who already possess it. Kierkegaard's insistence on the distinction between preferential and agapic love is thus complicated, first, by his claim that one who truly loves will not attend to this distinction and, second, by his admission that the difference between the two is in practice unrecognizable to the unredeemed human gaze. For how are the uninitiated to grasp it?

In "Love Builds Up," Kierkegaard states explicitly that "there is nothing, nothing at all, that cannot be done or said in such a way that it becomes upbuilding, but whatever it is, if it is upbuilding, then love is present. . . . There is no word in the language that in itself is upbuilding, and there is no word in the language that cannot be said in an upbuilding way and become upbulding if love is present" (WL, 212–13). The same claim appears much earlier, in *Fear and Trembling,* when we are told that Abraham may express his love in a manner that contradicts his ethical duty, and by implication in any manner whatsoever.[12] In *Works of Love* the category of the *hidden* serves as the repeated reminder of love's undecidability. As we have seen, Kierkegaard regards works of love as lacking in any surefire mark of recognition (*kendetegn*), just as he regards the *source* of love as likewise hidden, incommensurable with the finite. This claim is in accord with the Kantian sentiments that pervade *Works of Love;* love is hidden, both in its genesis and its effect. If hiddenness problematizes the distinction between eros and agape by rendering it unrecognizable, the occasional suggestion (in both pseudonymous and veronymous works) that hiddenness itself is to be a *criterion* of a work of love subverts the distinction entirely. The Kantian demarcation of inner and outer is breached by the contentious claim that a work, which gains recognition as a work of love, is thereby disqualified from being such.[13] Hiddenness becomes love's one outward sign. Here again, we see the distinctions that seem foundational to the text undermined by irony. The distinctions remain in force but show themselves to be either unusable (as is the case with distinctions that must remain merely theoretical) or incomprehensible (as spiritual meaning is to those whom the spirit eludes) or, finally, self-negating. The latter occurs when a distinction is employed in a manner contrary to the aim it was initially to serve, as is the case when hiddenness becomes the self-conscious goal of a supposedly self-effacing love, or when the distinction between love of other and love of self is used only for self-aggrandizement. Like Plato's *pharmakon,* the sign of writing's privilege and danger, hiddenness has the potential to both define and efface works of love.[14]

Masks and Metamorphoses: Kierkegaard's Elusive Agent

The undecidability that pervades Kierkegaard's discussion of works as signs of love affects, too, the identity of the speaking/writing/acting agent. Love of neighbor, understood as a total abandonment of self in favor of the other, is difficult to distinguish from an unqualified self-absorption.[15] Kierkegaard goes so far as to suggest that the neighbor who is to test our love need not actually exist: "The concept 'neighbor' is actually the redoubling of your own self, 'the neighbor' is what thinkers call 'the other,' that by which the selfishness in self-love is to be tested. As far as thought is concerned, the neighbor does not need to exist. If someone living on a desert island mentally conformed to this commandment, by renouncing self-love he could be said to love the neighbor" (WL, 21). Difficult as this is to reconcile with Kierkegaard's claim, a few chapters later, that the neighbor is not the "other I" but the "first you" (WL, 53), it seems very much in the spirit of the penultimate chapter of the text, "The Work of Love in Recollecting One Who is Dead." There the remembering of the dead is lauded for its evident selflessness, given the inability of the dead to reciprocate, but this embrace of the other is quickly brought into proximity with its opposite. When the neighbor is dead, the "first you" is a somewhat diminished force, after all, and the I is free to create this "other" to order. While this may seem an unlikely scenario, given the emphasis Kierkegaard places on loving the neighbor we see, without wishful alteration,[16] the malleability of the dead leads one to recollect that the pseudonyms often create the object of their worship or fascination, and most particularly when the otherness of the object is stressed. In *Either–Or*, A expresses a suspiciously high degree of anxiety over the contents of the seducer's diary, suggesting that he is its author; *Repetition's* Constantin Constantius claims to have authored the young man, whose every word, he assures us, is ventriloquism, leaving us to wonder whose voice we are hearing; and, in a jaw-dropping footnote in the *Concluding Unscientific Postscript*, Climacus suggests that the figure of Abraham may himself be the poetic creation of de Silentio.[17] If the distinction between self and other is compromised in *Works of Love*, as it so clearly is in the earlier pseudonymous writings, what becomes of the difference between love of self and love of other?

Climacus asserts, in *Philosophical Fragments*, that any attempt to conceptualize the unknown (to "grasp it securely") will result in an arbitrary idolatry. The pseudonyms, who long for their others, draw the object of their worship back into the circle of the same, as soon as they would guarantee that it is the Other that they worship. Climacus proclaims that, dialectically speaking, the absolute other is no different from the same. This admission renders suspect the central enterprise of *Fragments*, which was to derive the other (Christianity) from the same (the Socratic), an effort inaugurated repeatedly under the phrase, "if it is to be otherwise (*hvis det skulle være anderledes*)."[18] In this way, *Fragment's* attempt to arrive at Christianity through the abstract negation of Socratic self-sufficiency is unveiled and exposed to criticism. Whether Climacus's philosophical venture is understood as a demonstration of the inevitable solipsism of the intellect, or, on another reading, as opening the way for a relation to the Other that is not situated under either category, the binary opposition of Socratic and Christian is in any event undermined. The erosion of the distinction between self and other, implicit both in *Works of Love's* incongruous descriptions of *Kjerlighed* and *Philosophical Fragments'* anomalous delineation of Christianity, entails the disruption of the subject's identity; the confusion that, in turn, surrounds the identity of the author of *Works of Love* corresponds to the fragmentation that threatens its reader.

The vertiginous shifts in identity so familiar in the pseudonymous works have invaded Kierkegaard's most Apollonian of texts. Is the narrator of *Works of Love* a solipsist or a mouthpiece of the divine? Textual evidence points to both conclusions. If, as Kierkegaard insists, genuine works of love are to remain hidden, his own texts become (and he gestures somewhat transparently in this direction) candidates for this distinction by virtue of their own indirection. Might not Love have produced these deliberations on love? Perhaps. Providence may have guided Kierkegaard's pen. But we have been told that love does not dwell on itself, while Kierkegaard's texts are nothing if not self-referential. Does the text then demonstrate the necessity for grace by revealing the bankruptcy (i.e., the ultimately self-enclosed nature) of all human efforts? Kierkegaard the sober scribe and unbribable observer, documenting the deeds of love with impeccable objectivity, possibly a bearer, incognito, of divine wisdom, fades before the spectacle of Kierkegaard the interested or even depraved observer, proving by his very proof of love (the absurd notion of a visible hiddenness) that he lacks it. Nose against the glass, pleading for admission to the kingdom of hidden immediacy, incapable of ceasing to do and be all the things that make admission a more than moot possibility, he remains in all his guises a sign, a mirror, of you and me. What do we see in this mirror? Do we really love, as Constantin asks of the young man in *Repetition*? Judge for yourselves; certitude is impossible, and in the end probably undesirable. Through these metamorphoses, the subject is shown to be disseminated and is surely in no way in possession of transparent inwardness, unless we mean by this a "secret interiority" hidden first and foremost from *hin Enkelte,* the single individual. "Subjectivity is Untruth," Climacus remarks in the *Postscript.*[19] Consciousness lends itself to an all too clear-cut distinction between self and other that Kierkegaard would undermine. Like Rousseau, Kierkegaard locates the genesis of consciousness in its capacity to reflect, to compare self and other. The goal of a higher immediacy, or Christian consciousness, would, among other things, involve the radical revisioning of this distinction. In reading *Works of Love,* just as with the pseudonymous writings, we are left with the question of what we really know of the individual, be it self or other, who exists on the far side of the opposition between fallenness and autonomy, undefined and disseminated. If I have captured the logic of Kierkegaard's texts, and their implication for our self-knowledge, we have something very like that of Derrida's. John Caputo says it like this: "The ultimate, radical logic of the pure gift is to remove the gift entirely from the field of intentionality and willing, from pure hearts and cunning deceivers, from good will and bad, from human will or divine. That is to shift to a giving that is not human at all, neither Abrahamic nor pharisaical nor Matthean, neither selfish nor altruistic, neither ethical nor religious."[20]

Foes of deconstruction who were scandalized by the voluntarism of the God of *Fear and Trembling* seize upon *Works of Love* as proof of Kierkegaard's credentials as a responsible theologian. *Works of Love* reassures by reasserting the claim of the universal and of duty on the individual, and the incommensurability between the ethical and the religious in *Fear and Trembling* seems to have vanished. Yet the unreflective action[21] that Kierkegaard calls

Kjerlighed in *Works of Love* would seem to have little time or need for the Kantian distinctions invoked. Though the Law and Love may indeed "know one and the same thing" (WL, 106), there is a life-and-death difference, we are told (and not just by Kierkegaard), between the two. In contrast to *Fear and Trembling,* then, the law is not "sublated," but the coincidence and the difference between love and the law in *Works of Love* is rendered uncertain, so the trembling remains. While "the law" signifies clarity and judicial precision, the love that is sheer action seems "not human at all."[22]

In Pursuit of the Gift: Kierkegaard and Derrida

Kierkegaard's *Works of Love* posits an opposition between love of other and love of self that the text then deconstructs. The distinction is undermined by placing in question the subject's ability to draw the distinction in any actual context, as well as by suggesting diametrically opposed identities for the author of the text. At times, *Works of Love* seems the creation of one unable to free himself from concerns of which agape is either blissfully ignorant or heedless. At other times, the text is vaunted as itself a work of love, as when it is hinted (in the chapter "The Work of Love in Praising Love") that a speaker who truly praises love must have made himself appear self-loving to his contemporaries (WL, 374). (Kierkegaard seems to have felt confident on this point.) The final line of the chapter refuses to decide the question of the narrator's identity: "If, then, someone undertakes to praise love and is asked whether it is actually out of love on his part that he does it, the answer must be: 'No one else can decide this for certain; it is possible that it is vanity, pride—in short, something bad, but it is also possible that it is love'" (WL, 374).[23] No mention is made of whether the author himself could "decide this for certain."

In Kierkegaard's writings, the deconstructive maneuvers that anticipate Derrida's—the undermining of authorial intent and the repudiation of the distinction between the privileged term in a binary opposition and its other—are deployed most often in the context of the notion of human sinfulness. The mere mention of sin in *Fear and Trembling* razes the conceptual edifice that was to separate knights of faith from their murderous alter egos, just as sin is understood to thwart both Judge Wilhelm's struggle for autonomy and Constantin's pursuit of repetition. Whether the suggestion arrives in a package from Jutland[24] or in the unmotivated pronouncement, "upon this concept [sin], . . . [ethics] is shipwrecked,"[25] Kierkegaard's readers soon recognize that the vanity of the intellect and its distinctions, as well as the dizzying vacillations in the identity of his narrators (of pseudonymous and veronymous texts alike), are linked by Kierkegaard to the reality of sin.

Needless to say, when commentators speak to the affinities between Kierkegaard and postmodernism in general, or Kierkegaard and Derrida in particular, sinfulness is not the first banner hoisted up the flagpole.[26] Post-Nietzsche and post-Heidegger, the concept of sin seems the intellectual remains of a thwarted sadism and of onto-theological will to power. Merold Westphal opposes the tendency to exclude religious discourse and, with it, the "possibility of a robustly religious post-modernism."[27] Westphal attributes this tendency to misapplication of Heidegger's critique of onto-theology:

> Climacus makes it clear, as Heidegger does not, that the critique of onto-theology is adverbial and not substantive. It concerns the *how* of our relation to our most ultimate other without excluding any answers to *what* (or *who*) that other might be. . . . What the critique of ontotheology precludes is not that these claims [the "metaphysical claims of orthodox Christianity"] may be true but that they, or any analogous claims . . . can become a first principle in terms of which we can possess and embody the total intelligibility we seek. . . . To expose the futility and danger of putting God to work on philosophy's terms is one thing; to show that there is no God whose work is our highest task is quite another. Heidegger does not follow Climacus in making this distinction in his critique of onto-theo-logy. Perhaps this helps to explain why so much contemporary postmodernism bandies the term "onto-theo-logy" about as if it signified a successful attempt to make the world safe for atheism.[28]

My aim in this essay is not to make room for a religious postmodernism but for a more limited claim, namely, that the depth of the resonance between Derrida's work and Kierkegaard's is minimized if we abstract from the notion of sin. Derrida himself demonstrates this, I claim, in his reading of *Fear and Trembling* offered in *The Gift of Death*.

What Derrida draws attention to in *Fear and Trembling* and in Abraham's biblical trial is the aspect of sacrifice involved in all decisions. Derrida reads Abraham's binding of Isaac as revealing the sacrifice implicit in all duty to an other. The story, he says, represents "the most common and everyday experience of responsibility,"[29] namely, the experience that, given finitude and death, the fulfillment of responsibility to one person or cause requires the abandonment of others, a state of affairs always and everywhere valid, as Derrida says, in our starving world. In fulfilling a duty, I also betray "those I love in private, my own, my family, my son, each of whom is the only son I sacrifice to the other, every one being sacrificed to every one else in this land of Moriah that is our habitat every second of every day."[30] The dilemmas that Derrida describes, constant and troubling as they are, are the daily bread of Kierkegaard's tragic hero.[31] Our freedom as ethical beings consists always in choices that are to some degree constrained by interior and exterior limits. The only way to escape this situation would be to take refuge in Kant's noumenal realm, in the luxury of timeless and unconditioned acts of freedom.[32] Derrida of course steers clear of this costly refuge, and, in his reading of Kierkegaard's *Fear and Trembling,* the conflicts intrinsic to ethical existence are what is understood to give rise to fear and trembling. For, in contrast to the tragic hero in Kierkegaard's account, Derrida's "agent" cannot provide universal justification for her or his actions.

The sacrifice made by de Silentio's knight of faith is not, however, as Derrida suggests, the embracing of the sacrifices inherent in finitude. Abraham's willingness to sacrifice Isaac removes him from the life of uneasy compromise shouldered by the tragic hero and elevates him, by virtue of his renunciation of all finite ends, to a higher duty and a higher reward. His sacrifice is aimed at ending sacrifice, but not in the sense intended by scholars of the Hebrew scriptures. Rather, it is the renunciation of earthly fatherhood with its provisional autonomy in the hopes of gaining an unrestricted hegemony: a choice precisely to reject all forced choices (which all real choices are). In renouncing the forced choices by which one has identified with a community, a language, a family, and a culture, in withdrawing from the realm of the universal, Abraham would attain a second immediacy, an im/possible enjoyment of unity with the Other. Though de Silentio concedes in Problema III that no individual could fulfill the rigorous ethical qualifying rounds for knighthood in the order of faith, Abraham himself is portrayed (in Problema I and II) as having acceded to a life of higher duty to which all might aspire.[33] Derrida, perhaps out of filial loyalty, does not point out the return on Abraham's sacrifice.[34] Or perhaps it is de Silentio who has failed to do justice to Abraham's sacrifice, distorting it even as he would vindicate it. Carried away by his dialectical fervor, de Silentio banishes Abraham's fear and trembling even as he curtails his relevance for existing individuals. He pulls himself up short with the reminder: "up to now I have assiduously avoided any reference to the question of sin and its reality."[35] The merman of Problema III finds himself unable to fulfill his ethical duty, or, what is practically the same thing, he is unable to assure himself that he has done so. Having suspended the ethical for a purely immanent telos, the merman is left only with a possibility for faith. The situation of the merman is analogous to that of Derrida's Abraham: unable to forge a determinate identity through ethical striving.

Are Derrida and de Silentio in essential agreement, then, as to what the Abraham story teaches about human existence? What is the force of de Silentio's mention of sin? Is it merely a reminder of the inevitable limits of human living and loving, limits that Derrida so well portrays? The tendency in Kierkegaard's authorship is to distinguish between guilt (*Skyld*), which arises from finitude, and sin (*Synd*), which has its point of departure in a willed refusal of the Other. This notion of sin, entailing as it does the paralysis of the will[36] and a profound ignorance of oneself, bears with it, I would claim, a far more radical interrogation of the subject than that which has its point of departure in the notion of guilt (finitude). Sin disseminates agency in a thoroughgoing way, and the opacity that haunts the pseudonyms' quest for identity underlines this fragmentation. Though Kierkegaard seems at times to reify the notion of a sinful, self-enclosed humanity, incapable of recognizing or loving another, he nevertheless gestures repeatedly to the interruption of this state by divine initiative (by the other). In this connection, Kierkegaard's suggestion that the individual may become an instrument of God reiterates the undecidability of agency. As you will recall, "there is nothing, nothing at all, that cannot be done or said in such a way that it becomes upbuilding, but whatever it is, if it is upbuilding, then love is present" (WL, 212–13). Just as the earlier pseudonymous works use the Christian notion of sin to portray the interruption of philosophical hybris and dreams of totality, so, too, does the authorship as a whole gesture to the possibility (or is it the necessity?) of otherness invading an individual's despairing certitudes. Though always intent on the assault on bourgeois complacency as his first line of business, there is good reason to claim that Kierkegaard undermines both forms of self-certainty.[37] And in *The Gift of Death,* Derrida does so as well.

Though Derrida does not discuss the manner in which Abraham's sacrifice is nullified by de Silentio's explication,[38] he is surely cognizant of the tendency of seemingly "pure" gifts to reveal themselves as instances of canny investment. *The Gift of Death* raises this problematic in its treatment of the repeated assurance of heavenly rewards in the Gospel of Matthew. Chapter 4 of *Gift of Death* addresses the disturbing dissonance in the Mattheian injunctions against hypocrisy. The demand for sacrifice without thought of reward gives way in Matthew to an odd sotto voce reassurance that the reward will indeed be forthcoming.[39] This awareness of the certainty of compensation shifts the performance from gift to closed economy in much the same way that Abraham's sacrifice to end all sacrifice would, at least in de Silentio's version, free him from the compromised character of the everyday and make him whole. In Matthew, according to Derrida,

> the heart will . . . be . . . wherever you save real treasure, that which is not visible on earth, that whose capital accumulates beyond the economy of the terrestrial visible or sensible, that is, the corrupted or corruptible economy that is vulnerable to moth, rust, and thieves. . . . This infinite and dissymmetrical economy of sacrifice is opposed to that of the scribes and pharisees, to the old law in general. . . . It always presupposes a calculation that claims to go beyond calculation, beyond the totality of the calculable as a finite totality of the same.[40]

If this description may be said to parallel Kierkegaard's description of sinfulness, of the well-nigh inevitable detour of the gift into the circle of the same, *The Gift of Death* nevertheless ends on a note that recalls us to the possibility of the gift. After quoting Nietzsche's terse summary of the Christian economy, of "God personally immolating himself for the debt of man

. . . from love" followed by his incredulous "can you believe it," Derrida
remarks that "what makes this rhetorical question possible may . . . disturb
the structure of it."[41] There is, in other words, something in what Nietzsche
understands by belief that undermines his own attempt to reject it. Kierkegaard's and Derrida's accounts, then, resemble one another in this: though
both would claim that human willing is insufficient to guarantee the purity
of a gift, insufficient to prevent its appropriation by narrow prudence, they
also remind us that humanity is also incapable of hindering its birth.
De Silentio's Abraham merely demonstrated the former's inability to circumscribe the latter's deed.

Kierkegaard and Derrida struggle to make room for transcendence by
showing the failure of our practical and intellectual attempts to exclude it.
They seek a justice based on something "other" than the self-serving aims
of finite loyalties and rival orthodoxies. But, as Kierkegaard was well aware,
there is always the risk of betraying one's own higher aims. Kierkegaard
himself seems overly partial to a pedagogy that would define human nature
as self-enclosed—a totalizing claim all its own. At its best, deconstruction
reflects the given undecidability of our actions and the indeterminate identity
of the agent. Yet at other times deconstruction's longing for "the pure gift,"
and its accompanying vilification of the established order, also erects its own
violent orthodoxy. In studying Derrida's secret agent, one is tempted to claim
that, "[f]or Derrida, the only way to break the circle of self-aggrandizement
and wage-labor—earthly or heavenly—in which the gift is inevitably trapped
is the dissemination of intentional subjects and identifiable objects."[42] The
trouble is, there is no way to guard against subversion of giving—no way
and no need to "break" a circle of aggrandizement that is always already
broken; the version of dissemination just quoted leads one to believe that
there *is* a subject to be dismantled, not just the always already disseminated
subject. In our better moments we know this, and surely Derrida does as
well: Caputo confirms "[Derrida's] analysis shows the difficulty of keeping
the true coin of faith separate from the counterfeit coin of a credit system,
that there is nothing to guarantee that the one will not become the other,
nothing that says it cannot reverse itself and turn into its opposite, that it
does not already contain its opposite."[43] Richard Kearney makes this point,
too, when he says that "desire beyond desire—as precisely that desire for the
gift beyond the commerce of daily transaction—both is and is not outside
the circle of exchange."[44] But was the telltale language of "guarding" and
"breaking" merely accidental, or is it part and parcel of a desire for a pure
gift that all too easily becomes the desire for a graspable alterity, and all too
readily provides the motive for despising humble everyday loving and the
usually mixed motives that underlie it? If so, deconstruction exhibits a violence of its own, not dissimilar to that associated with the desire for closure
and absolute sovereignty.

Positing an absolute other as a guarantee that we do not stay in the circle of the same is like positing an absolute depravity to make sure that we do not become (as Kierkegaard feared) complacent, bourgeois Christians. A self-defeating gesture, if nevertheless the bread and butter of daily life and a common theological move. Kierkegaard reifies, at times, a notion of sin that is exclusive of all natural goodness; Derrida's vigilance in rejecting all ortho-doxies, all forms of closure, can signify a wholesale rejection of the needs and habits of finitude. An unqualified transcendence, just like a deified im-manence, has its dangers. At their worst moments, Derrida and Kierkegaard posit as our enemy the circle of the same, which is, after all, always already interrupted—and we live our lives only within this circle and can meet each other only there. At their best, they remind us of precisely this.

Notes

1. Søren Kierkegaard, *The Concept of Anxiety*, trans. Reidar Thomte and Albert B. Anderson (Princeton, N.J.: Princeton University Press, 1980), 20. All citations of Kierkegaard's works will be to volumes in *Kierkegaard's Writings*, pub-lished by Princeton University Press.

2. The introduction to *The Sickness unto Death* distinguishes repeatedly be-tween that which may be claimed from a human standpoint ("humanly speak-ing") and that which is proclaimed from a Christian standpoint ("Christianly speaking"). The necessity for the distinction is rooted in Anti-Climacus's later assertion that "interpreted Christianly, sin has its roots in willing, not in knowing, and this corruption of willing affects the individual's consciousness" (95). The difference between the two standpoints thus resists mediation.

3. *Works of Love* also underlines the "chasmic abyss between the God-man and every other person," which is "fixed" by the Law. Kierkegaard, *Works of Love,* 101. Hereafter WL.

4. Louis Mackey, "A Ram in the Afternoon: Kierkegaard's Discourse of the Other," in *Points of View: Readings of Kierkegaard* (Tallahassee: Florida State Uni-versity Press, 1986), 102–40.

5. The distinction in question here is between a pagan (human) and a Chris-tian understanding of love: "One must . . . take care to make it clear that the praise of erotic love and friendship belongs to paganism, that the *poet* actually belongs to paganism" (WL, 44).

6. I have in mind de Silentio's rapt admiration for Abraham's attainment of second immediacy, Constantin's fascination with the young man's initial ability to love, and Vigilius Haufniensis's absorption in spirit's incipient movements, a state from which he himself is far removed. See my "Eternity Lies Beneath: Autonomy and Finitude in Kierkegaard's Early Writings," *Journal of the History of Philosophy* 35, no. 1 (1997): 83–103.

7. Josiah Thompson noted Kierkegaard's repeated sounding of the theme of a lost immediacy in his *The Lonely Labyrinth: Kierkegaard's Pseudonymous Works* (Carbondale: Southern Illinois University Press, 1967). Though Thompson's

work on Kierkegaard, particularly his biography, routinely comes in for substantial criticism, his emphasis on the centrality of the notion of immediacy in Kierkegaard's authorship is well placed. The significance of Kierkegaard's denigration of reflection and the implications of this for his authorship—for his relation to German Romanticism and his shaping of the Christian ideal—remains an important issue in Kierkegaard studies. See Thompson, *Kierkegaard* (New York: Random House, 1973) and Alastair Hannay, *Kierkegaard* (Cambridge: Cambridge University Press, 2001), 317–41.

8. Jacques Derrida, *Of Grammatology*, trans. Gayatri Chakravorty Spivak (Baltimore: Johns Hopkins University Press, 1974), 259–68.

9. This self-interrogation is present in *Works of Love*'s suggestion that love itself is blind to the very distinction that the text is concerned to establish, in *Training in Christianity*'s critique of Christian art, and in *For Self-Examination*'s condemnation of the Christian poet. *Practice in Christianity*, 254–57, and *For Self-Examination; Judge for Yourselves*, ch. 1.

10. Owen Barfield, "The Meaning of the 'Literal,' " in *The Rediscovery of Meaning and Other Essays* (Middletown, Conn.: Wesleyan University Press, 1977), 32–43.

11. Kierkegaard, *Philosophical Fragments*, 22, 28.

12. Kierkegaard, *Fear and Trembling*, 70.

13. *Works of Love* proclaims that the deeds in question "must be done *outwardly* in self-sacrificing unselfishness" (WL, 365). Though Kierkegaard, in developing this claim, does not go so far as to argue that recognition of a work of love would deprive it of its moral worth, he is, I would guess, far from blind to the apparent dissonance between this statement and his earlier extended praise of love's cheerful indifference to its outward manifestations. The demand that one who would praise love must "make himself into the self-lover" is advanced as part of a "poetical venture" requiring that "one forget how the world is" (WL, 371), but such ventures are of necessity far removed from love's urgent business. For an alternate reading of this passage, see M. Jamie Ferreira, *Love's Grateful Striving: A Commentary on Kierkegaard's "Works of Love"* (Oxford: Oxford University Press, 2001), 76–83, 234–38.

14. Jacques Derrida, "Plato's Pharmacy," in *Dissemination*, trans. Barbara Johnson (Chicago: University of Chicago Press, 1981), 61–172.

15. William McDonald argues that what goes by the name of *Kjerlighed* in *Works of Love* is in no straightforward sense distinguishable from the detested Hegelian Absolute. "Love in Kierkegaard's Symposia," unpublished manuscript (Department of Philosophy, University of New England, New South Wales).

16. M. Jamie Ferreira argues cogently that the lessons in love's indifference to repayment, which Kierkegaard claims we learn in loving the dead, must not be viewed in abstraction from his insistence on love's attention to and acceptance of the other's concrete actuality (Ferreira, *Love's Grateful Striving*, 209–27). At the same time I would suggest that certain conflicts in *Works of Love* (between the necessity and dispensability of the other; between the inevitability and inadvisability of drawing reflective distinctions between the loving and the unloving) are not accidental features of the text to be explained away. Readings of Kierkegaard that focus primarily on questions of the orthodoxy of the veronymous

works tend to overlook crucial continuities in style and structure between the pseudonymous and veronymous texts. This has the effect of undermining what I take to be Kierkegaard's most important contribution: the force of his insistence on the limits of our knowledge.

17. Kierkegaard, *Concluding Unscientific Postscript*, 500–501 n.

18. Kierkegaard, *Fragments*, 13.

19. Kierkegaard, *Postscript*, 207.

20. John D. Caputo, "Instants, Secrets, and Singularities," in *Kierkegaard in Post/Modernity*, ed. Martin J. Matustik and Merold Westphal (Bloomington: Indiana University Press, 1995), 236.

21. WL, 182–91. Cf. Nietzsche's discussion of the purely grammatical distinction between doer and the deed, cause and effect, and so on in *The Genealogy of Morals*, trans. Walter Kaufmann and R. J. Hollingdale (New York: Random House, 1967), 45.

22. Caputo, "Instants, Secrets, Singularities," 236.

23. Joseph Westfall brought this quotation to my attention. His discussion of this passage in the current draft of his dissertation, "Writing and the Paradox," alerted me to the way in which this question reverberates throughout Kierkegaard's authorship.

24. This is the form in which Judge Wilhelm claimed to have received the text of the sermon "The Upbuilding That Lies in the Thought That in Relation to God We Are Always in the Wrong" (EO, 2:337).

25. Kierkegaard, *The Concept of Anxiety*, 17.

26. Mark Dooley's deconstructive reading of Kierkegaard is an excellent case in point. He aligns Kierkegaard's ethics with Derrida's later political thought, but he makes no bones about his intention to highlight only a certain "thread" within Kierkegaard's thought in order to "keep this thinker at the cutting edge of contemporary ethical and political debate" (xix). I find Dooley's book original and instructive in its careful analysis of the similarities in the political views of Kierkegaard and Derrida. My sense is, however, that certain key affinities between Kierkegaard and Derrida are neglected in such a selective approach. See *The Politics of Exodus: Kierkegaard's Ethics of Responsibility* (New York: Fordham University Press, 2001).

27. Merold Westphal, "Kierkegaard's Climacus: A Kind of Post-Modernist," in *International Kierkegaard Commentary: Concluding Unscientific Postscript to "Philosophical Fragments,"* ed. Robert Perkins (Macon, Ga.: Mercer University Press, 1997), 53–71.

28. Ibid., 61.

29. Jacques Derrida, *The Gift of Death*, trans. David Wills (Chicago: University of Chicago Press, 1995), 67.

30. Ibid., 69.

31. De Silentio lets his philosophically minded reader in on the fact that *Fear and Trembling's* notion of ethics relies on that set forth in Hegel's *Philosophy of Right*. The tragic hero, who exists within the confines of the ethical stage, is caught in a conflict between the claims of more and less inclusive social wholes. See Kierkegaard, *Fear and Trembling*, 54, and G. W. F. Hegel, *The Philosophy of Right*, trans. T. M. Knox (Oxford: Oxford University Press, 1967), pt. III.

32. See my "Søren Kierkegaard and the Uncanny: The Endangered Moral Agent," in *Anthropology and Authority: Essays on Søren Kierkegaard* (Amsterdam: Rodopi, 2000), 60–62. See also Immanuel Kant, *Religion within the Limits of Reason Alone,* trans. Theodore M. Green (New York: Harper and Row, 1960), 20.

33. By virtue of his willingness to sacrifice.

34. Caputo makes this point eloquently: "After all, even Abraham's sacrifice—is this not what deconstruction shows, even though Derrida, out of filial respect, does not bring it up?—is not absolutely safe, absolutely removed, absolutely safeguarded from hidden, subterranean, unconscious, unwanted, unwilled motivations that would turn it into the reverse of what it means to be (*vouloir*)? The 'merit' of deconstruction . . . is to put us on the alert to the way things can pass into their opposite, the way they can turn around and reverse themselves . . . so that they produce effects diametrically opposed to what they intend (*vouloir dire*)." *The Prayers and Tears of Jacques Derrida: Religion without Religion* (Bloomington: Indiana University Press, 1997), 220. Geoffrey Hale notes that if Problema I or II could justify Abraham's "leap," then the religious sphere would represent an "only apparent transgression of the ethical." See Hale, *Kierkegaard and the Ends of Language* (Minneapolis: University of Minnesota Press), 143.

35. Kierkegaard, *Fear and Trembling,* 98 n.

36. In "Arminian Edification: Kierkegaard on Grace and Free Will," Timothy Jackson argues that Kierkegaard would follow Augustine in the belief that "postlapsarian humanity [is] . . . unable not to sin." Jackson claims Kierkegaard's understanding of human freedom is distinguished from Augustine's "quite strong view of predestination" only in this: that the former would insist that, though "we cannot independently reach for the gift of salvation . . . we can either accept or refuse it." "Arminian Edification," in *The Cambridge Companion to Kierkegaard,* ed. Alastair Hannay and Gordon D. Marino (Cambridge: Cambridge University Press, 1998), 235–56, see esp. 236–37 and 248–49.

37. Kevin Newmark highlights the subject's opacity in his reading of Kierkegaard's treatment of Antigone: "To the extent that she must recognize her truth in an ineradicable debt to an inaccessible other, Antigone's future can be constructed only by a detour through this secret inheritance. But as a result of this construction of self permanently interrupted through the other's secret, her coherency as a subject will always be radically fragmented." "Secret Agents: After Kierkegaard's Subject," *MLN* 112 (1997): 719–52. I am much indebted to Newmark's insights in this essay.

38. The closest he comes to such a hermeneutics of suspicion is to grant that "demystifiers of . . . [Abraham's] calculation . . . might say he played his cards well." *Gift of Death,* 97.

39. Matthew 6.1–4.

40. Derrida, *Gift of Death,* 98, 107.

41. Ibid., 115.

42. Caputo, "Instants, Secrets, and Singularities," 231.

43. Ibid., 232.

44. Richard Kearney, "Desire of God," in *God, the Gift, and Postmodernism,* ed. John D. Caputo and Michael J. Scanlon (Bloomington: Indiana University

Press, 1999), 129. Kearney argues that, in our search for "the desire beyond desire," we should heed the "injunctions" of both faith and knowledge, without granting absolute authority to either. Alterity is no blanket refutation of scientific claims, no mere irrationalism. Newmark paraphrases Ricoeur on Kierkegaard to the same effect: "Kierkegaard's writing about those elements in existence that, from the point of view of comprehending [totalizing] thought can only be called paradoxical, absurd, or offensive, is something far different than a simple proclamation of irrationalism." Newmark, "Secret Agents," 728–29. See Paul Ricoeur, "Two Encounters with Kierkegaard: Kierkegaard and Evil; Doing Philosophy after Kierkegaard," in *Kierkegaard's Truth: The Disclosure of the Self,* ed. Joseph H. Smith (New Haven, Conn.: Yale University Press, 1981), 313–42.

10

ART, EROTICISM, AND
SADOMASOCHISTIC SACRIFICE
IN SØREN KIERKEGAARD AND
ISAK DINESEN

John Vignaux Smyth

The relation to the opposite sex has also been made into
the meaning and earnest of life—into true Christianity.
　　　　　　　　—Søren Kierkegaard, Journals

A friend is not what philosophy calls the necessary other,
but rather the superfluous third.
　　　　　　　　—Søren Kierkegaard, Either–Or

God . . . the first to have slain me.
　　　　　　　　—Kevilina Burbank, "Scandalous to Taste"

KIERKEGAARD AND DINESEN (KAREN BLIXEN) are two of Denmark's best-
known writers, but the broad significance of her response to his "Diary of
a Seducer" (from Either–Or) in her last novella, Ehrengard (1962), remains to
my knowledge largely ignored. Kierkegaard specialists, even feminist ones,
have not as yet regarded Ehrengard as a heavy hitter in the field of Kierkegaard
analysis, while Dinesen specialists have tended to focus on her "feminist"
reversal of the "Diary" without engaging her reading of Kierkegaard on his
(and her) own terms. This essay seeks to redress these omissions, while developing what I hope are novel readings of texts by both authors concerning
the relation between art, eroticism, mimesis, and sacrifice, among other top-
ics. Kierkegaard's most important texts on the erotic are Either–Or and The
Concept of Dread (The Concept of Anxiety). In the first, the focus is on the
relation between eroticism, aesthetics, and ethics; this I will pursue via Dinesen's treatment; in the second, the focus is on the relation between eroticism, guilt, and religious sacrifice—a relation that includes what nowadays
might be called sadomasochism—and this I will pursue independently. We
will thus see a continuity between what Kierkegaard calls the aesthetic, ethical, and religious spheres, a continuity that revolves around the relation
between mimesis and sacrifice (and mimesis, sex, and violence) in a way that

might recall the mimetic-sacrificial theory of René Girard—for whom sac-rificial phenomena are always imitative in origin and structure, and for whom secular sadomasochism is an extension of religious sacrifice. I begin, however, with some brief references to another theorist of the relation between sac-rifice and mimeticism, Theodor Adorno, because he wrote extensively on sacrifice in *Kierkegaard: Construction of the Aesthetic* (1933), and more exten-sively still on relations between mimesis, sacrifice, art, fashion, and eroticism in his last monumental book, *Aesthetic Theory.* I have argued elsewhere that Adorno's insights into Kierkegaard are far more "Kierkegaardian" than many seem to think.[1]

Adorno was hardly original in regarding sacrifice as a key to understand-ing Kierkegaard's view of religion (and everything else), but, like Kenneth Burke, he is notorious for regarding the three Kierkegaardian "stages" or "spheres"—aesthetic, ethical, religious—as a more or less technical and ab-stract articulation of a sacrificial mythology that is partially blind to sacrificial insights Kierkegaard achieves in the detail of his work. This is not to say that Kierkegaard is wrong in his basic view, later echoed in different ways by Durkheim, Kafka, Beckett, Burke, Girard, Bataille, and many others, that sacrifice is a key to religion, but that, according to Adorno—and this is the rub—Kierkegaard's overall trinitarian architecture falls prey to a mistake, or cluster of mistakes, whose sacrificial character he is well aware of when it comes to his aesthetes like Johannes the Seducer. Thus the "aesthetic" Kier-kegaard himself provides the key to a critical theory of Kierkegaard that turns him into an indispensable thinker for Adorno. As Walter Benjamin's contemporary review of Adorno's book astutely prophesied, the future of his work is to a significant degree contained in his early book on Kierkegaard. Despite being often stereotyped as a stereotypical Marxist critic of the pu-tatively "bourgeois" Dane, Adorno in fact provides a sacrificial "Construc-tion of the Aesthetic" that is to a significant degree both Kierkegaard's and his own (as his translator, Hullot-Kentor, notes, the subtitle equivocates).[2] This is also true for Isak Dinesen, whose treatment of the Kierkegaardian relation between the aesthetic and the erotic is both a eulogy of her coun-tryman and a playful confrontation with him. Adorno provides a theoretical rehabilitation of Kierkegaard's aesthetic sphere (as against views that see it as negated by the ethical and religious—hence the spheres are usually called "stages"), and Dinesen's novelistic one; but in both, sacrifice and mimesis play a pivotal role.

I have written elsewhere of Adorno's critique of Kierkegaard's "idealism" and praise of his "materialism."[3] What makes Adorno so antipathetic to many Kierkegaardians is not only his "Marxist" approach, but his rejection of what they take to be philosophically central in Kierkegaard's work (the existential leap, the self, absolute subjectivity, the three spheres, and so on) in favor of a mimetic and sacrificial power that, radical as it may be, joins Kierkegaard to religious orthodoxy. (Adorno himself says theological interpretations are generally superior to psychological interpretations because they stress to the utmost Kierkegaard's sacrificial "paradoxy" [K, 105].) Sacrificial mimesis, in both Kierkegaard and Adorno, is not the dialectical synthesis of ideal and material, or subjective and objective, but occurs "where the dialectical stops" (as Adorno remarks of the "blocked truth" that manifests itself beyond dialectics [K, 101])—and remains necessarily material, a matter of form, as we shall see in *The Concept of Dread*. This does not stop mimesis from being "spiritual"; on the contrary, as the orthodox *imitatio* suggests, it concerns precisely the "sacred" supplement to philosophy or dialectic.

The two crucial Kierkegaardian references in *Ehrengard* are to *Either–Or* (extensively, via the "Diary of a Seducer") and to *Fear and Trembling* (briefly, but at a key moment in Dinesen's erotic narrative). I shall begin my reading of *The Concept of Dread* and *Ehrengard* by quoting two of Adorno's references to these texts. The first concerns Adorno's summary that "woman because of her immediacy is essentially aesthetic, but just because she is essentially this, the transition to the religious is also direct. Feminine romanticism is in the very next instant the religious" (K, 104–105). According to Adorno, this erotic connection, indeed near identity, between the aesthetic and religious "bypasses the [sacrificial] logic of the spheres" precisely by highlighting their sacrificial constitution. Like Adorno, Dinesen also affirms Kierkegaard's insights into the close connection between the erotic–aesthetic and the religious, even or especially at moments (such as the one just mentioned, in which the feminine is identified with immediacy as opposed to masculine reflection) in which charges of sexism might seem most justified. The second reference is more concentrated, concerning Adorno's claim that "Abraham, as the subject of a 'dialectical lyric' [*Fear and Trembling*], is an allegorical name for the objective (one could almost say physical) dynamic of the spheres" (K, 97). This almost "physical" aspect of Kierkegaard's intellectual construct is precisely its sacrificial one, incarnated in his affirmation of Abraham as the notorious "teleological suspension of the ethical" in religious sacrifice (albeit miraculously transformed from human to animal, from one "kid" to another): the notorious Kierkegaardian construction of the sacrificial-religious as such. "Physical" may sound peculiar in this hyper-intellectual context of the relation between aesthetic, ethical, and religious spheres, or in the context of a Christian spiritualism, but we may recall that even in Christianity the sacrifice of the mass, while "purely" symbolic—a definite improvement over animal sacrifice, as Abraham's was over human sacrifice—retains the physical signs of bread and wine (whose symbolic status was of course at the center of the violent crisis of the reformation) for human flesh and blood. The mass bears the "figural" traces of physical sacrifice in the very gesture that abolishes physical sacrifice.[4] Here, mutatis mutandis, we observe that Adorno's deconstruction of Kierkegaard differs from Jacques Derrida's. Derrida assimilates

Kierkegaard's God to the structure of subjectivity or interiority conceived in terms of the relation to the "absolutely other," and conceives Abraham's sacrifice in terms of the instant of decision and absolute sacrificial "leap."[5] But this notion of the sacred as a structure of absolute otherness and incommensurability belongs firmly to that element in Kierkegaard that Adorno criticizes as a sacrificial mythology applied to reason itself, in which "the absolute difference of God is itself bound to [the illusion of] autonomous spirit as God's systematic negation" (K, 113). Mimesis, by contrast, always presupposes the kind of commensurability that properly belongs to the religious according to *The Concept of Dread*. Not absolute otherness and incommensurability provides the critical limit or "end" of reason, according to Adorno, but mimesis itself: "*Ratio* without mimesis is self-negating. Ends, the *raison d'être* of *raison,* are qualitative, and mimetic power is effectively the power of qualitative distinction."[6] To see how mimesis informs the sacrificial and the erotic in Kierkegaard, we turn now to *The Concept of Dread*.

Eroticism, Guilt, and Genius

The main body of *The Concept of Dread* advertises itself as a secular psychology of guilt or sin, as opposed to an ethics or religious dogmatics (represented in the introduction). But while dread is said to mediate the relation between possibility and actuality, psychology itself qua science is said to be idealistic: that is, it cannot deal with actuality or freedom as such, conceived as a synthesis of the ideal and material, but only with their possibility—in this case, thus, the possibility of possibility and the possibility of actuality.[7] Dogmatics, by contrast, presupposes the actuality of freedom and guilt or sin (like any conventional criminal justice system or ordinary ethical judgment).

   This redoubling of the argument, its attempt to conceive the concept of possibility to the second power, makes *The Concept of Dread* a notoriously difficult text in which rigor is difficult to distinguish from sophistry. Just as the *Philosophical Fragments* conceives history and freedom as a coming into existence within a coming into existence, a possibility within a possibility, so "dread is freedom's reality as a possibility for possibility" (CD1, 39). Hence Kierkegaard's psychology and its subject matter stand in a specular relation. Psychology cannot explain either freedom or sin (supposing these to exist); it can only posit their possibility. But this is exactly how dread is analyzed: as first positing the possibility of freedom, and then positing the further possibility of guilt as its consequence (CD1, 41). Dread, like psychology, is a *speculative* activity in which the mind reflects on itself. Dread defines a crucial aspect of the structure of *actual* speculation. Because the text constantly speaks in religious language and starts from the biblical account of the Fall, it is tempting to dismiss its claim to be "scientific" and psychological as opposed to dogmatic. But since its analysis of the structure of religious language and experience, as we shall see, is devoted very largely to a deconstruction of the very kind of sacrificial mythology that Adorno chides in his *Kierkegaard* (but which he also identifies as the most important and deceptive "content" of the religious paradox [K, 105]), and since the text constantly denies that it is providing any kind of ethical claim, it seems legitimate to regard it as providing in part an analysis of various manifestations of what nowadays might be called "guilt-complex," as well as a cluster of related psychological and psychosomatic phenomena—including shame, sexual modesty, masochism, and superstition. It is also notable that where Kierkegaard alludes directly to the New Testament in his analysis of the "demoniacal," he has nothing whatever to say about possession by the devil or any purely spiritual doctrine or superstition, but begins by alluding to such thoroughly psychosomatic disorders as "an exaggerated sensibility, an exaggerated irritability, nervous affections, hysteria, hypochondria, etc." (CD1, 122). Though the text makes no claim to explain these disorders as such or in detail, it does claim that they must be understood in relation to the kind of sacrificial aberrations that are its primary focus.

The Concept of Dread begins with the biblical Fall and its consequence in sexual shame or modesty (as the blush will be the central erotic motif in *Ehrengard*). But while it is emphatic about the significance of sexuality as an expression of spirit conceived as "a synthesis of the soulish and the bodily" (CD1, 39), it is careful to counter the "ethical misunderstanding of it as the sinful" (CD1, 63)—"by sin sensuousness became sinfulness" (CD1, 57)—ascribing this on the one hand to the idealist and anti-corporeal prejudice of rationalism (CD1, 53), and on the other to the Christian positing of sexuality as "the extreme point of the synthesis" between body and soul (CD1, 72). Nevertheless, we are told, "without sin there is no sexuality, and without sexuality no history" (CD1, 44), and "the concept of bashfulness (shame)" derives its structure from its initial content as an ignorance that is oriented toward this knowledge (CD1, 61). "In bashfulness there is dread" because spirit "is not merely qualified by relation to body but by relation to body with the generic difference," without this necessarily entailing any sexual impulse as such; hence "the dread in bashfulness is so prodigiously ambiguous" (CD1, 61), a dread present equally in ignorance of the erotic and "in all erotic enjoyment" (CD1, 64). In apparently dialectical terms, we are informed "with Greek candor" that dread belongs to the erotic experience because the latter is constituted by spirit (as synthesis) while simultaneously excluding spirit from its "culmination" (presumably copulation or orgasm) as though spirit were "a third party" compelled to hide itself (CD1, 64). As synthesis of body and mind, spirit expresses itself in the erotic experience as beauty; but as soon as spirit is posited in opposition to the body "the erotic is at an end. Hence the highest pagan expression is that the erotic is the comical"; and "the spirit's expression for the erotic is that it is at once beauty and the comical" (CD1, 62). I shall pass over here Kierkegaard's sacrificial suspension of sexuality in the service of its "paradoxical" preservation in Christian marriage, transfigured "in such a way that the sexual is forgotten and only remembered in forgetfulness" (CD1, 72). Like the teleological suspension of the ethical in *Fear and Trembling*, this suspension of the sexual in the service of its Christian preservation seems to have a sacrificial victim, here woman, whose "spiritual destiny" is associated with the most vulgar sexist stereotypes attributed alternately to scripture and to Romanticism: woman is more sensuous than man ("shown at once by her bodily organism"); "silence is not only woman's highest wisdom, but also her highest beauty"; "ethically regarded, woman culminates in procreation"; and so on (CD1, 58–60). In this connection, the passage cited earlier (from Adorno) concerning woman's immediate passage from erotic-aesthetic to religious spheres is arguably an index of her sacrificial status, and the "tedious vacuity" that Kierkegaard dialectically attributes to demoniacal dread could hardly find more banal expression than in these fortunately brief passages (which also betray, in their tendentious comparisons of Greek and Christian conceptions of gender, all the aberrance that Paul de Man, in his essay on "The Concept of Irony," attributes to Kierkegaard's historicism).[8] The Kierkegaard of "Against Christendom," who compares modern Christian marriage to a priest offering a couple a knife, provides an appropriately sacrificial antidote to this "Christian" view of gender.

The view of history and "spiritual destiny" proposed by Kierkegaard's analysis of dread or anxiety proper, however, is a different matter, providing a relentless critique of various modes of sacrificial ideology within as well as outside of Christian culture. The pagan world, first, is analyzed in terms of its self-fulfilling confusion of history and fate, which "may mean two things exactly opposite, since it is a unity of necessity and chance," a unity "ingeniously expressed by representing fate as blind, for that which walks forward blindly walks just as much by necessity as by chance" (CD1, 87). "One can say therefore of fate as Paul says of an idol, that 'it is nothing in the world'—but the idol nevertheless is the object of the pagan's religiousness." Fate, like the oracle, is studiously ambiguous, though the latter's tragedy obviously lies not in its ambiguity as such, "but in the fact that the pagan could not forbear to take counsel of it" (CD1, 87). Whereas the concept of guilt does not "in the deepest sense emerge in paganism," since, if it had, it "would have foundered upon the contradiction that one might become guilty by fate" (CD1, 87)—which would amount to a "mistaken concept of original sin" (CD1, 88)—sin, nevertheless, is akin to fate in coming into being "neither as a necessity nor by chance, and therefore to the concept of sin corresponds providence" (CD1, 88). (Note that in this analysis the conceptual difference between fate and providence is strictly limited to the positing of guilt as the possibility of freedom—as neither necessity nor chance—

and that any theological reification of providence in this context is therefore as unwarranted as that of fate itself.) Within the Christian world, "genius" represents the simultaneous perspicuity and aberrance of fate: "Fate is nothing; it is the genius himself who discovers it, and the deeper his genius is, the more deeply he discovers it; for that figure is merely the anticipation of providence" (CD1, 89). Though admittedly Kierkegaard leaves room for a higher or theological form of providence by artificially confining his definition of genius to "immediate spirit, which genius always is (only that it is immediate spirit *sensu eminentiori*)" (CD1, 88), in reality this merely means that "genius is outside the general" (CD1, 90), that is, that its positing of generality is always mediated by particular concretion, or that spirit is never posited beyond its definition as synthesis of the general and the concrete. However conceptually deep—and in proportion to the extent that concretion has previously served his genius—the genius is prone to be slave to the concrete: the military genius will fight only on the fourteenth of June "because that was the date of the Battle of Marengo" (CD1, 89). Note, nevertheless, that this *immediate* mimetic subservience—exaggerated, in part, because Kierkegaard wants to deflate genius in the service of the spiritual—finds a definite *reflective* analogy in his own analysis of what it means to say that "original sin is growing" (CD1, 47). It is growing because—while all sin requires a qualitative act of choice—quantitatively and "psychologically speaking" the "more" of sin that has come into existence since Adam has "a terrible significance," such that "the future seems to be anticipated by the past" (CD1, 82). The reflective mimesis posited here, which is *inductive*, takes on the same form as the immediate mimesis of genius, which is in essence a repetition compulsion. Wholly abstractly formulated (as in the case of sensuality), "the instant sin is posited, the temporal is sin" (CD1, 82); or in a psychological nutshell, *"dread of sin produces sin"* (CD1, 65).

The inductive psychology of sin, a reflective or Christianized transformation of fate into a demonic sense of providence, conforms to the structure of what René Girard, in his mimetic theory of sacrifice, calls "masochist induction" or self-fulfilling masochist prophecy. The mimetic structure here—no longer hidden by superstitious ciphers—is clarified in Kierkegaard's unpacking of the apparent psychological paradox concerning dread of sin: "Here the formula is: *The individual in dread, not of becoming guilty, but of being regarded as guilty, becomes guilty*"—"the utmost 'more' in this direction [being] that [an] individual from his earliest awakening is so placed and influenced that for him sensuousness has become identical with sin" (CD1, 67). Adorno complains that Kierkegaard's critique of Hegel's logicization of the concepts of mediation and transition is merely in the service of an opaque and idealistic notion of "the leap" (K, 90); but here the *actual* pattern of psychological mediation (however much Kierkegaard speaks of a leap "beyond psychology") is clear: either one imitates others (the masochist sensualist) or one imitates oneself (the genius, whose "autonomy" is just as rich in masochist self-fulfillment). Genius "is great by reason of its belief in fate, whether it conquers or falls, for it conquers by itself and falls by itself, or rather both come about by fate," and "he is never greater than when he falls by his own act," when he "discovers the doubtful reading in the text and then collapses" (CD1, 90). The doubtful reading may be a false alarm, but as Kafka concluded in "The Country Doctor" (a story also about the relation between archaic religion and modern sadomasochistic eroticism): "A false alarm on the night bell once answered—it cannot be made good, not ever."[9] The principle of mimetic mediation, we find, is everywhere in Kierkegaard's text the *actual* substitute for logical or dialectical mediation, and it everywhere meets us where (as Adorno puts it) the dialectic stops. Dialectically corresponding to genius in the Christian age (genius is technically also "spiritless" because defined as immediacy), the "spirit-less man" is superficially indistinguishable from the spirited one, "possess[ing] truth—not as truth, be it noted, but *as rumor and old wives' tales*" (CD1, 85, my emphasis) in a way "which corresponds exactly to pagan fetishism," except that "above all a charlatan is its real fetish" (CD1, 86), that is, a fetish raised to the second power, a worship of the mimetic principle itself. Meanwhile, if "dread dialectically determined in view of fate" (CD1, 86ff.) is thoroughly mimetic, "dread dialectically defined in view of guilt" (CD1, 92ff.) is thoroughly sacrificial: "To the oracle of paganism corresponds the sacrifice of Judaism" (CD1, 93). Indeed it is precisely the mimetic repetition of sacrifice that ultimately leads to "scepticism with respect to the act of sacrifice itself" (CD1, 93), since the need to repeat the sacrifice betrays its inefficacy. The Judaic (and pagan) sacrificial principle is ultimately discredited as based on a primitive confusion between being thought guilty and guilt, between mimetic semblance and reality, and between self and other, whereas the "higher" (Christian) form of guilt should not be a fear of "being thought guilty . . . but fear of being guilty" (CD1, 97). Nevertheless, we have just seen that the masochistic or self-sacrificial confusion of the two remains endemic to the Christian world, and the masochistic structure of sin remains fully operative in its properly Christian definition insofar as guilt is said to be posited by moral freedom precisely as a lack of freedom: "the opposite of freedom is guilt [not necessity]" (CD1, 97). Hence the "higher" dread of doing evil has its own pathologies, no less inductive in character than the "lower": notably, when "dread throws itself despairingly into the arms of remorse," which in turn "discovers the consequence before it comes" and masochistically "interprets the consequence of sin as penal suffering." "In other words, remorse has become insane" (CD1, 103). These, we are told, are some of "the psychological attitudes which freedom assumes towards sin, or *the psychological states approximating sin,*" which do not pretend "to explain sin ethically" (CD1, 105, my emphasis).

Whereas dread of evil "viewed from a higher standpoint, is in the good," and "the bondage of sin is an unfree relation to the evil," "the demoniacal [conceived as 'dread of the good'] is an unfree relation to the good" (CD1, 106). Here Kierkegaard takes his departure from the demons of the gospels, which are either "legion" or mute, arguing that mimetic multiplicity and "shut-upness" (CD1, 110) may equally signify demoniacal dread. But he is again careful to distinguish the demoniacal conceived as a psychological state or mental pathology from sin, especially insisting that "we must give up every fantastic notion of a pact with the devil, etc." (CD1, 109), which led formerly to a tendency to punish the sufferer. Accordingly, his exposition begins by juxtaposing the sacrificial severity employed in Christian tradition against the demoniac with the "therapeutic" purgation (powders, pills—"and then clysters!" [CD1, 108]) employed by modern physicians. The former is explained as the result of a spiritual over-identification with the sufferer ("convinced that after all in the last resort the demoniac himself . . . must wish that every cruelty and severity might be employed against him" [CD1, 108]), the latter by an over-physical and somatic, even genetic approach that under-identifies and hence also underestimates how "even divers of those men who want to deal with this phenomenon come themselves under the same category" (CD1, 109). The prodigious ambiguity of the demoniacal derives from the fact "that in a way it belongs to all spheres, the somatic, the psychic, the pneumatic," covering "a far greater field than is commonly supposed," and demonstrating how "a disorganization in one [sphere] shows itself in the others" (CD1, 109).

Without claiming to comprehend the myriad psychosomatic modes of what we might nowadays call "mania," Kierkegaard's analysis concentrates on two modes of discontinuity, defined in terms of "shut-upness" or reserve, and "the sudden." Muteness or reserve expresses itself as an increasingly compulsive tendency to talk to oneself and ultimately to "involuntary revelation" (CD1, 114–15), a compulsion that can be triggered by the most trivial contact. Indeed the category of "revelation" (with all its religious resonance) is here said to be "the same" (CD1, 113) whether it entails the most sublime or the most ridiculous, since both derive from the sheer positing (or mimetic) power of expression or communication as such: "Here applies the old saying, that if one dare utter the word, the enchantment of the magic spell is broken, and hence it is that the somnambulist wakes when his name is called" (CD1, 113). Meanwhile, inasmuch as "communication is in turn the expression for continuity, and the negation of continuity is the sudden" (CD1, 115), the latter is the temporal mode of that negation of continuity defined by reserve, a negation that precisely inasmuch as it recognizes no law is an expression of unfreedom (CD1, 116). In this connection, nota bene, mimesis is once more the principal category. Not only do we hear that "[m]imic art is able to express the sudden, though this does not imply that this art as such is the sudden," and that "the suddenness of the leap . . . lies within the compass of mimic art" (a demoniac parody of the qualitative leap itself), but that "*Mephistopheles is essentially mimic*" (CD1, 117, my emphasis). Hence the demoniac expresses itself as commonly in terms of "sociability" (CD1, 122) as in terms of superficial reserve; and insofar as the sudden cannot be fully reconciled with the representations of mimic art ("because that would interrupt the lines [of the mimetic drama]"), the demoniac can nevertheless equally be represented as "the vacuous, the tedious," which are comic expressions for reserve (CD1, 118–19).

Kierkegaard's mimetic definition of the devil explains much that would otherwise remain opaque in the text as a whole. His opening analysis of Genesis "associate[s] no definite thought with the serpent" (CD1, 43); indeed the lure to symbolic interpretation of the serpent is wittily regarded as itself a temptation of the serpent, a temptation specifically "to be *spirituel*" ("I am no lover of *esprit*" [CD1, 43]). Roger Poole's analysis of this problem of interpretation may be of help here because it implicitly chides previous commentary for failing sufficiently to recognize the problem. His own solution (appealing to an erudition that perceives in the Danish what is opaque to English readers) is disarmingly simple: observing the frequency of "s" sounds in the Danish original at this and other relevant points in the text, Poole suggests in deconstructivist or postmodernist fashion that we should identify the devil with this literal or textual hissing itself.[10] Here, one might say, is an interpretation of evil *à la lettre* with a vengeance! But Poole's chapter on *The Concept of Dread*—a chapter almost exclusively devoted to an empirical demonstration of this claim about the ubiquity of the textual hiss—offers an insight that might be regarded as instructive and misleading in almost equal measure. What is instructive is that his insistence on the material letter does go some way toward explaining Kierkegaard's own pointed repudiation of "esprit" and the "spirituel" at this juncture—though Poole does not draw attention to this detail as such. What is misleading, however, is that his interpretation is presented as though it stood independent of Kierkegaard's own argument in general and, rather astonishingly, without any reference to the subsequent mimetic definition of evil in particular. By contrast, I claim that the refusal to be tempted by symbolic interpretation of the serpent follows directly from the mimetic definition of the devil, who might therefore in principle be represented in any form whatsoever and must strictly speaking be represented by none. Precisely the temptation to externalize temptation as though "it come[s] from without" (CD1, 43) is at issue; or, more precisely (inasmuch as mimetic temptation *does* in one sense come from without), to essentialize and reify a mere form, to *spiritualize the material*. Poole is thus quite right in his textualist insistence on material form, but quite misguided to divorce this materialism from the mimetic principle that indeed explains in precisely what sense, according to Kierkegaard's reasoning (as Adorno recognized), the "materialist" explanation of "spiritual" phenomena is precisely the right one.

While Kierkegaard makes no claim to explain guilt ethically, mimetic mediation is everywhere the limit of his psychological dialectic. This illuminates not only such metaphorical details as where fate is called the "secret friend" of genius—as though fate were not merely something, but *someone* to be imitated—but also the entire conceptual genealogy of original sin. Rejecting the notion that Adam is tempted from without—either by the serpent or by God's prohibition ("even though it is certain both from pagan and from Christian experience that man's desire is for the forbidden" [CD1, 37])—Kierkegaard constructs his analysis on a mimetic logic that mediates relations between external and internal along the "materialist" lines suggested above. Thus his interpretation of Eve's mediation, while maintaining that dread is more natural to woman than to man, denies that this is an imperfection: "If there is to be any question of imperfection, it consists in something else, namely, in the fact that in dread she seeks support beyond herself in another, in man" (CD1, 42). Similarly, Adam's first sin derives from his reversal of this "natural" pattern of mimetic dependence; but the argument from woman's natural weakness is only provisional since "Adam and Eve are merely a numerical repetition" (CD1, 42), entirely equal from the perspective of spirit, and it is the pattern of repetition itself that is ultimately decisive. Thus when the predisposition to sinfulness is located in the fact of generation, the hackneyed issue of sexual desire (and the desire for the prohibited, for transgression) takes backseat to quantitative or material reproduction as such: "*It is the fact of being derived which predisposes the individual* [to sin], without for all that making him guilty" (CD1, 43).

More strikingly still—especially since Kierkegaard here emancipates himself altogether from the biblical myth (which is described as externalizing what is internal)—when it comes to explaining in precisely what sense Adam himself is neither tempted nor punished from without, we are told:

> This naturally has tormented many thinkers. The difficulty, however, is one we need only smile at. Innocence is indeed well able to talk, inasmuch as in language it possesses the expression for everything in the spiritual order. In view of this one need only assume that Adam talked with himself. The imperfection in the [biblical] account, that another speaks to Adam about what he does not understand, is thus eliminated. Adam was able to talk. From this it does not follow that in a deeper sense he was able to understand the word uttered. This applies above all to the distinction between good and evil, which is made in language, to be sure, but is only intelligible to freedom. (CD1, 41)

We face in this passage a linguistic materialism that not only explicitly divorces language from understanding, and is presented as the limit of psychological analysis (CD1, 41), but also explains why "the existence in this sense of a thousand Adams signifies no more than one" (CD1, 42). Kierkegaard's supposed existentialist individualism is accordingly not (or at least not here) in any genuine contradiction with a collectivist or evolutionary conception of the origin of language; on the contrary, Adam's language is explicitly compared both to "a kind as imperfect as that of children when they are learning to recognize an animal on the ABC card" (CD1, 42) and to the mimeticism of the animal that "is able to understand the mimic expression and movement in the speaker's voice, without understanding the word" (CD1, 40–41). Hence too, like Kafka in "Investigations of a Dog,"[11] Kierkegaard rejects pseudo-scientific talk of egoism or self-interest as "dissolv[ing] into tautology, or else one resorts to *esprit*" in continuity with the kind of natural philosophy that "has found this egoism in the whole creation" (CD1, 70): "when one would explain sin by selfishness, one becomes involved in confusions, since on the contrary it is true that by sin and in sin selfishness comes into being" (CD1, 71). Such selfishness is merely the dialectical equivalent of demoniac sociability, of collectivity, so that bondage to sin is compared precisely to "a game men play where two are concealed under a cloak, *appearing to be one person,* and while one speaks the other gesticulates without any pertinence to what is being said" (CD1, 106, my emphasis). The innate sinfulness of selfishness and sexuality are intertwined masochist misinterpretations conterminous with the mimetic ("satanic") deformations of collective history.

★　★　★

Paul de Man's essay "The Concept of Irony" praises Friedrich Schlegel's philosophical allegory of sex in *Lucinde*—of "making the beast with two backs" (as the phrase goes)—for its deployment of literal and figural, physical and symbolic, modes that fail to achieve synthesis: sex here is focus of a radical irony that "represents a threat to all assumptions one has about what a text should be"[12] because it exposes the arbitrariness of relations between the (literal) body and the (ideal) figure. Though crediting Kierkegaard's *The Concept of Irony* as "the best book on irony that's available,"[13] he accuses Kierkegaard's "historicism" of attempting, in his reading of Schlegel and others, to repress the irony that he elsewhere so well understands. However, here at least, far from sheltering history from the mimetic-sacrificial arbitrariness or "impertinence" of the relation of matter and mind, of gesture and voice, body and figure, as de Man alleges—the mimetic fusion of Kierkegaard's cloaked men is (as Shakespeare says of love) "at random from the truth"—Kierkegaard squarely makes that relation into the origin and engine of human history.[14]

Isak Dinesen and Johannes the Seducer

I turn now to Dinesen's *Ehrengard* because it shows to what extent sacrificial mimesis is also at stake in her revolutionary elaboration of the "Diary of a

Seducer," where the artist, Herr Cazotte, is the mimetic-sacrificial focus, playing the mediatory role of both the genius and "Satan" in the garden of Venusberg, and where his erotic mediation is skillfully interwoven with the development of political history. The central problem of artistic interpretation in the tale—Cazotte twice confronts Ehrengard in front of a statue of Leda and the Swan—concerns how one reacts, or should react, to a mimesis of rape: a "symbolic rape." Cazotte's own picture of Ehrengard, titled *The Bath of Diana,* might be said to be symbolic rape to the second power (Diana's violation being visual). At the center of the story, Dinesen's concern, like Kierkegaard's, is the relation between literal and symbolic, physical and psychological violence—imaged by the relation, as Cazotte puts it, between *blood outside and inside the human body* (in particular between violence and sexuality). Cazotte, following Johannes's stricture that "artistic" seducers aim not necessarily for physical penetration, but for whatever consummation is artistically appropriate to the women in question, sets out to produce in Ehrengard *symbolic blood,* blood *inside* the body, a blush.

Dinesen's novella is normally, and up to a point correctly, read as a kind of feminist response to Kierkegaard's novella in *Either–Or.* Cazotte plays the role of a Johannes (though his Christian names, Johann Wolfgang, are significantly those of Goethe)[15] who attempts to seduce Ehrengard by painting her nude portrait without her knowledge, hoping that she will privately recognize herself in the picture (she will be shown from behind), blush rose-pink like the lights of the Alpen-Gluhen, and be "fallen, broken and lost." Even though she will marry another, this will be her erotic initiation, and Cazotte's role, he flatters himself, will be irreplaceable: her erotic sacrifice to him will provide the model and engine of her erotic life.[16] Perhaps. But Ehrengard discovers that Cazotte's picture of her bathing every morning is under way, and instead of responding like the masculinized Diana (dismembering her voyeuristic "rapist"), she gives him permission to continue; while he in turn reports this in a letter to an older woman friend, signing himself "Yours in fear and trembling" (E, 257). Thus a connection is established between the sacrificial eroticism of *Either–Or* and the religious sacrifice of Kierkegaard's Abraham. The feminist ambivalence here, just as in Ehrengard's reaction to the sculpture of Leda, lies in the fact that she acquiesces to the "form" of rape in the very assertion of feminine agency (like Diana she is "masculinized") that overturns actual relations of dominance and submission.

Meanwhile, a reversal of the Johannes fantasy of erotic dominance (Johannes himself insists that gender opposition is in large part an "artistic fiction," a kind of "myth of nature") takes place via a political subplot that concerns the conceivable end of Germanic principalities and their dynasties (the date being roughly 1840).[17] Cazotte has successfully initiated Prince Lothar into the erotic, just as he hopes to initiate Ehrengard, by acting as mimetic model to this young man (who is first described in feminized terms reminiscent of a Victorian virgin, indifferent to sex, twin to the masculinized

Ehrengard) so that he marries and provides an heir. Since the child is conceived prior to the marriage, its existence has to be kept secret in the court
of Venusberg; and when it is kidnapped by a competing branch of the family,
Ehrengard takes matters into her own hands, follows the child on a horse
named Wotan (like Venus mastering Mars), symbolically castrates the kidnapper by bloodying his nose—a castration story that occurred in the same
room is explicitly recounted—and is then discovered in the Blue Boar Inn
(recalling the castrating boar of Venus and Adonis?) by her fiancé, Kurt.
Unable to tell him immediately (for political reasons) who the child really
is, she is saved by the arrival of Cazotte, whom she pretends has fathered
the child with her—and at this point the painter blushes deeply, thus bluntly
reversing the original plan of seduction (E, 268ff.). Here we have the quasi-
feminist reversal.

This reversal seems clear enough when compared to the apparently vulgar
chauvinist consummation of the "Diary," where Johannes, having presumably finally copulated with Cordelia, reflects that women in her position
might rather wish to be transformed into plants (as per the sacrificial metamorphoses of Greek myth) than continue to live on. At the end of *Ehrengard,*
in a kind of coda, Cazotte is pointedly absent from Ehrengard's wedding,
having an affair with an actress in Rome while painting a portrait of the
pope. (Perhaps it would be too painful to be present; perhaps the actress is
an antidote to Ehrengard. . . . Dinesen's refusal to interpret is as pointed as
the pointed details.) The reversal, however, is not simple: Ehrengard, after
all, has put her trust in Cazotte, positing a symbolic copulation between
them that causes him to blush instead of going pale at the thought of the
inevitable challenge to a duel with Kurt. The blush itself, image of symbolic
violence, blood *inside* the body—beauty, as *Much Ado about Nothing* puts it,
"printed in blood"—is a traditional emblem of interpretive ambivalence,
signifying innocence and guilt, modesty and shame, resistance and complicity,
and so on. Like absence of blood on the wedding sheet in Dinesen's "The
Blank Page" (as we shall see momentarily), it means "nothing," being constituted by potentially contradictory meanings. Similarly, when Cazotte first
asks Ehrengard what she is thinking in front of the statue of Leda and the
Swan, she reddens slightly and says "nothing" (E, 243)—and Cazotte tells
us he believes her (though saying one is thinking of "nothing" is usually a
euphemism, and the slight blush might seem to signify just that). The second
time they pass the statue—these two occasions are clearly pivotal to the
overall structure of the story—he again wonders if she is thinking nothing;
and it is at this point that she turns slightly pale and encourages him to finish
his picture (actively acquiesces to her symbolic "rape") while he signs his
epistolary account of these events "In fear and trembling." As in Kierkegaard's book of that title, "fear and trembling" seems to signify an acknowledgment of the sacrificial form or structure at stake in the very narrative

that leads to the overturning or attenuation of sacrificial violence, the acknowledgment of reciprocity. The signs of red and white (as in Shakespeare's *Venus and Adonis*) are *pharmacological* signs—ambivalent like the mimetic *pharmaka* famously analyzed by Derrida in Plato, and connected even etymologically (as both Derrida and Girard have stressed in that context) to the ambivalence of the *pharmakos,* the sacrificial victim. Like the *pharmakos* in Girard's theory, the blush is both guilty and innocent at the same time.[18]

"The Blank Page" confirms this pattern.[19] The best stories, we are told, say "nothing," just as the blank royal wedding sheet hung out by the nuns, along with all the bloodied ones, says "nothing": it means either that the bride was not a virgin or is merely accidental, a quirk of physiology. (The parallel with *Ehrengard* is further emphasized by the image of the holy ghost descending on the virgin Mary with beating wings, like Zeus raping Leda, just as *Ehrengard* itself superimposes images of the holy family on Greek myth, the virgin Mary on the modest Diana, and so on. Both stories are told by old women who, like the nuns, have sacrificed the physical erotic.) The best stories say "nothing," we are told, not because they are really void of content, but because their meaning is mediated by something outside the story, excluded from the representation as such—as the marriages of Lothar and Ludmilla, Ehrengard and Kurt, are mediated by Cazotte, and marriage in "The Blank Page" is monitored by the nuns. Cazotte, it will be said, is a seducer; the nuns chaste. But here lies the key to Dinesen's choice of Cazotte's subject matter: alternately nudes and Catholic priests. The erotic can be understood only in relation to what is excluded from the erotic, marriage in relation to what is excluded from marriage. The pattern is homologous with that of Girardian sacrifice, where legitimate structures are always mediated by the excluded scapegoat—or with the mimetic-sacrificial structure of Samuel Beckett's *Molloy* (to take a systematic example of psychical geography) where "Turdybaba" means the environs of the town Turdy exclusive of the town, the excluded mediator, Turdy itself.[20]

The question of who has "ravished" whom, the individual psychology of *Ehrengard* such as it is, accordingly gives way to a more general pattern of structural mediation. Cazotte follows Johannes in purporting to provide a "theory" of erotics and aesthetics—an erotic aesthetics—situated at the juncture of such quasi-polar opposites as theory and practice, reflection and immediacy, ideal and material, abstract and concrete, symbolic and literal, musical and visual, and so on (E, 219ff.). (Cazotte is compared to Pan both because Pan is cloven-hooved like the devil, and because he is a musician. He is named after a poet, Goethe, among other things because he provides the literary synthesis, so to speak, of painting and music: Dinesen's text itself, about a painter, is explicitly staged in musical movements.) Other dualisms such as red/white, Protestant/Catholic, Christian/pagan, serious/comic, military/erotic, religious/erotic, and so on are also at play. Dinesen's text mimics

Kierkegaardian dialectic and, like Kierkegaard, provides no dialectical solution (recall his attack on Hegelian mediation as merely abstract), but rather focuses on the mimetic-sacrificial figure as such, Cazotte, as essential mediator. Cazotte opens the story as a mimetic model in the Girardian sense: he is the erotic model required for Lothar to desire erotically. He is also necessary—in Dinesen's narrative, not merely his own fantasy—to the eroticization of the relation between Ehrengard and her fiancé (hitherto relating "platonically," as brother and sister). As mimetic model, he reminds us of the mimic "essence" of the devil in *The Concept of Dread*: he himself says he is the snake in the garden of Venusberg necessary to provide a properly objective view of paradise and a moral education for Ehrengard, who hitherto has accepted conventional morality, that of her warrior family, as a kind of codicil of nature (E, 232). Like the mimetic *pharmakon* in Plato, Cazotte—principle of both artistic and erotic mimesis—is both "moral" and "satanic." He is the poison necessary for the cure.

In *Either–Or*, as cited in my epigraph, A generalizes the principle of triangular mediation when he defines a friend, not as what philosophy calls the necessary other (a properly dialectical relation), but rather "the superfluous third."[21] Johannes implements this principle when he traitorously befriends and becomes amorous adviser to Cordelia's would-be lover Edward, accurately predicting that this will greatly facilitate transference. (Incidentally, Joakim Garff has recently made the original argument that such transference does not stop with volume 1, and that Judge Wilhelm's peculiar "ethical" interest in Johannes/A may have something to do with his wife's interest in the same direction.)[22] But while *Ehrengard* may thus be said to use the mimetic indications of *Either–Or* as springboard, Dinesen generalizes and expands the mimetic principle in a way that amounts to a genuinely original meditation on that text, and which might recall the openly pandemic mimetic principle of *The Concept of Dread* rather than anything fully explicit in *Either–Or* itself. To be sure, Kierkegaard's ethical and religious pseudonyms emphasize the dread and despair that lurk repressed behind the putatively aesthetic perspective of Johannes and his like, the masochist element implicit in his quasi-sadistic assertion of erotic dominance. But Cazotte's structural role is more important than his personal feelings; he conjoins the erotic and religious in his paintings, and his ethical position cannot be reduced to the "amorality" apparently espoused by Johannes. He appears not only to accept with grace the reversal of roles that the story metes out to him, but to understand that this structural possibility is inherent in the *symbolics of blood*, the blush itself. In "fear and trembling," he understands that his role is also sacrificial. Necessary to the "legitimate" marriages of the text, he is excluded from legitimate eros, like the priests and cardinals he paints alongside his nudes.

That Dinesen is concerned with the sacrificial structure of exclusion, beyond any simple feminist reversal, is demonstrated by a striking detail that has to do precisely with Cazotte's "femininity." Johannes himself recommends that the male seducer adopt a certain strategic "feminine modesty" to blunt his masculine features, but in Cazotte's case this goes much further than strategy, and straightforward readings of the undoing of his "chauvinism" must eventually run up against the problem that, in the context of Cazotte's mimetic role, the opposition between male and female is no more stable than that between red and white, erotic and religious, good and bad, musical and painterly, and so on—both Ehrengard and Lothar, as previously mentioned, are evidently "cross-gendered" like Diana. Accordingly, Dinesen gives Cazotte a mother but no father, and this leads ingeniously to one of the central tropes of the text when he fantasizes that Ehrengard's military father is his own, making their relation into a kind of "heavenly incest" (E, 247). The movement from male to female is associated with a movement from violence to symbolic violence (chess metaphors are prominent at this point), from war (rape) to love (art)—tropes that are traditional enough (also recalling the proverbial "androgyny" of the artist figure). But the trope of incest is startling and very much Dinesen's own: here we see the fundamental importance of the sacrificial structure whereby legitimate erotic (and religious) relations are founded on illegitimate ones, and, in the case of incest, perhaps *the* illegitimate one. (We may recall Beatrice's objection to marriage in *Much Ado about Nothing,* that all men are her brothers.) In most religions, like the Greek, incest is indeed "heavenly"—regularly performed by the gods though outlawed to humans. (Girard argues that this accords with his sacrificial theory whereby the gods, and holy men like Oedipus, are originally scapegoat figures, routinely accused of all the worst crimes like parricide and incest before being transfigured into *pharmacological* principles of the sacred.) The relation between Cazotte and Ehrengard is imaged in terms of at least three major transgressions: incest, rape, and infidelity. This relation, crucial to the story, must itself be sacrificed by the story—or, to be precise, enacted only symbolically, in a "heavenly" way. The "happy endings" of the tale (which is itself described as a comedy *or* tragedy, *pharmakon*-like) are predicated on this sacrifice, this "incestuous" exclusion of the very figure that has made them possible. Like the devil in *The Concept of Dread,* as we have seen, Cazotte's role as "Satan" is essentially mimic or mimetic—Dinesen's "reply" to Kierkegaard's seducer is deeply Kierkegaardian. The principle of mimesis, the poet-painter-musician-devil (Goethe/Cazotte/Pan), is now—as in Plato, mutatis mutandis—the *pharmakon/pharmakos* necessary to both political stability (the tenuous continuation of the aristocracy) and erotic development. I have said that the mimetic-sacrificial structure of the text is more general in significance than its "feminist" reversal as such. But Dinesen clearly *is* concerned with the problem of the relation between social and sexual emancipation: she superimposes, so to speak, Ehrengard's emancipation (dated carefully in the nineteenth century) on the classical mythical models of Diana, Venus, and Leda, and the Christian Virgin—and no doubt by implication too, on the so-called sexual revolution of the early 1960s, the period of composition. Ehrengard's complicity in the composition of *The Bath of Diana* shows why the mimesis of Leda's rape is the "nothing" at the heart of the tale. Regarded thematically, the statue depicts (divine) rape; regarded "musically," so to speak, it offers the bare form of sexual intercourse, a mere mimesis of rape. Put bluntly, Cazotte's question to Ehrengard in front of the statue might be formulated: "What do you think of the *form* of sexual intercourse?" (This is the kind of question taken up nowadays by so-called pro-sex feminism.) Mimesis as such means "nothing."

Taken together, *The Concept of Dread* and Dinesen's response to the "Diary of a Seducer" unfold a remarkably relentless sacrificial analysis of eroticism and so-called aesthetics—one that is perhaps implicit in *Either–Or* as a whole (as Adorno claimed) but whose mimetic structure is arguably concealed by the bifurcation into the deconstructive "aesthetic" modes of the *Either* and the "ethical" modes of the *Or* (in the journals Kierkegaard himself frankly identifies ethics with the domain of imitation), and whose sacrificial structure is formally announced only in the "religious" texts. In *Ehrengard* and *The Concept of Dread,* in any event, the erotic turns out to be the focus of a mimetic-sacrificial principle that not only explodes aesthetics in the conventional sense (as the *Either* already implies)—the analysis of "genius" in *The Concept of Dread* is more like a pathology of superstition and masochism than an ordinary aesthetics—but makes of the erotic a form, perhaps *the* modern form, of the sacred in a Girardian sense. As in Kafka's "A Country Doctor," modern sexuality turns out to be a secularized and sadomasochistic mutation of sacred violence, a kind of *pharmakon*-cure for its own disease.[23] Hence my opening epigraph from Kierkegaard himself: "The relation to the opposite sex has also been made into the meaning and earnest of life—into true Christianity."

Notes

1. René Girard's views are well known, and his mimetic-sacrificial theory of religion and sexuality can be found throughout his work. Adorno does not enjoy the best of reputations among Kierkegaardians: at the March 2001 International Kierkegaard Forum at Augusta State University, for example, the Derridean Mark Dooley (whose interesting paper I introduced) made it publicly clear he thought Adorno one of the very worst guides to understanding Kierkegaard. Roger Poole, in private conversation, seemed similarly to regard Adorno's critique of Kierkegaard as predictably Marxist and uninteresting.

2. See the introduction to Theodor Adorno, *Kierkegaard: Construction of the Aesthetic,* ed. and trans. Robert Hullot-Kentor (Minneapolis: University of Minnesota Press, 1989). Henceforth K.

3. John Vignaux Smyth, "Sacrificial Materialism in Kierkegaard and Adorno," in *Idealism without Absolutes: Philosophy and Romantic Culture,* ed. Arkadi Plotnitsky (Albany: State University of New York Press, 2003).

4. *Pace* Adorno, Burke, Derrida, and many others, John Milbank, in "The Sublime in Kierkegaard," in *Post-Secular Philosophy: Between Philosophy and Theology,* ed. Philip Blond (London: Routledge, 1998), 131–56, makes a brave and up to a point compelling argument for reading Kierkegaard's portrayal of "Abraham's sacrifice of Isaac as an anti-sacrifice because it is a completely pointless sacrifice . . . not at all a foundational sacrifice" in service of "the institution of the *polis,*" "a self-cancelling will to sacrifice, since undertaken in the conviction that the moment of sacrifice will never arrive" (144). However great the anti-sacrificial tension in Kierkegaard's "trembling" account, it must nevertheless be observed that the moment of sacrifice does arrive for the surrogate ram, whatever Abraham's "convictions" about his son. (Mark Dooley's response to my question at the March 2001 International Kierkegaard Forum at Augusta about the sacrificial "content" of *Fear and Trembling,* that its sacrificial theme is primarily "metaphorical," seems to me correct only insofar as the structure of sacrifice is itself "metaphorical," substituting animal for human, bread and wine for flesh and blood, and so on.)

5. Theodor Adorno, *Aesthetic Theory,* ed. and trans. Robert Hullot-Kentor (Minneapolis: University of Minnesota Press, 1997), 331.

6. Jacques Derrida, "Whom to Give to (Knowing Not to Know)," in *Kierkegaard: A Critical Reader,* ed. Jonathan Rée and Jane Chamberlain (Oxford: Blackwell, 1998), 53–74.

7. Søren Kierkegaard, *The Concept of Dread,* trans. Walter Lowrie (Princeton, N.J.: Princeton University Press, 1957), 44–45. Henceforth CD1.

8. Paul de Man, "The Concept of Irony," in *Aesthetic Ideology,* ed. Andrzej Warminski (Minneapolis: University of Minnesota Press, 1996), 163. (All this sexual stereotyping, moreover, is proposed in the face of Kierkegaard's insistence that Christian spirit does not recognize sexual opposition as such, and that Christ is accordingly never tempted sexually [CD1, 71].)

9. Franz Kafka, *Complete Stories,* ed. Nahum N. Glatzer (New York: Schocken, 1971), 225. For an indication of the remarkably explicit mimetic-sacrificial structure of "The Country Doctor," see my "Music Theory in Late Kafka," *Angelaki* 3, no. 2 (1998): 169–81.

10. See Roger Poole's chapter on *The Concept of Dread* in *Kierkegaard: The Indirect Communication* (Charlottesville: University Press of Virginia, 1993).

11. "I know that it is not one of the virtues of dogdom to share with others food that one has once gained possession of. . . . [T]hat is not selfishness, but the opposite, dog law, the unanimous decision of the people, the outcome of their victory over egoism, for the possessors are always in a minority" (Kafka, *Complete Stories,* 288). This "victory over egoism," nota bene, is the consequence of mimetic unanimity.

12. De Man, "Concept of Irony," 169.

13. Ibid.

14. De Man remarks that Schlegel's passage, a section of *Lucinde* called "A Reflection," "got Hegel and Kierkegaard and philosophers in general, and other

people too, very upset." The basic problem is not that Schlegel allegorizes philosophy as sex, which is fully "worthy of [philosophical or dialectical discourse]," but as "something much more specific than that [the act of coition]," combining two "radically incompatible" codes, physical and philosophic/psychic (169). Yet we have just seen in *The Concept of Dread* a specific allusion to the "culmination" of what de Man coyly calls "something much more specific," something that explicitly expels the spirit as "third party" from the very dialectical synthesis of body and soul that is supposed to constitute it. Indeed, none other than Friedrich Schegel is cited (in connection with the relation of modesty and lust) on the very same page in which Kierkegaard underlines "the prodigious contradiction that the immortal spirit is characterized as sex."

15. Roger Poole's original suggestion, made at the March 2001 International Kierkegaard Forum in Augusta, that Goethe is important to the structure of *Either–Or* finds rich confirmation in Dinesen's choice of names.

16. "Ehrengard," in *Anecdotes of Destiny and Ehrengard* (New York: Vintage, 1993), 234, 245. Henceforth E.

17. The opening line of the story begins: "One hundred and twenty years ago." The posthumous date of publication is 1962.

18. Similarly, *pharmakon* means both "poison" and "remedy" (as applied to writing and mimesis in Plato). Girard invokes Derrida on this topic in *Violence and the Sacred,* trans. Patrick Gregory (Baltimore: Johns Hopkins University Press, 1978), 296–97. Derrida's famous analysis occurs in "La Pharmacie de Platon," in *La Dissemination* (Paris: Editions du Seuil, 1972).

19. Dinesen, *Last Tales* (New York: Vintage, 1991), 99–105. Since the story is so short, I have omitted specific page references.

20. See Smyth, *The Habit of Lying: Sacrificial Studies in Literature, Philosophy, and Fashion Theory* (Durham, N.C.: Duke University Press, 2002), ch. 5, for analysis of this mimetic-sacrificial pattern in Beckett.

21. This definition of friendship occurs in "The Rotation Method," the ironic essay that identifies aesthetics with arbitrariness.

22. I refer to Garff's lecture at the March 2001 International Kierkegaard Forum at Augusta, "The esthetic is above all my element."

23. See note 9.

11

KIERKEGAARD AND DERRIDA: BETWEEN TOTALITY AND INFINITY

Mark Dooley

IN A NUMBER OF RECENT PUBLICATIONS,[1] I have suggested that the most appropriate way to consider the similarities between Kierkegaard and Derrida is to determine how they each differ from Levinas. On my interpretation, the claim that Kierkegaard has much more in common with Levinas than with Derrida ignores the vast differences that obtain between Kierkegaard and Levinas at a philosophical, political, and religious level, differences that are not so obvious in the case of the Kierkegaard-Derrida relationship. The same rejoinder can be mounted against those who claim that Derrida has much more in common with Levinas than he does with Kierkegaard. While there is, of course, an affinity between Levinas and Derrida, there are once again differences that, I contend, make all the difference.

I can metaphorically encapsulate what I am arguing here by saying that if all three thinkers strive to deconstruct the borders separating Athens from Jerusalem, Levinas does so because he ultimately wishes to sack Athens and reclaim the Holy City, while Kierkegaard and Derrida, on the other hand, simply want to afford free passage to those intending to travel between the two. Unlike Levinas, who identifies Hegel as a reductio ad absurdum of philosophy's hubristic attempt to assimilate and incorporate difference and otherness, Kierkegaard and Derrida, while no less worried by Hegel's totalizing tendencies, are nevertheless significantly more Hegelian in their approach. All three, that is, take issue with Hegel because he is insufficiently Jewish, or because he privileges Greek above Jew and philosophy above religion. But if Kierkegaard and Derrida share Levinas's concerns in this regard, they are still thinkers who owe more of a debt to Hegel than to anyone else. On my reading, thus, Derrida and Kierkegaard are figures committed to ensuring that the system remains open, that it remains free of the homogenizing impulses of onto-theology, and that it safeguards the interests of the singular in the face of the universal. This does not mean, however, as is the case with Levinas, that they want to occupy a site outside the system, but rather that they seek to sensitize it to the fact that it is without beginning and without end, that it is without any clearly identifiable origin or final telos.

In stating all of this, I am cognizant of the fact that in "Existence and Ethics"[2] Levinas chides Kierkegaard for not being sufficiently Hegelian, and also that Derrida in the course of his discussion of Kierkegaard in *The Gift of Death*,[3] tries to urge us to read Kierkegaard and Levinas as thinkers for whom the religious and the ethical are somewhat synonymous. Such considerations do not, however, alter my belief that Kierkegaard and Derrida lie between the two extremes of Hegel and Levinas. For, in the first instance, I think that Levinas's critique of Kierkegaard in "Existence and Ethics" is predicated upon a plethora of the most alarming misconceptions and misconstructions, the result of which is probably the most unfortunate reading of Kierkegaard available in the contemporary literature. Second, it is true, as Derrida argues, that there is no clear distinction between the ethical and the religious for both Kierkegaard and Levinas. But we should abjure from making too much of this, for there are subtle yet important differences between what Kierkegaard means by the ethical and the religious and what Levinas means when he employs the same terminology. What I think we should take from Derrida's observation is that there are a number of thinkers—Ricoeur, Marion, Levinas, Kierkegaard, and Derrida himself—for whom the distinction between the ethical and the religious is more than a little fuzzy. This should not, however, blind us to the fact that each of these philosophers employs very singular and specific definitions of ethics and religion that, in many cases, bear only ostensive similarity to one another.

With that acknowledged, let me now say a little about why my attempt to forge a stronger alliance between Kierkegaard and Derrida, as figures who occupy a place between Hegel's Athens and Levinas's Jerusalem, exercises both Derrideans and Kierkegaardians alike. That is, in showing why I have earned the censure of certain Derrideans and some Kierkegaardians, I hope to be in a better position to say why I think both factions have been looking at the wrong point of contact between Kierkegaard and Derrida, and also to say why I think it might better serve the purposes of both groups to rethink the nature of this relationship.

For a number of years, I have found myself in the position of trying, on the one hand, to convince Derrideans that Kierkegaard is more deconstructive than they tend to believe, and that ultimately Derrida shares much more with Kierkegaard than with Levinas, as well as trying to convince Kierkegaardians of the strict observance that Derrida is much more akin to Kierkegaard than they have heretofore presupposed. While many Derrideans tend to be sympathetic toward Kierkegaard, they are not prepared to go the distance with me when I say that the latter has a notion of politics and the state that is deconstructive through and through. For them, Kierkegaard, while sharing many literary and even proto-ethical tactics and insights with

Derrida, is nonetheless still too individualistic, isolationist, and inward-looking to be considered a full-fledged deconstructionist. In other words, he lacks what is essential for those of a deconstructive mind-set—the stress on the social, relational, and cultural network in which all selves are situated. According to Kierkegaard, so their argument goes, what is fundamental is one's personal relationship to God at the expense of the relationship to the neighbor. As such, there is too much stress on inwardness to the detriment of one's social alliances.

Moreover, Kierkegaard's appeal to Christianity, they continue, renders him insufficiently undecidable in matters of faith; unlike Derrida who privileges a messianic openness to the future above any determinate messianism or concrete religious structure, Kierkegaard is too confident that salvation is to be gained through Christianity alone. He is, in short, too Christocentric, in that he favors the militancy of a Pauline Christianity over and above the gentle appeal to the other in whose face is marked the trace of God. In this, as John Caputo argues, he has much more in common with the early Heidegger whose Christianity assumes a strident form than with Derrida's quasi-Jewish Augustinianism. This accusation assumes its most visceral form in Levinas's critique of Kierkegaard cited earlier. For him, Kierkegaard initiated a philosophy of the hammer that was eventually to result in Heidegger's collusion with Nazism. For Levinas, Kierkegaard's extreme agonizing over his own self, without sufficient regard to his responsibility to others, is what generated the violence of the "teleological suspension of the ethical." This is, alas, an interpretation that still has some life left in it.

If Derrideans are, therefore, suspicious of Kierkegaard because of his robust individualism, his strident Lutheranism, and his violence, Kierkegaardians are no less suspicious of Derrida for what they see as his trivializing of the tradition, his whimsical approach to serious philosophical, ethical, and theological issues, and his general insouciance about the implications of his work for society and the academy. Whereas Kierkegaard has a notion of selfhood that accommodates others, Derrida has, they argue, no such sense of self. His is not so much a deconstruction as a *destruction* of selfhood, community, and value. As such, he bears a greater resemblance to the aesthete of volume 1 of *Either–Or*, for whom endless play is substituted for meaningful reflection on the self and its role in society.

For both Sylvia Walsh and Ronald Hall,[4] Derrida is an irresponsible ironist, one for whom questions of truth and ultimate meaning are irrelevant. Unlike Socrates whom Kierkegaard lauds as a positive ironist, Derrida ironizes simply for its own sake without regard to the consequences. He affirms nothing in the process of decrying everything. Consequently, he is without commitment, preference, or earnestness. Deconstruction, thus, encourages nihilism, a total abnegation of the self, and political anarchy. If they are correct in this, such Kierkegaardians argue, all attempts to demonstrate that

Kierkegaard is a proto-deconstructionist are doing the latter more ill than good.

What I wish to argue for the remainder of this paper is that the Derrideans and Kierkegaardians about whom I have spoken paint pictures of both figures that amount to little more than caricatures. In so doing, they have failed to spot that what is most essential in both authors is that which allies them most significantly. If people like Walsh and Hall could let go of their deep suspicions of Derrida as a sneering nihilistic iconoclast, if they could loosen the Lutheran straitjacket in which their Kierkegaard is entrapped, and if Derrideans could begin to see that Kierkegaard's religiousness is not what separates him from Derrida, but is his most deconstructive gesture, then I believe the profile of both men as individuals who have much to contribute at both an ethical and political level will have been enhanced enormously. This can only be good news for all those interested in giving a new impetus to left-wing Continental thought at a time of global economic and political transmogrification. Kierkegaard and Derrida can, I believe, act as useful prods in the direction of a sensitive and sensible response to the harsher features of "third way" politics.

I want to begin defending my claim that Kierkegaard and Derrida ought to be considered as thinkers occupying a place somewhere between Hegel's Athens and Levinas's Jerusalem by stating that I don't think it a good idea to push, as many Derrideans have in the past, the connection between these figures at the level of the aesthetic; that is, I agree with John Caputo when he urges that we should abjure from making too much of the comparisons between the Kierkegaard of volume 1 of *Either–Or* and the early Derrida. I say this not only because it gives rise to accusations that Derrida is more like the "unhappiest man" than the knight of faith, but also because it obfuscates the more potent similarities to be found at the levels of the ethical and the religious. I have always believed that we would be better served by looking to texts such as *Fear and Trembling, The Sickness unto Death, Practice in Christianity,* and *Works of Love* for points of contact and comparison between these two authors. For in these texts we read a Kierkegaard who shares the Derridean aversion to the extremes of totality and infinity, Hegelian unity and Levinasian diversity, absolute narcissism and what Levinas calls "total altruism." For both Kierkegaard and Derrida, the circle of exchange—a metaphor for one's relationship to the other—turns neither, as in the case of Hegel, on a full balance of payments, nor, as in the case of Levinas, on a total deficit, but on what we might call, following Johannes de Silentio, John Caputo, and Derrida himself, a slightly "mad economics."

If Hegel strives to reinforce the identity of the self through a dialectical sublation of difference, and if Levinas urges us to become hostages to the other to the point of substitution, or to the point at which we abandon the self in an act of total altruism, Kierkegaard and Derrida instruct that while the self can neither become fully present to itself nor fully negated, it has nevertheless the capacity to continually reweave and reconsider itself in response to appeals from those with whom it has not formerly identified. Put otherwise, in contradistinction to the accusations made by some Derrideans and Levinasians to the effect that Kierkegaard is interested only in personal salvation to the detriment of social relations, I maintain that Kierkegaard's notion of identity is predicated upon an openness to others who serve to make the system tremble both from within and without.

Similarly, in opposition to people like Hall and Walsh, who argue that Derrida is without a sense of self whatsoever, I suggest that Derrida's theory of identity is as durable as that proposed by Kierkegaard. For both theories identify selfhood as being constituted by a sameness that is continually being challenged by difference. Unlike Hegel's theory of identity amid difference, theirs is not one that, as stressed above, prioritizes and privileges sameness and presence above difference and otherness. Neither does it seek to nullify sameness in the name of difference. Rather, it strives to ensure that the same does not lose sight of the fact that it is always co-implicated with otherness, and that this otherness keeps it from closing in upon itself. Simply put, both Kierkegaard and Derrida insist that we always already are embedded within a socio-historical matrix, and because this matrix is contingently configured, it can easily afford refuge to the unforeseen and unexpected strangers and foreigners who show up at its borders. In this scenario, the borders of the self, the home, or the state are not walls of exclusion; nor do they represent the point at which we are under threat of becoming hostages. They are rather a means of safeguarding the security of the home, of the *oikonomia,* while concomitantly ensuring that it does not become a monolith founded on the objectionable principles of social, sectarian, and racial division.

Derrida explains this position most poignantly in the following excerpt from an interview recorded in 1986:

> There is no narcissism and non-narcissism; there are narcissisms that are more or less comprehensive, generous, open, extended. What is called non-narcissism is in general but the economy of a much more welcoming, hospitable narcissism, one which is much more open to the experience of the other as other. I believe that without a movement of narcissistic reappropriation, the relation to the other would be absolutely destroyed, it would be destroyed in advance. The relation to the other—even if it remains asymmetrical, open, without possible reappropriation—must trace a movement of reappropriation in the image of oneself for love to be possible. . . . Love is narcissistic.[5]

This remarkable statement suggests quite clearly that there can be no relationship to the other that does not presuppose a relationship to oneself. If there were no such circle of reappropriation between self and other, love would not be possible. In such a case, the self would simply be the other.

If the wheels of desire are to continue turning, the other must never be reduced to the same and the same must never surrender itself fully to the other. While, contrary to what Levinas maintains, narcissism is inescapable, it is also necessary to break the spell of full narcissism in favor of hospitable narcissism; or, to put it in simpler terms, just because the self cannot twist free of its socio-linguistic cum historical matrix, it does not follow that it cannot admit those who were once strange and different into its sense of identity. Owning a home does not prevent me from becoming a good host. It is, if anything, a precondition for becoming a host worthy of the name. This is why Derrida enjoins us to "give economy a chance," why he asks us to ensure that the borders separating oneself from the other remain supple and flexible, while at the same time recognizing that such borders cannot be totally dismantled. "I" will always be separated from the other on the basis of "my" singular experience of the world, or on the basis of "my" unique place in a socio-linguistic constellation from which there is no escape. What Derrida calls "singularity," and what Kierkegaard refers to as "residual incommensurability," is this experience of ineluctable and inescapable finitude.

If, as I have been contending, Kierkegaard and Derrida avoid the extremes of absolute narcissism and total altruism, they are nonetheless thinkers whose work is replete with Hegelian and Levinasian gestures. That is, while both strive to highlight the dangers of Hegelian totalization, they each affirm Hegel's deconstruction of the transcendental subject in favor of a theory of identity that is fully relational. As Derrida makes clear in "Violence and Metaphysics,"[6] and as Kierkegaard's entire theory of the stages of existence suggests, reciprocal recognition is a fundamental feature of both theories of selfhood. This is why I strongly disagree with those who, like Ronald Green and Christopher Norris, argue that Kierkegaard and Derrida display strong neo-Kantian tendencies. Neither author commits himself to a strong transcendental position in either philosophy or ethics. Both are true Hegelians insofar as they propound a view of identity that is predicated upon being-with-others in context, and also insofar as they each consider that dialectical, dialogical, and contextual setting as being the framework in which ethical obligation arises. *Sittlichkeit,* in other words, is privileged above the Kingdom of Ends.

That said, however, it is Kierkegaard's and Derrida's *Jewish* streak, or their Levinasian sensibility, that ensures that they maintain a healthy critical disposition in relation to the ethical as formulated by Hegel. Both authors decry Hegel's sacrifice of all things Jewish on the altar of dialectical reason. Of course, when I talk of their Jewishness I do not wish this to be confused with any organized structure. What I have in mind is their biblical or religious sensitivities, along with their emotional appeals on behalf of singularity and the poor existing individual. It is this Jewishness that lies behind

Kierkegaard's claim that Hegel's world historical process is without an ethics, and behind Derrida's haunting question that marks the opening of *Glas:* "what, after all, of the remain(s), today, for us, here, now, of a Hegel?"[7] as well as behind his equally evocative deconstruction of *savoir absolu* throughout the tortured and blood-stained periphrases of *Circumfession.*[8]

Their Jewishness is obvious also in their equally intense distrust of the type of strong family-values that, for Hegel, ensures the effectiveness of *Sittlichkeit.* Both Kierkegaard and Derrida, in *Fear and Trembling* and *Glas,* respectively, alert us to the dangers for ethics and genuine responsibility of "the family," or of a sense of identity that is founded on clearly demarcated borders, and that is resistant to the idea that identity is always already disturbed from within by multifarious forces that have no obvious place on the family tree.

Moreover, it is their Levinasian Jewishness that makes them suspicious of closure, or of a notion of history that is premised on dialectical reconciliation and the surmounting of all loss. It is for this reason that Kierkegaard and Derrida resist the Hegelian notion that history has a deep underlying teleological momentum, that it has a purpose or a mission. For them, as stated earlier, existence, by its very nature, is fully contingent. Consequently, it does not unfold like a book with regularity, but is subject to all sorts of unpredictable vicissitudes. In a manner that resembles the serpentine wandering of "writing" before it is contained in an artificial frame or border, the future of an existing individual is not so clearly defined. It is errant and directionless. So when Kierkegaard seeks to undermine the pretensions of Hilarius Bookbinder, and when Derrida endeavors to show us how the Book is deconstructed from within by the disseminating drift of *ecriture,* they are not urging us, as some have maintained, to surrender to a play of signifiers, but to keep an eye on what remains after the world-historical process has come to an end. Kierkegaard and Derrida, that is, try to sensitize us to the remains and fragments, to the singularities and individualities, that have been expelled from the system.

Their Jewishness allows them, thus, to raise a voice against Hegel's tendency to deify the state at the expense of singularity and individuality. In both *Fear and Trembling* and *Practice in Christianity,* Kierkegaard identifies as his target the Hegelian idea, propounded in the *Philosophy of Right,* that the laws of the state are the material manifestation of God's divine design on earth. As Anti-Climacus stresses in *Practice in Christianity:*

> But that the established order has become something divine, is a falsehood brought about by ignoring its own origin. . . . The deification of the established order . . . is the smug invention of the lazy, secular human mentality that wants to settle down and fancy that now there is total peace and security, now we have achieved the highest. . . . Every human being is to live in fear and trembling, and likewise no established order is to be exempted from fear

and trembling. Fear and Trembling signify that we are in the process of becoming; and every single individual, likewise the generation, is and should be aware of being in the process of becoming. (PC, 88)

All states and communities, Anti-Climacus argues, are composed of existing individuals who are subject to contingency, chance, and time. Hence, they are in a constant process of becoming and change; their origins are not clearly identifiable because no *existing* individual can assume a vantage point outside of time and history.

The Hegelian contention that most offends Kierkegaard and Derrida is that it is possible to take up a purely objective viewpoint once history and becoming have been stilled. Such an idea presupposes that we can indeed do what only God seems capable of—that is, observe the world once the subjective and objective poles of the system have been fully reconciled. Both authors repudiate this Hegelian excess by emphasizing how gripped by temporality we are, and how futile our metaphysical and onto-theological attempts to cheat time have proven to be. They insist, thus, that no state can assume that it has achieved the highest, for as long as human beings change so too will their communities and states. The order of law—or in Hegel's jargon, the ethical or universal sphere—can never be confused or conflated with perfect justice. In Kierkegaard's vernacular, the ethical is not the religious.

So while both Kierkegaard and Derrida embrace Hegel's theory of social ethics, they are nevertheless deeply cognizant of the deleterious consequences that such a theory may generate if unchecked by, in Levinasian terms, "a biblical perspective which transcends the Greek language of intelligibility—as a theme of justice and concern for the other as other, as a theme of love and desire which carries us beyond the finite Being of the world as presence."[9] The deification of the established order, or the attempt to domesticate God in the very fabric of the state, presupposes a partisan and sectarian God, one who would be willing to take the side of one group of people over another. It is a way of justifying what states do in the name of God, irrespective of how many are killed, maimed, or tortured in the process. For, on this interpretation, God endorses the powers that be.

But for Kierkegaard and Derrida, any careful scrutiny of subjectivity and temporality shows that the established order did not come into existence through the intercession of the divine, but through fear and trembling, or through an uncertain and very tentative process. Hence, what is important for both is to maintain a sensitivity to the fact that Hegel's account of memory, recollection or *anamnesis,* is one that is questionable in the extreme. This is so because it is based on the quite dubious belief that we can somehow fully recover ourselves from the manifold layers of tradition that have preceded us, and that there is indeed a way of clearly ascertaining what obtained at the beginning or at the origin. In this account there is no place for the fear and trembling of which Anti-Climacus speaks, no place for the vagaries of time and chance, no accommodation for the view that the ideal of self-presence may just be an effect of subterfuge.

The Book of World History has a definite beginning, middle, and end. All writing is assigned a place or a paragraph in the pages of the system, within its borders or frame. Derrida, however, objects to this by insisting that all borders and frames are arbitrarily constructed, and, consequently, that wherever there are such borders one is liable to find traces of those who were strategically excluded. To think about writing, thus, or to meditate on what has fallen between the lines of the Book, is also, Derrida instructs, to meditate on "the production of a system of effacement," in which the trace of those whose voices have been silenced through exclusion is "rendered unreadable." The meditation on writing is, he continues, "a meditation on this *absolute weakness,* the weakness of what you are calling the victim."[10] So the most appropriate way to think about writing is, according to Derrida, to account for it in terms of effacement, unreadability, exclusion, and victimhood.

For Kierkegaard, likewise, the Book of World History effaces the singular in an effort to deify the universal. It presupposes that we can somehow reclaim the past through an act of what Hegel calls "productive memory," or that we can, to paraphrase Constantin Constantius, enter eternity through the back door. But life for Constantin is a forward-moving process, one that denies to the subject a way of recapturing loss and providing certainty. For him, as for the majority of the pseudonyms, the future is the whole of which the past is merely a part. As with Derrida, the emphasis is on a repetition forward, rather than on a recollection backward. Eternity, in other words, is something that can only be hoped for in fear and trembling, or in what Derrida calls "undecidability."

Memory or repetition, thus, is marked by a past that has never been present to a currently existing individual. The metaphor of the circle that is appropriated by Hegel to signal *Geist's* dialectical trajectory from beginning to end is deconstructed in the works of Kierkegaard and Derrida by way of a reflection on "the catastrophe of memory,"[11] or the inability of the subject to fully recollect herself from the multitudinous layers of history and tradition that antedate her. On this account, the self is always already cut from the origin. It is impossible for the established order or the state to proclaim, therefore, that it is somehow a material manifestation of God's divine design, or that it is driven by a deep underlying teleological dynamism. For such proclamations serve only to conceal the fact that there is much we have indeed forgotten and that the self is always out of joint with itself. The illusion of self-presence, or of the possibility of full narcissistic reappropriation, is exposed through a Jewish consciousness that is alert to the fact that loss is integral to life.

So, *pace* Walsh and Hall, Derrida does not deny that we belong to a socio-historical framework and that we realize a sense of identity and self through our interactions with others within that context. He is, rather, in agreement with the Kierkegaardian belief that we are always already before the law, ineluctably situated with others in the ethical sphere of existence. However, he is, again in a similar fashion to Kierkegaard, denying that we can fully gather ourselves up through the process of recollection advanced by Hegel. What both seek to avoid, in so doing, is the deification of the established order, or the violence of a totality that believes that it has a divine imprimatur.

We could say, as I have argued many times before in different contexts, that Kierkegaard and Derrida reject the politics of statehood in favor of a politics of exodus.[12] A politics of exodus is one in which the power of the state is tempered by a critical vigilance that keeps us sensitive to those whose welfare is not served by the prevailing orthodoxy. In other words, it recognizes the value of the state and its laws, for the law protects as well as threatens, but it also recognizes, as Drucilla Cornell remarks, that the law can, if left unchecked, become a monster. Kierkegaard sees such an approach to the political in religious terms. But this should not unduly frighten Derrideans, for Kierkegaard's religiousness is, on my reading at least, quite in keeping with what Derrida has been referring to lately as his "religion without religion."[13] It is also worthy of note that it was Derrida himself who described his own critical approach as a "politics of exodus."[14] My strong belief is that Kierkegaard's religiousness is not incorporated into his view of selfhood because of a need to achieve personal salvation at the expense of one's societal obligations, for such a view ignores entirely the Kierkegaardian contention discussed earlier that eternity cannot be accessed through the back door. Rather, his religiousness takes the form of a *teleological* suspension of the ethical, and not, as Levinas claims, a simple *suspension* of the ethical. As such, the religious for Kierkegaard is not to be equated with the view of someone like John Milbank, for whom salvation is only possible within a specifically Christian framework, but ought to be considered as a way of keeping the ethical, qua *Sittlichkeit,* honest and open to its past and its possibilities.

The teleological suspension of the ethical could be recast in Derridean and Hegelian jargon as an interruption of the circle of the same in the name of singularity or difference. In more contemporary Derridean parlance, it could be described as a suspension of the law in response to justice. For the notion presupposes not that there is a way of cutting oneself off from the ethical, but that one remains within the ethical economy while concomitantly seeing to it that it does not close in upon itself, that it does not become a pure economy founded on exclusion. Just as it is impossible, according to Derrida, to negate oneself in a pure affirmation of the other to the point of substitution, so too, according to Kierkegaard, it is equally impossible to negate one's factical situatedness in an effort to make contact with the infinite. The politics of exodus, while appealing to a Levinasian sensitivity to ensure the honesty of the law, does not, however, encourage us to try to escape the law. What religiousness of this sort *does* encourage us to realize is that selfhood is a process in which, to use the language of Anti-Climacus, necessity and possibility, or finitude and infinitude, are forever keeping each other in check. For Kierkegaard, despair is the price to be paid when one opts for the purely finite or for pure infinity.

What appears to mark Kierkegaard off from Derrida in this regard is the fact that Kierkegaard is an avowed Christian and Derrida is not; Derrida's messianic openness to the future, as I said at the outset, appears to be at odds with Kierkegaard's penchant for a particular determinate messianism. However, I think the differences here are somewhat factitious. In the first place, Kierkegaard's Christianity should not be confused with the confessional faith of Christendom; it was precisely against the established church that the majority of his most trenchant polemics were, of course, directed. What needs to be kept in mind, thus, is that his is a call to *practice* Christianity. He wants his reader to tame the pure economy of the ethical with what Paul Ricoeur terms a "logic of superabundance," or what Derrida likes to call the "logic of the gift." In both cases, the emphasis is not on what we are required to do by law, for anyone wishing to avoid sanction will do just that, but on how we can make our laws a little more forgiving and merciful. Forgiveness and mercy are both "religious" categories that require a temporary suspension of the law, or a teleological suspension of the ethical, in the name of the one for whom the law has become a monster. They are acts of superabundance insofar as they require much more than we are required to do in order to fulfill our legal obligations.

However, Kierkegaard understands just as much as Derrida that there can be no pure experience of the religious, that one can never be unconditionally merciful, forgiving, or altruistic. For there is no possibility of my ever being able to negate my ethical self (the self that has been shaped through the process of recognition in *Sittlichkeit*) so as to become, as Levinas urges, an unconditional hostage to the other. Finitude for both Kierkegaard and Derrida, to repeat, can never be negated in favor of infinitude. As such, total altruism would only be possible after finitude had been surmounted, something that seems impossible for two thinkers so committed to the view that existence is fully punctuated by temporality. But if both believe it to be impossible, they nevertheless encourage their readers to take a risk on such an impossibility. Both want to keep the circle between the self and the other as loose and as flexible as is possible without trying to get outside the circle. They both want us to begin with Levinas's impossible notion of total altruism as a way of avoiding the Hegelian extreme of absolute narcissism. Put

otherwise, Kierkegaard and Derrida appropriate this impossible and unconditional Levinasian command as a way of ensuring that the conditional laws
of the state do not become too conditional.

Both Hegel and Levinas, I want to contend, believe in what Derrida
referred to in a recent interview with me as the "becoming possible of the
impossible."[15] This suggests that they are each committed to the view that
it is indeed possible to surmount the residual incommensurability that separates me from my neighbor, albeit in entirely different ways and directions.
In the case of Hegel, this means that the self can become fully reconciled to
itself through a complete and harmonious reconciliation of opposition. For
Levinas, on the other hand, it means an act of self-abnegation to the point
where the circle of reappropriation is totally shattered. For Kierkegaard,
however, we can never be more than "near-dwellers," for, as he argues in
Works of Love, altruistic acts of self-denial can only serve to regulate the
irrepressible urge toward self-love. For Derrida, likewise, unconditional hospitality, forgiveness, justice, and all the other so-called undeconstructibles that
have punctuated his most recent writings are employed to show that there
can never be more than a *temporary* suspension of the law of state or home
(*oikonomia*) in response to singular appeals for justice. This suggests, as Derrida goes on to say in my conversation with him, that God is not, as it is
for Hegel and Levinas, what is possible, but rather is "*the* impossible, the
singular . . . pure hospitality." "God," he continues, "is the name of the limit,
the absolute limit, absolute transcendence, absolute immanence. Each time
I write 'the absolute' I think of 'absolution,' the moment when the debt is
remitted absolutely" (23). But, of course, as I have been arguing, for both
Kierkegaard and Derrida there is no way of stitching up loss or of recovering
oneself absolutely from the vagaries of contingency, no way of dissolving the
tension between the finite and the infinite. Neither author thinks it possible
to become one with God, either through the self-relationship or by way of
one's relationship with the neighbor. Both, however, desire the impossible,
desire that which keeps the possible from becoming confused with necessity,
while at the same time appreciating that it is just that—*impossible.*

Kierkegaard's Christianity beyond Christendom and Derrida's prophetic
religion without religion, in other words, offer a *via-media* between Athens
and Jerusalem, between total conjunction and infinite interruption. I see
Derrida as having brought to its logical conclusion the deconstruction of the
religions of the Book initiated by Kierkegaard over a century before. For
Kierkegaard saw the inherent dangers in a philosophical position that sought,
as in the case of Hegel, to use the incarnation as a way of welding church
and state together. That is why the God of which Kierkegaard speaks is, as
I have argued, more Jewish than Christian—if by "Christian" one means the
God of Christendom, of the determinate, doctrinal, and confessional form
of Christianity. His God is one who cannot be recollected through dialectical

wizardry. Neither is it the God of the Talmud, one so wholly other that it evades all form of dialectical circumscription to the point where it is rendered wholly unrecognizable. It is rather a God who calls us, as Anti-Climacus instructs, into active service on behalf of the "most wretched," or on behalf of those about whom no mention is made in Hegel's text. As such, Kierkegaard's God is both jew-greek and greek-jew, one who calls not for admiration but for imitation. It is a God of whom little trace can be found in history, for, in contradistinction to the God of Hegel who has made peace with the established order, this is a God who is both inside and outside the established order, one who seeks to infuse the state with fear and trembling so as to keep it flexible and malleable.

Such a God is one of faith, in that, like Blanchot's account of the Messiah showing up at the gates of Rome, we can never be certain whether he has indeed come. The direct discourse of the religions of the Book gives way here to the indirect communication of the *incognito*. Consequently, due to our factical situatedness we can never know if the offensive figure who moves erratically beneath the lines of the pseudonymous discourses urging us to teleologically suspend the ethical is actually the messiah. In Kierkegaard's account, as well as in Derrida's, the messiah can never show up in any state or church to proclaim that the kingdom has come. For that is the product of a "lazy secular mentality" that believes that it has reached the highest. Rather, because no state can claim that it is the highest, for all the reasons stated earlier, the kingdom for both thinkers is always to come.

There are those who might argue that Derrida's account of *khora, différance,* and undecidability, while sharing some of the same general features as Kierkegaard's account of faith, is still much less determinate and robust. In response, I can only say that I believe such critics have still not fully appreciated the radical nature of Kierkegaard's politics of exodus, his religion without religion. I might also rejoin by saying that, like Derrida, Kierkegaard is not in a position to advance a theory of religion that is predicated upon any form of immanentism, or upon a notion of God as being totally outside time, one whose source, miraculously enough, has traced itself in time. He is in the same position as Derrida, insofar as all this poor existing individual has to draw upon is a past that leads nowhere definite. Going beyond this is a matter for faith and groundless hope. This is why religion for both men is not discussed in terms of doctrine and dogma, but rather in terms of *praxis,* or of how best to keep the circle of sameness and self-aggrandizement from becoming a barrier to those whose only hope is for a merciful response, or for a gift beyond the logic of exchange. They each encourage a religious consciousness that does not seek to subvert the claims that the ethical makes upon the self, but that seeks to keep the ethical *truly* universal. They show us a way of being religious, that is, after the demise of established religion and its foundational aspirations.

Let me say, to conclude, that I believe the distance between Kierkegaardians and Derrideans on these matters is not all that great, but it is, for the time being at least, serving to keep alive a split that is, as stated above, unhelpful to the cause of this form of Continental thought. My hope is that in the not-too-distant future, people on both sides will begin to see the potential of an approach that characterizes these thinkers as both Greeks and Jews, as both loyal subjects of Athens and devout denizens of Jerusalem. When that time eventually comes around, my expectation is that we shall get books that no longer dwell on casuistic distinctions, but on how the work of both men can be used to engender a new and timely political vision. It is my belief that the politics of globalization and centralization requires an urgent response in the form advanced by a politics of exodus. My sincere hope is that the proponents of totality and those of infinity may soon come to realize that it is only by working in tandem, as Kierkegaard and Derrida suggest, that such a politics will eventually take root.

Notes

1. See Mark Dooley, *The Politics of Exodus: Søren Kierkegaard's Ethics of Responsibility* (New York: Fordham University Press, 2001); "The Politics of Exodus: 'Hospitality' in Derrida, Kierkegaard, and Levinas," in *The International Kierkegaard Commentary: Works of Love,* ed. Robert L. Perkins (Macon, Ga.: Mercer University Press), 167–192; and "The Politics of Statehood vs. a Politics of Exodus: Heidegger, Kierkegaard, and Levinas," in *Søren Kierkegaard Newsletter,* no. 40 (August 2000): 11–17. See also my "Private Irony vs. Social Hope: Derrida, Rorty, and the Political," *Cultural Values* 3, no. 3 (July 1999): 263–90, and "The Civic Religion of Social Hope: A Response to Simon Critchley," *Philosophy and Social Criticism* 27, no. 5 (2001): 35–58, for reasons why I believe it ill-advised to push the Derrida-Levinas connection too far.

2. Emmanuel Levinas, "Existence and Ethics," in *Kierkegaard: A Critical Reader,* ed. Jonathan Rée and Jane Chamberlain (Oxford: Blackwell, 1998), 26–38.

3. Jacques Derrida, *The Gift of Death,* trans. David Wills (Chicago: University of Chicago Press, 1995).

4. See Sylvia Walsh, *Living Poetically: Kierkegaard's Existential Aesthetics* (University Park: Pennsylvania State University Press, 1994), esp. 243–66, and Ronald Hall, *Word and Spirit: A Kierkegaardian Critique of the Modern Age* (Bloomington: Indiana University Press, 1993), esp. 164–206.

5. Jacques Derrida, "There is No *One* Narcissism (Autobiophotographies)," in *Points . . . : Interviews, 1974–1994,* ed. Elisabeth Weber (Stanford, Calif.: Stanford University Press, 1995), 199.

6. Jacques Derrida, "Violence and Metaphysics," in *Writing and Difference,* trans. Alan Bass (London: Routledge, 1978).

7. Jacques Derrida, *Glas,* trans. John P. Leavey Jr. and Richard Rand (Lincoln: University of Nebraska Press, 1986), 1.

8. Jacques Derrida, *Circumfession,* trans. Geoffrey Bennington (Chicago: University of Chicago Press, 1993).

9. Emmanuel Levinas, "Ethics of the Infinite," in *Dialogues with Contemporary Continental Thinkers,* ed. Richard Kearney (Manchester, England: Manchester University Press, 1984), 56.

10. Derrida, *Points,* 389.

11. See my "The Catastrophe of Memory: Derrida, Milbank, and the (Im)Possibility of Forgiveness," in *Questioning God,* ed. John D. Caputo, Mark Dooley, and Michael J. Scanlon (Bloomington: Indiana University Press, 2001), 129–52, for an account of the way in which Derrida accounts for the paucity of memory.

12. See note 1 above.

13. For a full analysis of Derrida's "religion without religion," see John D. Caputo, *The Prayers and Tears of Jacques Derrida* (Bloomington: Indiana University Press, 1997). See also Jacques Derrida, "Hospitality, Justice, and Responsibility: A Dialogue with Jacques Derrida," in *Questioning Ethics,* ed. Richard Kearney and Mark Dooley (London: Routledge, 1999), 65–83.

14. See Jacques Derrida, "Deconstruction and the Other," in *Dialogues with Contemporary Continental Thinkers,* 120.

15. "The Becoming Possible of the Impossible: A Conversation with Jacques Derrida," in *A Passion for the Impossible: John D. Caputo in Focus,* ed. Mark Dooley (forthcoming).

12

EMPTY COMMUNITY: KIERKEGAARD ON BEING WITH YOU

Jason Wirth

> Obligation alienates the ego: it becomes the you of an
> absolutely unknowable other.
> —Jean-François Lyotard[1]

> The field of emptiness in which such a world comes
> about is none other than the field of the rebirth of the
> self—where heaven and earth are born anew in the
> Great Death.
> —Keiji Nishitani[2]

ALASDAIR MACINTYRE CONCLUDED HIS seminal reflection *After Virtue*[3] with a dire scenario: If his account of the ruins of the moral condition is correct, one needs, amid the loss of a discursive and thereby defensible account of any kind of virtuous life, the formation of local forms of community within which the language of virtue again becomes audible. The new dark ages are upon us, but unlike the last dark ages in which the dangers present to moral life were conspicuous, the latest disaster is mute and has gone largely unnoticed. "This time however the barbarians are not waiting beyond the frontiers, they have already been governing us for quite some time. And it is our lack of consciousness of this that constitutes part of our predicament" (AV, 263). Indeed, among the clamor of ceaseless moral debates, there survives plenty of moral language, but it has become unhinged, decontextualized, as if, as in MacIntyre's "imaginary situation," fragments of the language of science had survived an attempted annihilation of science, and were later rediscovered, but without a template by which to make general sense of what was at stake in scientific activity (AV, 2). One might recreate experiments without any sense of why or how science valued experiments. Analogously, the same would be true in the irresolvable clashes of emoting agents, each arguing according to their personal preferences or intuitions or feelings without any kind of context in which standards would emerge to resolve competing claims. "There seems to be no rational way of securing moral agreement in our culture" (AV, 6).

Hence it could be inferred from MacIntyre's arguments that we live in an age of untold irresponsibility. Not only has the language of virtue ceased to be able to offer compelling accounts of how best to articulate and then seek to fulfill our responsibilities, but rather responsibility has become so enervated that it cannot yet even respond to its irresponsibility. If I understand MacIntyre's point, what we are being asked is not to answer in this or that particular way. One cannot answer if one does not (a) realize that one has heretofore been unable to answer and thereby (b) never had an understanding of the nature of responsibility despite having exerted abundant energy in seemingly responsible activities. To put this more directly: To be responsible, one must first have been asked something, understand what that something is, and then be able to respond. If I am able to respond, this means that I must have some sense of what it means to respond and to whom I owe a response. Again, inferring from the sense of MacIntyre's argument, the catastrophe can be most fundamentally put this way: Amid the emotivist chaos and its illusion of responsible activity, *we* hardly even know that something is being asked of *us*. It is the difficulty of this we, even a lost *we* or a *we* that comes to know itself in having failed to be responsible, a difficulty that I believe MacIntyre, for all his virtues, grossly underestimates, that I would like to reflect upon in what follows.

It was Nietzsche who first saw the subterranean secret hidden in most accounts of responsibility. The language of obligation (guilt, *die Schuld,* after all, is a debt) and of being answerable to someone beyond oneself first implies that one has some kind of self and that it recognizes its penitent and humble self as already in a state of obligation. In *Zur Genealogie der Moral,*[4] responsibility [*Verantwortlichkeit*] begins when I become answerable for my own future (GM, II/1, 39). I have become *berechenbar, regelmäßig, notwendig,* calculable or predictable, regular or rule-bound, and necessary or inevitable (GM, II/2, 39). Responsibility becomes power over oneself and over destiny (GM, II/2, 40), self-maintenance in order to fulfill one's debts. It is the formation of a self-maintaining self through the breeding of an animal with a conscience. And how is this animal bred? In the same way all animals are trained: with pain. The field of operations is the memory, and mnemonic techniques are employed to get a sense of self to stick, to rob the memory of its capacity to discharge and unload its stimuli and shed what one has become. "A thing must be burnt in so that it stays in the memory: only something which continues *to hurt* stays in the memory" (GM, II/3, 41). In this context I am, for instance, reminded of "survivor guilt" among those who somehow managed to persevere through experiences of unfathomable trauma. What does a death camp survivor have to feel guilty about? What did Job have to feel guilty about? They did nothing to deserve what happened to them, but now they can no longer forget the degraded selves that they have become. And this movement advances as soon as the survivors so

internalize their own putrefaction that they become grateful to their tor-
mentors for letting them live.[5] The *conatus*, the endeavor to preserve oneself,
what Nietzsche called *die Selbstsucht*, is the covertly poisonous fruit of responsibility. It is the manifestation of a condition of distress. I am I and, as
such, I owe my benefactor/tormentor for giving me myself. Modern moral
communities are unions of the self-interested, conglomerations of the *conatus*,
to which Lyotard pointedly asked, "Could we begin with the dispersion,
without any nostalgia for the self?" (D, 110).

Hence, in *Götzen-Dämmerung*,[6] in his remarkable discussion of the four
great errors, Nietzsche lists the error of the free will as an example of an
error based on the attribution of "imaginary causes." Yet the goal of the
doctrine of the free will, which was, after all, a Christian "discovery," was
not to make one feel good about one's innate capabilities. It was the theologian's way of making humankind "responsible" (*verantwortlich*) "in their
sense of the word." "One has disrobed Becoming of its innocence
[*Unschuld*] if being this or that way is traced back to the will, to intentions,
to acts of responsibility: the doctrine of the will was essentially invented for
the purpose of punishment, i.e., of *wanting-to-find-guilty*" (GD, sec. 7, 977;
my translation). Even Kant, whose categorical imperative Nietzsche said
"smells of cruelty," needed the intelligible ideal of freedom, itself, *strictu sensu*,
a reasonable fiction but not a fact and not admissible to the tribunal of the
understanding [*Verstand*]. Without freedom, Kant argued already in the first
Kritik, the idea of responsibility would become unintelligible. If I cannot
choose *x*, I cannot be said to have been responsible to have chosen *x*, that
is, that I *ought* to have chosen *x* (A554/B 582–A 555/B 583). Without
responsibility, the project of ethics would be lost and community would be
sundered.

Yet, in Nietzsche's own words, this theological sense of responsibility was
responsibility in the theologian's "sense of the word." To what or to whom
is one responding when one finds canonical ethical responsibility irresponsible? The *Übermensch*, otherwise than the *conatus*, obliged Nietzsche, although this call was not the call to be an *Übermensch*, to actualize some
perfected state with the predicates appropriate to that state. In some strange
sort of way, one might say that Nietzsche was called, as Heidegger read the
call of the conscience, "from afar to afar." Nietzsche, the one who interrogated the *value* of values, the *good* of the good, was called beyond moral
accountability and beyond community, the herd, that is, responsible mem-
bership in shared predicates of goodness.

Hence, in a strange way that would need to be very carefully developed,
Nietzsche, in the solitude of his crooked paths where he walked, utterly
alone, leaping from mountain peak to mountain peak, can be said to be a
"repetition" of Kierkegaard's Abraham (and more recently and equally compelling, Derrida's),[7] who Johannes de Silentio tells us, "knows it is beautiful

to be born as the single individual who has his home in the universal, his friendly abode, which immediately receives him with open arms if he wants to remain in it. But he also knows that up higher there winds a lonesome trail, steep and narrow; he knows it is dreadful to be born solitary outside of the universal, to walk without meeting one single traveler" (FT, 76).

When God called Abraham, Abraham responded without hesitation. "Here I am." But to what did God call Abraham and who or what is it that issues such a call? From a communitarian perspective, God called Abraham to madness, to a "teleological suspension of the ethical." The ethical stage, for Kierkegaard, is the work of articulation, disclosure, by which a community understands its shared sense of the Good. Community is traditionally built upon the betrayal of secrets and the rule of daylight. "As soon as I speak, I express the universal, and if I do not do so, no one can understand me" (FT, 60). Yet, from an ethical perspective (the Good for us), Abraham can only appear as a murderer. What could Abraham say? What could one say that would make sense of this? The call to sacrifice what reason construes, to the best of its ability, to be the shared good of the human condition, is the call to sacrifice the intelligibility, indeed, the discursivity, of the Good. "Speak he cannot; he speaks no human language" (FT, 114).[8] With the movement of faith, Abraham is called to sacrifice his son. Ethically, sacrifice is always murder, yet Abraham, in accepting the call, sacrificed his own life as an agent in any conceivable moral community.

Yet Abraham is not a self-indulgent killer in the middle of some erotic errancy and drunken *Sehnsucht.* Abraham felt utterly responsible to his son. He loved his son more than himself, and Abraham had a deep sense of his ethical responsibilities. It was out of the deepest sense of responsibility that, in responding to God's call—a call that demanded that he sacrifice intelligibility to the moral community—his ethical responsibilities appeared irresponsible. Ethics has never done enough for the Good that does not call us to repeat moral rules and imitate hagiographic exemplars, but that individuates one before the utter singularity of the Good. As Johannes de Silentio trembles before the earthquake of responsibility to God,[9] trembling as ethical ground becomes violently tremulous, sleepless before the violence erupting within responsibility itself, he finds Abraham singled out to be altogether singular before and by that which speaks in an utterly singular way. One may be "secure" in the universal, but in faith one is "kept in a state of sleeplessness" (FT, 78), "constantly kept in tension" (FT, 79), as "the individual relates himself as the single individual absolutely to the absolute" (FT, 70). Here the uneven number is higher than the even number, and the paradox is that "interiority is higher than exteriority" and "incommensurable" with it (FT, 69). Hence, the "single individual simply cannot make himself understandable to anyone" (FT, 71).

This is the paradox, or, to use Derrida's term, the *aporia,* of responsibility:

that one can only sacrifice what one loves, what one has preserved in responsibility as one's own (all the way down to the very intelligibility of our
moral community, our family of meaning), in the name of a higher responsibility (to what is not our own, not of our world, and not akin to our family
of meaning) that renders ethical responsibility irresponsible, yet which, in its
turn, can only appear as ethically irresponsible. And, indeed, this is how
Silentio reads "the hard saying" of Luke 14.26: "If anyone comes to me and
does not hate his own father and mother and wife and children and brothers
and sisters, yes, and even his own life, he cannot be my disciple" (FT, 72).
This μισειν is not the hatred in the hearts of the loveless. It is the hatred of
those who know and cherish the call of love, and hence it is a hatred that
emerges out of the very love that one is called to refuse. It is the refusal of
love for one's own as ever having been responsible enough.

Finally, then, who or what is this singularity that calls one to hate what
one loves and love what one hates and to do so in such a way that one will
be hated as the traitor to the moral community? It is not a universal silence
at the heart of all ethical discourse, which continually frustrates an ethical
discourse's authority to make successful evaluative judgments. It is not the
silence of a Socrates who, as Kierkegaard claimed in his thesis *The Concept
of Irony,* led, like an angry God, all positive claims, ethical or otherwise, back
to the unremitting silence of the negative. Such silence, Socratic or otherwise, is a tragic silence,[10] and, in the catastrophe of moral discourse, we can
all, at least in principle, recognize the silent murderer that eviscerates the
force of a common account of the Good. We can all cry for ourselves as
akin to the tragic hero, left silent by the wrath of the gods as they annihilate
our ethical idolatries. God does not index the Christian community's claim
to know God and to be able to respond appropriately, what Nietzsche dismissed as "Platonism for the people" (i.e., a communal understanding of the
Good). But neither is it an abstract silence that greets our most earnest moral
inquiries. Such a silence is conceptual, and, as such, is ethical,[11] and, as
Kierkegaard reminds us, there is security even in tears.[12] Kierkegaard called
the tears of tragic silence "infinite resignation," and it is the shirt whose
"thread is spun with tears, bleached with tears; the shirt is sown in tears—
but then it also gives protection better than iron or steel" (FT, 45).
One cannot cry for Abraham, for he can say nothing to us, not even that
we are lost. Or to the extent that one who cannot speak meaningfully can
say anything, he says, "Do not weep for me, but weep for yourself"[13]
(FT, 66).

Abraham, then, addresses the absolute alterity of the Good in the second
person, while the tragic hero can only address the utterly other in the third
person (FT, 77). As Lyotard phrased it: "What you judge to be the Lord's
call is the situation of *you* when *I* is deprived of experience, 'estranged,'

'alienated,' disauthorized. You do not therefore have the experience of the Lord nor even of alienness" (D, 115–16). The Good is therefore never just *the* Good. It is rather the very face to face with the utterly singular, with the incomprehensible call to responsibility, that becomes the thought of *my* death—a possessive pronoun by which Heidegger, for example, meant, not intelligible ownership, but that which manifests in the world as that which does not belong to the world's referential totality, but which, unlike all of *my* worldly predicates, cannot be taken away from *me*. The call of death is that meaning is neither an exclusive nor foundational predicate of the Good. But my death is already also the thought of *your* death and hence not only do *I* not have the Good, but *we* do not have the Good as a set of predicates either implicitly or explicitly circulating in a community of meaning. Abraham knows this "dreadful responsibility of loneliness" (FT, 114). Yet if I am not only called to *our* Good, that is, a communitarian Good, and if the Good is not reducible to MacIntyre's demand that "the good of life is life in search of the Good," for this already gives the prerogative of the name of the Good to the community at the expense of the singular, to whom am I called? Not to the idea of silence, for silence speaks, albeit such that it keeps its secret, thus dissimulating itself in the very movement of communicating itself. As Derrida put it: "God keeps silent about his reasons" (GD, 58), otherwise "he wouldn't be God, we wouldn't be dealing with the Other as God or with God as *wholly other* [*tout autre*]. If the other were to share his reasons with us by explaining them to us, if he were to speak all the time without any secrets, he wouldn't be the other, we would share a type of homogeneity" (GD, 57).

This calls for the community whose founding act of goodness remains secret. It is a call to a community that somehow wants to talk about secrets. But secrets, precisely because they are secrets, leave the one who would tell such secrets two possibilities. One can betray the secret, to bring the secretive into the light of day, to make the infinite finite and the nothing something. Or one can let the secret be what it is. One can let the secret speak without betraying itself, without demanding that the secret lose its secrecy as the price of it communicating itself. In a word, such secretive communication, such rendering secrets audible in their secrecy, is the love of secrets.

Indeed, this is the call to love, toward what some of the Mahāyāna Buddhists called the *mahā-karunā*, the Great Compassion, born of the Great Death (the dissolution of the ego). For Kierkegaard, the return back from the great silence of Mount Moriah gives rise to *agape* as it leaps away from erotic love as fickle and erratic, as moving from love project to love project, as did Johannes in "The Seducer's Diary," in its relentless performance of the rotation method. Nor does it settle for Judge Wilhelm's horror before such errancy and his desperate defense of the still waters of marriage and the constancy of matrimonial devotion and fidelity and other ethical stabilities that dissipate and enervate the tremulous questions and movements of desire that rock the universal. Rather it lets the Neighbor be.

And how is one to think this secret love, which is not the love of *my* neighbor, but, as Kierkegaard argued in *Works of Love*,[14] *the* neighbor, as if, somehow, my love for the one who is not me, indeed, for all ones who are not, for everyone is not me, is also self-love precisely because I too am a neighbor to myself. "*Neighbor* is what philosophers would call the *other,* that by which the selfishness in self-love is to be tested" (WL1, 37).

Such secretive self-love is not erotic love because *eros* in the aesthetic stage loves a constant flow of objects precisely because this vortex of desire must fundamentally love only itself. All that *eros* holds onto as it jettisons each and every beloved after it has taken momentary possession of them, as if it were a muted Don Giovanni, compiling a list of conquests (been there, done that) as long as it could muster, is *eros itelf*.[15] In wanting only itself, it moves from object to object, omnivorous and prodigal, wanting everything, *but one at a time and each for only a moment.*

Ethical love, by contrast, is the demand of the responsible ego, of the one that finds the means of communicating its responsibilities to itself and to others. But this too is not the Great Compassion, which loves only the neighbor, each and every neighbor, including itself as neighbor. This is the love of the singular, and, I daresay, the love of the secret, of the neighbor qua secret, as that tremulous mystery that has always already evaded the grasp of the universal and toward which I am called in love, in the letting go of demands, in the relinquishing of the desire that the secret be other than it is, other than a secret.

Love is the relinquishment of the demand that the secret be otherwise than a secret. It is the Great Compassion, *agape* as the generosity that allows the singular its singularity, beyond all ethical loves and hence beyond all ethical communities. Indeed, such love of all neighbors, of the community united only by the secrecy of its secrets, is the kind of love that moved Abraham to tell his most tremulous neighbor, "Here I am." It is a love fraught with the earthquakes of singularity and the impossibility of love taking stock properly of all of its responsibilities.

Yet, if the Good is wholly other, where is it? Where is the neighbor when the neighbor is everywhere and thereby nowhere? On the one hand, it is nowhere in specific, for the wholly other is, as Derrida tells us, wholly other—*tout autre est tout autre*! On the other hand, every other—*tout autre*—is wholly other.[16] I am called everywhere; every other is wholly other and hence one remains responsible not only to our community, but also to the one(s) that the communitarian already refused. After all, not far from Mount Moriah, the Holy Place divides itself into the war between Christian, Jew, and Muslim, all of whom claim that it is *their* holy place (GD, 70). To have spent time writing this essay is not to have spent time feeding the poor, or learning new languages, or teaching more students. Every time I or we have chosen what is mine or ours, the knight of good conscience has already, in the name of responsibility, sacrificed responsibility. The community constructed on the good conscience of its possession of the proper predicates of goodness has always sacrificed, even in the best of times, the Good itself.[17] Yet newspapers and television shows work themselves into frenzies of self-righteousness and make themselves giddy with the cruel joys of finger-pointing. But what then of the responsibility to the Good that does not sacrifice responsibility in the name of having articulated our responsibilities, but remains responsible to the ineluctable irresponsibility of the most responsible acts of responsibility? One might then say of the incommunicable Neighbor that must be continually witnessed, that demands the irreducibility of love to sympathy (and its orgies of communication: tears, moral self-righteousness, the birth of nations, etc.): that the Great Compassion expresses the sovereign proposition: *that I only love you.* For the secret of love is the love of secrets.[18]

Sovereign community is not founded on an inside that, in partaking in particular predicates of goodness, sets itself against its outside, that is, against its neighbors. *Mahā-karunā* is akin to the solar generosity found in both Nietzsche's *Zarathustra* and Kierkegaard's birds of the air and lilies of the field. It refuses its own place in the sun, and, after the Great Death of its humanity, comes back from the Pure Land, from the Nothing, from the irreducible alterity of You, wanting to love like the sun, which, like nature, does not have her favorites.[19] Concluding with Nishitani:

> The sun in the sky makes no choices about where to shine its rays and shows no preferences as to likes or dislikes. There is no selfishness in its shining. This lack of selfishness is what is meant by non-ego, or "emptiness" (*sunyata*). (RN, 60)

Notes

1. Jean-François Lyotard, *The Differend: Phrases in Dispute* (Minneapolis: University of Minnesota Press, 1988), 115. Henceforth D.

2. Keiji Nishitani, *Religion and Nothingness,* trans. Jan van Bragt (Berkeley and Los Angeles: University of California Press, 1982), 283. Henceforth RN.

3. Alasdair MacIntyre, *After Virtue,* 2d ed. (Notre Dame, Ind.: University of Notre Dame Press, 1984). Henceforth AV.

4. I am using, with some emendations of my own, *On the Genealogy of Morality* (1887), ed. Keith Ansell-Pearson and trans. Carol Diethe (Cambridge: Cambridge University Press, 1994). Henceforth GM, followed by essay number and aphorism number, and then by translation page.

5. Cf. Alphonso Lingis, *The Community of Those Who Have Nothing in Common* (Bloomington: Indiana University Press, 1994): "The one being tortured is not being asked to declare true what he knows to be false. The torturer demands that he confess that he is incapable of making sense, that his body is incapable of lucidity and discernment, that it is nothing but corruption and putrefaction" (147). Henceforth CN.

6. *Götzen-Dämmerung* (1888), in *Werke in drei Bänden*, vol. 2, ed. Karl Schlechta (Munich: Carl Hanser Verlag, 1956). Henceforth GD.

7. Jacques Derrida, *The Gift of Death* (1992), trans. David Wills (Chicago: University of Chicago Press, 1995). Henceforth GD. Søren Kierkegaard, *Fear and Trembling; Repetition* (1843), trans. Howard V. Hong and Edna H. Hong (Princeton, N.J.: Princeton University Press, 1990), 76. Henceforth FT.

8. Derrida: "The first effect or first destination of language therefore involves depriving me of, or delivering me from, my singularity. By suspending my absolute singularity in speaking, I renounce at the same time my liberty and my responsibility" (GD, 60). See also Mark Taylor, "Sounds of Silence," in *Kierkegaard's Fear and Trembling: Critical Appraisals,* ed. Robert L. Perkins (Tuscaloosa: University of Alabama Press, 1981), 165–88. "The ethicist believes all forms of silence to be deceptive and deceitful. Secrecy and concealment unravel the very moral fabric of a society" (180).

9. Silentio contrasts his own insomnia with the minister who sleeps well at night and who "can just as well sleep until the last quarter hour before he has to speak" about Abraham (FT, 52) and who knows no fear and trembling before the impossibility of responsibility (we have always failed; we are always already guilty). He also contrasts himself with the assistant professors, expert producers of critical editions and bureaucrats of the idea, secure with their permanent positions and their "future in a well-organized state," but who "have hundreds, yes, even thousands of years between them and the earthquakes of existence" (FT, 62–63).

10. Johannes de Silentio is quite clear about this: Socrates is an "intellectual tragic hero" (FT, 117), and Socratic ignorance is "the infinite resignation" (FT, 69). Although faith can only break through after infinite resignation, faith transcends it.

11. Cf.: "The tragic hero is still within the ethical. He allows an expression of the ethical to have its τελος in a higher expression of the ethical" (FT, 59). "I *think* myself *into* the hero; I cannot think myself into Abraham" (FT, 33).

12. "In infinite resignation there is peace and rest" (FT, 45).

13. Silentio is quite clear about this: the tragic poet says of his hero: "Weep for him, for he deserves it" (FT, 66). "The tragic hero needs and demands tears" (FT, 61). Yet one "cannot weep over Abraham. One approaches him with a *horror religiosus*" (FT, 61).

14. Søren Kierkegaard, *Works of Love: Some Christian Reflections in the Form of Discourses* (1847), trans. Howard V. Hong and Edna H. Hong (New York: Harper and Row, 1962). Henceforth WL1.

15. "However joyous, however happy, however indescribably confident, instinctive and inclinational love, spontaneous love, can be itself, it still feels

precisely in its most beautiful moment the need to establish itself, if possible, more securely" (WL1, 44–45).

16. "The next human being—he is one's neighbor—this the next human being in the sense that the next human being is every other human being" (WL1, 70).

17. Cf. Lingis: "In our rational collective enterprises we find, in principle, nothing alien to us, foreign, and impervious to our understanding; we find only ourselves. We do not, like the Balinese, find in our institutions, public works, and community gatherings the visitation of alien spirits, demonic and divine forces, or pacts made with the forces of volcanoes and rivers and skies" (CN, 6).

18. See Peter Fenves's fine study *"Chatter": Language and History in Kierkegaard* (Stanford, Calif.: Stanford University Press, 1993). "But a secret that can never be communicated under any condition and that therefore breaks every injunction to keep a secret cannot form a cult or a cultic community and cannot to this extent foster communion" (148). "If, however, philosophy ceded a place to the inconceivable and incomprehensible, it could concede a unique moment of secrecy, and by making this concession, it could have a chance to communicate something other than the appearance of communication" (148–49). In this respect, I am also reminded of the remarkable conclusion to Andrei Tarkovsky's masterpiece *The Sacrifice* (1986), in which Alexander burns the house down, knowing that this act cannot directly communicate the secret.

19. "Love of one's neighbor, on the other hand, is self-renouncing love, and self-renunciation casts out all preferential love just as it casts out all self-love—otherwise self-renunciation would also make distinctions and would nourish preference for preference" (WL1, 67).

13

Kierkegaard on Hamlet: Between Art and Religion

Richard Kearney

Part One

Kierkegaard's reflections on Hamlet are not as frequent as one might expect given their common destiny as introspective melancholy Danes. But the reflections that do exist are tantalizing, if characteristically oblique. Over half of these are to be found in an appendix to the fourth and final part of *Stages on Life's Way* (1845), already a multi-layered work composed by multiple pseudonyms (William Afham, A Married Man, Frater Taciturnus) and published by yet another pseudonymous character called "Hilarius Bookbinder." More exactly, the appendix on *Hamlet* is part of a supplementary text to the main concluding part, "'Guilty?'/'Not Guilty?': A Story of Suffering—An Imaginary Psychological Construction," by Frater Taciturnus. The supplement is called a "Letter to the Reader," and the appendix on *Hamlet* therefore is really more of an appendix to an appendix. Its exact title reads "A Side-glance at Shakespeare's *Hamlet*." The text in question thus lies coiled like the inner seam of a multi-layered Danish pastry.

My hypothesis in what follows is that if every text, as the hermeneutic model suggests, involves someone talking about something to someone, then this one is, when closely decrypted, nothing more nor less than Kierkegaard talking about Kierkegaard to himself.

To make matters even more intriguing, the "side-glance" a *Hamlet* is itself prefaced by two brief allusions to *Hamlet* within the "'Guilty?'/'Not Guilty'" text itself. The first of these hints that "if it so happens that an individual who was great by virtue of his inclosing reserve offers himself as a subject for poetic treatment . . . we sneak up to admire."[1] Though Kierkegaard does not mention Hamlet by name here, a note by the editors and translators, Hong and Hong, leaves us in little doubt that it is Hamlet who is being referred to. Later in the text, but still before we get to the appendix proper, Kierkegaard makes his first explicit, albeit still indirect, pronouncement on Hamlet: "The esthetic hero must have his opposition outside himself, not in himself. That this is not the case in Hamlet is perhaps precisely the anomaly—more on that later."[2] And Kierkegaard will remain true to his promise. The appendix when it does come later, in however cursory and lapidary a form, will indeed make much of the fact that Hamlet fails as an esthetic hero precisely because the opposition is *within,* rather than *outside* of, himself. But before proceeding to a detailed textual analysis of what Kierkegaard actually *does* offer in his "side-glance" at *Hamlet,* let me first take a look at one or two other brief references that Kierkegaard makes to his Danish predecessor in some of his other works, in particular *The Concept of Dread* and *Concluding Unscientific Postscript,* both also written in the mid-1840s.

★   ★   ★

In the *Concept of Dread* (1844), where we might expect to find the most elaborate references to Hamlet—given his famously melancholic disposition—we must content ourselves with a single allusion. It comes in the context of Kierkegaard's own quasi-autobiographical discussion (via the pseudonym of Vigilius Haufniensis) of the relationship between what he calls "shut-up" characters and "revelation." In "poetic existences"—such as his own and Hamlet's—we are told that the "most subtle contradiction" of "shut-upness" manifests itself as a will to revelation which goes incognito. On the surface, shut-upness operates demonically to transform "revelation" into a "mystification"—even as it may continue surreptitiously to will it. But this leads to a second contradiction in that the very form of expression that one uses to expose the inner secrets and subterfuges of the shut-up poetic existence is that of "monologue" or "soliloquy"—someone talking to him/herself. To break the silence of shut-upness is to make these inaudible self-to-self speeches audible. "For its talk," says Kierkegaard, "is precisely monologue, and hence when we would characterize a shut-up we say that he talks to himself. But here I essay only to give everything 'an understanding but no tongue,' as said the shut-up Hamlet warningly to his two friends."[3] And yet the irony is unavoidable, is it not? *Both* Kierkegaard *and* Hamlet were shut-up soliloquizers whose respective published soliloquies are considered among the most celebrated of modern letters!

For Kierkegaard the dilemma is the following: *either* to respond demoniacally to revelation (by remaining shut-up); *or* to respond authentically (by "assuming the responsibility for it in freedom").[4] In the case of the former—that is, the demoniacal—the revelation will out in any case, generally through an involuntary glance, lapsus, or gesture: what Kierkegaard calls the "sudden." Indeed, Kierkegaard—or at least his pseudonym Vigilius Haufniensis—comes very close here to anticipating Freud's description of unconscious parapraxis. He describes the "sudden" as a symptom of "psychic unfreedom."[5] And ironically the more the *will to shut-upness* (or what he also calls "close reserve") wins out over the *will to revelation,* the more certain it is, we are told, that this demoniacal repression will result in an outburst of unwilled "ventriloquism": an uncontrolled lapse of self-exposure at the least expected moment. The demoniacal thus expresses itself as the "sudden" exposure of the inner secret, the degree of suddenness being proportional to the prior degree of suppression. The opposite of such shut-upness and suddenness is "communication" and "continuity," which the author insists are the idioms of "salvation." The demoniacal—like the sudden, terrible, almost insane outbursts that express it—is, we are told, "dread of the good."[6]

So the question one can hardly resist here is this: Is Hamlet an authentic character in whom the will to salvation wins out over shut-up "close reserve" and "entrenchment in the ego"?[7] Or is he a demoniacal character condemned to psychic unfreedom and dread?

★ ★ ★

In Kierkegaard's two subsequent texts that refer to Hamlet—*Concluding Unscientific Postscript* (1846, by Johannes Climacus) and, more importantly, in *Stages on Life's Way* (1845, published by the Hilarius Bookbinder)—we find some hints of a solution. In the former work, the author first assumes what seems like an odd position in associating Hamlet with comic rather than tragic contradiction. He defines the difference between the two as follows: "the tragic is *suffering* contradiction, and the comic is *painless* contradiction."[8] And he then goes on to cite Hamlet "swearing by the fire tongs" as an example of the comic insofar as there is a contradiction between the solemnity of the oath and the reference—that is, to the inane fire tongs—that annuls the oath.

But Kierkegaard reverts to a more tragic understanding of Hamlet's attitude to contradiction when he comments on his famous existential question, "to be or not to be." The analysis here is dense and difficult, but very telling. It goes like this. Whereas from an *objective* or purely scientific point of view the question of existence is "indifferent" and "leads away from the subjective individual," Hamlet shows us that "existence and non-existence have only subjective existence."[9] Which prompts the following surmise:

> At its maximum, this way will lead to a contradiction, and to the extent that the subject does not become totally indifferent to himself, this is merely an indication that his objective striving is not objective enough. At its maximum, it will lead to the contradiction that only objectivity has come about, whereas subjectivity has gone out, that is, the existing subjectivity that has made an attempt to become what in the abstract sense is called subjectivity, the abstract form of an abstract objectivity. And yet, viewed subjectively, the objectivity that has come about is at its maximum either a hypothesis or an approximation, because all eternal decision is rooted specifically in subjectivity.[10]

Kierkegaard goes on to claim that the objective way of mathematics and science lays claim to a "security" that is totally incompatible with the question of "what it means to exist."[11] And because of this the objective way thinks it has staved off "madness" that lies in constant wait for the "subjective way," since the latter is incapable of distinguishing between lunacy and truth as expressions of "inwardness."[12]

This does not, of course, stop Kierkegaard from rejoining that the determination of our "objective age" to get rid of inwardness and existence may itself involve its own kind of "lunacy." One may state something that is objectively true and still be a lunatic, Kierkegaard brazenly reminds us![13]

But perhaps Kierkegaard's most telling comment on Hamlet in *Concluding Unscientific Postscript* comes when the author claims that "to pray is just as difficult as to play the role of Hamlet."[14] An intriguing statement! Just as the greatest of actors can spend their entire lives trying to get this role right, so too learning to become subjective, that is, learning to exist and to know what it means to die, are tasks that demand, not an instant, not a week, month, or year, but a lifetime. "To be finished with life before life is finished with one is not to finish the task at all."[15] Which is why the true greatness of a tragic hero is that he/she does not die until the final act when death has had time to gain "infinite reality in pathos."[16] The greatest hero is the one who can wait, keep vigil, procrastinate. And though Kierkegaard does not explicitly mention Hamlet here, it is impossible not to suppose that he is still teasing out the analogy made two pages earlier between (a) praying, (b) existing, and (c) playing the role of Hamlet! In all three cases, the readiness is all. But the matter is not, as we shall see, quite as simple as it seems.

★ ★ ★

It is, no doubt, in *Stages on Life's Way* that Kierkegaard comes clean—or at least as clean as he ever comes—on his attitude to Hamlet. This work, as the McKinnon Concordance shows, contains over half of all Kierkegaard's references to Hamlet (ten out of twenty, to be precise). In the "Side-glance" appendix mentioned earlier, Kierkegaard's narrator, Frater Taciturnus, confesses that he is "engrossed" by the claim that "*Hamlet* is a Christian drama."[17] This claim is attributed to a certain Börne who shares the determination, in common with two of his contemporaries, Heine and Feuerbach, to have nothing to do with the "religious." But precisely because of this, says Taciturnus, these thinkers offer a unique insight into the religious. The author plays with a curious analogy here: just as a jealous lover can know as much about the erotic as a happy one, so those offended by the religious can be just as insightful about it as believers. And in an age where great believers are few and far between, we should, says the author, be grateful that we have at least "a few really clever people who are offended (by religion)."[18]

After this mischievous preparatory remark, Kierkegaard's pseudonym comes to his main statement on the matter: "Börne says of *Hamlet*: 'It is a Christian drama.' To my mind this is a most excellent comment. I substitute only the word a 'religious' drama, and then declare its fault to be not that it is that but that it did not *become* that or, rather, that it *ought not* to be drama at all."[19] Once unpacked, this dense formulation seems to be saying that *Hamlet* should be considered a *failed religious drama*. Or to be more precise, *Hamlet* is a work that should have been properly *religious,* and therefore not an *aesthetic* drama at all. Or else, it should have been properly *aesthetic* and therefore not a *religious* work at all. The fact is, however, that it is neither. It falls between the religious and aesthetic stools and so, as T. S. Eliot would famously pronounce a half century later, *Hamlet is a dramatic failure.* This is not, of course, to deny that it is the most fascinating drama ever written. *Hamlet,* as both Kierkegaard and Eliot were aware, is the literary character who most fascinates modern minds. And neither, I suspect, would have been surprised by the statistic that Hamlet is the most written about person in Western civilization after Jesus and Napoleon.

Kierkegaard's pseudonym spells out his evaluation of *Hamlet* as a failed religious drama as follows. If Shakespeare deprives Hamlet of religious presuppositions and doubts that conspire against him and prevent him from acting, then he is merely a "vacillator" in a comedy. In other words, if Hamlet is not paralyzed with genuinely religious visions and misgivings, there is no good reason for him not to proceed with the summons to avenge his father's murder and restore Denmark to its former state. But Kierkegaard does not think that Shakespeare *does* make Hamlet religious in this manner, and so the play fails to be the great religious drama it ought to have been and could have been.

So how *should* Shakespeare have written this play according to the author of the "Side-glance"? Well, first, Hamlet's grandiose plan to become the avenger to whom vengeance belongs should have been confronted from the start with the religious prohibition on revenge killing. A reference to Romans 12.19 is cited in a note: "Never try to get revenge: leave that to Retribution. As Scripture says: 'Vengeance is mine—I will pay them back. . . . If your enemy is thirsty give him something to drink. . . . Do not be mastered by evil, but master evil with good.'" But since one does not see Hamlet "sink religiously under (his revenge) plan," his conscience stricken by such biblical prohibitions, one expects quick action as in a normal revenge tragedy where one deals only with "external" obstacles. Alas, however, in the case of *Hamlet* there seem to be neither internal subjective religious doubts nor external objective obstacles to action—yet Hamlet fails to act. And as a result, the whole vacillating, procrastinating drama becomes one huge introspective psychodrama where Hamlet's misgivings take on a purely psychological form of "dialectical repentance"—a non-religious and ultimately unfounded repentance that, in Taciturnus's reckoning, "comes too early." As a result, Hamlet comes across as simply "morbidly reflective."

Returning to the guiding idea of a Revenge Plan that Hamlet sets himself but fails to realize, Taciturnus argues as follows: "If the plan remains fixed, then Hamlet is a kind of loiterer who does not know how to act; if the plan does not remain fixed, he is a kind of self-torturer who torments himself for and with wanting to be something great. Neither of these involves the tragic."[20] In short, without the presence of the religious, *Hamlet* simply degenerates into (a) a revenge hero who cannot live up to his purpose, or (b) a reflective melancholic with no real purpose at all who analyzes himself to death in the name of some empty (i.e., a-religious, a-moral) imago.

Taciturnus then goes on to repeat his arguments on the basis of the *either* esthetic *or* religious model, concluding once again, for a second time, that *Hamlet* is *neither* properly esthetic *nor* properly religious. (Anticipations of Derridean aporetics perhaps?)

> If Hamlet is kept in purely *esthetic* categories, then what one wants to see is that he has the demonic power to carry out such a resolution. His misgivings have no interest whatsoever; his procrastination and temporizing, his postponing and his self-deluding enjoyment in the renewed intention at the same time as there is no outside hindrance merely diminish him, so that he does not become an esthetic hero, and then he becomes a nonentity.[21]

On the other hand, "if he is *religiously* oriented, his misgivings are extremely interesting, because they give assurance that he is a religious hero."[22] But this, were it the case, would not lead to good drama either because it would belong to the order of the "interior being" where alone such religious misgivings could have their "essential significance." In short, trying to make a good drama out of the religious struggles of subjective inwardness is like trying to make a silk purse from a pig's ear. It simply cannot be done.

If it could be done, Kierkegaard seems to be saying (via his pseudonym) that he, S. K., might well have tried his hand at religious drama himself! But religious drama is, according to the above logic, a contradiction in terms—at least for our modern age of Reformed Christianity where the religious gravitates inward toward subjective solitude and away from external action. (Frater Taciturnus contrasts this to medieval Catholicism where a zealous believer *could* become "a tragic hero for the sake of the Church just as the Roman did for his country," that is, still observing the "esthetic" categories of Aristotelian drama as the "imitation of an action." In other words, for premodern Roman Catholics the idea of being a militant actor on behalf of a religious messianic politics—that is, a saintly agitator, crusader, missionary, or martyr—was still a possibility. But for modernity this is no longer a realistic option.)

In sum, either Hamlet's dilemma is religious, and therefore inappropriate for dramatic action, or it is esthetic, and therefore appropriate for dramatic action. It cannot be both at once. That Shakespeare tried to achieve the impossible—by seeking to compose a religious drama—is to his credit. But it does not and cannot take from the inevitable failure of the enterprise.

★ ★ ★

Yet Taciturnus has not totally given up. In the same "Side-glance" appendix, he resolves on a third tack. What, he asks, if Shakespeare had allowed Hamlet to *carry out* his plan of action—in keeping with the dramatic demands of the esthetic model—and then, having murdered Claudius (and perhaps Gertrude too), realized his sin and collapsed back into an attitude of genuine religious repentance *after the event*? In sum, first the evil action, then the good introspection and revelation. First the esthetic (imitation of an action), then the religious (pardon and peace).

But *this* third scenario is also impossible, for no matter how subtly dialectical one tries to manage such a move, it would ultimately make for a moralizing-sermonizing tract where the esthetic action of revenge is used merely to make a religious point. In that instance, the drama would be no more than a means toward an end, a pre-text for a pre-established doctrine, the moral of the story having been set from the start—rendering the action of the drama entirely redundant. In short, the only way such a scenario could work would be as religious propaganda—a prospect almost as unpalatable for Kierkegaard, it seems, as political propaganda. (Incidentally, it is just such a religious reading that René Girard proposes in *Shakespeare: Les Feux de l'envie*.)[23] It could thus be argued that *Hamlet* exposes the folly of mimetic desire and sacrificial revenge in favor of a true Christian revelation: No to revenge, yes to providence and peace!

This is how Kierkegaard has his pseudonym, Taciturnus, tease out his final, yet still self-defeating attempt to save Hamlet as religious drama:

> If Hamlet is to be interpreted religiously, one *must* either allow him to have conceived the plan, and then the religious doubts divest him of it, or do what to my mind better illuminates the religious (for in the first case there could possibly be some doubt as to whether he was capable of carrying out his plan)—and give him the demonic power resolutely and masterfully to carry out his plan and *then* let him collapse into himself and into the religious until he finds peace there. A drama, of course, can never come from this; a poet cannot use this subject, which should begin with the last and let the first shine out through it.[24]

So it would seem that, for Kierkegaard, Hamlet is neither a religious hero nor an esthetic (tragic) hero but something in between. Neither fish nor fowl. A hybrid creature. In short an esthetic-religious mess. Perhaps not unlike Kierkegaard himself.

★ ★ ★

In the piece immediately following the "Side-glance at Shakespeare's *Hamlet*," Taciturnus makes a supplementary and useful distinction between the two kinds of hero. By way of trying to get a final fix (if that were possible) on what Kierkegaard is really getting at, I think it might be worth-while bearing with Taciturnus on this ostensibly labored point. So let's take one last spin of the dialectical wheel.

The *tragic-esthetic hero* is, we are now told, great by suffering in such a way that he conquers in the external—what "uplifts the spectator while he weeps for the dying one."[25] As such the suffering of the tragic hero "must arouse fear and cleanse the passions," provoking the spectator's sympathies, which differ within the various views of the world.[26] No surprises here—standard Aristotelian poetics.

Now, by contrast, the *religious hero* is great by suffering *without conquering in the external,* and therefore without inviting the spectator to be purified (as Aristotle put it) through pity and fear. The religious hero, in other words, is someone "emancipated from externals" and from the tragic world of ac-tions and passions. But precisely *because* of this, he is uniquely capable of that "qualitative qualification that is reserved for the religious, where a farthing is worth just as much as kingdoms and countries."[27] One thinks here not only of the Gospel allusions to the widow and her farthing or the kingdom of heaven as a mustard seed, but also of the passages in *Hamlet* itself where the hero observes how important it is "to find quarrel in a straw" (4.4.55), or to realize "when our deep plots do pall (fail)" that "there's a divinity that shapes our ends,/ Rough-hew them how we will" (5.2.9–11).[28] But, Kier-kegaard insists, Hamlet does not ultimately pass muster when it comes to the religious category. Why? Because as we learn from a Journal entry of 1844 (deleted from the "Side-glance" appendix to *Stages on Life's Way*): "The mistake in Shakespeare is precisely that Hamlet does not have religious doubts. If he does not have them, then it is sheer nonsense and indecision if he does not settle the matter straight away."[29]

★ ★ ★

Because (according to Kierkegaard) Hamlet does not have religious doubts, he does not qualify as a religious hero; and because he does not settle the matter straight away in a dramatic act, he does not qualify as a tragic hero. So what, we might ask at this point, is Hamlet to Kierkegaard that he should weep for him? Apart from the fact that both are morbidly reflective Danes—enough perhaps in itself to justify the connection—there would seem to be other, less avowed, reasons.

First, it would seem obvious that Kierkegaard himself had keen concerns during the writing of *Stages on Life's Way* in 1844–45 about his own vocation as a religious individual. Indeed his view of himself is probably not much different than that of Hamlet: namely, that he is (a) too interior, subjective, shut-up, and inactive to be properly tragic, provoking sympathy and fear in his readers; and (b) too full of morbid reflection ever to be able to make a proper leap of faith! In short, Kierkegaard sees in his compatriot Hamlet a symptomatic embodiment of the in-between condition he once confessed to—namely, being too religious to fit into the esthetic category of Climacus but not religious enough to meet the religious category of Anti-Climacus.

Second, Kierkegaard appears to identify with Goethe's remark about Hamlet that in "relation to his body his soul was an acorn planted in a flower pot which at last breaks the container."[30] The Dane of Copenhagen seems to have shared with the Dane of Elsinore a deep sense not only of being ill fitted for his task in life, incapable of heroic action or passionate love, but also of being shackled with a summons to amend a wrong that cannot be atoned for. (I am thinking here of Kierkegaard's father's cursing of God and misbehavior with his maid; and of Hamlet's father's "foul deed done in his days of nature" and his mother's incestuous relation with Claudius.) Indeed, Kierkegaard must have been fascinated by the way in which Hamlet is caught in the paralyzing bind of his father's double injunction: remember me/I cannot tell you what to remember. And he must have been equally intrigued by the second double injunction of the ghost-father, namely: (a) prevent the bed of Denmark from becoming a foul place of incest; but (b) "contrive against thy mother naught." In short, you must act, but you can't act!

Indeed it could be said that this is not entirely dissimilar to Kierkegaard's own personal sense of paralysis and paradox following his famous Easter conversion experience of 1848: he initially believed he had received a direct summons from God to "speak out"—only to revert subsequently to the esthetic and pseudonymous ploys of "indirect communication." Reflecting upon the event afterward, Kierkegaard was horrified by his own demonic hubris at supposing himself to be a chosen martyr of God—like the medieval hero-martyrs he considers so anachronistic in "Side-glance." This critical reflection was later to be corroborated by his disapproval of the self-proclamation of Pastor Adler as chosen advocate of divine mission, recorded at length in the pages of *Authority and Revelation* (1848). Kierkegaard's ultimate sentiment seems to have been that of the spectator of tragic aberration: "there but for the grace of God go I. . . ."

The fact, moreover, that for both Kierkegaard and Hamlet the legacies of their heavenly father and their ghostly father were at times so diabolically intermixed (Derrida might say "contaminated") made their language, and their lives, a process of inevitable and ineluctable deconstruction.

Third and finally, it is almost certain that Kierkegaard saw in Hamlet's relationship to Ophelia a mirror image of his own relationship to Regine Olsen. The vehemence of Kierkegaard's criticism of Hamlet in this regard—as failing to live up to his "secret" religious mission by distracting himself with Ophelia and loving her almost by default—surely betrays a veiled criticism of his own behavior. The analogy between Kierkegaard-Regine and Hamlet-Ophelia is not explicitly mentioned in *Stages on Life's Way,* but it surfaces in the following entry in his Journal. Let us read the passage deliberately in light of our above hypothesis:

> *Hamlet and Ophelia.* Hamlet cannot be regarded as really being in love with Ophelia. It must not be interpreted in this way, even though psychologically it is quite true that a person who is going about hatching a great plan is the very one who needs momentary relaxation and therefore can well use a love affair. Yet I do not believe that Hamlet is to be interpreted this way. No, what is indefensible in Hamlet is that, intriguing in grand style as he is, he uses a relationship to Ophelia to take the attention away from what he actually is keeping hidden. He *misuses* Ophelia. This is how it should be interpreted, and one can also add that precisely because he is so overstrained he almost goes so far that momentarily he actually is in love.[31]

                    ★   ★   ★

And yet in spite of all, and especially in spite of Kierkegaard's complaint about how "incredible" he finds it that "Goethe has taken such great pains to uphold *Hamlet*,"[32] Kierkegaard himself feels compelled to conclude his own published "Side-glance" with this admission: "On a specific point, one may have a doubt . . . and yet agree on the one opinion that has been the opinion of one and two and three centuries—that Shakespeare stands unrivaled, despite the progress the world will make, that one can always learn from him, and the more one reads him, the more one learns."[33] That this final admission is ostensibly inconsistent with all the criticisms of *Hamlet* that precede it is typical of Kierkegaard's own deeply contradictory, not to say aporetic, approach to this play of plays.

Part Two: Some Notes on a Deconstructive Reading

Since this volume is specifically concerned with continental and deconstructive readings of Kierkegaard, let me conclude with some remarks on Derrida's allusions to *Hamlet* in *Spectres of Marx*—and see what relevance, if any, they might have for our above analysis.

I use the term "allusions" advisedly. Derrida at no point offers a consistent argument about Hamlet. Yet his *Spectres of Marx* opens with several direct quotations from the play, makes passing references throughout, bears a mention of the "work of mourning" in its subtitle, and actually carries (in its English edition) a front-cover representation of Hamlet confronting his ghost-father. And of course, both *Hamlet* and *Spectres of Marx* are concerned with "spectres," that is, the influence of the returned dead (*les revenants*) on the living. For Hamlet, the specter in question was his own father. For Derrida, it is the less personal surrogate father-figure of Marx (and by historical extension, Shakespeare himself).

In spite of this obvious difference, the logic of posthumous influence is, Derrida suggests, similar in both cases. It is, as he says in the "Exordium," the "*non-contemporaneity with itself of the living present.*"[34] One is prompted, in the light of our above analysis of Kierkegaard's "side-glance," to think here of what the latter had to say about the out-of-kilter temporality of Shakespeare's failed attempt at a religious drama (where the end informs the beginning); or again, of Kierkegaard's intriguing references to "ventriloquism" and the "sudden" as the eruption of non-continuous time.

But before teasing out such matters, let's see what Derrida himself has to say about this spectral temporality—or what he calls "spectropoetics." The context is that of trying to do justice to those who are no longer—or not yet—part of the "living present"; and the passage in question culminates, tellingly for our purposes, with a citation from *Hamlet:*

> To be just: beyond the living present in general—and beyond its simple negative reversal. A spectral moment, a moment that no longer belongs to time, if one understands by this word the linking of modalized presents (past, present, actual present: "now," future present). We are questioning in this instant, we are asking ourselves about this instant that is not docile to time, at least to what we call time. Furtive and untimely, the apparition of the specter does not belong to that time, it does not give time, not that one: "Enter the ghost, exit the ghost, re-enter the ghost" (*Hamlet*).[35]

Derrida's first chapter, entitled "Injunctions of Marx," then opens with an explicit citation from act 1, scene 5 of *Hamlet*. The passage in question concerns the episode where Hamlet and his companions are sworn to silence by the ghost; yet we know, since it is the opening act of the play, that the matter will not rest there. Though Hamlet does indeed admonish his guards, "And still your fingers on your lippes, I pray," he goes on to immediately state his deep unease at the fact that while he is not responsible for what has occurred he is obliged nonetheless to "set it right." The voice from the past is summoning him to his future. "The time is out of joint: Oh cursed spite,/ That ever I was born to set it right."

Derrida then proceeds to invoke the opening reference to another ghost, this time in Marx's *Communist Manifesto*—"A specter is haunting Europe— the specter of communism." He suggests the following analogy between the two kinds of ghost:

> As in *Hamlet,* the Prince of a rotten State, everything begins by the apparition of a specter. More precisely by the *waiting* for this apparition. The anticipation is at once impatient, anxious, and fascinated: this, the thing ("this thing") will end up coming. The *revenant* is going to come. It won't be long. But how long it is taking. Still more precisely, everything begins in the imminence of a *re*-apparition, but a reapparition of the specter as apparition *for the first time in the play*.[36]

Derrida does not hesitate to suggest that "in the shadow of a filial memory, Shakespeare will have often inspired Marxian theatricalization."[37] A strange use of the future anterior tense here! Or as he puts it, invoking Valéry's famous text on the "'European Hamlet,' *Shakespeare qui genuit Marx* . . . (and a few others)."[38] (We are inclined to include Kierkegaard and Derrida himself, of course, among these other few, but more of that anon.) What the specter represents for Hamlet, as later for Marx and others, is a "Thing that is not a thing."[39] Or as Derrida says: "One does not know what it *is*." One does not know if it corresponds to a name or an essence or any specific identity; and yet this invisible thing looks at us even though we cannot look at it. "The Thing meanwhile looks at us and sees us not see it even when it is there. A spectral asymmetry interrupts here all specularity. It desynchronizes, it recalls us to anachrony."[40]

Derrida calls this the "visor effect," namely, the impression that "we do not see who looks at us." Or more specifically in the case of Hamlet's father, "Even though in his ghost the King looks like himself ('As thou art to thy selfe,' says Horatio), that does not prevent him from looking without being seen: his apparition makes him appear still invisible beneath his armor."[41] Derrida claims that this definition of the *visor effect* will be presupposed by everything he, Derrida, has to say on the subject of the specter in general. And as will become more obvious later in the book, what is at issue is not just Marx and Marxism but the whole "spectropoetics" of messianicity in general, that is, the very religious structure of existence as "religion without religion."

Now replace the specters of Hamlet or Marx with the Holy Ghost of messianic Christianity, and we are no longer a million miles away from Kierkegaard. Indeed, if we compare (a) what Kierkegaard has to say about Hamlet not being sufficiently "religious" in his doubts, with (b) Kierkegaard's contrasting analysis of his true religious hero, Abraham, in *Fear and Trembling*, we can read the entire analysis of spectral logic in a more evidently Kierkegaardian light. The following description by Derrida of Hamlet's response to his ghostly father could, I submit, as easily have been written about Abraham's response to the voice of the angel in *Fear and Trembling* (or, for that matter, about Levinas's religious response to the summons of the infinite Other): "This spectral *someone other looks at us*, we feel ourselves being looked at by it, outside of any synchrony, even before and beyond any look on our part, according to an absolute anteriority . . . and asymmetry, according to an absolutely unmasterable disproportion."[42] More specifically, we might consider the relevance of this analysis for the notion of messianic commitment or summons—the very thing that, according to Kierkegaard, Hamlet would have had to be more struck by if he were to be a properly religious character:

> Here anachrony makes the law. To feel ourselves seen by a look which it
> will always be impossible to cross, that is the *visor effect* on the basis of which
> we inherited from the law. Since we do not see the one who sees us, and
> who makes the law, who delivers the injunction (which is, moreover, a
> contradictory injunction), since we do not see the one who orders "swear,"
> we cannot identify it in all certainty, we must fall back on its voice. The
> one who says "I am thy Father's Spirit" can only be taken at his word. An
> essentially blind submission to his secret, to the secret of his origin: this is a
> first obedience to the injunction. It will condition all the others. It may
> always be a case of still someone else. Another can always lie, he can disguise
> himself as a ghost, another ghost may also be passing himself off for this
> one.[43]

In short, how can we ever be sure which kind of ghost, holy or unholy, is
here before us if, as Derrida says elsewhere, "every other is every other"
(*tout autre est tout autre*)? And the simple answer is: we *can't* be sure.

Moreover, this question of the undecidability of the spectral injunction
is in turn related, for Derrida, to the dilemma of mourning. Nothing is
worse for the work of mourning, notes Derrida, than confusion about the
identity of the one dead and gone. "One *has to know* who is buried where—
and *it is necessary* (to know—to make certain) that, in what remains of him,
he remain there. Let him stay there and move no more."[44] Or as the colloquial
expression goes when someone is finally buried: *requiescat in pace*. May they
rest in peace! Now Hamlet, as we know, is notorious as someone who *cannot*
properly mourn his dead father precisely because he cannot properly identify
his father's nature or his past (e.g., "those foul deeds committed in [his] days
of nature whose very tale would harrow up [his, Hamlet's] soul" etc.). It is,
of course, true for anyone who has lost a loved one at sea or in some natural
disaster to want to "recover and identify" the body so that the work of
mourning can take place. But this is experienced as an even deeper anxiety
by Hamlet, for not only has he missed his father's burial (he was "too late"
returned from Wittenberg), but he can't even be sure that the paternal specter who is summoning him to murder his uncle is really his father at all—
or at least the father he thought he knew!

Hamlet, like the ghost who confronts him, is riven with undecidability—
and so is unable to mourn (his father), to love (his mother), to desire (Ophelia), or to act (by taking revenge on Claudius). But, in Kierkegaard's reading,
this undecidability is even more accentuated. For we recall, by Taciturnus's
account, that Hamlet is not only confused by the undecidable vision of an
invisible ghost—a thing that is nothing; he is doubly confused in that he has
no real religious experience of a God who forbids revenge (e.g., "Vengeance
is mine says the Lord!"). In short, Kierkegaard's Hamlet is deprived of both
an earthly father and a divine one. And the same might—who knows?—
have even been true of Kierkegaard himself in certain "non-religious"
moments of vacillation, inaction, or faithlessness—moments almost too

disturbing to be admitted or acknowledged. For remember, not only did Kierkegaard have a most troubled relation with his own father (who cursed God and crushed his own son), but he himself experienced moments of deep hesitation and confusion—especially prior to his famous Easter conversion of 1848. (An experience during which he felt summoned by God to speak out and write directly in his own name and voice. And why, one might legitimately ask, was it a "conversion" if he was already converted?)

★ ★ ★

But there is, I think, another key point at which the Kierkegaardian and Derridean readings of *Hamlet* overlap. Derrida concludes the second chapter of his Marx book by stating that the "deconstructive procedure" he practices attempts to put into question our inherited "onto-theological" notions of historical time by way of thinking another kind of temporality or "historicity." This, says Derrida, would allow us to think "another opening of eventness as historicity that permitted one not to renounce, but on the contrary to open up access to an affirmative thinking of the messianic and emancipatory promise as promise."[45] As *promise,* insists Derrida, and "not as onto-theological or teleo-eschatological program or design."[46] Derrida's deconstructive thinking seeks to preserve this very promise by inscribing the "possibility of the reference to the other, and thus of radical alterity and heterogeneity" (i.e., of *différance*); and this in turn signals the impossibility of the present ever being fully contemporaneous or identical with itself.[47] So doing, deconstruction maintains the indestructibility of "emancipatory desire," which is, Derrida concludes, the very condition of "re-politicization," or perhaps even of "another concept of the political."[48]

In light of this rather "upbeat" deconstructive reading of Hamlet's undecidability, we can, I submit, reinterpret Kierkegaard's verdict on *Hamlet* in a variety of ways. Let me outline, by way of conclusion, at least three.

First hypothesis: Kierkegaard was incapable of moving from a traditional Christian understanding of the religious to a deconstructive understanding of religion-without-religion as "messianicity"—and so he was unable to appreciate the positive implications of Hamlet's *failure* as a "religious hero" (in the traditional sense). In other words, the problem with Kierkegaard, on this account, would be that he hadn't read Derrida. Or to put it more plainly, he wasn't deconstructive enough—that is, sufficiently to realize that Hamlet's undecidable reflectiveness is actually a very good and profoundly religious thing, once one accepts the notion of "religion without religion."

Second hypothesis: Kierkegaard failed to move beyond the old alternatives of the esthetic versus the religious to embrace a new category of the *political.* There is not one mention of the political in all of Kierkegaard's references to Hamlet. Contrariwise, one might note that there is not one of Derrida's references to Hamlet in *Spectres of Marx* that is *not political.* Had

Kierkegaard espoused such a new concept of the political, he might have been able to escape the paralyzing either/or of esthetic versus religious options to which he condemns Hamlet.

Third hypothesis: Kierkegaard is also anticipating, in his "Side-glance" at *Hamlet* and other texts, Derrida's rethinking of the religious and the political. Read in this manner, in tune with commentators like Caputo and Dooley, Kierkegaard may be construed as a "radical hermeneut" whose deconstructive reading of Hamlet as *neither esthetic nor religious in strictu sensu* is already opening up a new sense of that very "event-ness as historicity" that Derrida sees as the precondition of emancipatory desire.[49] By this account, *Works of Love* and other signed works may be seen as prefiguring the possibility of just such a new politics.

Such a new politics might, I suggest, signal the following six features:

1. a commitment to action in fear and trembling—that is, in tolerance and vigilance;
2. a way of acting and suffering in the world so that the inwardly subjective and reflective is never sacrificed to the dictates of the purely "objective" and impersonal imperatives of the global techno-capitalist network;
3. a way of reflecting and acting "religiously"—that is, "messianically" in Derrida's terms, or "in light of the Kingdom" in Kierkegaard's terms—so that the impossible tasks of justice, pardon, and hospitality (these three great works of love) become more and more possible in each instant of decision and commitment;
4. a deconstructive-existential hermeneutic that tempers our instinctive rush to judgment and condemnation in favor of more refined and discerning judgments;
5. a new political practice based on Hamlet's insight that "memory" is indispensable and that amnesty can never be founded upon amnesia: for the "story" of the father needs to be told, the adversary's "rights of memory" need to be honored, so that the repetitive cycles of mimetic desire and revenge may be overcome; and
6. an acknowledgment, finally, that the best kind of politics is one open to endless responsibility and the surprise of the unexpected—the possibility of the impossible.

Read in this proto-deconstructive way, Kierkegaard may be conceived as a kind of Derrida *avant la lettre*. Maybe. It's possible. But I'm not absolutely certain. The ghost of Hamlet that migrated into Kierkegaard's reading of *Hamlet* is not, I think, identical to the one that migrated into Derrida's— however similar on questions of non-synchronous time, undecidability, and the logic of the spectral. For when it comes to specters and spirits, as Derrida reminds us, "there is *more than one of them* and they are heterogeneous."[50]

This irreducible heterogeneity of ghosts is perhaps itself a guarantee of the heterogeneity of Kierkegaardian and Derridean readings.

That question remains open. But one thing is sure: new concepts of the "religious" and the "political" urgently need to be opened up and thought through in our postmodern age of growing indifference and indifferentiation. And if either Kierkegaard (as read through Derrida) or Derrida (as read through Kierkegaard) can help us in this task, which I suspect they can, we must be grateful.

Notes

1. Kierkegaard, *Stages on Life's Way,* ed. and trans. Howard V. Hong and Edna H. Hong (Princeton, N.J.: Princeton University Press, 1988), 230.

2. Ibid., 407.

3. Kierkegaard, *The Concept of Dread,* trans. Walter Lowrie (Princeton, N.J.: Princeton University Press, 1954), 114. Henceforth CDI.

4. Ibid.

5. Ibid., 116.

6. Ibid.

7. Ibid., 115.

8. Kierkegaard, *Concluding Scientific Postscript,* trans. David Swenson and Walter Lowrie (Princeton, N.J.: Princeton University Press, 1941), 514 (my italics). Henceforth CUPI.

9. Ibid., 193.

10. Ibid., 194.

11. Ibid.

12. Ibid.

13. This is also relevant, of course, to the basic hermeneutic distinction—so important to Dilthey, Heidegger, and Gadamer—between *Verstehen* and *Erklaren,* and more generally, between *Geistwissenshaft* and *Naturwissenshaft.*

14. CUPI, 163.

15. Ibid., 164.

16. Ibid., 165.

17. SLW, 453.

18. Ibid., 452.

19. Ibid. (my emphasis).

20. Ibid., 453.

21. Ibid.

22. Ibid., 454.

23. René Girard, *Shakespeare: Les Feux de l'envie* (Paris: Grasset, 1990), 331ff.

24. SLW, 454 (my emphasis).

25. Ibid., 455.

26. Ibid., 454, 636.

27. Ibid., 455.

28. Quotations come from *The Tragedy of Hamlet, Prince of Denmark,* ed. Sylvan Barnet (New York: New American Library, 1963).

29. JP 1561, n.d., 1844. Kierkegaard is here referring to Rötscher, a Hegelian "systematician" who in Kierkegaard's view interpreted Hamlet "rightly" as being "morbidly reflective," and was ultimately obliged in his analysis of the "psychical development of esthetic characters" to use "existential categories such as the leap" (SLW, 635–36; from the draft to the "Side-glance" passage). In the same Journal entry, JP 1561, entitled "Rötscher," Kierkegaard again cites Börne's "en passant" remark that Hamlet is a "Christian Tragedy." In the section on "The Romantic Arts" in his *Lectures on Aesthetics*, trans. J. M. Knox (Oxford: Oxford University Press, 1998), with which Kierkegaard would have certainly been familiar, Hegel discusses *Hamlet* in his contrast between Greek and modern tragedy. He points out that Hamlet's character is rooted in a collision similar to that treated by two Greek tragedians—Aeschylus in the *Choephori* and Sophocles in *Electra*—namely, the father is murdered and the mother has married the murderer. But the big difference is that while the Greek dramas portray the tragic actions as "ethical," Shakespeare's drama does not. In the case of *Hamlet*, the plot is purely *personal*. It is a play not about social or ethical action but about arbitrary internal conflict—indeed, the inability to take action.

> Whereas in the Greek poets the King's death does have an ethical justification, in Shakespeare it is simply and solely an atrocious crime and Hamlet's mother is guiltless of it. Consequently the son has to wreak his revenge only on the fratricide King in whom he sees nothing really worthy of respect. Therefore the collision turns strictly here not on the son's pursuing an ethically justified revenge and being forced in the process to violate the ethical order, but on Hamlet's *personal character*. His noble soul is not made for this kind of energetic activity; and full of disgust with the world and life, what with decision, proof, arrangements for carrying out his resolve, and being bandied from pillar to post, he eventually perishes owing to his own hesitation and a complication of external circumstances. (*Aesthetics,* 1225–26)

In short, if we were to use Kierkegaard's categories here, we would say that for Hegel there is no real ethical basis to Hamlet's predicament, nor a religious basis for that matter, but a purely subjective one.

The concern of *Hamlet*, as of many other modern tragedies, is that of "characters" and their inner "conflicts." The greatness of classical Greek tragedy, for Hegel, is that its heroes were confronted by circumstances in which, having solidly identified themselves "with the one ethical 'pathos' that alone corresponds to their own already established nature, they necessarily come into conflict with the opposite but equally justified ethical power" (*Aesthetics,* 1226). By contrast, modern romantic characters like Hamlet are placed from the outset in a vast "field of more or less accidental circumstances and conditions within which it is possible to act in this way or in that" (that is, in an arbitrary rather than necessary fashion). As a result, says Hegel, "the conflict, for which the external circumstances do of course provide the occasion, lies essentially in the character to which the individuals adhere in their passion, not because of any substantial justification but because they are what they are once and for all" (ibid.). Modern heroes like

Hamlet do not act out of an "inherently ethical pathos" but rather from "chance"; and they make their decisions according to their own wishes and needs. And since the aims and motivations of the "inner subjective life" are all *particular*—rather than *universal* as in Greek drama—ethical considerations are not an "essential" or "objective" part of the drama. But when it comes to the portrayal of "directly present life and inner greatness of soul," claims Hegel, Shakespeare's characters are incomparable. Even Goethe and Schiller, he insists, cannot achieve anything like the "inner force and height of passion" of Shakespeare's heroes.

The lever of modern romantic tragedy, Hegel goes on to surmise, is what he calls the "personal tragedy of inner discord" (*Aesthetics*, 1229). "Indecision," "vacillation," "weakness of irresolution," "perplexity about the reasons that are to guide decision," "the swithering of reflection," and so on. These are all characteristics of the modern romantic hero left to his own devices and deprived of the external necessity of action (*Sittlichkeit*). In modern as opposed to classical tragedy, Hegel explains, "such dithering figures generally appear by being themselves in the grip of a twofold passion which drives them from one decision or one deed to another simultaneously." And to put this vacillation and discord into the same character must always involve, deems Hegel, "much awkwardness" (ibid.). Why? Because, in Hegel's considered view, "mental distraction into opposed interests has its source partly in a vagueness and stupidity of mind, partly in weakness and immaturity" (ibid.). But worst of all, says Hegel, is when the modern dramatist portrays such indecision of the whole character "as a sort of perverse and sophistical dialectic and then . . . makes it the main theme of the entire drama, so that truth is supposed to consist precisely in showing that no character is inwardly firm and self-assured" (*Aesthetics*, 1229). Now while Hegel goes on to invoke Shakespeare as a modern dramatist who *avoids* such portrayals of "vacillating characters inwardly divided against themselves" (ibid.), it is almost impossible not to see Shakespeare's *Hamlet* as a perfect example of such a portrayal.

Hegel goes on to try and retrieve Shakespeare's main tragic characters, including Hamlet and Romeo and Juliet, as somehow reflecting some "necessary correspondence" between inner conflicts and outer circumstances. But his explanation is, to my mind, less than convincing. Here is how he contrasts normal modern tragedy (which he holds in low esteem) with the Shakespearean exception to the rule: In modern tragedy, he writes,

> the tragic denouement is displayed as purely the effect of unfortunate circumstances and external accidents which might have turned out otherwise and produced a happy ending. In this case the sole spectacle offered to us is that the modern individual with the non-universal nature of his character, his circumstances, and the complications in which he is involved, is necessarily surrendered to the fragility of all that is mundane and must endure the fate of finitude. But this mere affliction is empty, and, in particular, we are confronted by purely horrible external necessity when we see fine minds, noble in themselves, perishing in such a battle

against the misfortune of entirely external circumstances. Such a history
may touch us acutely, and yet it seems only dreadful and we feel a pressing
demand for a necessary correspondence between the external circumstances and what the inner nature of those fine characters really is. It is
only from this point of view that we can feel ourselves reconciled in e.g.,
the fate of Hamlet or Juliet. Looked at from the outside, Hamlet's death
seems to be brought about accidentally owing to the fight with Laertes
and the exchange of rapiers. But death lay from the beginning in the
background of Hamlet's mind. The sands of time do not content him. In
his melancholy and weakness, his worry, his disgust at all the affairs of life,
we sense from the start that in all his terrible surroundings he is a lost
man, almost consumed already by an inner disgust before death comes to
him from outside. (*Aesthetics,* 1231–32)

But even if we credit Hegel's positive reading of *Hamlet,* we are still left with
his conclusion that even this modern tragedy leaves us feeling a woe that is only
"a grievous reconciliation, an unhappy bliss in misfortune" (ibid.). In short, the
typical emotion of the lost, beautiful, unhappy soul.

The main difference, we may conclude, between Kierkegaard's and Hegel's
reading of *Hamlet* is that the former considers it both a religious and esthetic
failure (without any explicit mention of its ethical function), whereas Hegel
praises it as an esthetic success, albeit far removed from the ethical catharsis and
necessity of Greek tragedy and not yet able to offer insight into the non-grievous
reconciliation of Christian providence and peace.

30. Kierkegaard, *Either/Or,* vol. 1, trans. David F. Swenson and Lillian Marvin
Swenson (Princeton, N.J.: Princeton University Press, 1959), 209.

31. JP, 2:1562, n.d., 1854. Moreover, in light of this Journal entry we might
reread a curious passage from the sketch to the section on the religious and tragic
heroes cited above from *Stages on Life's Way,* a passage not included in the published text but entitled, tellingly, "What is it to be a hero?" It is hard not to read
this unpublished passage without thinking of (a) Kierkegaard's imaginary male
character (who fails to be a properly religious hero) as a version of himself and
(b) of his imaginary female character (who fails to be a properly esthetic heroine)
as a version of Regine (SLW, 637). Of his imaginary failed hero, the author
writes: "If he, my character, had been a hero in the ordinary sense, he would
have had to become that demonically by saying: I see that my idea of existence
requires that she must go, ergo, and that this road over her leads me to my great
goal. On the other hand, he must not say conversely that for him the main point
was that he should suffer more than she. That is a religious hero. He is the
greatest hero who wins the most.—He is the greatest hero who suffers the most.
(Feuerbach in *Wesen des Christenthum* is scandalized at Pascal's life, that it is a
story of suffering . . .)." Of his imaginary failed heroine, Kierkegaard writes: "She
also could have become a heroine, but only esthetically. I have not wished to
keep her that way, for a new light should fall upon his sympathy; how it pains
him that she breaks with the idea." To which the author adds this seemingly
confessional aside: "If she had become a heroine, I would have bowed before

her (although the esthetic interests me less) for there is nothing I would rather do than bow; would to God that there were someone to bow before; most people, however, believe that there is a great deal to stoop for in the world." Then we stumble upon this self-disparaging and somewhat mock-heroic observation: "I am *poetice et eleganter* (in a poetic and refined way) a street inspector; I think of the two chamberlains who opened the door for Napoleon and said: The Emperor. Anyone could be made a hero if he will confide in me. I shall bring him into mortal danger; then it will turn out all right. Baggesen's lines fit most people (the majority):

> Our Lord took a piece of sausage meat
> and said: Become a man
> Become sausage-witted and sausage-happy."

(SLW, "Selected Entries from Kierkegaard's Journals and Papers Pertaining to *Stages on Life's Way*," 636–37).

32. See "Selected Entries" in SLW, 635.

33. SLW, "Side-glance," 454.

34. Jacques Derrida, *Spectres of Marx*, trans. Peggy Kamuf (London: Routledge, 1994).

35. "Exordium," in ibid., xx.

36. Ibid., 4.

37. Ibid., 5.

38. Ibid.

39. Ibid., 6.

40. Ibid., 7.

41. Ibid.

42. Ibid.

43. Ibid., 8–9.

44. Ibid., 9.

45. Ibid., 74–75.

46. Ibid.

47. Ibid.

48. Ibid.

49. See John Caputo, "Repetition and *Kinesis:* Kierkegaard on the Foundering of Metaphysics," in *Radical Hermeneutics* (Bloomington: Indiana University Press, 1987), 11–35. See also Mark Dooley, *The Politics of Exodus* (New York: Fordham University Press, 2001).

50. Derrida, *Spectres of Marx*, 75.

CONTRIBUTORS

Jacob Bøggild, assistant professor, Institute for Nordic Languages and Literature, Aarhus University, Denmark, is the author of *Ironiens Tænker: Tænkningens Ironi. Kierkegaard læst retorisk* [*The Thinker of Irony: The Irony of Thinking. Kierkegaard Read Rhetorically*] and numerous articles on Kierkegaard in both Danish and international publications and periodicals.

John D. Caputo, David R. Cook Professor of Philosophy, Villanova University, is the author of *On Religion; More Radical Hermeneutics: On Not Knowing Who We Are; Deconstruction in a Nutshell: A Conversation with Jacques Derrida; The Prayers and Tears of Jacques Derrida: Religion without Religion; Against Ethics: Contributions to a Poetics of Obligation with Constant Reference to Deconstruction;* and numerous other books and articles.

Mark Dooley, John Henry Newman Scholar in Theology, University College–Dublin, is author of *A Passion for the Impossible: John D. Caputo in Focus,* as well as numerous articles on Kierkegaard; editor of *The Politics of Exodus: Kierkegaard's Ethics of Responsibility;* and co-editor of *Questioning God* (with John D. Caputo and Michael J. Scanlon) and *Questioning Ethics* (with Richard Kearney).

Joakim Garff, lecturer and researcher at the Søren Kierkegaard Research Center, University of Copenhagen, is author of *SAK, Søren Aabye Kierkegaard: En Biografi* [*SAK, Søren Aabye Kierkegaard: A Biography*] and *"Den Søvnløse": Kierkegaard læst æstetisk/biografisk* [*"The Sleepless": Kierkegaard Read Aesthetically/Biographically*], and co-author of *Skriftbilleder: Søren Kierkegaards journaler, notesbøger, hæfter, ark, lapper og strimler* [*Typefaces: Søren Kierkegaard's Journals, Notebooks, Pamphlets, Sheets, Scraps, and Strips*]. He is co-editor of *Søren Kierkegaards Skrifter* [*Søren Kierkegaard's Writings*], a new Danish edition of Kierkegaard's writings, as well as of *Kierkegaardiana.*

Robert Gibbs, professor of philosophy, University of Toronto, is author of *Why Ethics? Signs of Responsibilities* and *Correlations in Rosenzweig and Levinas,* and co-author of *Reasoning after Revelation: Dialogues in Postmodern Jewish Philosophy.* He has written numerous articles that deal extensively with questions in contemporary Continental philosophy and its relations to Jewish thought.

Elsebet Jegstrup is adjunct professor of philosophy at Elon University and formerly associate professor of philosophy at Augusta State University. She is the author of many articles on Kierkegaard and is currently working on a book titled "A Questioning of Justice: Continental Concerns." She organized the International Kierkegaard Forum held at Augusta State University in March 2001 and co-founded the Georgia Continental Philosophy Circle.

Richard Kearney is Charles Seelig Professor in Philosophy, Boston College, and visiting professor, University College–Dublin. He is the author of *Strangers, Gods, and Monsters: Interpreting Otherness; The God Who May Be: A New Hermeneutics of Religion; On Stories; The Wake of Imagination;* and *Poetics of Imagining.* He has edited a number of books, among them *The Continental Philosophy Reader; Paul Ricoeur: Hermeneutics of Action;* and *Continental Philosophy in the Twentieth Century.*

John Llewelyn, formerly reader in philosophy at the University of Edinburgh, visiting professor of philosophy at the University of Memphis, and the Arthur J. Schmitt Distinguished Visiting Professor of Philosophy at Loyola University of Chicago, is author of *Seeing Through God; Appositions of Jacques Derrida and Emmanuel Levinas; The HypoCritical Imagination: Between Kant and Levinas; Emmanuel Levinas: The Genealogy of Ethics; The Middle Voice of Ecological Conscience;* and *Derrida on the Threshold of Sense.*

Roger Poole is currently a visiting fellow at the Faculty of Divinity at Cambridge University, where he directs the research project Kierkegaard after Postmodernism. He is the author of *Towards Deep Subjectivity* and *Kierkegaard: The Indirect Communication;* co-author (with Henrik Stangerup) of *Dansemesteren [The Laughter Is on My Side];* and is a contributor to the *Cambridge Companion to Kierkegaard.* He is chairman of the Søren Kierkegaard Society of the United Kingdom.

Vanessa Rumble, associate professor of philosophy, Boston College, has published numerous articles on Kierkegaard, Scandinavian culture, and psychoanalysis. She serves currently as president of the Søren Kierkegaard Society (USA), and she is working on a book on Kierkegaard and the legacy of German romanticism.

John Vignaux Smyth, professor and chair of the Department of English, Portland State University, is author of *The Habit of Lying: Sacrificial Studies in Literature, Philosophy, and Fashion Theory; A Question of Eros: Irony in Sterne,*

Kierkegaard, and Barthes; as well as numerous articles and essays in philosophy and literature. His poetry appears in the March 2003 issue of *Grand Street.*

Jason Wirth, associate professor of philosophy and chair of Division 1 (Philosophy, Communications, and Fine Arts), Oglethorpe University, is author of *The Conspiracy of Life: Meditations on Schelling and His Time* and *The Ages of the World,* a translation with introduction of Schelling's *Die Weltalter.* He is the editor of *Schelling Now.* He is the co-founder and current chair of the Georgia Continental Philosophy Circle.

David Wood, professor in the Department of Philosophy, Vanderbilt University, is author of *Philosophy at the Limit; The Deconstruction of Time; Thinking after Heidegger;* and *The Step Back: Towards a Negative Capability.* He has edited ten volumes in Continental philosophy, including *Derrida: A Critical Reader* and *Of Derrida, Heidegger, and Spirit,* and is currently working on *Things at the Edge of the World* and a work on philosophy and trees.

INDEX

Abraham, 1, 21–22, 25, 76–79, 82, 100, 105, 134, 161, 165, 167, 170–71, 173, 181–82, 197, 216–18, 220, 222, 235
abyss, 14, 31, 37, 41, 107, 174
accountability, 104, 216
accountancy, 128–29
acoustic illusion, 99
actuality, 7, 35, 75, 79, 175, 182
Adam, 61, 185, 189–90
addressee, 72, 86, 143, 148, 153
admiration, 22, 76, 78–80, 174, 211
Adorno, Theodor, 180–85, 189, 196–97
Aeschylus, 240
affirmation: of Abraham, 2, 181; deconstruction and, 6, 37; of the gift, 23; irony and, 39; of the justice to come, 30; negation and, 208; repeating forward and, 138
Agacinski, Sylviane, 8, 87
agape, 163–64, 166, 169, 220
alienation, 56, 74, 96–97, 120, 144, 214, 219, 223
allegory, 87, 190
alterity, 3, 6, 11, 146, 161, 173, 218, 221, 237
altruism, 202, 204, 209
ambiguity, 18–19, 22, 27, 38, 90, 123, 134, 138, 184, 187
analogy, 91, 136, 165, 185, 227, 232, 234
anamnesis, 206–207
anonymity, 48, 96, 157
Anthropology, 93, 178
anticipation, 77–79, 93, 162, 185, 229, 234
Anti-Climacus, 80, 163, 211–12, 232; and becoming in time, 206–207 (*see also* becoming); and deconstruction, 26; and God, 35, 40, 210; the idealist, 75, 79; and *Practice in Christianity,* 175; and *The Sickness Unto Death,* 174

Antigone, 118, 121–25, 127, 177
anxiety: anxious, 125; and cause and effect, 116; and *The Concept of Anxiety,* 161, 179; and decadence and acoustic tone, 51, 70; and form, 51, 62; and love, 132, 145, 156 (*see also* love); and mourning, 236; and reflection, 122–24; and "The Seducer's Diary," 167; and "sympathetic antipathy and antipathetic sympathy," 126
apology, 68, 116
apostle, 14, 27, 99, 100–101, 118–21, 123–24, 126
appearance(s), 43, 91, 138, 161, 223
appropriation, 7, 77, 82, 173
approximation, 226
Archilocus, 56
Aristotle, 45, 93, 104, 129, 231
arithmetic, 94–95, 129–30
atheism, 170
Athens, 199, 200, 202, 210
atonement, 124
Augusta State University, 9, 196
Augustine, 22, 177
authenticity/authentic, 32, 53, 62–63, 69, 225–26
authority, 18, 26, 39, 78, 112, 150, 164, 178, 218, 232
autonomous, 125, 151, 182, 225
autopsy, 77

Baggesen, Jens, 89, 243
Barfield, Owen, 165, 175
Barit, Julian, 139

www.ingramcontent.com/pod-product-compliance
Ingram Content Group UK Ltd.
Pitfield, Milton Keynes, MK11 3LW, UK
UKHW022112140225

455125UK00007B/194